Cognitive Technologies

Managing Editors: D. M. Gabbay J. Siekmann

Editorial Board: A. Bundy J. G. Carbonell
M. Pinkal H. Uszkoreit M. Veloso W. Wahlster
M. J. Wooldridge

Advisory Board:

Luigia Carlucci Aiello
Franz Baader
Wolfgang Bibel
Leonard Bolc
Craig Boutilier
Ron Brachman
Bruce G. Buchanan
Anthony Cohn
Artur d'Avila Garcez
Luis Fariñas del Cerro
Koichi Furukawa
Georg Gottlob
Patrick J. Hayes
James A. Hendler
Anthony Jameson
Nick Jennings
Aravind K. Joshi
Hans Kamp
Martin Kay
Hiroaki Kitano
Robert Kowalski
Sarit Kraus
Maurizio Lenzerini
Hector Levesque
John Lloyd

Alan Mackworth
Mark Maybury
Tom Mitchell
Johanna D. Moore
Stephen H. Muggleton
Bernhard Nebel
Sharon Oviatt
Luis Pereira
Lu Ruqian
Stuart Russell
Erik Sandewall
Luc Steels
Oliviero Stock
Peter Stone
Gerhard Strube
Katia Sycara
Milind Tambe
Hidehiko Tanaka
Sebastian Thrun
Junichi Tsujii
Kurt VanLehn
Andrei Voronkov
Toby Walsh
Bonnie Webber

For further volumes:
http://www.springer.com/series/5216

Laura Kallmeyer

Parsing Beyond Context-Free Grammars

PD Dr. Laura Kallmeyer
SFB 833
Universität Tübingen
Nauklerstr. 35
72074 Tübingen
Germany
lk@sfs.uni-tuebingen.de

Managing Editors
Prof. Dr. Dov M. Gabbay
Augustus De Morgan Professor of Logic
King's College London
Dept. Computer Science
London WC2R 2LS
United Kingdom

Prof. Dr. Jörg Siekmann
Forschungsbereich Deduktions- und
Multiagentensysteme, DFKI
Stuhlsatzenweg 3, Geb. 43
66123 Saarbrücken, Germany

Cognitive Technologies ISSN 1611-2482
ISBN 978-3-642-14845-3   e-ISBN 978-3-642-14846-0
DOI 10.1007/978-3-642-14846-0
Springer Heidelberg Dordrecht London New York

Library of Congress Control Number: 2010933793

ACM Computing Classification (1998): I.2.7, F.4, J.5

© Springer-Verlag Berlin Heidelberg 2010
This work is subject to copyright. All rights are reserved, whether the whole or part of the material is concerned, specifically the rights of translation, reprinting, reuse of illustrations, recitation, broadcasting, reproduction on microfilm or in any other way, and storage in data banks. Duplication of this publication or parts thereof is permitted only under the provisions of the German Copyright Law of September 9, 1965, in its current version, and permission for use must always be obtained from Springer. Violations are liable to prosecution under the German Copyright Law.
The use of general descriptive names, registered names, trademarks, etc. in this publication does not imply, even in the absence of a specific statement, that such names are exempt from the relevant protective laws and regulations and therefore free for general use.

Cover design: KünkelLopka GmbH, Heidelberg

Printed on acid-free paper

Springer is part of Springer Science+Business Media (www.springer.com)

Preface

Given that context-free grammars cannot adequately describe natural languages, grammar formalisms beyond CFG that are still computationally tractable are of central interest for computational linguists. However, despite the considerable interest in such formalisms and in their various parsing algorithms, a coherent textbook that allows access to the large body of knowledge on polynomial-time parsing beyond context-free grammars has not been available so far. Textbooks on parsing covered mainly context-free grammars while mentioning more powerful formalisms only very briefly.

This want of a detailed presentation of grammar formalisms and parsing beyond CFG is addressed with this book. The book provides an extensive overview of the formal language landscape between CFG and PTIME. It moves from Tree Adjoining Grammars to Multiple Context-Free Grammars and then to Range Concatenation Grammars while explaining available parsing techniques for these formalisms. The text is enriched with many illustrations and examples coming with the different formalisms and algorithms. This makes the book accessible to anybody familiar with basic notions of CFG parsing. It is useful both for researchers and students in computational linguistics and in formal language theory.

Tübingen, *Laura Kallmeyer*
June 2010

Acknowledgments

First of all and most importantly, I want to thank my colleague Wolfgang Maier. We taught two courses at the University of Tübingen and one course at the European Summer School in Logic, Language and Information (ESSLLI) in 2008 in Hamburg, all of them covering the topic of parsing beyond context-free grammars. The idea to write this textbook arose out of these courses and much material from the course slides was reused when writing the book. The course preparations and the related discussions of the subject were crucial for achieving a good understanding of the topic and being able to cover it in a textbook. Also, when writing the book, I frequently discussed its content and structure with Wolfgang. Therefore one can say that without Wolfgang's help the book would not look as it does and, furthermore, it would very probably not exist at all.

The suggestion to write a textbook on parsing beyond context-free grammars came from Carl Vogel who participated in our ESSLLI course on this topic. I am grateful for this suggestion; it made me for the first time seriously consider the idea of covering the course material in a book.

While writing this book, I was financed by an Emmy Noether Grant from the German Research Foundation DFG (Deutsche Forschungsgemeinschaft).

Contents

1 Introduction 1
  1.1 Formal Grammars and Natural Languages 1
  1.2 Parsing Beyond CFGs 5
  1.3 What This Book Is Not About 7
  1.4 Overview of the Book 8
      1.4.1 Grammar Formalisms for Natural Languages 8
      1.4.2 Parsing: Preliminaries 8
      1.4.3 Tree Adjoining Grammars 8
      1.4.4 MCFG and LCFRS 9
      1.4.5 Range Concatenation Grammars 9
      1.4.6 Automata 10
  1.5 Some Basic Definitions 10
      1.5.1 Languages 10
      1.5.2 Context-Free Grammars 11
      1.5.3 Automata 12
      1.5.4 Trees 14

2 Grammar Formalisms for Natural Languages 17
  2.1 Context-Free Grammars and Natural Languages 17
      2.1.1 The Generative Capacity of CFGs 17
      2.1.2 CFGs and Lexicalization 20
      2.1.3 Mild Context-Sensitivity 23
  2.2 Grammar Formalisms Beyond CFG 26
      2.2.1 Tree Adjoining Grammars 26
      2.2.2 Linear Indexed Grammars 31
      2.2.3 Linear Context-Free Rewriting Systems 33
      2.2.4 Multicomponent Tree Adjoining Grammars 33
      2.2.5 Multiple Context-Free Grammars 36
      2.2.6 Range Concatenation Grammars 36
  2.3 Summary 38

3 Parsing: Preliminaries ... 41
3.1 Parsing as Deduction ... 41
3.1.1 Motivation ... 41
3.1.2 Items ... 42
3.1.3 Deduction Rules ... 44
3.2 Implementation Issues ... 44
3.2.1 Dynamic Programming ... 44
3.2.2 Chart Parsing and Tabulation ... 46
3.2.3 Hypergraphs ... 47
3.3 Properties of Parsing Algorithms ... 48
3.3.1 Soundness and Completeness ... 48
3.3.2 Complexity ... 49
3.3.3 Valid Prefix Property ... 51
3.4 Summary ... 51

4 Tree Adjoining Grammars ... 53
4.1 Introduction to Tree Adjoining Grammars ... 53
4.1.1 Definition of TAG ... 53
4.1.2 Formal Properties ... 58
4.1.3 Linguistic Principles for TAG ... 63
4.1.4 Extended Domain of Locality and Factoring of Recursion ... 65
4.1.5 Constituency and Dependencies ... 68
4.2 Equivalent Formalisms ... 70
4.2.1 Tree-Local MCTAG ... 70
4.2.2 Linear Indexed Grammars ... 72
4.2.3 Combinatory Categorial Grammars ... 72
4.3 Summary ... 74

5 Parsing Tree Adjoining Grammars ... 77
5.1 A CYK Parser for TAG ... 77
5.1.1 The Recognizer ... 77
5.1.2 Complexity ... 82
5.2 An Earley Parser for TAG ... 82
5.2.1 Introduction ... 82
5.2.2 Items ... 83
5.2.3 Inference Rules ... 85
5.2.4 Extending the Algorithm to Substitution ... 88
5.2.5 The Parser ... 91
5.2.6 Properties of the Algorithm ... 92
5.2.7 Prefix Valid Earley Parsing ... 93
5.3 An LR Parser for TAG ... 96
5.3.1 Introduction ... 96
5.3.2 Construction of the Automaton ... 99
5.3.3 The Recognizer ... 101
5.3.4 Valid Prefix Property ... 107

5.4 Summary 107

6 Multiple Context-Free Grammars and Linear Context-Free Rewriting Systems 109
6.1 Introduction to MCFG, LCFRS and Simple RCG 109
    6.1.1 MCFG and LCFRS 110
    6.1.2 Formal Properties 117
    6.1.3 Applications 122
6.2 Equivalent Formalisms 125
    6.2.1 Set-Local Multicomponent TAG 125
    6.2.2 Minimalist Grammars 126
    6.2.3 Finite-Copying LFG 126
6.3 Summary 128

7 Parsing MCFG, LCFRS and Simple RCG 131
7.1 CYK Parsing of MCFG 131
    7.1.1 The Basic Algorithm 131
    7.1.2 The Naïve Algorithm 134
    7.1.3 The Active Algorithm 136
    7.1.4 The Incremental Algorithm 139
    7.1.5 Prediction Strategies 141
7.2 Simplifying Simple RCGs 142
    7.2.1 Eliminating Useless Rules 142
    7.2.2 Eliminating ε-Rules 143
    7.2.3 Ordered Simple RCG 145
    7.2.4 Binarization of the Rules 147
7.3 An Incremental Earley Parser for Simple RCG 149
    7.3.1 The Algorithm 149
    7.3.2 Filters 154
7.4 Summary 155

8 Range Concatenation Grammars 157
8.1 Introduction to Range Concatenation Grammars 157
    8.1.1 Definition of RCG 157
    8.1.2 Applications 164
8.2 Relations to Other Formalisms 167
    8.2.1 Literal Movement Grammars 167
    8.2.2 CFG, TAG and MCFG 170
8.3 Summary 173

9 Parsing Range Concatenation Grammars 177
9.1 Basic RCG Parsing 177
    9.1.1 CYK Parsing with Passive Items 178
    9.1.2 Non-directional Top-Down Parsing 179
    9.1.3 Directional Top-Down Parsing 180

XII   Contents

		9.1.4 Optimizations 183
	9.2	Parsing with Constraint Propagation 184
		9.2.1 Range Constraints 185
		9.2.2 CYK Parsing with Active Items 186
		9.2.3 Earley Parsing 188
	9.3	Summary 190

10 Automata 193
    10.1 Embedded Push-Down Automata 193
        10.1.1 Definition of EPDA 193
        10.1.2 EPDA and TAG 197
        10.1.3 Bottom-Up Embedded Push-Down Automata 197
        10.1.4 k-Order EPDA 199
    10.2 Two-Stack Automata 200
        10.2.1 General Definition 200
        10.2.2 Strongly-Driven Two-Stack Automata 202
    10.3 Thread Automata 204
        10.3.1 Idea 204
        10.3.2 General Definition of TA 206
        10.3.3 Constructing a TA for a TAG 208
        10.3.4 Constructing a TA for an Ordered SRCG 209
    10.4 Summary 213

Appendix A: Hierarchy of Grammar Formalisms 215

Appendix B: List of Acronyms 217

Solutions 219

References 235

Index 245

1

Introduction

1.1 Formal Grammars and Natural Languages

Since the 1980s it has been known that context-free grammars (CFGs) are not powerful enough to describe all phenomena we encounter in natural languages. Examples that show the limitation of CFGs are cross-serial dependencies in Dutch, as in (1), and in Swiss German (Shieber, 1985; Bresnan et al., 1982) and so-called unbounded scrambling phenomena (Becker, Rambow, and Niv, 1992; Rambow, 1994) in, for instance, German and Korean. A German scrambling example is given in (2).

(1) ... dat Jan Piet de kinderen zag helpen zwemmen
  ... that Jan Piet the children saw help   swim
  '... that Jan saw Piet help the children swim'

(2) ... dass des Verbrechens der Detektiv   den Verdächtigen
  ... that the crime$_{gen}$ the detective$_{nom}$ the suspect$_{acc}$

  dem Klienten zu überführen   versprochen hat
  the client$_{dat}$ to prove guilty of promised has
  '... that the detective has promised the client to prove the suspect guilty of the crime'

Let us express the relation between a noun and the verb it depends on by mapping a verb and its nominal arguments to the same terminal symbol. If we do this for the two example sentences, we obtain the following: The cross-serial dependencies as in (1) yield a string $abcabc$, which, when iterated, amounts to a dependency pattern as in the copy language $\{ww \,|\, w \in \{a,b,c\}^+\}$. For scrambling, all permutations of the noun phrases preceding the verbs are grammatical (though, depending on the lexical material they are filled with, these permutations are more or less felicitous). This leads to patterns $ababab$ (see (2)), $aabbab$, $abbaab$, $babaab$, ... This amounts to the language $\{\pi(w')w \,|\, w = a_1 \ldots a_n \in \{a, b, \ldots\}^*, w' = a_1^{k_1} \ldots a_n^{k_n}$, where k_i is the number

L. Kallmeyer, *Parsing Beyond Context-Free Grammars*, Cognitive Technologies,
DOI 10.1007/978-3-642-14846-0_1, © Springer-Verlag Berlin Heidelberg 2010

of nominal arguments of a_i and π is a permutation}. Both phenomena, crossserial dependencies and scrambling, cannot be described using only CFGs.

In an attempt to specify the formal properties of natural languages, Joshi introduced the notion of mild context-sensitivity (1985) that proposes that a grammar formalism that is adequate for dealing with natural languages should 1. extend CFGs, 2. be able to describe a limited amount of crossing dependencies, 3. be polynomially parsable and 4. generate only languages of constant growth. The latter means, roughly, that if we order the word lengths we find in a language, then the difference between two subsequent elements is limited by a constant.

The first two conditions formulate minimal requirements that are widely accepted. Any grammar formalism proposed for natural languages satisfies these constraints. The other two conditions formulate limitations of the generative capacity of the grammar formalisms we choose for natural languages. The property of constant growth has been questioned for natural languages since there are some phenomena where, when iterating them, the word length seems to grow exponentially. These are case stacking in Old Georgian (Michaelis and Kracht, 1997) and Chinese number names (Radzinski, 1991). It should be noted, however, that the generalizations for Old Georgian cannot be verified since there are no speakers of this language today, and for Chinese number names, it is not completely clear to what extent this is really part of the syntax. Therefore it is still an open question whether natural languages are of constant growth.

Given these facts, different extensions of CFG have been proposed for processing natural languages. Within this book, we restrict ourselves to formalisms that satisfy at least the first three constraints, i.e., in particular, we treat only formalisms generating polynomial languages.

The weakest extension we will cover in this book is Tree Adjoining Grammar (TAG), originally introduced in (Joshi, Levy, and Takahashi, 1975). TAGs extend CFGs in the following way: In a CFG, in each derivation step we rewrite non-terminals with strings of terminals and non-terminals. In terms of the corresponding derivation tree, we substitute a new tree (the root being the left-hand side non-terminal and the daughters being the right-hand side elements of the corresponding production) for a leaf with a non-terminal label. In TAG, we can even insert new trees somewhere inside the already derived tree, and not only at leaves. In other words, we can replace an internal node with a new tree. This new tree can contribute two non-adjacent parts to the terminal string. Figure 1.1 gives examples of how the yields of elementary structures can look in the different formalisms. In a CFG, the yield of a non-terminal A is a single string γ. The example for TAG shows the result of an adjunction where the subtree between the two A nodes is a tree from the grammar that has been adjoined. Its yield has two components, namely the two non-adjacent strings γ_1 and γ_2.

TAGs have been shown to be able to model a large range of linguistic phenomena in an adequate way (Abeillé, 1988; Abeillé, 2002; Kroch, 1987;

1.1 Formal Grammars and Natural Languages 3

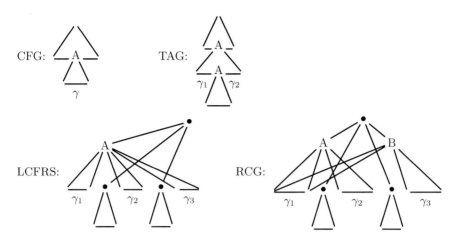

Fig. 1.1. Yields of non-terminals in different formalisms

Kroch, 1989; Frank, 1992; Frank, 2002) and several large coverage grammars have been implemented using TAG, among others for English (XTAG Research Group, 2001) and French (Abeillé, 2002; Crabbé, 2005).

Extending the idea of having non-adjacent portions of the terminal string in the yield of an element from the grammar leads to Linear Context-Free Rewriting Systems (LCFRSs) (Vijay-Shanker, Weir, and Joshi, 1987; Weir, 1988) and the equivalent Multiple Context-Free Grammars (MCFGs) (Seki et al., 1991). In these grammars, non-terminals can span tuples of strings and the productions specify how to compute the span of the left-hand side non-terminal from the spans of the right-hand side terminals. In terms of trees, this leads to trees with crossing branches. Figure 1.1 shows an example where the yield of the non-terminal A consists of the three non-adjacent strings γ_1, γ_2 and γ_3.

For some natural language phenomena, TAGs are too limited to provide a linguistically adequate analysis, for instance for certain extraction phenomena and word order variations in so-called free word order languages (Kroch and Joshi, 1987; Becker, Joshi, and Rambow, 1991; Kahane, Candito, and de Kercadio, 2000). An example for the latter are scrambling configurations such as (2). Some of the extensions proposed for this reason fall into the class of LCFRS. Furthermore, more recently, LCFRSs have attracted considerable interest in the context of data-driven parsing since they can be extracted in a very natural way both from constituency treebanks (Maier and Søgaard, 2008; Kallmeyer and Maier, 2010) and from dependency treebanks (Kuhlmann, 2007; Kuhlmann and Satta, 2009). Constituency treebanks are sets of sentences that are equipped with tree-shaped syntactic structures where the internal nodes are labeled with non-terminal syntactic categories such as VP and NP. In contrast to this, dependency treebanks are sets of

4   1 Introduction

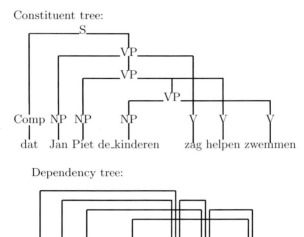

Fig. 1.2. Constituent and dependency tree for (1)

sentences that are equipped with tree-shaped syntactic structures where the words in a sentence represent the nodes of the tree while the edges correspond to dependency relations. See Figure 1.2 for an example.

In LCFRS, we have a linearity condition that signifies that a single portion of the terminal string cannot belong to the spans of two different non-terminals that are not derived from each other (i.e., that do not stand in a dominance relation in the derivation tree). If we drop this constraint, we obtain Range Concatenation Grammars (RCGs) (Boullier, 2000b), the most expressive formalism that we will present in this book. In an RCG, a terminal node can be part of two subtrees of the derivation tree whose root nodes do not stand in any dominance relation. The example in Figure 1.1 shows a case where two non-terminals, A and B, both have two non-adjacent strings as yields where the first component of both yields is the same: A has a yield consisting of the strings γ_1 and γ_2 while B has a yield consisting of the strings γ_1 and γ_3.

To get a better understanding of the idea behind RCGs, think of the non-terminals as predicates that are true for the string tuples that are in their yields. In an RCG, it is possible to require more than one predicate to be true for a certain yield. It would be possible for instance to generate structures as shown in Figure 1.3 for so-called gapping phenomena. Here, the noun *broccoli* is the object of both the first and the second VP.

From a formal point of view, RCGs are particularly interesting because they generate exactly the class of all polynomial languages. Furthermore, RCGs can model some natural language phenomena that even LCFRSs cannot deal with. These are long-distance scrambling in languages such as German (Becker, Rambow, and Niv, 1992; Boullier, 1999a) and some phenomena that

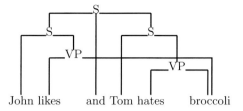

Fig. 1.3. A possible RCG tree for gapping constructions

have been argued not to be of constant growth (Radzinski, 1991).[1] Finally, RCGs are closed under intersection and allow us to model different aspects of natural language in parallel (Sagot, 2005). Therefore, restricted forms of RCGs can be exploited for machine translation (Søgaard, 2008).

As a summary, Figure 1.4 shows the hierarchy of language classes that we will deal with in this book.

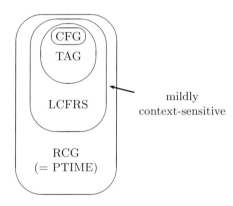

Fig. 1.4. The language hierarchy treated in this book

1.2 Parsing Beyond CFGs

The focus of this book is on parsing algorithms for the above-mentioned formalisms. We will concentrate on symbolic approaches only.

The parsing strategies and the automata presented throughout the book are all extensions of the strategies that have been developed for CFGs (see

---

[1] Note however that for scrambling other extensions of TAG have been proposed, such as V-TAG (Rambow, 1994) and TT-MCTAG (Lichte, 2007), which are probably more adequate from a linguistic point of view.

Grune and Jacobs (2008) for an extensive overview of CFG parsing). More concretely, we will extend the bottom-up and top-down parsing techniques from CFGs to the more powerful formalisms treated in this book.

We will see how the different ways to extend CFGs adopted in the different formalisms influence the parsing complexity. A central aspect is always the maximal number of non-adjacent strings that can occur in the yield of an elementary structure where an elementary structure can be a tree from the grammar as in the case of TAG or a non-terminal node as in the case of LCFRS. In LCFRS terminology, this number is called the *fan-out* of the grammar. For TAG, we can have at most two non-adjacent parts in the yield, i.e., we have fan-out 2, and we obtain a parsing complexity of $\mathcal{O}(n^6)$. For LCFRS, if we have maximal k non-adjacent parts in the yields (fan-out k), we can do parsing in $\mathcal{O}(n^{3k})$ if the grammar is binarized.

Since we are mainly interested in natural language processing, we have to assume that our grammars are highly ambiguous. As a consequence, if we want to perform an efficient parsing, we have to use tabulation techniques, i.e., we have to make sure we can reuse partial results and thereby avoid having to compute the same sub-analysis several times. This is one of the reasons why we will present parsing as a deductive process (Pereira and Warren, 1983; Shieber, Schabes, and Pereira, 1995) where, in every step, we deduce a new partial result from results we have already found. We assume that our algorithms are implemented as chart parsers (Kay, 1986). This means that we have a structure (the chart) that serves to store all our intermediate partial results. We add new results that we can deduce from the results already in the chart as long as possible. Once this process stops because we cannot find any more new results, we check whether the chart contains a result that represents a possible parse for our input string.

The goal of this book is twofold: On the one hand we aim at giving a complete picture of the formal grammar landscape extending CFGs in the spirit of mildly context-sensitive grammars. For this reason, we give detailed formalizations of the different formalisms; we list their formal properties, sometimes with proofs, and we also give application examples that motivate the need for these formalisms. On the other hand, we provide a detailed description of symbolic parsing algorithms that have been developed for these formalisms. We will show how traditional CFG parsing techniques can be extended to the more powerful grammar frameworks covered in this book.

Besides providing a thorough formalization of the presented material, we give numerous examples and list a large range of problems at the end of each chapter whose solutions can be found at the end of the book. This way, the book is useful not only for advanced researchers but also for students who have only just started studying this field. Furthermore, the book may be used as a textbook on which a course on advanced symbolic parsing algorithms can be based.

Though some prior knowledge of formal grammar theory and parsing is of course helpful when reading this book, it is not a necessary requirement.

The book is self-contained; it introduces all the mathematical concepts and all aspects of CFG parsing that are needed to be able to follow it.

1.3 What This Book Is Not About

There are several grammar formalisms used for natural languages that are left aside in this book.

A first group concerns formalisms that have a very high expressive power and, as a consequence of this, generate more than polynomial languages. The most prominent formalisms of this type are Lexical Functional Grammar (LFG) (Kaplan and Bresnan, 1982; Bresnan, 2001) and Head-Driven Phrase Structure Grammar (HPSG) (Pollard and Sag, 1994). These formalisms follow a different tradition, compared to the grammars we deal with. All the formalisms covered in this book are motivated by the goal to extend the expressive power as far as necessary beyond CFG (necessary to describe all natural language phenomena) while keeping it as restricted as possible in order to guarantee computational tractability. This amounts to the aim of finding a grammar formalism that, by itself, gives already a close characterization of the class of natural languages. LFG and HPSG do not subscribe to this line of grammar design since they provide formalisms that are very powerful and that, by themselves, do not tell us anything about the class of natural languages. Only the concrete grammars of course characterize a natural language.

A second set of formalisms that are only briefly mentioned but not treated in detail are the different types of vector grammars proposed in the context of natural language processing. A vector grammar is a grammar whose elements are sets, for instance sets of rewriting rules or sets of TAG trees. Whenever an element from such a set is used in a derivation, all the other elements from the same set must be used as well. Depending on how elements from the same set have to be added, we obtain a large range of different formalisms with different properties. Examples are Matrix Grammars (Dassow and Păun, 1989), unordered Vector Grammars (Cremers and Mayer, 1973), tree-local and set-local multicomponent TAG (Joshi, 1985; Weir, 1988), non-local MCTAG with dominance links (Becker, Joshi, and Rambow, 1991) and Vector-TAG with dominance links (Rambow, 1994).

A third group of grammar formalisms that are not treated in this book are the different types of Categorial Grammar such as Combinatory Categorial Grammar (CCG) (Steedman, 2000) and Abstract Categorial Grammar (ACG) (de Groote, 2001). The way these grammars are defined is different from the grammar formalisms covered in this book since categorial grammars are deduction-based logical frameworks. In this book, we concentrate on rewriting grammars, i.e., grammars whose rules define the way parts of an already generated structure can be rewritten. Such grammars present straight-forward extensions of CFG.

Another important topic in the context of parsing that is left aside as well is dependency parsing. The reason is that, in general, dependency parsing is data driven and not rule-based and therefore presents a different approach to parsing, compared with the rule-based symbolic parsing algorithms presented in this book. See for instance (Merlo, Bunt, and Nivre, 2010) for a series of recent papers on dependency parsing.

1.4 Overview of the Book

The book is structured into ten chapters where the first three chapters serve as introduction while the next six chapters cover the different extensions of CFG and their respective parsing algorithms. Chapter 10 introduces different automata models that generate the string languages of the formalisms introduced in the preceding chapters.

1.4.1 Grammar Formalisms for Natural Languages

In Chapter 2 we explain why CFGs are too limited for natural languages. In particular, we give the proof from Shieber (1985) that Swiss German is not context-free because of its cross-serial dependencies. CFGs can describe nested dependencies but they are too limited to deal with the crossing dependencies we encounter in some natural languages. We also introduce the notion of mild context-sensitivity, a property that Joshi (1985) has put forward as a reasonable characterization of the type of grammar formalism needed for natural languages. Finally, we motivate the different extensions of CFG that we will treat in this book. We give an overview over these formalisms, the languages they generate and the way they are related to each other.

1.4.2 Parsing: Preliminaries

Chapter 3 introduces notions about parsing that are relevant for this book. We introduce the framework of parsing as deduction (Shieber, Schabes, and Pereira, 1995) that will be used throughout the book to specify parsing algorithms. We then explain some basic notions about tabulation and chart parsing. Furthermore, we list some properties of parsing algorithms such as complexity and prefix validity that oftentimes will be subject to investigation in the context of the different algorithms presented in the course of the book.

1.4.3 Tree Adjoining Grammars

The fourth and fifth chapter cover the smallest extension of CFG presented in this book, namely Tree Adjoining Grammars (TAG). Chapter 4 introduces the formalism while Chapter 5 deals with different parsing techniques for TAG.

TAGs (Joshi and Schabes, 1997) only slightly extend CFGs. The additional power stems from the adjunction operation that permits us to replace internal nodes in a tree with new trees from the grammar. TAGs have been extensively used for modeling natural languages; we give several examples of TAG analyses for natural language phenomena. The string languages of TAG have several closure properties and a pumping lemma for TAG has been shown.

We explain different parsing algorithms for TAG that apply strategies from CFG parsing to the specific needs of TAG parsing. In particular, we describe a CYK-style bottom-up parser, an Earley bottom-up parser with top-down prediction and a proposal for LR parsing. We discuss various aspects of these algorithms, such as the prefix validity of different types of Earley parsing algorithms for TAG.

1.4.4 MCFG and LCFRS

Chapters 6 and 7 deal with Linear Context-Free Rewriting Systems (LCFRSs) (Vijay-Shanker, Weir, and Joshi, 1987) and the equivalent Multiple Context-Free Grammars (MCFGs) (Seki et al., 1991) and simple Range Concatenation Grammars (SRCGs) (Boullier, 1998a). These formalisms extend CFGs by allowing non-terminals to have a sequence of non-adjacent strings as yields. They are particularly well suited for modelling discontinuities which occur frequently in natural languages. In Chapter 6 we introduce the formalism, discuss its formal properties and present some applications.

Chapter 7 then presents different types of CYK and Earley parsing algorithms that have been proposed for these grammars. In this chapter, we also introduce several normal forms for SRCG such as ε-free SRCGs, ordered SRCGs and binarized SRCGs and we show how to transform an arbitrary SRCG into an equivalent SRCG in one of these normal forms. All these normal forms of course have an impact on parsing complexity.

1.4.5 Range Concatenation Grammars

The next chapter introduces Range Concatenation Grammars (RCGs) (Boullier, 2000b). RCGs have the greatest generative capacity among the formalisms presented in this book. They generate the entire class of all polynomially parsable languages. The formalism keeps the idea from LCFRS and SRCG that non-terminals can span sequences of terminal strings. But it extends this by allowing a single string to be part of the yields of different non-terminal nodes that are not derived from each other. In other words, one can reuse terminal strings in different contexts.

We present the formalism and discuss several restricted forms of it. Furthermore, we discuss its relation to other formalisms, namely to CFG, TAG, MCFG and Literal Movement Grammar (LMG) (Groenink, 1996). A restricted form of the latter, so-called *simple* LMG, is equivalent to RCG. We give the transformation algorithm from TAG to specific types of SRCG.

Concerning parsing, we discuss in Chapter 9 the extensions of standard parsing algorithms such as CYK and Earley to the specific needs of RCG.

1.4.6 Automata

Chapter 10 finally presents several automata models that generate the string languages of some of the formalisms from the previous chapters.

Extended Push-down Automata (EPDA) (Vijay-Shanker, 1987) recognize the class of Tree-Adjoining Languages (TALs) and are a natural extension of Push-down Automata (PDA). An alternative automata model for TAL is Two-Stack Automata (2-SA) (Becker, 1994), which we present as well. A restricted variant of 2-SA is Strongly-driven Two-Stack Automata (SD-2SA) (Villemonte de la Clergerie and Pardo, 1998; Alonso Pardo, Nederhof, and Villemonte de la Clergerie, 2000), explicitly aiming at an elegant representation of different parsing strategies.

The most powerful automata model treated in this book are Thread Automata (TA) (Villemonte de la Clergerie, 2002) that recognize all Linear Context-Free Rewriting Languages (LCFRLs). The strategy of a TA for LCFRS follows an incremental top-down restricted bottom-up recognition strategy. Therefore one of the Earley algorithms presented in Chapter 6 for simple RCG can be seen as a deduction rule-based formulation of a TA for simple RCG.

1.5 Some Basic Definitions

In the following, we introduce some basic notions and facts related to formal grammars and formal languages that will be referred to in the course of the book. We follow standard definitions presented, e.g., in (Hopcroft and Ullman, 1979).

1.5.1 Languages

First, we introduce some definitions related to the notion of languages.

Definition 1.1 (Alphabet, word, language).

1. *An* alphabet *is a non-empty finite set* X.
2. *A string* $x_1 \ldots x_n$ *with* $n \geq 1$ *and* $x_i \in X$ *for* $1 \leq i \leq n$ *is called a non-empty word on the alphabet* X. X^+ *is defined as the set of all non-empty words on* X.
3. *A new element* $\varepsilon \notin X^+$ *is added:* $X^* := X^+ \cup \{\varepsilon\}$.
   For each $w \in X^*$, *the concatenation of* w *and* ε *is defined as follows:* $w\varepsilon = \varepsilon w = w$.
   ε *is called the* empty word, *and each* $w \in X^*$ *is called a word on* X.

4. A set L is called a language *iff there is an alphabet X such that $L \subseteq X^*$.*

Definition 1.2 (Homomorphism).
For two alphabets X and Y, a function $f : X^* \to Y^*$ is a homomorphism iff for all $v, w \in X^*$: $f(vw) = f(v)f(w)$.

Definition 1.3 (Length of a word).
Let X be an alphabet, $w \in X^*$.

1. *The* length *of w, $|w|$ is defined as follows: if $w = \varepsilon$, then $|w| = 0$. If $w = xw'$ for some $x \in X$, then $|w| = 1 + |w'|$.*
2. *For every $a \in X$, we define $|w|_a$ as the number of as occurring in w: If $w = \varepsilon$, then $|w|_a = 0$, if $w = aw'$, then $|w|_a = |w'|_a + 1$ and if $w = bw'$ for some $b \in X \setminus \{a\}$, then $|w|_a = |w'|_a$.*

1.5.2 Context-Free Grammars

In the following, we introduce context-free grammars and the languages they generate and we list a range of properties they have.

Definition 1.4 (Context-free grammar).
A context-free grammar (CFG) *is a tuple $G = \langle N, T, P, S \rangle$ such that*

1. *N and T are disjoint alphabets, the* non-terminals *and* terminals *of G,*
2. *$P \subset N \times (N \cup T)^*$ is a finite set of* productions *(also called* rewriting rules*). A production $\langle A, \alpha \rangle$ is usually written $A \to \alpha$.*
3. *$S \in N$ is the* start symbol.

Definition 1.5 (Language of a CFG).
Let $G = \langle N, T, P, S \rangle$ be a CFG. The (string) language $L(G)$ of G is the set $\{w \in T^* \mid S \stackrel{*}{\Rightarrow} w\}$ where

- *for $w, w' \in (N \cup T)^*$: $w \Rightarrow w'$ iff there is a $A \to \alpha \in P$ and there are $v, u \in (N \cup T)^*$ such that $w = vAu$ and $w' = v\alpha u$.*
- *$\stackrel{*}{\Rightarrow}$ is the reflexive transitive closure of $\Rightarrow$:*
  - *$w \stackrel{0}{\Rightarrow} w$ for all $w \in (N \cup T)^*$, and*
  - *for all $w, w' \in (N \cup T)^*$: $w \stackrel{n}{\Rightarrow} w'$ iff there is a v such that $w \Rightarrow v$ and $v \stackrel{n-1}{\Rightarrow} w'$.*
  - *for all $w, w' \in (N \cup T)^*$: $w \stackrel{*}{\Rightarrow} w'$ iff there is a $i \in \mathbb{N}$ such that $w \stackrel{i}{\Rightarrow} w'$.*

A language L is called context-free *iff there is a CFG G such that $L = L(G)$.*

Definition 1.6 (Useful symbol).
Let $G = \langle N, T, P, S \rangle$ be a CFG. A $X \in (N \cup T)$ is called useful *if there are $\alpha, \beta \in (N \cup T)^*$ and $w \in T^*$ such that $S \stackrel{*\{\Rightarrow}{\alpha}} X\beta \stackrel{*\{\Rightarrow}{w}}$.*
Otherwise, A is called useless.

Definition 1.7 (Normal forms).
Let $G = \langle N, T, P, S \rangle$ be a CFG. G is

- in Chomsky normal form *(CNF)* iff all productions have either the form $A \to BC$ or $A \to a$ with $A, B, C \in N, a \in T$.
- in Greibach normal form *(GNF)* iff all productions have the form $A \to a\alpha$ with $a \in T, \alpha \in N^*$.

Proposition 1.8 (Pumping lemma for context-free languages).
Let L be a context-free language. Then there is a constant c such that for all $w \in L$ with $|w| \geq c$ it holds that $w = xv_1yv_2z$ with

- $|v_1v_2| \geq 1$,
- $|v_1yv_2| \leq c$, and
- for all $i \geq 0$: $xv_1^i yv_2^i z \in L$.

Proposition 1.9. *Context-free languages are closed under homomorphisms, i.e., for alphabets T_1, T_2 and for every context-free language $L_1 \subset T_1^*$ and every homomorphism $h : T_1^* \to T_2^*$, $h(L_1) = \{h(w) \,|\, w \in L_1\}$ is a context-free language.*

Proposition 1.10. *Context-free languages are closed under intersection with regular languages, i.e., for every context-free language L and every regular language L_r, $L \cap L_r$ is a context-free language.*

Proposition 1.11. *The copy language $\{ww \,|\, w \in \{a,b\}^*\}$ is not context-free.*

Proposition 1.12. *For every CFG G,*

- *there exists a CFG G' that does not contain useless symbols such that $L(G) = L(G')$.*
- *there exists a CFG G' in Chomsky normal form such that $L(G) \setminus \{\varepsilon\} = L(G')$.*
- *there exists a CFG G' in Greibach normal form such that $L(G) \setminus \{\varepsilon\} = L(G')$.*

Proofs of these propositions can be found for example in (Hopcroft and Ullman, 1979).

1.5.3 Automata

The productions of CFGs are rewriting rules that describe how to generate words from a start symbol by repeatedly rewriting a left-hand side symbol of a production with its right-hand side string. Such grammars are generative devices.

A different way to characterize a language is a device that, given an input word w, performs certain actions and, after a certain number of steps, eventually accepts or rejects w. Such devices are for instance automata such as Finite

State Automata (FSA) and Push-Down Automata (PDA). An automaton is a recognizer in the sense that it recognizes the words belonging to a specific language. Oftentimes it can be extended to a parser, i.e., a device that not only accepts the words belonging to a given language but that also outputs their analysis.

Definition 1.13 (Finite State Automaton).

1. A Finite State Automaton *(FSA) M is a quintuple* $\langle Q, \Sigma, \delta, q_0, F \rangle$ *such that*
   - Q *is a finite set of states.*
   - Σ *is a finite set, the input alphabet.*
   - $\delta : Q \times \Sigma \to \mathcal{P}(Q)$ *is the transition function (where* $\mathcal{P}(Q)$ *is the power set of* Q*).*
   - $q_0 \in Q$ *is the initial state.*
   - $F \subseteq Q$ *is the set of final states.*
2. *The* transition closure $\hat{\delta} : Q \times \Sigma^* \to \mathcal{P}(Q)$ *of an FSA M is defined as follows:*
   - $\hat{\delta}(q, \varepsilon) := \{q\}$ *for all* $q \in Q$.
   - *For all* $a \in \Sigma, w \in \Sigma^*$: $\hat{\delta}(q, wa) := \{p \mid$ *there is a* $r \in \hat{\delta}(q, w)$ *such that* $p \in \delta(r, a)\}$.
3. *The* string language *accepted by an FSA M is*

$$L(M) := \{w \mid \hat{\delta}(q_0, w) \cap F \neq \emptyset\}.$$

Proposition 1.14. *The set of languages accepted by FSAs is the set of regular languages (Hopcroft and Ullman, 1979).*

Definition 1.15 (Push-Down Automaton).

1. A Push-Down Automaton *(PDA) M is a tuple* $\langle Q, \Sigma, \Gamma, \delta, q_0, Z_0, F \rangle$ *with*
   - Q *is a finite set of states.*
   - Σ *is a finite set, the input alphabet.*
   - Γ *is a finite set, the stack alphabet.*
   - $q_0 \in Q$ *is the initial state.*
   - $Z_0 \in \Gamma$ *is the initial stack symbol.*
   - $F \subseteq Q$ *is the set of final states.*
   - $\delta : Q \times (\Sigma \cup \{\varepsilon\}) \times \Gamma \to \mathcal{P}_{fin}(Q \times \Gamma^*)$ *is the transition function.* ($\mathcal{P}_{fin}(X)$ *is the set of finite subsets of* X*).*
2. *An* instantaneous description *of a PDA is a triple* (q, w, γ) *with*
   - $q \in Q$ *is the current state of the automaton,*
   - $w \in \Sigma^*$ *is the remaining part of the input string, and*
   - $\gamma \in \Gamma^*$ *is the current stack.*

3. For all $q, q' \in Q, a \in \Sigma \cup \{\varepsilon\}, w \in \Sigma^*, Z \in \Gamma, \alpha, \beta \in \Gamma^*$:
   $(q, aw, Z\alpha) \vdash (q', w, \beta\alpha)$ iff $\langle q', \beta \rangle \in \delta(q, a, Z)$.
   $\stackrel{*}{\vdash}$ is the reflexive transitive closure of $\vdash$.
4. The language accepted by M with a final state is

$$L(M) := \{w \mid (q_0, w, Z_0) \stackrel{*}{\vdash} (q_f, \varepsilon, \gamma) \text{ for a } q_f \in F \text{ and a } \gamma \in \Gamma^*\}.$$

The language accepted by M with an empty stack is

$$N(M) := \{w \mid (q_0, w, Z_0) \stackrel{*}{\vdash} (q, \varepsilon, \varepsilon) \text{ for a } q \in Q\}.$$

The two modes of acceptance are equivalent, i.e., for each language L there is a PDA M_1 with $L = L(M_1)$ iff there is a PDA M_2 with $L = N(M_2)$.

Proposition 1.16. *The set of languages accepted by PDAs is the set of all context-free languages (Hopcroft and Ullman, 1979).*

1.5.4 Trees

Many of the formalisms treated in this book are concerned with trees; we therefore need the following basic definitions of trees.

Definition 1.17 (Directed Graph).

1. *A* directed graph *is a pair $\langle V, E \rangle$ where V is a finite set of* vertices *and $E \subseteq V \times V$ is a set of* edges.
2. *For every $v \in V$, we define the* in-degree *of v as $|\{v' \in V \mid \langle v', v \rangle \in E\}|$ and the* out-degree *of v as $|\{v' \in V \mid \langle v, v' \rangle \in E\}|$.*

E^+ is the transitive closure of E and E^* is the reflexive transitive closure of E.

Definition 1.18 (Tree).

1. *A* tree *is a triple $\gamma = \langle V, E, r \rangle$ such that*
   - *$\langle V, E \rangle$ is a directed graph and $r \in V$ is a special node, the* root *node.*
   - *γ contains no cycles, i.e., there is no $v \in V$ such that $\langle v, v \rangle \in E^+$,*
   - *only the root $r \in V$ has in-degree 0,*
   - *every vertex $v \in V$ is accessible from r, i.e., $\langle r, v \rangle \in E^*$, and*
   - *all nodes $v \in V - \{r\}$ have in-degree 1.*
2. *a tree is* ordered *if it has an additional* linear precedence *relation $\prec \in V \times V$ such that*
   - *$\prec$ is irreflexive, antisymmetric and transitive,*
   - *for all v_1, v_2 with $\{\langle v_1, v_2 \rangle, \langle v_2, v_1 \rangle\} \cap E^* = \emptyset$: either $v_1 \prec v_2$ or $v_2 \prec v_1$ and if there is either a $\langle v_3, v_1 \rangle \in E$ with $v_3 \prec v_2$ or a $\langle v_4, v_2 \rangle \in E$ with $v_1 \prec v_4$, then $v_1 \prec v_2$, and*

- *nothing else is in $\prec$.*

A vertex with out-degree 0 is called a leaf. The vertices in a tree are also called nodes.

We use Gorn addresses for nodes in ordered trees: The root address is ε, and the jth child of a node with address p has address pj.

Definition 1.19 (Labeling). *A* labeling *of a graph $\gamma = \langle V, E \rangle$ over a signature $\langle A_1, A_2 \rangle$ is a pair of functions $l : V \to A_1$ and $g : E \to A_2$ with A_1, A_2 possibly distinct.*

Definition 1.20 (Syntactic tree).
   Let N and T be disjoint alphabets of non-terminal and terminal symbols. A syntactic tree *(over N and T) is an ordered finite labeled tree such that $l(v) \in N$ for each vertex v with out-degree at least 1 and $l(v) \in (N \cup T \cup \{\varepsilon\})$ for each leaf v.*

Definition 1.21 (Tree Language of a CFG).
   Let $G = \langle N, T, P, S \rangle$ be a CFG.

1. *A syntactic tree $\langle V, E, r \rangle$ over N and T is a* parse tree *in G iff*
   - $l(v) \in (T \cup \{\varepsilon\})$ *for each leaf v,*
   - *for every $v_0, v_1, \ldots, v_n \in V$, $n \geq 1$ such that $\langle v_0, v_i \rangle \in E$ for $1 \leq i \leq n$, there is no $u \notin \{v_1, \ldots, v_n\}$ with $\langle v_0, u \rangle \in E$ and $\langle v_i, v_{i+1} \rangle \in \prec$ for $1 \leq i < n$, it holds that $l(v_0) \to l(v_1) \ldots l(v_n) \in P$.*
2. *A parse tree $\langle V, E, r \rangle$ is a* derivation tree *in G iff $l(r) = S$.*
3. *The* tree language *of G is*

$$L_T(G) = \{\gamma \mid \gamma \text{ is a derivation tree in } G\}.$$

Definition 1.22 (Weak and Strong Equivalence).
   Let F_1, F_2 be two grammar formalisms.

- *F_1 and F_2 are* weakly equivalent *iff for each instance G_1 of F_1 there is an instance G_2 of F_2 that generates the same string language and vice versa.*
- *F_1 and F_2 are* strongly equivalent *iff for both formalisms the notion of a tree language is defined and, furthermore, for each instance G_1 of F_1 there is an instance G_2 of F_2 that generates the same tree language and vice versa.*

2
Grammar Formalisms for Natural Languages

2.1 Context-Free Grammars and Natural Languages

2.1.1 The Generative Capacity of CFGs

For a long time there has been a debate about whether CFGs are sufficiently powerful to describe natural languages. Several approaches have used CFGs, oftentimes enriched with some additional mechanism of transformation (Chomsky, 1956) or with features (Gazdar et al., 1985) for natural languages. These approaches were able to treat a large range of linguistic phenomena.

However, in the 1980s Stuart Shieber was able to prove in (1985) that there are natural languages that cannot be generated by a CFG. Before that, Bresnan et al. (1982) made a similar argument but their proof is based on the tree structures obtained with CFGs while Shieber argues on the basis of weak generative capacity, i.e., of the string languages.

The phenomena considered in both papers are cross-serial dependencies. Bresnan et al. (1982) argue that CFGs cannot describe cross-serial dependencies in Dutch while Shieber (1985) argues the same for Swiss German. Swiss German has case marking; therefore dependencies are visible on the strings and one can show that the string languages are not context-free.

Let us first consider the Dutch data from (Bresnan et al., 1982).

(3) ... dat Jan de kinderen zag zwemmen
     ... that Jan the children saw swim

'... that Jan saw the children swim'

In (3), we have two verbs and two noun phrases. The links mark the dependencies between these: *the children* is an argument of *swim* while *Jan* is an argument of *saw*. The dependency links are in a crossing configuration. This phenomenon can be iterated, as shown in (4) and (5).

(4) ... dat   Jan Piet de kinderen zag helpen zwemmen
    ... that Jan Piet the children saw help   swim

'... that Jan saw Piet help the children swim'

(5) ... dat   Jan Piet Marie de kinderen zag helpen leren zwemmen
    ... that Jan Piet Marie the children saw help   teach swim

'... that Jan saw Piet help Marie teach the children to swim'

In principle, an unbounded number of crossed dependencies is possible. However, except for the first and last verb any permutation of the NPs and the verbs is grammatical as well (even though with a completely different dependency structure since the dependencies are always cross-serial). Therefore, the string language of Dutch cross-serial dependencies amounts roughly to $\{n^k v^k \mid k > 0\}$, which is a context-free language.

Bresnan et al. (1982) argue that the strong generative capacity of CFGs is too limited for the Dutch examples. A weakness of the argument is however that an argument about syntactic structure makes always certain theoretical stipulations. Although it is very probable, it does not absolutely prove that, even using different syntactic theories, there is no context-free analysis for the Dutch examples. It only shows that the syntactic structures Bresnan et al. (1982) think the appropriate ones cannot be obtained with a CFG.

Shieber's argument about Swiss German cross-serial dependencies is more convincing since it relies only on the string language, i.e., it concerns the weak generative capacity of CFGs. Swiss German displays the same dependency patterns as Dutch in examples such as (3)–(5). The crucial difference is that Swiss German has case marking. Let us consider the Swiss German data.

(6) ... das   mer em Hans   es huus   hälfed   aastriiche
    ... that we Hans$_{DAT}$ house$_{ACC}$ helped paint

'... that we helped Hans paint the house'

(7) ... das   mer d'chind   em Hans   es huus   lönd hälfe aastriiche
    ... that we   the children$_{ACC}$ Hans$_{DAT}$ house$_{ACC}$ let   help paint

'... that we let the children help Hans paint the house'

In Swiss German, as in Dutch, the dependencies are always cross-serial in these examples. But, since we have case marking, permutations of the noun phrases would lead to ungrammatical sentences. This is why Shieber was able to show that Swiss German (as a string language) is not context-free.

Proposition 2.1.
The language L of Swiss German is not context-free (Shieber, 1985).

The argumentation of the proof goes as follows: We assume that L is context-free. Then the intersection of a regular language with the image of L under a homomorphism must be context-free as well. We find a particular homomorphism and a regular language such that the result obtained in this way is a non-context-free language. This is a contradiction to our assumption and, consequently, the assumption does not hold.

Shieber considers sentences of the following form:

(8) ... das mer d'chind em Hans es huus haend
 ... that we the children$_{ACC}$ Hans$_{DAT}$ house$_{ACC}$ have
 wele laa hälfe aastriiche
 wanted let help paint
 '... that we have wanted to let the children help Hans paint the house'

Swiss German allows constructions of the form *(Jan säit)* ('Jan says')*das mer (d'chind)^i (em Hans)^j es huus haend wele (laa)^i (hälfe)^j aastriiche*. In these constructions the number of accusative NPs *d'chind* must equal the number of verbs (here *laa*) selecting for an accusative and the number of dative NPs *em Hans* must equal the number of verbs (here *hälfe*) selecting for a dative object. Furthermore, the order must be the same in the sense that if all accusative NPs precede all dative NPs, then all verbs selecting an accusative must precede all verbs selecting a dative.

The following homomorphism f separates the iterated noun phrases and verbs in these examples from the surrounding material:

$f(\text{``d'chind''}) = a$ $\quad$ $f(\text{``Jan säit das mer''}) = w$
$f(\text{``em Hans''}) = b$ $\quad$ $f(\text{``es huus haend wele''}) = x$
$f(\text{``laa''}) = c$ $\quad$ $f(\text{``aastriiche''}) = y$
$f(\text{``hälfe''}) = d$ $\quad$ $f(s) = z$ otherwise

To make sure we concentrate only on the constructions of the described form, we intersect $f(L)$ with the regular language $wa^*b^*xc^*d^*y$. Whenever we have a sentence whose image under f is in the intersection, this sentence has the form *(Jan säit) das mer (d'chind)^i (em Hans)^j es huus haend wele (laa)^k (hälfe)^l aastriiche* for some $i, j, k, l \geq 0$. Furthermore, because of the constraints we observe in Swiss German, $i = k$ and $j = l$. Therefore, the result of this intersection is $\{wa^i b^j xc^i d^j y \mid i, j \geq 0\}$, a language that is not context-free.[1] Consequently, the original language L, Swiss German, is not context-free either.

Alternatively, one can also reduce Swiss German to the copy language $\{ww \,|\, w \in \{a, b\}^*\}$ by appropriate homomorphisms and an intersection with a regular language (see Problem 2.2 for more details). For grammar formalisms whose language classes are closed under homomorphisms and intersection with regular languages, this means the following: If such a formalism cannot generate the copy language, then it is not powerful enough to describe all natural languages. Therefore, the fact that a formalism can generate the copy language is often considered a necessary condition for the ability to describe natural languages.

2.1.2 CFGs and Lexicalization

Besides the fact that the generative capacity of CFGs is too weak to describe all natural languages, CFGs cannot be strongly lexicalized. A set of grammars can be strongly lexicalized if, for every grammar in this set, we can find a strongly equivalent lexicalized grammar in the same set. This property is sometimes claimed useful for formalisms intended to describe natural languages (Schabes, 1990; Joshi and Schabes, 1997).

Lexicalized grammars are grammars where each rewriting rule contains at least one terminal. On the one hand, lexicalized grammars are computationally interesting since in a lexicalized grammar the number of analyses for a sentence is finite (if the grammar is finite of course). On the other hand, they are linguistically interesting since, if we assume that each lexical item comes with the possibility of certain partial syntactic constructions, we would like to associate it with a set of such structures.

Another linguistic aspect of lexicalized grammars is that they relate oftentimes immediately to dependency structures since combinations during derivation can be interpreted as dependencies. This link is investigated in detail in (Kuhlmann, 2007).

Lexicalization is particularly useful for parsing since the lexical elements give us a strong indication for which rewriting rules to use, i.e., they help to restrict the search space during parsing.

A lexicalized grammar can never generate the empty word ε. Therefore, in the following we consider only languages that do not contain ε.

Definition 2.2 (Lexicalized Grammar). *A grammar is* lexicalized *if it consists of*

- *a finite set of elementary objects of finite size each associated with a nonempty lexical item (called its* anchor*),*

---

[1] To see that, we can intersect this language with the regular language $a^*b^*c^*d^*$, which leads to $\{a^i b^j c^i d^j \,|\, i, j \geq 0\}$. This language can be shown to be non-context-free using the pumping lemma for context-free languages.

2.1 Context-Free Grammars and Natural Languages

CFG rewriting step $\alpha A \beta \Rightarrow \alpha X_1 \ldots X_k \beta$ with production $A \rightarrow X_1 \ldots X_k$

Corresponding tree substitution:

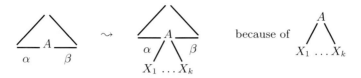

Fig. 2.1. Context-free derivation steps as substitution

- and an operation/operations for composing these structures that do not copy, erase or restructure unbounded components of their arguments.

The objects might be for instance productions as in CFG or trees as in TAG or tree descriptions ("quasi trees") as in D-Tree Substitution Grammar (Rambow, Vijay-Shanker, and Weir, 2001).

An elementary object can contain more than one lexical item. We then call the set of its lexical items a *multicomponent anchor*.

Lexicalized grammars are *finitely ambiguous*, i.e., no sentence of finite length can be analyzed in an infinite number of ways. Consequently the recognition problem for lexicalized grammars is decidable.

Definition 2.3 (Lexicalization).
A formalism F can be strongly (weakly) lexicalized by a formalism F' if for any finitely ambiguous grammar G in F there is a lexicalized grammar G' in F' such that G and G' are strongly (weakly) equivalent.

CFG can be weakly lexicalized by CFG since for each CFG whose string language does not contain ε, a weakly equivalent lexicalized CFG can be found, namely the one in Greibach Normal Form (GNF) (see Hopcroft and Ullman (1979)).[2] However, the derivation trees obtained with the original CFG and the one in Greibach Normal Form are different in general.

In order to show that CFGs cannot be strongly lexicalized by CFGs, we show that they cannot be strongly lexicalized by Tree Substitution Grammars, a formalism that is strongly equivalent to CFG. Therefore, we now introduce Tree Substitution Grammars.

We can consider context-free derivation steps as tree substitutions since a non-terminal leaf is replaced with a tree of height 1 (one mother node and n daughters) as depicted in Figure 2.1.

Extending the height of the trees permitted leads to Tree Substitution Grammars:

---

[2] A CFG is in Greibach Normal Form if each production is of the form $A \rightarrow a\,x$ with $A \in N, a \in T, x \in (N \cup T)^*$.

Definition 2.4 (Tree Substitution Grammar).

A *Tree Substitution Grammar (TSG)* consists of a quadruple $\langle T, N, I, S \rangle$ such that

- T and N are disjoint alphabets, the *terminals* and *non-terminals*,
- I is a finite set of syntactic trees, and
- $S \in N$ is the *start symbol*.

We call the syntactic trees in I the *elementary trees*.

Every elementary tree is a *derived* tree and we can obtain larger derived trees from existing ones by replacing some of the non-terminal leaves with elementary trees having the same non-terminal as root label. Such operations are called *substitution*.

Definition 2.5 (Substitution).

Let $\gamma = \langle V, E, r \rangle$ be a syntactic tree, $\gamma' = \langle V', E', r' \rangle$ an initial tree and $v \in V$. $\gamma[v, \gamma']$, the result of *substituting* γ' into γ at node v is defined as follows:

- if v is no leaf or $l(v) \neq l(r')$, then $\gamma[v, \gamma']$ is undefined;
- otherwise, $\gamma[v, \gamma'] := \langle V'', E'', r'' \rangle$ with $V'' = V \cup V'' \setminus \{v\}$ and $E'' = (E \setminus \{\langle v_1, v_2 \rangle \mid v_2 = v\}) \cup E' \cup \{\langle v_1, r' \rangle \mid \langle v_1, v \rangle \in E\}$.

A leaf that has a non-terminal label is called a *substitution node*.

A sample substitution is shown in Figure 2.2 where the *John*-tree with root node label NP is substituted into the NP substitution node in the *laughs* tree.

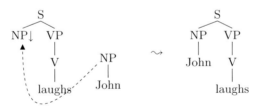

Fig. 2.2. Sample substitution

A tree is *completed* if all leaves are labeled by terminals. The tree language $T(G)$ of a TSG G is the set of all completed derived trees that have the root label S. The string language of G is then the set of strings yielded by the trees in the tree language.

TSGs are weakly equivalent to CFGs and each CFG is a TSG.

Proposition 2.6. *CFG cannot be strongly lexicalized by TSG (Schabes, 1990; Joshi and Schabes, 1997).*

Proof. Consider the CFG G with productions $S \to S\,S$, $S \to a$. Assume that there is a strongly equivalent lexicalized TSG G'. Then each tree in the tree language is derived from some initial tree t with a leaf labeled with a such that the path between this leaf and the root has a constant length n. Below this leaf nothing can be added, i.e., each tree derived from t still has a path of length n. Let n_{max} be the maximal path length between root and leaf with label a in the initial trees of G'. Then there is no derived tree in the tree language of G' such that all paths have a length $> n_{max}$. But such trees exist in the tree language of G. Contradiction. □

Then, trivially, CFGs cannot strongly lexicalize CFGs either.

The reason why TSG cannot strongly lexicalize CFG is that in a TSG we always add material below one of the leaves. Consequently, TSGs do not permit the distance between two nodes in the same elementary tree to increase. One way to overcome this is to allow not only leaves but also internal nodes to be replaced with new elementary trees. This leads to tree-rewriting grammars with adjunction, i.e., to Tree Adjoining Grammars.

2.1.3 Mild Context-Sensitivity

Once it was clear that CFGs were not powerful enough to describe all natural language phenomena, the question of the appropriate context-sensitive formalism for natural languages arose. In an attempt to characterize the amount of context-sensitivity required, Aravind Joshi introduced the notion of mild context-sensitivity (1985). This is a term that refers to classes of languages, not to formalisms.

Definition 2.7 (Mildly context-sensitive).

1. A set $\mathcal{L}$ of languages is mildly context-sensitive *iff*
   a) $\mathcal{L}$ contains all context-free languages.
   b) $\mathcal{L}$ can describe cross-serial dependencies: There is an $n \geq 2$ such that $\{w^k \mid w \in T^*\} \in \mathcal{L}$ for all $k \leq n$.
   c) The languages in $\mathcal{L}$ are polynomially parsable, i.e., $\mathcal{L} \subset PTIME$.
   d) The languages in $\mathcal{L}$ have the constant growth property.
2. A formalism F is mildly context-sensitive *iff* the set $\{L \mid L = L(G)$ for some $G \in F\}$ is mildly context-sensitive.

The constant growth property roughly means that, if we order the words of a language according to their length, then the length grows in a linear way. E.g., $\{a^{2^n} \mid n \geq 0\}$ does not have the constant growth property. The following definition is from Weir (1988).

Definition 2.8 (Constant Growth Property).

Let X be an alphabet and $L \subseteq X^*$. L has the constant growth property *iff* there is a constant $c_0 > 0$ and a finite set of constants $C \subset \mathbb{N} \setminus \{0\}$ such that for all $w \in L$ with $|w| > c_0$, there is a $w' \in L$ with $|w| = |w'| + c$ for some $c \in C$.

As already mentioned, mild context-sensitivity is introduced as a property of a set of languages. So far, it has not been possible to identify a grammar formalism that generates the largest possible mildly context-sensitive set of string languages. The closest approximation we know of are *Linear Context-Free Rewriting Systems (LCFRSs)*, introduced in (Vijay-Shanker, Weir, and Joshi, 1987; Weir, 1988), and equivalent formalisms such as *set-local Multicomponent Tree Adjoining Grammars (MCTAGs)* (Weir, 1988), *Multiple Context-Free Grammars (MCFGs)* (Seki et al., 1991) and *simple Range Concatenation Grammars (simple RCGs)* (Boullier, 2000b). However, recent research on certain types of MCTAG suggests that there might be mildly context-sensitive grammar formalisms that are not comparable with LCFRS and equivalent formalisms, i.e., that generate languages that cannot be generated by LCFRS and vice versa (Kallmeyer and Satta, 2009).

There are different ways to show the constant growth property for a specific formalism. Oftentimes, constant growth follows from a pumping lemma. If there is no pumping lemma, then one might show the constant growth property of a language class by showing the semilinearity (Parikh, 1966) of the languages. Constant growth follows from semilinearity.

Let us introduce semilinearity.

First, we define for $\langle a_1, \ldots, a_n \rangle, \langle b_1, \ldots, b_n \rangle \in \mathbb{N}^n$ and $m \in \mathbb{N}$ that $\langle a_1, \ldots, a_n \rangle + \langle b_1, \ldots, b_n \rangle := \langle a_1 + b_1, \ldots, a_n + b_n \rangle$ and $m \langle a_1, \ldots, a_n \rangle := \langle ma_1, \ldots, ma_n \rangle$.

A Parikh mapping is a function counting for each letter of an alphabet the occurrences of this letter in a word w:

Definition 2.9 (Parikh mapping).

Let $X = \{a_1, \ldots, a_n\}$ be an alphabet with some (arbitrary) fixed order of the elements. The Parikh mapping $p : X^* \to \mathbb{N}^n$ (with respect to this order) is defined as follows:

- For all $w \in X^* : p(w) := \langle |w|_{a_1}, \ldots, |w|_{a_n} \rangle$ where $|w|_{a_i}$ is the number of occurrences of a_i in w.
- For all languages $L \subseteq X^* : p(L) := \{p(w) \mid w \in L\}$ is the Parikh image of L.

Two words are *letter equivalent* if they contain equal number of occurrences of each terminal symbol, and two languages are letter equivalent if every string in one language is letter equivalent to a string in the other language and vice-versa.

Definition 2.10 (Letter equivalent).

Let X be an alphabet.

1. *Two words $w_1, w_2 \in X^*$ are* letter equivalent *if there is a Parikh mapping p such that $p(w_1) = p(w_2)$.*
2. *Two languages $L_1, L_2 \subseteq X^*$ are* letter equivalent *if there is a Parikh mapping p such that $p(L_1) = p(L_2)$.*

2.1 Context-Free Grammars and Natural Languages

Definition 2.11 (Semilinear).

1. Let $x_0, \ldots, x_m$ with $m \geq 0$ be in $\mathbb{N}^n$ for some $n \geq 0$.
   The set $\{x_0 + n_1 x_1 + \cdots + n_m x_m \mid n_i \in \mathbb{N} \text{ for } 1 \leq i \leq m\}$ is a linear subset of $\mathbb{N}^n$.
2. The union of finitely many linear subsets of $\mathbb{N}^n$ is a semilinear subset of $\mathbb{N}^n$.
3. A language $L \subseteq X^*$ is semilinear iff there is a Parikh mapping p such that $p(L)$ is a semilinear subset of $\mathbb{N}^n$ for some $n \geq 0$.

Lemma 2.12. *The constant growth property holds for semilinear languages.*

Proof. Assume $L \subseteq X^*$ is semilinear and $p(L)$ is a semilinear Parikh image of L where $p(L)$ is the union of the linear sets $M_1, \ldots, M_l$. Then the constant growth property holds for L with

$c_0 := max\{\Sigma_{i=1}^n y_i \mid$ there are $x_1, \ldots, x_m$ such that
$\{\langle y_1, \ldots, y_n \rangle + n_1 x_1 + \cdots + n_m x_m \mid n_i \in \mathbb{N}\}$
is one of the sets $M_1, \ldots, M_l\}$ and

$C := \{\Sigma_{i=1}^n y_i \mid$ there are $x_1, \ldots, x_m$ such that
$\{x_1 + n_1 \langle y_1, \ldots, y_n \rangle + \cdots + n_m x_m \mid n_i \in \mathbb{N}\}$
is one of the sets $M_1, \ldots, M_l\}$. □

Parikh has shown that a language is semilinear if and only if it is letter equivalent to a regular language. The proof is given in (Kracht, 2003, p. 151). As a consequence, we obtain that context-free languages are semilinear.

Proposition 2.13 (Parikh Theorem).
Each context-free language is semilinear (Parikh, 1966).

Furthermore, each language that is letter equivalent to a semilinear language is semilinear as well since the Parikh images of the two languages are equal. Therefore, in order to show the semilinearity (and constant growth) of a language, it is sufficient to show letter equivalence to a context-free language.

As far as we know, Joshi's hypothesis that natural languages are mildly context-sensitive has been questioned only by two natural language phenomena that have been claimed to be non-semilinear, namely case stacking in Old Georgian (Michaelis and Kracht, 1997) and Chinese number names (Radzinski, 1991). The analyses of Old Georgian, however, are based on very few data since there are no speakers of Old Georgian today. Therefore, it is hard to tell whether there is really an infinite progression of case stacking possible. Concerning Chinese number names, it is not totally clear to what extent this constitutes a syntactic phenomenon. Therefore, even with these counterexamples, there is still good reason to assume that natural languages are mildly context-sensitive.

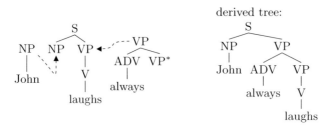

Fig. 2.3. TAG derivation for *John always laughs*

2.2 Grammar Formalisms Beyond CFG

We have seen that CFGs are not powerful enough to deal with all natural language phenomena. This is one of the reasons why we are interested in investigating extensions of CFG. We now introduce the different formalisms that will be treated in this book. The formalisms presented in this section will be defined in detail in the corresponding chapters on parsing. This section aims only at providing an intuition of how these formalisms extend CFG, how they model natural language phenomena and how they are related to each other.

2.2.1 Tree Adjoining Grammars

The Formalism

Starting from Tree Substitution Grammars, if we allow also for replacing internal nodes with new trees, we obtain Tree Adjoining Grammars. Tree Adjoining Grammar (TAG, Joshi, Levy, and Takahashi (1975; Joshi and Schabes (1997)) is a tree-rewriting formalism. A TAG consists of a finite set of syntactic trees (so-called *elementary trees*). Starting from the elementary trees, larger trees are derived by substitution (replacing a leaf with a new tree) and adjunction (replacing an internal node with a new tree). In case of an adjunction, the tree being adjoined has exactly one leaf that is marked as the *foot node* (marked with an asterisk). Such a tree is called an *auxiliary* tree. When adjoining it to a node n, in the resulting tree, the subtree with root n from the old tree is attached to the foot node of the auxiliary tree. Non-auxiliary elementary trees are called *initial* trees. A derivation starts with an initial tree. In a final derived tree, all leaves must have terminal labels.

For a sample derivation see Figure 2.3 where the tree for *John* is substituted for the subject NP slot while the auxiliary tree for the modifier *always* adjoins to the VP node in the tree of *laughs*.

The internal nodes in $I \cup A$ can be marked as *OA* (obligatory adjunction) and *NA* (null adjunction, i.e., no adjunction allowed). Furthermore, for nodes that are not *NA*, one can specify the set of auxiliary trees that can be adjoined at that node.

As a second example, Figure 2.4 shows a TAG for the copy language and Figure 2.5 shows a sample derivation using the trees from this grammar. (*NA* stands for "null adjunction", i.e., no adjunction allowed at that node. *OA* stands for "obligatory adjunction", i.e., adjunction mandatory at that node.) In this TAG, the *NA* constraints are crucial since they make sure that the adjunction always targets the middle S node. Without adjunction constraints, it is not possible for TAG to generate the copy language.

Fig. 2.4. TAG for the copy language

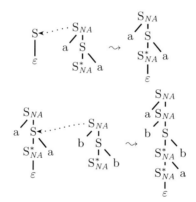

Fig. 2.5. A sample derivation of a word in the copy language

TAG derivations are represented by derivation trees (unordered trees) that record the history of how the elementary trees are put together. A derived tree is the result of carrying out the substitutions and adjunctions, i.e., the derivation tree describes uniquely the derived tree. Each edge in a derivation tree stands for an adjunction or a substitution. The edges are labeled with Gorn addresses. E.g., the derivation tree in Figure 2.6 indicates that the elementary tree for *John* is substituted for the node at address 1 and *always* is adjoined at node address 2 (the fact that the former is an adjunction and the latter is

Fig. 2.6. TAG derivation tree for *John always laughs*

a substitution can be inferred from the fact that the node at address 1 is a leaf that is not a foot node while the node at address 2 is an internal node).

The fact that TAGs are able to generate the copy language indicates that they are powerful enough to describe cross-serial dependencies. An actual analysis has been proposed in (Kroch and Santorini, 1991); it is shown in Figures 2.7 and 2.8.

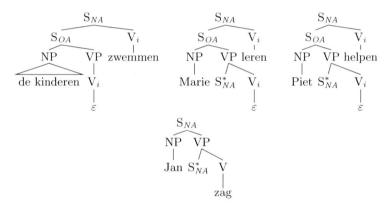

Fig. 2.7. TAG for cross-serial dependencies

Lexicalization

As we have seen in Section 2.1.2, in order to lexicalize CFGs one has to extract recursive sub-trees (with root and some leaf having the same non-terminal symbol) and put them into extra structures. This leads to a set of trees with an adjunction operation, i.e., to a TAG.

As an example, consider again the CFG in Figure 2.9 that cannot be lexicalized using only substitution. With adjunction, a lexicalization of this CFG is possible. The corresponding TAG is given in Figure 2.9.

In general it can be shown that CFGs can be lexicalized by TAGs and, furthermore, TAGs are closed under strong lexicalization. I.e., for each grammar that is a CFG or a TAG, there is a strongly equivalent lexicalized TAG (LTAG) (Schabes, 1990; Joshi and Schabes, 1997).

2.2 Grammar Formalisms Beyond CFG   29

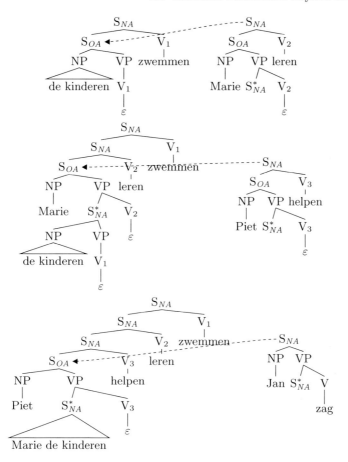

Fig. 2.8. Derivation of (5) using adjunction

CFG: $S \to SS,$ $S \to a$ Strongly equivalent LTAG: $\begin{array}{c} S \\ | \\ a \end{array}$ $\begin{array}{c} S \\ \wedge \\ S^* \ S \\ | \\ a \end{array}$

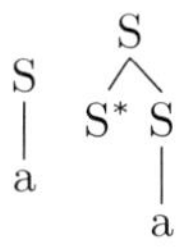

Fig. 2.9. CFG and strongly equivalent lexicalized TAG

Extended domain of locality and factoring of recursion

Because of the move to larger trees (compared to CFGs) and the addition of adjunction, TAGs have some properties that make them particularly interesting for natural language processing.

TAG elementary trees allow to express locally dependencies such as filler-gap dependencies, even if they are 'unbound'. This is why TAG is said to have an *extended domain of locality*. Two properties are crucial for obtaining this extended domain of locality: TAG elementary trees can be arbitrarily large (but have to be finite), and recursion can be factored away because of adjunction. Consequently, even so-called unbounded dependencies can be captured locally, i.e., inside single elementary trees (Kroch, 1987; Frank, 1992; Frank, 2002). Because of the constraints that hold for adjunction, in many cases one gets locality constraints for unbounded dependencies for free.

(9) a. **whom**$_i$ did John tell Sam **that Bill likes** t_i
    b. **whom**$_i$ did John tell Sam that Mary said **that Bill likes** t_i

As an example that illustrates this property of TAG, consider the derivation of (9a.) in Figure 2.10 with the recursive part being put in a separate tree that gets adjoined.

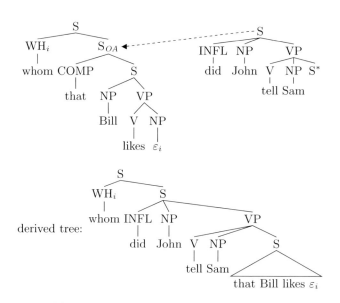

Fig. 2.10. Derivation for an unbounded dependency

When dealing with natural languages, one always uses *Lexicalized Tree Adjoining Grammars (LTAGs)*. The linguistic theory implemented within LTAG is roughly as follows. The grammar contains extended projections of each lexical item (the elementary trees anchored by this lexical item). These extended projections satisfy certain linguistic principles that are not part of the TAG formalism itself. The extended projections are minimal in the sense that they contain slots only for the arguments of their lexical head. Recursion is factored away. Consequently, the set of elementary structures in the grammar is finite. Every constraint concerning larger structures (constraints on "unbounded dependencies") does not need to be stipulated but, instead, follows from the possibilities of adjunction in the extended projections.

We will give a more detailed discussion of LTAG for natural languages in Chapter 4.

2.2.2 Linear Indexed Grammars

Indexed grammars (IGs) were introduced by (Aho, 1968). An indexed grammar looks like a CFG except that the non-terminals are equipped with stacks of indices, i.e., besides the non-terminals N and the terminals T, we have an alphabet I of indices. In a derived sentential form x, non-terminals can be equipped with stacks of indices, i.e., $x \in (NI^* \cup T)^*$.

The productions in an IG have the form (i) $A \to \alpha$ or (ii) $A \to Bf$ or (iii) $Af \to \alpha$ with $A, B \in N, f \in I, \alpha \in (N \cup T)^*$. The first kind of production works like context-free productions while copying the stack of A to all non-terminals in α. The second kind of production adds a symbol to the stack of A while replacing A with B. The third kind of production deletes a symbol f from the stack of A and then works like the first kind of production.

As an example consider the IG for $\{a^{2^n} \mid n \geq 0\}$ with $N := \{S, A, B\}, I := \{f, g\}, T := \{a\}$ and productions $P := \{S \to a, S \to Ag, A \to Af, A \to B, Bf \to BB, Bg \to aa\}$. This grammar works as follows: For a word a^{2^n} with $n \geq 1$, we first apply the production $S \to Ag$ and then n times the production $A \to Af$. This leads to a non-terminal A with a stack of length n. Then the A is turned into a B, and, while reducing the stack, the B is doubled (with the production $Bf \to BB$). This happens $n-1$ times. Then we reach the last stack symbol and, while reducing this as well, we finally generate two terminals aa. Crucially, when doubling the B with $Bf \to BB$, the remaining stack is passed to both Bs in the right-hand side of the production. This guarantees that the two parts have the same number of as (since they have the same stacks). Figure 2.11 shows a sample derivation with this grammar.

An indexed grammar is called a *linear indexed grammar (LIG)* (Gazdar, 1988; Vijay-Shanker, 1987) if in a production $A \to \alpha$ or $Af \to \alpha$ the stack of A is copied only to one non-terminal in α.

We write the productions in a LIG as follows:

- $A[\ldots] \to X_1 \ldots X_i[\ldots] \ldots X_n$ with $X_j \in N \cup T$ for $j \neq i$, $X_i \in N$.
- $A[\ldots] \to B[f \ldots]$
- $A[f \ldots] \to X_1 \ldots X_i[\ldots] \ldots X_n$ with $X_j \in N \cup T$ for $j \neq i$, $X_i \in N$.

$$\begin{aligned}
S &\Rightarrow Ag & &\text{production } S \to Ag \\
&\Rightarrow Afg & &\text{production } A \to Af \\
&\stackrel{*}{\Rightarrow} Afffg \\
&\Rightarrow Bfffg & &\text{production } A \to B \\
&\Rightarrow BffgBffg & &\text{production } Bf \to BB \\
&\stackrel{*}{\Rightarrow} BfgBfgBfgBfg \\
&\stackrel{*}{\Rightarrow} BgBgBgBgBgBgBgBg \\
&\stackrel{*}{\Rightarrow} aaaaaaaaaaaaaaaa & &\text{production } Bg \to aa
\end{aligned}$$

Fig. 2.11. IG derivation for $a^{2^4} = a^{16}$

As an example consider the LIG for the copy language from Figure 2.12.

$$\begin{aligned}
&S_0 \to S[\#] \\
&S[..] \to aS_a[..] \quad S_a[..] \to S[a..] \\
&S[..] \to bS_b[..] \quad S_b[..] \to S[b..] \\
&S \to T \\
&T[a..] \to T[..]a \quad T[b..] \to T[..]b \\
&T[\#] \to \varepsilon
\end{aligned}$$

Fig. 2.12. LIG for the copy language

It has been shown that LIG and TAG are weakly equivalent (Vijay-Shanker, 1987; Vijay-Shanker and Weir, 1994).

When constructing a LIG that is equivalent to a given TAG, whenever an adjunction is performed, while traversing the adjoined tree, the stack can be used to keep track of the tree one has to go back to once the adjunction is finished. It needs to be passed along the path from the root to the foot node. Figure 2.13 shows the LIG one obtains when constructing an equivalent LIG for the TAG for the copy language given in Figure 2.4 along these lines.

$$\begin{aligned}
&\langle S, \alpha \rangle \to \varepsilon \\
&\langle S, \alpha \rangle \to \langle S_1, \beta_a \rangle [\langle \alpha, 0 \rangle] & &\langle S, \alpha \rangle \to \langle S_1, \beta_b \rangle [\langle \alpha, 0 \rangle] \\
&\langle S_1, \beta_a \rangle [\ldots] \to a \langle S_2, \beta_a \rangle [\ldots] & &\langle S_1, \beta_b \rangle [\ldots] \to b \langle S_2, \beta_b \rangle [\ldots] \\
&\langle S_2, \beta_a \rangle [\ldots] \to \langle S_3, \beta_a \rangle [\ldots] a & &\langle S_2, \beta_b \rangle [\ldots] \to \langle S_3, \beta_b \rangle [\ldots] b \\
&\langle S_2, \beta_a \rangle [\ldots] \to \langle S_1, \beta_a \rangle [\langle \beta_a, 2 \rangle \ldots] & &\langle S_2, \beta_a \rangle [\ldots] \to \langle S_1, \beta_b \rangle [\langle \beta_a, 2 \rangle \ldots] \\
&\langle S_2, \beta_b \rangle [\ldots] \to \langle S_1, \beta_a \rangle [\langle \beta_b, 2 \rangle \ldots] & &\langle S_2, \beta_b \rangle [\ldots] \to \langle S_1, \beta_b \rangle [\langle \beta_b, 2 \rangle \ldots] \\
&\langle S_3, \beta_a \rangle [\langle \alpha, 0 \rangle \ldots] \to \langle S, \alpha \rangle [\ldots] & &\langle S_3, \beta_b \rangle [\langle \alpha, 0 \rangle \ldots] \to \langle S, \alpha \rangle [\ldots] \\
&\langle S_3, \beta_a \rangle [\langle \beta_a, 2 \rangle \ldots] \to \langle S_2, \beta_a \rangle [\ldots] & &\langle S_3, \beta_b \rangle [\langle \beta_a, 2 \rangle \ldots] \to \langle S_2, \beta_a \rangle [\ldots] \\
&\langle S_3, \beta_a \rangle [\langle \beta_b, 2 \rangle \ldots] \to \langle S_2, \beta_b \rangle [\ldots] & &\langle S_3, \beta_b \rangle [\langle \beta_b, 2 \rangle \ldots] \to \langle S_2, \beta_b \rangle [\ldots]
\end{aligned}$$

Fig. 2.13. Equivalent LIG for the TAG from Figure 2.4

Productions of the Generalized CFG (start symbol is S):
$S \to f_1(A, B, C)$ $A \to f_2(A)$ $B \to f_3(B)$ $C \to f_4(C)$
$A \to f_5()$ $B \to f_5()$ $C \to f_5()$

Strings $\phi(t)$ yielded by the terms t:
$\phi(f_5()) := \langle \varepsilon, \varepsilon \rangle$,
$\phi(f_2(t)) := \langle aw_1, aw_2 \rangle$ where $\langle w_1, w_2 \rangle = \phi(t)$,
$\phi(f_3(t)) := \langle bw_1, bw_2 \rangle$ where $\langle w_1, w_2 \rangle = \phi(t)$,
$\phi(f_4(t)) := \langle cw_1, cw_2 \rangle$ where $\langle w_1, w_2 \rangle = \phi(t)$,
$\phi(f_1(t_1, t_2, t_3)) := \langle w_1 u_1 v_1 w_2 u_2 v_2 \rangle$
    where $\langle w_1, w_2 \rangle = \phi(t_1)$, $\langle u_1, u_2 \rangle = \phi(t_2)$, $\langle v_1, v_2 \rangle = \phi(t_3)$

Fig. 2.14. An LCFRS for $\{a^n b^m c^k a^n b^m c^k \mid n, m, k \geq 0\}$

LIGs themselves are not used for natural languages. Their interest lies in their relations to other formalisms, in particular in their equivalence to TAGs. Because of this equivalence, LIGs have been proposed for TAG parsing (Vijay-Shanker and Weir, 1993; Boullier, 1996).

2.2.3 Linear Context-Free Rewriting Systems

Linear Context-Free Rewriting Systems (LCFRSs) are introduced in (Vijay-Shanker, Weir, and Joshi, 1987; Weir, 1988). They are grammars that have an underlying context-free structure. More concretely, an LCFRS consists of

1. a generalized context-free grammar (GCFG) that generates a set of terms,
2. a yield function that specifies the strings yielded by these structures.

LCFRS is more powerful than TAG and LIG. More concretely, every TAG can be written as an LCFRS.

In an LCFRS, the yield $\phi(t)$ of a term t is a sequence of strings. A unique equation is associated with each production $A \to f(A_1, \ldots, A_n)$ in C. It describes how to compute the yield of a term $f(t_1, \ldots, t_n)$ from the yields of $t_1, \ldots, t_n$ and a bounded collection of new terminals. When computing the yield of a left-hand side from the yields of a right-hand side, we must neither copy nor erase.

As an example consider the LCFRS in Figure 2.14.

The languages generated by these grammars are mildly context-sensitive and they properly contain the languages generated by TAG. Figure 2.15 shows an example of an equivalent LCFRS for a given TAG.

2.2.4 Multicomponent Tree Adjoining Grammars

Multicomponent Tree Adjoining Grammars (MCTAGs) were first introduced in (Joshi, Levy, and Takahashi, 1975) as *simultaneous TAGs*, later redefined as *multicomponent TAGs (MCTAGs)* in (Weir, 1988; Joshi, 1985). The underlying linguistic motivation is the idea to separate the contribution of a lexical

2 Grammar Formalisms for Natural Languages

TAG for $L_4 = \{a^n b^n c^n d^n \mid n \geq 0\}$:

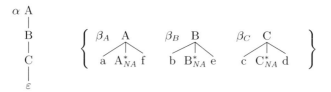

α: S
       |
       ε

β: a S d with children b S^*_{NA} c (where root is S_{NA})

Productions of the corresponding Generalized CFG (start symbol is α):
$\alpha \to f_\alpha(), \beta \to f_\beta()$ (no adjunctions),
$\alpha \to f_{\alpha:\varepsilon}(\beta), \beta \to f_{\beta:1}(\beta)$ (adjunctions of β).

Strings $\phi(t)$ yielded by the terms t:
$\phi(f_\alpha()) := \varepsilon$,
$\phi(f_\beta()) := \langle ab, cd \rangle$,
$\phi(f_{\alpha:\varepsilon}(t)) := \langle w_1 w_2 \rangle$ where $\langle w_1, w_2 \rangle = \phi(t)$,
$\phi(f_{\beta:1}(t)) := \langle aw_1 b, cw_2 d \rangle$ where $\langle w_1, w_2 \rangle = \phi(t)$.

Fig. 2.15. An LCFRS for a given TAG

item into several components. Instead of single trees, these grammars contain (finite) sets of trees. In each derivation step, a new set is picked and all trees from the set are added simultaneously, i.e., they are attached (by substitution or adjunction) to different nodes in the already derived tree.

As in TAG, a derivation starts from an initial tree and in the end, in the final derived tree, all leaves must have terminal labels (or the empty word) and there must not be any *OA* constraints left.

A sample MCTAG with a derivation is shown in Figure 2.16.

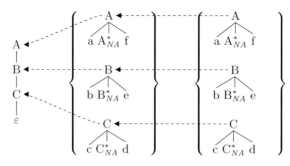

Derivation for *aabbccddeeff*:

Fig. 2.16. MCTAG for $L_6 = \{a^n b^n c^n d^n e^n f^n \mid n \geq 0\}$ with sample derivation

MCTAGs are linguistically interesting because they extend the domain of locality since the contributions of single lexical elements are separated into different trees. As an example, consider extractions out of complex NPs (Kroch, 1989) as in (10). A possible MCTAG analysis is shown in Figure 2.17.

(10) which painting$_i$ did you see a picture of t_i

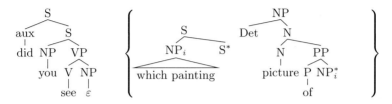

Fig. 2.17. MCTAG elementary trees for extraction from NP

An MCTAG is called *tree-local* iff in each derivation step, the nodes the new trees attach to belong to the same elementary tree. It is called *set-local* iff in each derivation step, the nodes the new trees attach to belong to the same elementary tree set. Otherwise it is called *non-local*. The derivation in Figure 2.16 for example is a set-local derivation. Usually, the term "MCTAG" without specification of the locality means "set-local MCTAG".

Concerning the respective generative capacity, it has been shown that tree-local MCTAGs are strongly equivalent to TAGs while set-local MCTAGs are weakly equivalent to LCFRSs. As an example, Figure 2.18 shows the LCFRS that is equivalent to the set-local MCTAG from Figure 2.16.

GCFG productions:
$\alpha \to f_\alpha(), \alpha \to g_\alpha(\beta_{A,B,C})$,
$\beta_{A,B,C} \to f_{A,B,C}()$,
$\beta_{A,B,C} \to g_{A,B,C}(\beta_{A,B,C})$.

Yield function ϕ:
$\phi(f_\alpha()) := \langle \varepsilon \rangle$,
$\phi(f_{A,B,C}()) := \langle a, b, c, d, e, f \rangle$,
$\phi(g_\alpha(t)) := \langle w_1 w_2 w_3 w_4 w_5 w_6 \rangle$ where $\langle w_1, w_2, w_3, w_4, w_5, w_6 \rangle = \phi(t)$,
$\phi(g_{A,B,C}(t)) := \langle w_1 a, w_2 b, w_3 c, d w_4, e w_5, f w_6 \rangle$
  where $\langle w_1, w_2, w_3, w_4, w_5, w_6 \rangle = \phi(t)$

Fig. 2.18. LCFRS for $L_6 = \{a^n b^n c^n d^n e^n f^n \mid n \geq 0\}$

2.2.5 Multiple Context-Free Grammars

Multiple Context-Free Grammars (MCFGs), (Seki et al., 1991), are very similar to LCFRSs. The non-terminals in an MCFG, in contrast to CFG, can yield sequences of terminals, i.e., their span can be discontinuous in the input. Each non-terminal has a fixed dimension that determines the number of components in its span. In other words, from a non-terminal of dimension k, k-tuples of terminal strings are derived. The dimension of the start symbol S is 1.

An MCFG, similar to the GCFG of an LCFRS, contains productions of the form $A_0 \to f[A_1, \ldots, A_k]$ where f is a function from a given set of functions F. The idea is that f describes how to compute the yield of A_0 (a $dim(A_0)$-tuple of terminal strings) from the yields of $A_1, \ldots, A_k$. f must be linear in the sense that each of its arguments is used at most once to compute the new string tuple. Note that the functions f are not required not to delete parts of their input as in the case of LCFRS. In other words, it might be the case that some of the arguments in the right-hand side of a production are not used to compute the yield of the left-hand side. However, even though deletion in the yield computation is allowed in MCFG and not in LCFRS, the two formalisms are weakly equivalent (Seki et al., 1991).

As an example consider the MCFG in Figure 2.19 that generates the language $\{a^n b^n c^n d^n \mid n \geq 1\}$.

Productions:
  $S \to f[A],\ A \to g[A],\ A \to h[\,]$.

Yield functions:
  $h[\,] = (ab, cd),\ g[(x_1, x_2)] = (ax_1 b, cx_2 d),\ f[(x_1, x_2)] = (x_1 x_2)$

Fig. 2.19. MCFG for $\{a^n b^n c^n d^n \mid n \geq 1\}$

MCFGs have been investigated mainly in the context of biological applications such as the modeling of RNA pseudoknotted structures (Kato, Seki, and Kasami, 2006). However, because of their equivalence to LCFRSs and set-local MCTAGs, they are useful for natural language processing as well.

2.2.6 Range Concatenation Grammars

If we incorporate the definitions of the yield functions in MCFG and LCFRS into the productions themselves, and, in addition, if we relax the conditions on the yield functions, we obtain *Range Concatenation Grammars (RCGs)* (Boullier, 2000b).

The idea of RCGs is roughly that the productions of RCGs (called *clauses*) rewrite predicates ranging over parts of the input by other predicates. As an example consider the clause $S(aXb) \to S(X)$. This clause signifies that the predicate S (a unary predicate) holds for a part of the input if (i) this part starts with an a and ends with a b and (ii) S also holds for the part between the a and the b.

The RCG with clauses $S(aXb) \to S(X), S(c) \to \varepsilon$ for example generates the language $\{a^n cb^n \mid n \geq 0\}$.

An RCG consists of an alphabet N of non-terminals (called predicates) of a fixed arity (this corresponds to the dimension from MCFG) where the special predicate S has arity 1. Furthermore, it has a terminal alphabet T and an alphabet of variables V. The clauses have the form

$$A(\alpha_1, \ldots, \alpha_{dim(A)}) \to \varepsilon$$

or

$$A(\alpha_1, \ldots, \alpha_{dim(A)}) \to A_1(\alpha_1^{(1)}, \ldots, \alpha_{dim(A_1)}^{(1)}) \ldots A_n^{(n)}(\alpha_1, \ldots, \alpha_{dim(A_n)}^{(n)})$$

where the predicates are from N and their arguments are words over $(T \cup V)$.

For a given clause, an instantiation with respect to a string $w = t_1 \ldots t_n$ maps all variables and all occurrences of terminals in the clause to ranges $\langle i, j \rangle$ with $0 \leq i \leq j \leq |w|$. A range $\langle i, j \rangle$ denotes the part of w between positions i and j. An instantiation must be such that all occurrences of a terminal t are mapped to a range whose yield is a t, and adjacent variables/occurrences of terminals in one of the arguments are mapped on adjacent ranges, i.e., ranges $\langle i, j \rangle, \langle k, l \rangle$ with $j = k$.

A derivation step consists of replacing the left-hand side of an instantiated clause with its right-hand side. The language of an RCG G is the set of strings w that satisfy the start predicate S, in other words, the set of w such that ε can be derived from $S(\langle 0, |w| \rangle)$.

RCGs are called *simple* if (i) the arguments in the right-hand sides of the clauses are single variables, (ii) no variable appears more than once in the left-hand side of a clause or more than once in the right-hand side of a clause, and (iii) each variable occurring in the left-hand side of a clause occurs also in its right-hand side and vice versa.

Simple RCGs are weakly equivalent to LCFRSs and MCFGs. RCGs in general however are more powerful; they generate exactly the class PTIME of polynomially parsable languages (Bertsch and Nederhof, 2001). They properly include the set of languages generated by LCFRS and even the maximal set of mildly context-sensitive languages. An example of a language that can be generated by a RCG but that is not semilinear is the language from Figure 2.20.

RCGs are equivalent to a restricted form of *Literal Movement Grammars (LMGs)* (Groenink, 1996), so-called *simple* LMGs. These grammars have rewriting rules that are like the ones in RCG with the additional constraints that (i) the arguments in the right-hand sides of the clauses are single variables, (ii) no variable appears more than once in the left-hand side of a clause and (iii) each variable occurring in the right-hand side of a clause occurs also

RCG for the language $\{a^{2^n} \mid n \geq 0\}$:
$S(XY) \rightarrow S(X)eq(X,Y)$
$S(a) \rightarrow \varepsilon$
$eq(aX, aY) \rightarrow eq(X,Y)$
$eq(a,a) \rightarrow \varepsilon$

A sample derivation (reduction to ε) for $w = aaaa$:
$S(X\ \ Y) \rightarrow S(X)\ eq(X,\ \ Y)$
$\quad\downarrow\quad\downarrow\qquad\ \ \downarrow\quad\ \ \downarrow\quad\downarrow$
$\langle 0,2\rangle\ \langle 2,4\rangle\qquad \langle 0,2\rangle\ \langle 0,2\rangle\ \langle 2,4\rangle$
$\ aa\quad\ aa\qquad\ \ aa\quad\ aa\quad aa$
With this instantiation, $S(\langle 0,4\rangle) \Rightarrow S(\langle 0,2\rangle)eq(\langle 0,2\rangle,\langle 2,4\rangle)$.
$S(X\ \ Y) \rightarrow S(X)\ eq(X,\ \ Y)\qquad S(a) \rightarrow \varepsilon\qquad eq(a,\ \ a) \rightarrow \varepsilon$
$\quad\downarrow\quad\downarrow\qquad\ \ \downarrow\quad\ \ \downarrow\quad\downarrow\qquad\qquad\downarrow\qquad\qquad\ \ \downarrow\quad\downarrow$
$\langle 0,1\rangle\ \langle 1,2\rangle\quad \langle 0,1\rangle\ \langle 0,1\rangle\ \langle 1,2\rangle\qquad \langle 0,1\rangle\qquad\ \langle 0,1\rangle\ \langle 1,2\rangle$
$\ a\qquad a\qquad\ a\qquad a\qquad a\qquad\quad\ a\qquad\qquad\ \ a\qquad a$
leads to $S(\langle 0,2\rangle) \Rightarrow S(\langle 0,1\rangle)eq(\langle 0,1\rangle,\langle 1,2\rangle) \stackrel{*}{\Rightarrow} \varepsilon$
$eq(a\ \ X\quad a\quad Y) \rightarrow eq(X,\ \ Y)\qquad eq(a,\ \ a) \rightarrow \varepsilon$
$\quad\ \ \downarrow\quad\downarrow\quad\ \downarrow\quad\downarrow\qquad\ \ \downarrow\quad\downarrow\qquad\qquad\downarrow\quad\downarrow$
$\langle 0,1\rangle\ \langle 1,2\rangle\ \langle 2,3\rangle\ \langle 3,4\rangle\quad \langle 1,2\rangle\ \langle 3,4\rangle\qquad \langle 1,2\rangle\ \langle 3,4\rangle$
$\ a\qquad a\qquad a\qquad a\qquad\ a\qquad a\qquad\qquad a\qquad a$
leads to $eq(\langle 0,2\rangle,\langle 2,4\rangle) \Rightarrow eq(\langle 1,2\rangle,\langle 3,4\rangle) \Rightarrow \varepsilon$

Fig. 2.20. RCG for $\{a^{2^n} \mid n \geq 0\}$

in its left-hand side. In contrast to RCG, an instantiation in a LMG maps variables to strings of terminals. Consequently, the terminals in a clause need not have corresponding terminals in the input and different occurrences of the same variable can be mapped to different occurrences of the same string. This is why with this restricted form of clauses one obtains a grammar formalism with the same generative capacity as RCGs.

2.3 Summary

In this chapter, we have given an overview of the different grammar formalisms that we will deal with in the course of this book.

The starting point was the observation that CFGs do not have enough expressive power to deal with natural languages. A formal proof of this fact has been given by Shieber (1985), showing that Swiss German is not context-free because of its cross-serial dependencies. Shieber was able to make an argument even on the basis of the weak generative capacity since Swiss German has case marking and therefore dependencies are visible even in the string language.

Another property that has been argued as being desirable for an adequate grammar formalism for natural languages is lexicalization. It has been shown that in general, CFGs cannot be strongly lexicalized.

From these shortcomings arises the need for more powerful formalisms. This has led to a rich variety of grammar formalisms that can be seen as more and more extending the properties of context-free grammars. In TAG, we allow not only replacing leaves with new trees as in CFG but we also allow internal nodes to be replaced with new trees. In LCFRS, we allow the yields of non-terminals to consist not only of single strings but of tuples of non-adjacent strings. In RCG, we even allow strings to be used several times in different contexts. All these grammar frameworks, and their respective equivalent formalisms, constitute a hierarchy of string languages as shown in Figure 2.21.

A notion that has proved an important concept in the characterization of grammar formalisms with respect to their relevance for natural languages is the notion of mild context-sensitivity, introduced by Joshi (1985). A class of languages is mildly context-sensitive if it contains all context-free languages, if it can describe cross-serial dependencies, if it contains only polynomial languages and if its languages are of constant growth. The language classes of TAG and of LCFRS in our hierarchy are mildly context-sensitive.

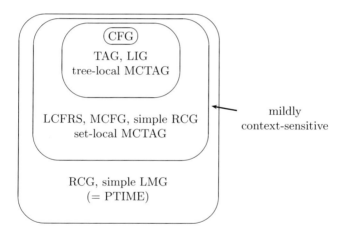

Fig. 2.21. The language hierarchy of the different grammar formalisms

Problems

2.1. Consider the language $L_2 = \{a^n b^n \mid n \geq 0\}$.

1. Give a CFG for L_2 with nested dependencies, i.e., such that for each word $a_1 \ldots a_n b_1 \ldots b_n$ (the subscripts mark the occurrences of the as and bs respectively) a_i and b_{n+1-i} are added in the same derivation step for all $1 \leq i \leq n$.

2. Show that for L_2 there is no CFG displaying cross-serial dependencies, i.e., no CFG such that for each word $a_1 \ldots a_n b_1 \ldots b_n$, a_i and b_i are added in the same derivation step for all $1 \leq i \leq n$ and, furthermore, different as are added in different derivation steps.

2.2. Similar to the argument of Shieber (1985) for Swiss German, one can apply first a homomorphism f, then intersect the result with some regular language, and then apply another homomorphism g in order to reduce the language of Swiss German to the copy language $\{ww \mid w \in \{a,b\}^*\}$. Find the corresponding homomorphisms and the regular language.

2.3. Consider the following CFG:
S → NP VP   NP → John
VP → ADV VP ADV → always
VP → V   V → laughs
Find a TSG that strongly lexicalizes this grammar.
Why is this lexicalization not satisfying from a linguistic point of view?

2.4.   1. Show that the copy language $\{ww \mid w \in T^*\}$ for some alphabet T is semilinear using the Parikh Theorem.
2. Show that $\{a^{2^n} \mid n \geq 0\}$ is not semilinear.

3
Parsing: Preliminaries

3.1 Parsing as Deduction

3.1.1 Motivation

There are different means of specifying a parsing algorithm. The most frequently used are a pseudo-code description of the algorithm and deduction rules.

The pseudo-code description has the advantage of being relatively close to the proper implementation. Consequently, implementing an algorithm given in pseudo-code is more or less immediate. However, the pseudo-code specification makes a lot of choices that actually do not belong to the parsing strategy of the algorithm. It introduces data structures and control structures.

Consider for example a CYK algorithm for CFGs in Chomsky Normal Form. The parsing strategy is a non-directional bottom-up strategy that starts by assigning categories to terminals and then, in each step, applies a production of the form $A \to BC$ by computing a new A from already found categories B and C. One can store the results in a chart as a data structure and, with respect to control structure, one can fill the chart row by row or diagonal by diagonal. A pseudo-code representation of the algorithm would also specify the latter. In contrast to this, a specification by means of deduction rules describes only the parsing strategy itself.

Deduction rules for the specification of parsing techniques have been proposed in (Pereira and Warren, 1983; Shieber, Schabes, and Pereira, 1995) and were further formalized in (Sikkel, 1997). Using deduction rules to describe parsing algorithms has several advantages: We can concentrate on the parsing strategy itself without having to worry about implementation details at the same time, proofs of soundness and completeness are easier to do and the complexity is easier to determine.

Throughout this book, we will use deduction rules to specify the parsing algorithms we present. Following Sikkel, we call a specification of an algorithm by means of deduction rules a *parsing schema*. Roughly, a parsing schema consists of the following parts: a characterization of intermediate parsing results, a specification of how to deduce new results from existing ones and the specification of a goal result. In the case of CYK, the intermediate results would be the categories we can find together with their spans and the goal result would be an S category that spans the entire input.

3.1.2 Items

A deduction rule is supposed to specify a single parsing step, for example "Based on the production $A \to BC$, from existing adjacent B and C categories, we can obtain a new A category." For this, we first need to characterize intermediate parsing results, such as an existing B category.

In the context of CYK, having found a category A means having found a tree with root category A and a span starting at position i in the input and ending at position j.[1] The inner structure of the parse tree rooted with A is not relevant for the subsequent use of this category in further parsing steps. Therefore, we abstract away from it in the representation of the parse tree.

In the following, as a running example, let us consider the CFG $G_{telescope}$ from Fig. 3.1.

$N = \{S, NP, VP, PP, D, P, N, V\}$, start symbol S,
$T = \{man, girl, John, Mary, telescope, saw, the, with\}$.

Productions:

S → NP VP	NP → D N	N → N PP
VP → VP PP	VP → V NP	PP → P NP
N → man	N → girl	N → telescope
D → the	NP → John	NP → Mary
P → with	V → saw	

Fig. 3.1. CFG $G_{telescope}$

In a parsing schema, the intermediate results are called *items*. In the case of CYK, we can characterize an item by the category A and the start and end positions i, j of the span. Therefore, in this case, we define an item as $[A, i, j]$ where $A \in N$ and $0 \leq i < j \leq n$ where n is the length of the input. We can assume $i < j$ since the grammars are in Chomsky Normal Form and therefore, no category can have an empty span (i.e., a yield ϵ).

As an example, consider the CYK items given in Fig. 3.2 for parsing the input sentence *Mary saw the man* with the CFG $G_{telescope}$ from Fig. 3.1. The

---

[1] Alternatively, the span could be specified by giving the start position and the length.

goal item, i.e., the result we need to find for a successful parse, is $[S,0,n]$ in the case of CYK.

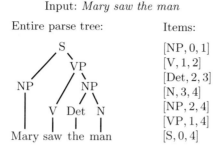

Fig. 3.2. Example: CYK items

In the case of CYK, we are dealing only with completed categories since we apply a production $A \to BC$ only when having found appropriate B and C categories. However, in other algorithms, we encounter intermediate results where some categories are completed while others are only predicted. As an example, consider the Earley algorithm, an algorithm that combines a top-down prediction with a bottom-up completion. Intermediate results of the Earley algorithm are such that, for a predicted category A, we have completed some of the daughters of A while the remaining daughters have been predicted. Such an intermediate result can be represented by an item containing a production with a dot in the right-hand side. This dot marks the position up to which the right-hand side has been recognized (i.e., completed). The part on the right of the dot is the predicted part. Such a production with a dot is called a *dotted production*.

Let us consider as an example again our grammar $G_{telescope}$. Starting from S, we can predict the production S → NP VP. Since nothing from the right-hand side has been completed, we characterize this prediction by the dotted production S → • NP VP. Once we have found the NP, we can move the dot over this category, which results in the dotted production S → NP • VP. This signifies that we have already found an NP and, in order to complete the left-hand side category S, we still need to find the predicted VP.

In addition to characterizing the dotted production, in an Earley algorithm, we need to characterize the span of the completed part of the right-hand side. This can be done again by giving its start and end positions. Consequently, Earley items have the form $[A \to \alpha \bullet \beta, i, j]$ with $A \to \alpha\beta \in P$ and $0 \leq i \leq j \leq n$.

Even in items containing only single categories instead of entire productions, we might want to distinguish between predicted and completed categories. This can be done either using a corresponding flag inside the items or using a dot that precedes (prediction) or follows (completion) the category.

Items consisting of a single category and its span are called *passive items* while items containing a dotted production and its span are called *active items*.

3.1.3 Deduction Rules

If we specify an algorithm using parsing schemata, we understand parsing as a deductive process. We can use deduction rules to describe how to deduce new items from existing ones. These rules establish a relation between antecedent items and consequent items. In most cases, there is actually only one consequent item. Eventually, in addition to checking on the existence of the antecedent items, we also need to check certain side conditions. Therefore, the general form of deduction rules in parsing schemata is as follows:

$$\frac{antecedent}{consequent} \; side \; conditions$$

where antecedent and consequent are lists of items. We can apply such a rule if the antecedent items can be deduced and the side conditions hold. Then, the consequent items can be deduced as well.

As an example consider again the *complete* step in the CYK algorithm, i.e., the step where, based on the existence of a production $A \to BC$, from adjacent B and C categories, we can deduce an A category. The corresponding deduction rule is as follows:

$$\frac{[B, i, j], [C, j, k]}{[A, i, k]} \quad A \to BC \in P.$$

An entire parsing schema consists of deduction rules, an axiom or axioms that can be notated as a deduction rule with an empty set of antecedent items, and a goal item or several goal items. Parsing succeeds if, for a given input, based on the parsing schema, it is possible to deduce a goal item.

Figure 3.3 gives the parsing schemata for CYK and Earley parsing of CFGs. As an example of parsing with the Earley algorithm given here, consider again the grammar $G_{telescope}$ from Fig. 3.1 and the input *Mary saw the man*. Figure 3.4 lists the items we obtain for this input. (Only the successful items are listed.)

3.2 Implementation Issues

3.2.1 Dynamic Programming

When dealing with natural languages, we are in general faced with highly ambiguous grammars. Deterministic parsing approaches such as $LL(k)$ parsing (Sippu and Soisalon-Soininen, 1990) are therefore not adequate.

There are two aspects arising from the ambiguity of natural language syntax:

3.2 Implementation Issues   45

CYK

Goal item: $[S, 0, n]$

Scan:

$$\frac{}{[A, i-1, i]} \quad A \to w_i \in P$$

Complete:

$$\frac{[B, i, j], [C, j, k]}{[A, i, k]} \quad A \to B\,C \in P$$

Earley

Goal items: $[S \to \alpha\bullet, 0, n]$
with $S \to \alpha \in P$

Axioms:

$$\frac{}{[S \to \bullet\alpha, 0, 0]} \quad S \to \alpha \in P$$

Predict:

$$\frac{[A \to \alpha \bullet B\beta, i, j]}{[B \to \bullet\gamma, j, j]} \quad B \to \gamma \in P$$

Scan:

$$\frac{[A \to \alpha \bullet a\beta, i, j]}{[A \to \alpha a \bullet \beta, i, j+1]} \quad w_{j+1} = a$$

Complete:

$$\frac{[A \to \alpha \bullet B\beta, i, j], [B \to \gamma\bullet, j, k]}{[A \to \alpha B \bullet \beta, i, k]}$$

Fig. 3.3. Parsing schemata for CYK and Earley parsing of CFGs

	Item	Operation
1.	$[S \to \bullet\ NP\ VP, 0, 0]$	axiom
2.	$[NP \to \bullet\ Mary, 0, 0]$	predict from 1
3.	$[NP \to Mary\ \bullet, 0, 1]$	scan from 2
4.	$[S \to NP \bullet VP, 0, 1]$	complete 1 with 3
5.	$[VP \to \bullet\ V\ NP, 1, 1]$	predict from 4
6.	$[V \to \bullet\ saw, 1, 1]$	predict from 5
7.	$[V \to saw\ \bullet, 1, 2]$	scan from 6
8.	$[VP \to V \bullet NP, 1, 2]$	complete 5 with 7
9.	$[NP \to \bullet\ Det\ N, 2, 2]$	predict from 8
10.	$[Det \to \bullet\ the, 2, 2]$	predict from 9
11.	$[Det \to the\ \bullet, 2, 3]$	scan from 10
12.	$[NP \to Det \bullet N, 2, 3]$	complete 9 with 11
13.	$[N \to \bullet\ man, 3, 3]$	predict from 12
14.	$[N \to man\ \bullet, 3, 4]$	scan from 13
15.	$[NP \to Det\ N\ \bullet, 2, 4]$	complete 12 with 14
16.	$[VP \to V\ NP\ \bullet, 1, 4]$	complete 8 with 15
17.	$[S \to NP\ VP\ \bullet, 0, 4]$	complete 4 with 16

Fig. 3.4. Successful Earley items obtained for *Mary saw the man*

1. On the one hand, strings can have more than one analysis. Consequently, we need to find some way to branch and pursue all of them.
2. On the other hand, different analyses can have common sub-analyses for certain substrings. In order to avoid computing these sub-analyses several

times, we need to find some way to reuse (partial) parse trees that we have already found.

Because of these needs, we have to implement a parser in such a way as to store intermediate parsing results, to pursue all of them and to retrieve them if needed in order to reuse them in a different context. This latter aspect is called *computation sharing* (Villemonte de la Clergerie, 2006). To achieve this, we follow an approach of *dynamic programming*, a term that was first introduced in Operational Research (Bellman, 1957). The underlying strategy is, roughly, that we have a set of results that can be reused at any time. This set increases during parsing.

The advantage of specifying an algorithm with deduction rules is that the items we deduce represent partial parsing results. The fact that once an item is deduced (computed), it can serve as antecedent in different rule applications corresponds to a sharing of the computation of this intermediate result. Therefore the framework of parsing as deduction yields a very natural formalization of a dynamic programming strategy.

3.2.2 Chart Parsing and Tabulation

In order to store intermediate parse results in a way that allows for an efficient retrieval, we use a table. Such tables are called *charts* and the storage of parse items in a chart is called *tabulation*.

In the context of CFGs, the CYK parser and the Earley parser (see Fig. 3.3 for the deduction rules) are typical chart parsers. Let us consider the CYK parser. Here the parse items have the form $[A, i, j]$. In order to allow for an efficient storage and retrieval of these items, we can number the non-terminals and then realize the chart as a 3-dimensional table $\mathcal{C}$ where the first dimension is the index of the non-terminal A, the second the start index i of the span and the third the end index j of the span.

Chart parsing in general works as follows: We have two structures, the chart C and an agenda $\mathcal{A}$, both initialized as empty. We then start by computing all items that are axioms, i.e., that can be obtained by applying rules with empty antecedents. Starting from these items, we extend the set as far as possible by subsequent applications of the deduction rules. The general chart parsing technique is sketched in Fig. 3.5.

The way the chart parsing algorithm is formulated here, we have only a recognizer. Whenever we find a goal item in the resulting chart, we can conclude that our input sentence is in the language generated by our grammar.

A chart parsing algorithm can be extended to a parser by adding backpointers to the items in the charts. The backpointers tell us about the origin of an item. Actually, since our grammars are ambiguous, there can be more than one way to deduce an item; therefore we need lists of backpointers. The chart together with the backpointers can be seen as a compact representation

$\mathcal{C} = \mathcal{A} = \emptyset$
for all items I resulting form a rule application with empty antecedent set **do**
    add I to $\mathcal{C}$ and to $\mathcal{A}$
end for
repeat
    remove an item I from $\mathcal{A}$
    for all items I' resulting from a rule application with antecedents I and items from $\mathcal{C}$ **do**
        if $I' \notin \mathcal{C}$ **then**
            add I' to $\mathcal{C}$ and to $\mathcal{A}$
        end if
    end for
until $\mathcal{A} = \emptyset$
if there is a goal item in $\mathcal{C}$ **then**
    output true
else
    output false
end if

Fig. 3.5. Chart parsing

CFG:
$T = \{a, b, c\}$
$N = \{S, A, B, C, D, T_a, T_b, T_c\}$
$S \to AC \quad S \to BD$
$A \to T_a A \quad A \to a$
$C \to T_b H \quad H \to CT_c \quad C \to T_b T_c$
$B \to T_a G \quad G \to BT_b \quad B \to T_a T_b$
$D \to T_c D \quad D \to c$
$T_a \to a \quad T_b \to b \quad T_c \to c$

j							
6	$S, ((\cdot,\cdot),(\cdot,\cdot))$	S		C	H	D	T_c, D
5					C	T_c, D	
4	B		G		T_b		
3			B	T_b			
2	A		T_a, A				
1	T_a, A						
0		1	2	3	4	5	i

Fig. 3.6. Chart for parsing $w = aabbcc$ with backpointers for the goal item

of a parse forest. The single parse trees can be read off the chart by starting from the goal item(s) and following the backpointers.

For an example see the ambiguous CFG in Fig. 3.6 and the sample chart for parsing *aabbcc* with the CYK algorithm. The figure shows the backpointers for the goal item $[S, 0, 6]$. There are two pairs of backpointers corresponding to the two syntactic analyses of the input.

3.2.3 Hypergraphs

As we have seen, a chart is a set of items. Each application of a deduction rule that has been used to create the chart describes dependencies between the items. These dependencies are between the set of antecedent items and the set of consequent items. The latter contains usually only a single element. This view on the items and their dependencies results in a structure that is

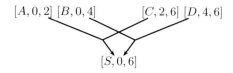

Fig. 3.7. Parts of the hypergraph for the chart in Fig. 3.6

a hypergraph (Gallo et al., 1993). In a probabilistic setting, we can assign weights to the nodes in the hypergraph and then realize k-best parsing as a search on the hypergraph (Klein and Manning, 2004; Huang and Chiang, 2005).

A hypergraph $\langle V, E \rangle$ consists of a set of nodes V and a set of hyperedges $E \in \mathcal{P}(V) \times \mathcal{P}(V)$. In other words, instead of linking a single node to a single node, the edges in hypergraphs link sets of nodes to sets of nodes.

As already mentioned, in the hypergraph that corresponds to a chart obtained from applying deduction rules, the items are the nodes while every application of a deduction rule can be seen as a hyperedge that links the set of antecedent items to the set of consequent items. The reversed hyperedges are the backpointers that are needed to extract entire parse trees from a chart. As an example of a hypergraph-based presentation of the deduction process, consider the fragment of the hypergraph for the chart in Fig. 3.6 that is shown in Fig. 3.7.

3.3 Properties of Parsing Algorithms

There are different properties of algorithms that are interesting to examine.

3.3.1 Soundness and Completeness

The most important property that a useful algorithm should have is to be sound and complete. Roughly, this means that the algorithm does what it is supposed to do. In the context of parsing, we say that an algorithm is sound and complete if for every grammar G and every input sentence w, the following holds: a) if the algorithm answers *yes*, then w is in the string language $L(G)$; and b) if w is in the string language $L(G)$, then the algorithm answers *yes*. The first property (a) is called *soundness*, the second property (b) is called *completeness*.

Given an algorithm specified with deduction rules, soundness and completeness can often be shown via an induction over the deduction rules. Take for instance the CYK algorithm from Fig. 3.3 that has the following rules:

3.3 Properties of Parsing Algorithms

Goal item: $[S, 0, n]$

Scan: $\dfrac{}{[A, i-1, i]} \quad A \to w_i \in P$

Complete: $\dfrac{[B, i, j], [C, j, k]}{[A, i, k]} \quad A \to B\,C \in P$

We can show the following property for the items generated by these rules, given a fixed grammar G and an input sentence $w = w_1 \cdots w_n$ with $w_i \in T$ for $1 \leq i \leq |w| = n$: For all $A \in N$ and all $0 \leq i < j \leq n$:

$$[A, i, j] \text{ iff } A \stackrel{*}{\Rightarrow} w_{i+1} \cdots w_j.$$

We can show this by induction over the length $l = j - i$ of the span.

1. The case $l = 1$ is covered by the **scan** rule since the only way to derive a string w of length 1 from a non-terminal A is by a rule $A \to w$. The **scan** rule guarantees that for every w_j and every $A \in N$, if there is a production $A \to w_j$, then $[A, j-1, j]$. On the other hand, since the **scan** rule is the only rule that allows us to derive items spanning only a single terminal, we also know that whenever $[A, j-1, j]$, then $A \stackrel{*}{\Rightarrow} w_j$.
2. The case $l > 1$ is covered only by the **complete** rule since its consequent items always have a span longer than 1. We can assume that the induction claim holds for the antecedent items since they have a lower length than the consequent item. Assume that $[A, i, k]$ was obtained by the **complete** rule. Then the production $A \to BC$ required by the side condition and $B \stackrel{*}{\Rightarrow} w_{i+1} \cdots w_j$ and $C \stackrel{*}{\Rightarrow} w_{j+1} \cdots w_k$ give us $A \stackrel{*}{\Rightarrow} w_{i+1} \cdots w_k$. On the other hand, if $A \stackrel{*}{\Rightarrow} w_{i+1} \cdots w_k$, $k > i+1$, then there must be a production $A \to BC$ as above and consequently, $[A, i, k]$.

If we apply our claim to the goal item, we obtain that a) if $[S, 0, |w|]$ then $S \stackrel{*}{\Rightarrow} w$ (soundness) and b) if $S \stackrel{*}{\Rightarrow} w$ then $[S, 0, |w|]$ (completeness).

See the solution of problem 3.2 for the proof of the soundness of the Earley algorithm.

3.3.2 Complexity

For a given grammar G and an input sentence $w \in T^*$, we call the *recognition problem* the task to decide whether $w \in L(G)$ or not. We distinguish between the *fixed* and the *universal* recognition problem.

- *Fixed recognition problem*: Assume a given grammar G (fixed). Then decide for a given input word w if $w \in L(G)$. In this case, the complexity of the problem is given only with respect to the size of the input sentence w, i.e., the size of the grammar is taken to be a constant. This is also sometimes called the *word recognition problem*.

- *Universal recognition problem*: Decide for an input grammar G and an input word w if $w \in L(G)$. In this case, we have to investigate the complexity of the problem in the size of the input sentence w and the grammar G.

Note that in real natural language applications, we often deal with very large grammars. Grammars extracted from treebanks for instance can easily have more than 10,000 or even 20,000 productions while the average sentence length is somewhere between 20 and 30. Therefore, for natural language processing, the complexity of the universal recognition problem is an important factor.

To characterize the complexity of a problem, we distinguish between the *time* and the *space* complexity. They depend on the length n of the input sentence w and (if the universal recognition problem is considered) the size of the grammar G.

We distinguish the following different complexity classes (Hopcroft and Ullman, 1979):

1. **P (PTIME)**: problems that can be solved deterministically in an amount of time that is polynomial in the size of the input. I.e., there is a constant c and a k such that the parsing of a string of length n takes an amount of time $\leq cn^k$.
   Notation: $\mathcal{O}(n^k)$.
2. **NP**: problems whose positive solutions can be verified in polynomial time given the right information, or equivalently, whose solutions can be non-deterministically found in polynomial time.
3. **NP-complete**: the hardest problems in NP. A problem is NP-complete if any problem in NP can be transformed into it in polynomial time.

The question whether the two classes P and NP are equal or not is an open question. Most people think however that NP is larger.

The specification of parsing algorithms via deduction rules facilitates the computation of the complexity of an algorithm (McAllester, 2002). In order to determine the time complexity, we have to calculate the maximal number of (different) rule applications that is possible. This depends on the most complex deduction rule in our parsing schema.

Take for instance again the CYK algorithm specified above. The most complex rule is the **complete** rule:

$$\frac{[B,i,j],[C,j,k]}{[A,i,k]} \quad A \to B\, C \in P.$$

In this rule, we have three different non-terminals that depend on each other since they occur in a single production and three different indices, all of them ranging either from 0 to $n-1$ (indices i and j) or from 1 to n (index k) where n is the length of the input sentence. Consequently, it holds for the number c of different possible applications of **complete** that $c \leq |P|n^3$. We therefore obtain for the fixed recognition problem where $|P|$ is treated as a constant, that the time complexity of this algorithm is $\mathcal{O}(n^3)$.

See the solutions of Problems 3.3 and 3.4 for the space complexity of the CYK algorithm and the time complexity of the Earley algorithm.

An example for a formalism where the fixed recognition problem is polynomial while the universal recognition problem is NP-complete are ID/LP grammars (Shieber, 1984). ID/LP grammars are like CFGs except that the specification of the immediate dominance relation is separated from the specification of linear precedence.

Take for instance a CFG production $A \to X_1 \ldots X_n$. Such a production specifies two relations, namely the *immediate dominance (ID)* relations between A and the X_i ($1 \leq i \leq n$) and the *linear precedence (LP)* relations between X_i and X_j for $i < j$. The idea underlying ID/LP grammars is to dissociate these two relations: The productions $A \to X_1, \ldots, X_n$ specify only ID relations while additional LP relations can be specified separately: $X_1 \prec X_2, X_2 \prec X_3, \ldots$. These LP relations are global, i.e., they hold for all right-hand sides of productions in the grammar.

For each ID/LP grammar, an equivalent CFG can be constructed. Therefore the fixed recognition problem for ID/LP (like the one for CFGs) is in P. The construction of the equivalent CFG however is such that the number of possible LP orders for $A \to X_1, \ldots, X_n$ can be $n!$. Therefore the universal recognition problem for ID/LP grammars is NP-complete (Barton, 1985).

3.3.3 Valid Prefix Property

An algorithm is said to have the valid prefix property (or to be prefix valid) if it considers only hypotheses consistent with the input seen so far. More precisely, whenever a partial parse tree spans a portion of the input ending at position j, the string $w_0 \ldots w_{j-1}$ must be the prefix of a word in the language.

Consider for example the two algorithms from Fig. 3.3, the CYK algorithm for CFGs in Chomsky Normal Form and the Earley algorithm. The CYK algorithm does not have the valid prefix property. For instance, given a grammar with productions $S \to AB$, $B \to BB$, $A \to a$, $B \to b$, for an input word bb, we can obtain an item $[B, 0, 1]$ that spans the input up to position 1, i.e., that yields the string b. However, there is no word in the language of this grammar that starts with a b since every word has to start with an a.

In contrast to this, the Earley algorithm has the valid prefix property if we assume that the grammar does not contain useless symbols (i.e., from every non-terminal, we can derive a set of terminal strings). This follows for instance from the soundness proof in the solution of Problem 3.2.

3.4 Summary

This chapter has introduced basic notions of parsing that are important for the chapters on parsing algorithms that will come later in the book.

In a first part, we have explained the framework of parsing as deduction. The idea is that the set of intermediate parsing results is characterized via deduction rules. This way of specifying a parsing algorithm has several advantages. Firstly, it separates the proper algorithm from control structures and data structures. By doing so, it allows a better understanding of the dependencies between parsing results. Furthermore, a formulation with deduction rules facilitates the tabulation of parsing results in a natural way. This leads to a chart parsing strategy where all intermediate results are stored in a chart and can be retrieved for reuse at any time. This is particularly important in applications where one is faced with highly ambiguous grammars as it is generally the case in natural language processing. Throughout the book, all parsing algorithms will be specified using deduction rules.

Besides the technique of defining parsing as a deductive process, we have also seen a range of properties of parsing algorithms that are important to investigate such as soundness and completeness, complexity and prefix validity.

Problems

3.1. (Deduction Rules for Earley Parsing)

Let us suppose that we are dealing only with CFGs whose productions have the form either $A \to a$ or $A \to aB$ where $A, B \in N$, $a \in T$.

For such grammars, we can simplify the Earley algorithm. Give the corresponding parsing schema.

3.2. Show that the Earley algorithm from Fig. 3.3 is sound.

In order to show this, show that the following holds:

If $[A \to \alpha \bullet \beta, i, j]$ then $S \stackrel{*}{\Rightarrow} w_1 \cdots w_i A \gamma \Rightarrow w_1 \cdots w_i \alpha \beta \gamma \stackrel{*}{\Rightarrow} w_1 \cdots w_j \beta \gamma$ for some $\gamma \in (N \cup T)^*$.

Note that this proves also the prefix validity of this algorithm.

3.3. (CYK space complexity)

What is the space complexity of the CYK algorithm given in this chapter?

3.4. Give the time complexity of the Earley algorithm from Fig. 3.3.

4
Tree Adjoining Grammars

4.1 Introduction to Tree Adjoining Grammars

In this section we introduce TAG. Besides giving the definition of the formalism, we briefly mention the linguistic principles underlying TAG in order to give an idea of the way TAG is used for natural language processing. The formal definitions are taken from (Kallmeyer, 2009).

4.1.1 Definition of TAG

Tree Adjoining Grammar (TAG, Joshi and Schabes (1997)) is a tree-rewriting formalism. A TAG consists of a finite set of trees (elementary trees). The nodes of these trees are labelled with non-terminals and terminals (terminals only label leaf nodes). Starting from the elementary trees, larger trees are derived by substitution (replacing a leaf with a new tree) and adjunction (replacing an internal node with a new tree). In case of an adjunction, the tree being adjoined has exactly one leaf that is marked as the foot node (marked with an asterisk). Such a tree is called an *auxiliary* tree. To license its adjunction to a node n, the root and foot nodes must have the same label as n. When adjoining it to n, in the resulting tree, the subtree with root n from the old tree is attached to the foot node of the auxiliary tree. Non-auxiliary elementary trees are called *initial* trees. A derivation starts with an initial tree. In a final derived tree, all leaves must have terminal labels.

In a TAG, one can specify for each node whether adjunction is mandatory and which trees can be adjoined.

(11) John seems to try to sleep

A sample TAG $G_{raising}$ for raising constructions such as (11) is shown in Fig. 4.1. This TAG (a lexicalized TAG) will be the running example for the next chapter for illustrating the different parsing algorithms. The subscripts *NA* and *OA* indicate adjunction constraints: *NA* signifies that for this node,

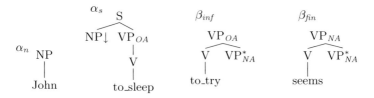

Fig. 4.1. A small LTAG $G_{raising}$ for raising constructions

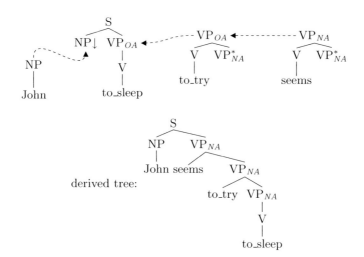

Fig. 4.2. A sample derivation in $G_{raising}$

adjunction is not allowed while OA signifies that adjunction is obligatory. The derivation for (11) using the TAG $G_{raising}$ is shown in Fig. 4.2.

Besides the definition of trees from Section 1.5, for TAG we need, specifically, the definitions of initial and auxiliary trees. In the following, we assume an alphabet N of non-terminal symbols and an alphabet T of terminal symbols. For the labels of the nodes in our elementary trees, we also allow the empty word ε, which acts like a terminal, i.e., only leaves can be labelled with ε.

Definition 4.1 (Auxiliary and initial trees).

1. *An* auxiliary tree *is a syntactic tree $\langle V, E, r \rangle$ such that there is a unique leaf f marked as foot with $l(r) = l(f)$. We write this tree as $\langle V, E, r, f \rangle$.*
2. *An* initial tree *is a non-auxiliary syntactic tree.*

Any leaf with a non-terminal label that is not a foot node is called a substitution node.

Now we can introduce TAG.

Definition 4.2 (Tree Adjoining Grammar).

A Tree Adjoining Grammar *(TAG)* is a tuple $G = \langle N, T, I, A, S, f_{OA}, f_{SA} \rangle$ where

- N, T are disjoint alphabets of non-terminal and terminal symbols,
- $S \in N$ is a specific start symbol,
- I is a finite set of initial trees, and A a finite set of auxiliary trees with node labels from N and $T \cup \{\varepsilon\}$,
- f_{OA} and f_{SA} are functions that represent adjunction constraints: $f_{OA} : \{v \mid v \text{ vertex in some } \gamma \in I \cup A\} \to \{0, 1\}$ and $f_{SA} : \{v \mid v \text{ vertex in some } \gamma \in I \cup A\} \to P(A)$ are functions such that $f_{OA}(v) = 0$ and $f_{SA}(v) = \emptyset$ for every v with out-degree 0.

Every tree in $I \cup A$ is called an elementary tree.

For a given node, the function f_{OA} specifies whether adjunction is obligatory (value 1) or not (value 0) and f_{SA} gives the set of auxiliary trees that can be adjoined. Only internal nodes can allow for adjunction; adjunction at leaves is not possible. As a notational convention, we often omit the functions f_{OA} and f_{SA} in the tuple notation, i.e., we write TAGs as $\langle N, T, I, A, S \rangle$.

In TAG, larger trees are derived from $I \cup A$ by subsequent applications of the operations substitution and adjunction. The substitution operation combines a syntactic tree and an initial tree into a new syntactic tree while adjunction combines a syntactic tree and an auxiliary tree into a new syntactic tree. Substitution was defined in Section 2.1.2, in the context of Tree Substitution Grammars.

Definition 4.3 (Adjunction).

Let $\gamma = \langle V, E, r \rangle$ be a syntactic tree, $\gamma' = \langle V', E', r', f \rangle$ be an auxiliary tree and $v \in V$. $\gamma[v, \gamma']$, the result of adjoining γ' into γ at node v, is defined as follows:

- if v is a leaf or $l(v) \neq l(r')$, then $\gamma[v, \gamma']$ is undefined;
- otherwise, $\gamma[v, \gamma'] := \langle V'', E'', r'' \rangle$ with
  - $V'' = V \cup V'' \setminus \{v\}$ and
  - $E'' = (E \setminus \{\langle v_1, v_2 \rangle \mid v_1 = v \text{ or } v_2 = v\})$
    $\cup\ E'\ \cup\ \{\langle v_1, r' \rangle \mid \langle v_1, v \rangle \in E\}\ \cup\ \{\langle f, v_2 \rangle \mid \langle v, v_2 \rangle \in E\}.$

Derived trees in TAG are trees that can be obtained by taking an elementary tree γ_e and adding derived trees $\gamma_1, \ldots, \gamma_n$ by adjunction or substitution at pairwise different nodes $v_1, \ldots, v_n$ in γ_e. Every elementary tree is itself a derived tree. We assume that in the course of a derivation, we use pairwise different instances of elementary trees. In other words, the same elementary tree can be used several times but this means that we use isomorphic copies of the elementary tree with pairwise disjoint node sets. See for example the derivation of (12) in Fig. 4.3 where the tree β_{inf} is used twice. We use different copies and therefore, in the resulting derived tree, we have for example

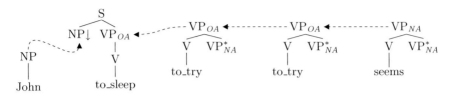

Fig. 4.3. Derivation of (12) in $G_{raising}$

two different nodes with terminal label *to_try*. In the following, we call γ an instance of $\gamma_e \in (I \cup A)$ if γ is isomorphic to γ_e.

(12) John seems to try to try to sleep

TAG derivations are represented by derivation trees that record the history of how the elementary trees are put together. A derived tree is the result of carrying out the substitutions and adjunctions, i.e., the derivation tree describes uniquely the derived tree. Each edge in a derivation tree stands for an adjunction or a substitution. The edges are labelled with Gorn addresses. E.g., the first derivation tree in Fig. 4.4 indicates that the elementary tree α_n for *John* is substituted for the node at address 1 and a tree derived from the elementary tree β_{inf} for *to_try* is adjoined at node address 2 to the tree α_s for *to_sleep*. The tree derived from *to_try* in turn is obtained by adjoining the elementary tree of *seems* to the root (address ε). Note that the distinctions between adjunctions and substitutions can be inferred from the nature of the node whose address labels the corresponding edge. If this address is the address of a substitution node, then we are dealing with a substitution; otherwise we are dealing with an adjunction.[1] Derivation trees are unordered trees.[2]

In the following definition, for each way to obtain a derived tree, we define immediately the corresponding derivation tree.

Definition 4.4 (Derived tree and derivation tree).
Let $G = \langle N, T, I, A, S \rangle$ be a TAG.

1. *Every instance γ' of a $\gamma \in I \cup A$ is a derived tree in G.*
   The corresponding derivation tree is $\langle \{v\}, \emptyset, v \rangle$ with $l(v) = \gamma$.
2. *For $\gamma_1, \ldots, \gamma_n$ derived trees in G with derivation trees $D_i = \langle V_i, E_i, r_i \rangle$ ($1 \leq i \leq n$) and for an instance $\gamma = \langle V, E, r \rangle$ of a $\gamma_e \in I \cup A$ such*

---

[1] Some authors actually mark adjunction with a dashed edge and substitution with a solid edge.
[2] We assume that once an adjunction or substitution is performed on a node, the node disappears (see the definitions of adjunction and substitution). This means that multiple adjunctions are not possible. Consequently, the order of adjunctions and substitutions on a tree does not matter for the resulting derived tree.

4.1 Introduction to Tree Adjoining Grammars   57

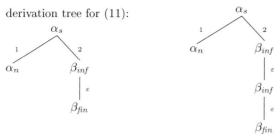

Fig. 4.4. Derivation trees in $G_{raising}$

that $\gamma, \gamma_1, \ldots, \gamma_n$ have pairwise disjoint sets of nodes, if there are pairwise different nodes $v_1, \ldots, v_n \in V$ with Gorn addresses $p_1, \ldots, p_n$ such that
- $\gamma' = \gamma[v_1, \gamma_1] \ldots [v_n, \gamma_n]$ is defined and
- $l(r_i) \in f_{SA}(v_i)$ for all $\gamma_i \in A$,

then γ' is a derived tree in G.
The corresponding derivation tree is $D = \langle V, E, r \rangle$ such that
- $V = \bigcup_{i=1}^{n} V_i \cup \{r\}$,
- $E = \bigcup_{i=1}^{n} E_i \cup \{\langle r, r_1 \rangle, \ldots, \langle r, r_n \rangle\}$,
- $l(r) = \gamma_e$ and
- $g(\langle r, r_i \rangle) = p_i$ for $1 \leq i \leq n$.[3]

3. These are all derived trees and derivation trees in G.

We call a derived tree that does not contain substitution nodes or vertices v with $f_{OA}(v) = 1$ a saturated *derived tree* and the corresponding derivation tree a saturated *derivation tree*.

This definition differs slightly from standard definitions. Here, we treat at once all adjunctions and substitutions performed on a single elementary tree. In the corresponding derivation tree, we combine a new root tree with all its daughters. In classical TAG definitions, these adjunctions and substitutions are oftentimes defined separately, i.e., each of them is considered a single derivation step that adds one edge to the derivation tree. The disadvantage of the classical definition is that, after having performed an adjunction on a tree γ, the addresses of nodes in γ below the adjunction site change. Consequently, when adjoining (or substituting) later to such a node, instead of the current address of this node, we need to take its address in its original elementary tree as the edge label in the corresponding derivation tree. This complication

---
[3] Note that there can be more than one derivation tree for a single derived tree since there might be more than one combination of adjunctions and substitutions with elementary trees leading to the same result. However, for a given derivation tree, the derived tree is uniquely determined.

is avoided here by choosing immediately all adjunction/substitution sites in an elementary tree.

Definition 4.5 (Tree language).
Let $G = \langle N, T, I, A, S \rangle$ be a TAG.

1. The tree language of G is $L_T(G) := \{\gamma \mid \gamma$ is a saturated derived initial tree in G with root label $S\}$.[4]
2. The string language of G is the set of yields of trees in $L_T(G)$.

4.1.2 Formal Properties

The class of languages generated by TAG (TAL) properly contains all context-free languages. Since every CFG can be considered a Tree Substitution Grammar (see Section 2.1.2) which, in turn, is a TAG with an empty set of auxiliary trees, CFL is clearly contained in TAL. In Chapter 2 we have already seen a TAG for a non-context-free language, namely the TAG for the copy language in Fig. 2.4, p. 27. Another example is the TAG for $L_3 := \{a^n b^n c^n \mid n \geq 0\}$ from the solution of Problem 4.1.

Note that TAGs without adjunction constraints, i.e., TAGs where adjunctions are never obligatory and where the set of adjoinable trees for a given node contains all auxiliary trees with the appropriate root label, also extend CFG but are less powerful than TAGs with adjunction constraints as defined here. Without adjunction constraints it is for instance not possible to generate $L_3 = \{a^n b^n c^n \mid n \geq 0\}$ (cf. solution of Problem 4.1).

One of the reasons why the TAG formalism is appealing from a formal point of view is the fact that it has nice closure properties (Vijay-Shanker and Joshi, 1985; Vijay-Shanker, 1987):

Lemma 4.6. *TALs are closed under union.*

This can be easily shown as follows: Assume the two sets of non-terminals to be disjoint. Then build a large TAG putting the initial and auxiliary trees from the two grammars together.

Lemma 4.7. *TALs are closed under concatenation.*

In order to show this, assume again the sets of non-terminals to be disjoint. Then build the unions of the initial and auxiliary trees, introduce a new start symbol S and add one initial tree with root label S and two daughters labeled with the start symbols of the original grammars.

Lemma 4.8. *TALs are closed under Kleene closure.*

---

[4] Sometimes TAG is defined without a start symbol S; then the last condition is omitted. The two versions (with or without start symbol) are equivalent.

The idea of the proof is as follows: We add an initial tree with the empty word and an auxiliary tree that can be adjoined to the roots of initial trees with the start symbol and that has a new leaf with the start symbol.

Lemma 4.9. *TALs are closed under substitution.*

In order to obtain the TAG that yields the language after substitution, we replace all terminals by start symbols of the corresponding TAGs.

As a corollary one obtains:

Lemma 4.10. *TALs are closed under arbitrary homomorphisms.*

Furthermore, TALs are also, like CFLs, closed under intersection with regular languages:

Lemma 4.11. *TALs are closed under intersection with regular languages.*

The proof in (Vijay-Shanker, 1987) uses extended push-down automata (EPDA), the automata that recognize TALs. We will introduce EPDAs in Section 10.1. Vijay-Shanker combines such an automaton with the finite state automaton for a regular language in order to construct a new EPDA that recognizes the intersection.

As a special case of Lemma 4.9 we obtain that TALs are closed under regular substitution (i.e., substitution with regular languages). With a theorem from Ginsburg (1966) we then get the following corollary:

Lemma 4.12. *TALs are closed under inverse homomorphisms.*[5]

To summarize, the closure properties of TALs are such that TALs form a substitution-closed *Full Abstract Family of Languages (Full AFL)*.[6]

We know from the pumping lemma for CFLs (Prop. 1.8) that in CFLs, from a certain string length on two parts of the string can be iterated ("pumped"). The proof idea is the following: Context-free derivation trees from a certain maximal path length on have the property that a non-terminal occurs twice on this path. Then the part between the two occurrences can be iterated. This means that the strings to the left and right of this part are pumped.

The same kind of iteration is possible in TAG derivation trees since TAG derivation trees are context-free (see Fig. 4.5). This leads to a pumping lemma for TALs (Vijay-Shanker, 1987).

A derived auxiliary tree β' can be repeatedly adjoined into itself. Into the lowest β' (low in the sense of the derivation tree) another auxiliary tree β''

---

[5] For a homomorphism f, the image of a language L under the inverse homomorphism f^{-1} is $f^{-1}(L) := \{x \mid f(x) \in L\}$.

[6] A set of languages forms a *Full AFL* if it is closed under intersection with regular languages, homomorphisms, inverse homomorphisms, union, concatenation and Kleene star.

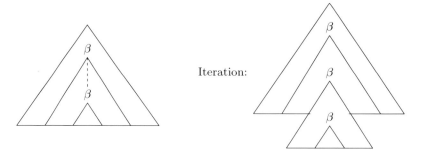

Fig. 4.5. Iteration in a TAG derivation tree

derived from β is adjoined. What does that mean for the derived tree? Let n be the node in β' to which β' can be adjoined and to which the final β'' is adjoined as well. There are three cases (see Fig. 4.6 for the corresponding derived trees before adjoining the final β''):

1. n is on the spine (i.e., on the path from the root to the foot node),
2. n is on the left of the spine, or
3. n is on the right of the spine.

Assume that the final β'' adds strings v_1 and v_2 on the left and right of the foot node.

Case 1: β' adds the two strings $w_1 w_2$ and $w_3 w_4$ on the two sides of its foot node. Adjunction to n adds new strings between w_1 and w_2 and between w_3 and w_4 respectively. This leads to strings

$x w_1 v_1 w_2 y w_3 v_2 w_4 z$ (no iteration of β')
$x w_1 w_1 v_1 w_2 w_2 y w_3 w_3 v_2 w_4 w_4 z$ (one iteration)
$x w_1 w_1 w_1 v_1 w_2 w_2 w_2 y w_3 w_3 w_3 v_2 w_4 w_4 w_4 z$
$x w_1 w_1 w_1 w_1 v_1 w_2 w_2 w_2 w_2 y w_3 w_3 w_3 w_3 v_2 w_4 w_4 w_4 w_4 z$
...
$\Rightarrow x w_1^n v_1 w_2^n y w_3^n v_2 w_4^n z$ in the string language for all $n \geq 0$.

Case 2: β' adds the two strings $w_1 w_2 w_3$ and w_4 on the two sides of its foot node. Adjunction to n adds new strings between w_1 and w_2 and between w_2 and w_3 respectively. This leads to strings

$x w_1 v_1 w_2 v_2 w_3 y w_4 z$ (no iteration)
$x w_1 w_1 v_1 w_2 v_2 w_3 w_2 w_4 w_3 y w_4 z$ (one iteration of β')
$x w_1 w_1 w_1 v_1 w_2 v_2 w_3 w_2 w_4 w_3 w_2 w_4 w_3 y w_4 z$
$x w_1 w_1 w_1 w_1 v_1 w_2 v_2 w_3 w_2 w_4 w_3 w_2 w_4 w_3 w_2 w_4 w_3 y w_4 z$
...
$\Rightarrow x w_1^{n+1} v_1 w_2 v_2 w_3 (w_2 w_4 w_3)^n y w_4 z$ in the string language for all $n \geq 0$.

Case 3: β' adds the two strings w_1 and $w_2 w_3 w_4$ on the two sides of its foot node. Adjunction to n adds new strings between w_2 and w_3 and between w_3 and w_4 respectively. This leads to strings

4.1 Introduction to Tree Adjoining Grammars

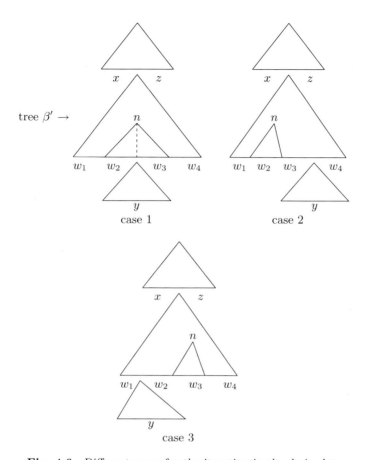

Fig. 4.6. Different cases for the iteration in the derived tree

$xw_1yw_2v_1w_3v_2w_4z$ (no iteration)
$xw_1yw_2w_1w_3w_2v_1w_3v_2w_4w_4z$ (one iteration)
$xw_1yw_2w_1w_3w_2w_1w_3w_2v_1w_3v_2w_4w_4w_4z$
$xw_1yw_2w_1w_3w_2w_1w_3w_2w_1w_3w_2v_1w_3v_2w_4w_4w_4w_4z$
...
$\Rightarrow xw_1y(w_2w_1w_3)^n w_2v_1w_3v_2w_4^{n+1}z$ in the string language for all $n \geq 0$.

Lemma 4.13 (Pumping Lemma for TAL). *If L is a TAL, then there is a constant c such that if $w \in L$ and $|w| \geq c$, then there are $x, y, z, v_1, v_2, w_1, w_2, w_3, w_4 \in T^*$ such that*

- $|v_1v_2w_1w_2w_3w_4| \leq c$,
- $|w_1w_2w_3w_4| \geq 1$, *and*

- *one of the following three cases holds:*[7]
    1. $w = xw_1v_1w_2yw_3v_2w_4z$ *and* $xw_1^n v_1 w_2^n y w_3^n v_2 w_4^n z$ *is in the string language for all* $n \geq 0$, *or*
    2. $w = xw_1v_1w_2v_2w_3yw_4z$ *and* $xw_1^{n+1}v_1w_2v_2w_3(w_2w_4w_3)^n yw_4z$ *is in the string language for all* $n \geq 0$, *or*
    3. $w = xw_1yw_2v_1w_3v_2w_4z$ *and* $xw_1y(w_2w_1w_3)^n w_2v_1w_3v_2w_4^{n+1}z$ *is in the string language for all* $n \geq 0$.

Proof. Let G be a TAG and let m be the maximum length of the yield of trees in the tree language of G where there is no β occurring twice on the same path in the derivation tree. $c_1 := m + 1$.

For any word with length $\geq c_1$, a β' as above can be iterated and one of the three cases above holds.

If inside β' and below the foot node of β' there are no other derived auxiliary trees adjoined into themselves (and one can always choose such a β'), then there is a constant c_2 such that $|v_1v_2w_1w_2w_3w_4| \leq c_2$ in all three cases.

Furthermore, since the length of the word is $> m$, β' can be chosen such that at least one of the four iterated parts w_1, w_2, w_3, w_4 is not ε.

Let $c := max\{c_1, c_2\}$. Then the pumping lemma holds for G with the constant c.

□

As a corollary, the following weaker pumping lemma holds:

Lemma 4.14 (Weak Pumping Lemma for TAL). *If L is a TAL, then there is a constant c such that if $w \in L$ and $|w| \geq c$, then there are $x, y, z, v_1, v_2, w_1, w_2, w_3, w_4 \in T^*$ such that*

- $|v_1v_2w_1w_2w_3w_4| \leq c$,
- $|w_1w_2w_3w_4| \geq 1$,
- $x = xv_1yv_2z$, *and*
- $xw_1^n v_1 w_2^n y w_3^n v_2 w_4^n z \in L(G)$ *for all* $n \geq 0$.

In this weaker version, the w_1, w_2, w_3, w_4 need not be substrings of the original word w.

A pumping lemma can be used to show that certain languages are not in the class of the string languages satisfying the pumping lemma.

---

[7] According to Vijay-Shanker (1987) the second and third case can be reduced to the first. But if this is true, it is not at all obvious: in the second and third case the parts that are iterated are not present in the original word x: in case 2, $w_2w_4w_3$ is no substring of x and in case 3, $w_2w_1w_3$ is no substring of x. This is why I prefer to stay with the three cases. It is true however that cases 2 and 3 are somehow weaker than case 1, i.e., a language not satisfying case 1 will probably not satisfy cases 2 or 3 either.

Lemma 4.15. *The double copy language $L := \{www \,|\, w \in \{a,b\}^*\}$ is not a TAL.*

Proof. Assume that L is a TAL.
Then $L' := L \cap a^*b^*a^*b^*a^*b^* = \{a^n b^m a^n b^m a^n b^m \,|\, n, m \geq 0\}$ is a TAL as well. Assume that L' satisfies the weak pumping lemma with a constant c.
Consider the word $w = a^{c+1}b^{c+1}a^{c+1}b^{c+1}a^{c+1}b^{c+1}$.
None of the w_i, $1 \leq i \leq 4$ from the pumping lemma can contain both as and bs. Furthermore, at least three of them must contain the same letters and be inserted into the three different a^{c+1} respectively or into the three different b^{c+1}. This is a contradiction since then either $|v_1| \geq c+1$ or $|v_2| \geq c+1$. □

Another example of a language that can be shown not to be a TAL, using the pumping lemma, is $L_5 := \{a^n b^n c^n d^n e^n \,|\, n \geq 0\}$ (see the solution of Problem 4.5).
Concerning mild context-sensitivity, we will see polynomial parsing algorithms for TAG in the next chapter. Furthermore, in Chapter 6, we will show that LCFRLs (the languages generated by LCFRSs) are semilinear and contain TALs. Consequently, TALs are mildly context-sensitive.

4.1.3 Linguistic Principles for TAG

In the preceding sections, we have introduced the TAG formalism. When using TAG for natural languages, we have additional linguistic principles that are respected (Frank, 1992; Frank, 2002; Abeillé, 2002). These principles are not part of the TAG formalism itself; some of them are even not formalized and remain therefore rather vague. But there is a general understanding that these principles should be more or less respected when designing a natural language TAG.

The linguistic principles underlying TAG are the following:

- **Lexicalization**: Each elementary tree has at least one non-empty lexical item, its lexical *anchor*. Elementary trees can even have more than one anchor.[8]
- **Predicate argument co-occurrence**: each predicate contains in the elementary tree associated with it argument slots (leaves with non-terminal labels, i.e., substitution nodes or foot nodes) for each of its arguments, i.e., for each of the elements it subcategorizes for including the subject.
- **Semantic anchoring**: elementary trees are not semantically void.
- **Compositionality principle**: an elementary tree corresponds to a single semantical unit.

---

[8] Empty words are also allowed but only in combination with at least one non-empty lexical element.

Only on the first two principles is there general agreement. The third one is adopted by most people but not completely respected in the XTAG grammar (where we have separate auxiliary trees for complementizers). The fourth one is very arguable since, in order to verify it, we need a definition of a single semantical unit which is not available in TAG and which depends very much on the semantic theory we use.

The fact that TAGs for natural languages are lexicalized enables us to perform a lexical selection preceding parsing. In other words, given an input string w, we first select all trees from our TAG that have lexical items occurring in w. We then use the sub-TAG obtained in this way for parsing.

Besides there being a general consensus for lexicalization, there is a general consensus on a condition on *Elementary tree minimality* (Frank, 2002), which requires that an elementary tree contain argument slots only for the arguments of its lexical anchor, and for nothing else. Most argument slots are substitution nodes, in particular the nodes for nominal arguments. See (13) for an example. (13b.) shows the elementary tree of the verb *gives* as used in (13a.).

(13) a. John gives a book to Mary

b.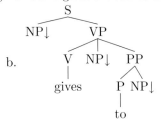

Sentential arguments however are realised by foot nodes (see (14) for an example). The reason is that we want to be able to extract material from sentential arguments (in long-distance dependencies such as (14c.)). Such extractions can be obtained by adjoining the embedding clause into the sentential argument.

(14) a. John thinks that Mary comes

b.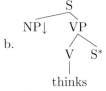

c. Whom does Paul think that Mary likes?

Modifiers always have auxiliary trees with the modified category being the foot node. Examples are given in (15) and (16).

(15) a. John quickly read the book

b.

(16) a. John read the yellow book

b.

4.1.4 Extended Domain of Locality and Factoring of Recursion

Compared to CFGs, TAGs have larger elementary structures and they allow for adjunction. Because of these two crucial properties, TAGs exhibit properties that are very useful for modelling natural languages.

In TAG, constraints such as the need of certain arguments for a predicate can be stated only within the local domains of elementary trees. But elementary trees can be arbitrarily large (provided they are finite) and, furthermore, because of the adjunction operation these local domains can comprise (slots for) elements arbitrarily far away from each other in the final derived tree. This is why TAG is often said to have an *extended domain of locality*. A related aspect is that the adjunction operation allows us to put recursive structures into separate elementary trees. This is often called *factoring of recursion*.

The extended domain of locality in combination with the factoring of recursion is crucial for the way TAG deals with unbounded dependencies and the constraints holding for them. The constraints are not explicitly stated in the grammar in the form of some additional constraint on derived trees but they follow from the form of the elementary trees (which is guided by the above-mentioned linguistic principles) and the possibilities of adjunction.

As an example consider wh-movement. There are several constraints that have been observed for wh-movement. These constraints are not equally strong (Kroch, 1987; Frank, 1992; Frank, 2002); some of them are language-dependent, others seem to be of a universal character.

- **Subjacency**: A moved element may not cross more than one category NP or S (cyclic movement via intermediate traces is allowed). Examples are given in (17):

  (17) a. * a book which Karen met the man that had written t
  b. ? a book which I read Andy's review of t
  c. ? a book which Karen asked who had read t

- **Condition on Extraction Domains (CED)**: Extractions from constituents not appropriately governed are not allowed. In particular, extractions from subjects and adjuncts are not possible. See (17a.) for an example.
- **Empty Category Principle (ECP)**: A trace must be properly governed. This means in particular that extractions of subjects from tensed or infinitival clauses with overt complementizers are not possible. Examples are given in (18).

(18) a. * which book did Lenny say that t was very boring?
b. * who did Lenny ask whether t had arrived yet?
c. * whom would Lenny have preferred for t to have married his daughter?

Adjunct extractions out of islands such as in (19) are combinations of subjacency and ECP violations.

(19) a. * why did Karen ask who had read this book t?
b. * why did Karen know that Steven had read the book t?

In the standard LTAG analysis (Kroch, 1987), the slot for moved element and the trace (i.e., the empty word) at the original position (sometimes called the gap) are in the same elementary tree. This follows from the linguistic principles mentioned above. As an example, see Fig. 4.7 for the LTAG analysis of (20). Note that the trees in this figure are not the elementary trees since some of the substitutions have already been performed. Fig. 4.7 shows only the adjunction that creates the long-distance dependency. As one can see here, there is actually no wh-movement in TAG since the wh-element does not change its position; it is already an extracted element with a trace left behind in the elementary tree. The adjunction only inserts more material between the extracted element and its trace.

(20) which book did Harvey say Cecile had read t

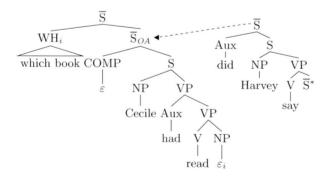

Fig. 4.7. Derivation for (20)

With this analysis and the principles for elementary trees, extraction from adjuncts as in (21) is correctly blocked since adjuncts are not present in the elementary trees of the lexical items they modify. Consequently, there is no elementary tree that might lead to a derivation for (21).

(21) * which movie did Georgette fall asleep after watching t?

For a wh-island violation as (22a.), the tree in (22b.) would be needed.[9]

(22) a. ? which book did Judy wonder who wrote t?

b.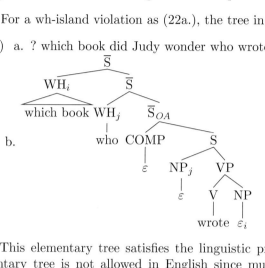

This elementary tree satisfies the linguistic principles. But such an elementary tree is not allowed in English since multiple fronted wh-elements are not possible in English. However, languages where such multiple fronted wh-elements are possible, e.g., Romanian, also allow wh-extraction out of an unbounded number of wh-islands.

So-called *that*-trace effects (ECP violations) also can be excluded by not allowing the corresponding elementary tree. For the analysis of (23a.), we would need the elementray tree given in (23b.). Such a tree does not exist in our grammar; consequently, there is no derivation for (23a.).

(23) a. * who did Alice say that t left?

b.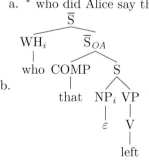

---

[9] Actually, for (22b.) and (23b.) to be elementary trees, the wh-phrases must be replaced with substitution nodes. We precompiled substitution here for better readability.

The examples in this section have shown that, for a large range of constraints for unbounded dependencies, it is possible to provide TAG analyses respecting the linguistic principles of TAG such that these constraints follow from the elementary trees, i.e., can be stated locally.

4.1.5 Constituency and Dependencies

As we have seen above, the *derived tree* gives the constituent structure of a sentence. The *derivation tree* records how the elementary trees of the grammar were put together in order to obtain the derived tree. In a lexicalized grammar, each node in the derivation tree corresponds to (at least) one lexical item of the input sentence.

For this section we adopt the linguistic principles explained above and we assume following (Frank, 1992; Frank, 2002) that all functional elements (complementizers, determiners, auxiliaries, negation) are part of the elementary trees of the lexical item they are associated with. Under this assumption, each substitution or adjunction corresponds to the application of a predicate to one of its arguments. Consequently, the derivation tree gives us the set of predicate-argument dependencies of a sentence and therefore the derivation tree is close to a semantic dependency graph (see Candito and Kahane (1998)).

This is the principal reason why in most approaches to LTAG semantics, semantics is computed on the derivation tree (Candito and Kahane, 1998; Joshi and Vijay-Shanker, 1999; Kallmeyer and Joshi, 2003; Kallmeyer and Romero, 2008) or, if two synchronous TAGs are used, the derivation tree can be considered the interface structure that links syntax to semantics (Shieber, 1994; Nesson and Shieber, 2006; Han, 2002).[10]

As an illustration, Figs. 4.8–4.13 show the analyses for the examples (24)–(29). (24) and (25) are simple examples for substitutions of NP and PP arguments. (26)–(28) are different constructions involving clausal complements. (26) is an example of a tensed complement clause; (27) is an ECM construction, i.e., the verb selects for an infinitival complement while assigning an accusative case to the subject of this complement.[11] (28) is an example of a control verb. Finally, (29) is a raising construction.

(24) John buys Bill a book

(25) John gives a book to Mary

(26) Bill hopes that John wins

(27) John expects [Bill to win]

---

[10] Note, however, that in some cases the derivation tree is not exactly the semantic dependency structure (Rambow, Vijay-Shanker, and Weir, 1995; Dras, Chiang, and Schuler, 2004; Frank and van Genabith, 2001).

[11] The case assignment is handled via features.

4.1 Introduction to Tree Adjoining Grammars   69

Fig. 4.8. Elementary trees and derivation tree for (24)

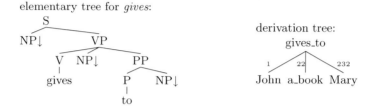

Fig. 4.9. Elementary trees and derivation tree for (25)

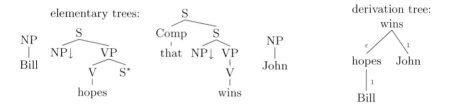

Fig. 4.10. Elementary trees and derivation tree for (26)

Fig. 4.11. Elementary trees and derivation tree for (27)

(28) John persuades Bill [PRO to leave]

(29) John seems to like Bill

Fig. 4.12. Elementary trees and derivation tree for (28)

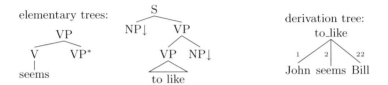

Fig. 4.13. Elementary trees and derivation tree for (29)

4.2 Equivalent Formalisms

4.2.1 Tree-Local MCTAG

For a range of linguistic phenomena, it has been proposed to separate the elementary trees of a TAG into distinct subtrees that can be adjoined to or substituted into different nodes in an already derived tree. A TAG where the elementary trees are grouped into sets is called a *multicomponent* TAG (MCTAG) (Joshi, Levy, and Takahashi, 1975; Weir, 1988). Depending on how the trees from a multicomponent are used, we distinguish different types of MCTAGs.

Definition 4.16 (MCTAG).
A multicomponent TAG (MCTAG) is a tuple $G = \langle N, T, S, I, A, \mathcal{A} \rangle$ where $G_{TAG} := \langle N, T, S, I, A \rangle$ is a TAG with elementary trees $I \cup A$, and $\mathcal{A}$ is a partition of $I \cup A$. $\mathcal{A}$ is called the set of elementary tree sets.[12]

For tree-local MCTAG we require that 1) whenever a tree from a tree set is used, all other trees from the same set must be used as well and 2) all trees from

---

[12] Note that this definition does not exclude the possibility that the same tree occurs in different sets or even several times in the same set. In this case, we consider that there are different trees that look exactly the same (i.e., that are isomorphic while having identical labels).

Furthermore, this definition differs from the definition in (Weir, 1988) in the sense that Weir defines elementary tree sets as sequences of elementary trees. However, the usual practice in more recent MCTAG publications is a definition as sets, which was actually already adopted by the first introduction of MCTAG under the name of simultaneous TAG in (Joshi, Levy, and Takahashi, 1975).

the same tree set must be added (adjoined or substituted) to nodes belonging to the same elementary tree. In the following, we will give a formalization of this property in terms of the underlying TAG derivation trees allowed in a tree-local MCTAG. In this derivation tree, the root must be labelled by an initial tree α such that the singleton $\{\alpha\}$ is in the grammar. Furthermore, for every pair of trees γ_1, γ_2 from the same elementary set and for every node v in the derivation tree, the number of γ_1-nodes among the daughters of v must be the same as the number of γ_2-nodes among the daughters of v.

Definition 4.17 (Tree-locality condition).
Let $G = \langle N, T, S, I, A, \mathcal{A} \rangle$ be an MCTAG, $G_{TAG} := \langle N, T, S, I, A \rangle$. Let $D = \langle V, E, r \rangle$ be the derivation tree of a saturated derived initial tree in G_{TAG}. D is a tree-local TAG derivation tree in G iff
(TL) $\{l(r)\} \in \mathcal{A}$ and for every $\Gamma \in \mathcal{A}$, $\gamma_1, \gamma_2 \in \Gamma$ and $v \in V$:
$|\{v' \mid \langle v, v' \rangle \in E \text{ and } l(v') = \gamma_1\}| = |\{v' \mid \langle v, v' \rangle \in E \text{ and } l(v') = \gamma_2\}|$.

Note that this characterization is different from the original definition of tree-locality that is based on a grouping of the elementary tree instances into instances of elementary tree sets. The original definition assumes that elementary tree instances, when used during a derivation, come in a specific set instance. The elements of such a set must all attach to nodes from the same elementary tree. Clearly, if our condition (TL) is satisfied, then we can partition the daughters of a node v into sets such that each set represents a tree set instance and the original tree-locality constraint is satisfied with respect to these sets.

Our formulation of tree-locality for MCTAG is taken from Kallmeyer (2009). It is motivated by the fact that its checking requires only counting and no grouping into tree sets. For parsing, our formulation of tree-locality is therefore preferable.

The tree language of a tree-local MCTAG G is then the subset of the tree language of G_{TAG} that can be derived with a tree-local TAG derivation tree with respect to G.

Tree-local MCTAGs are equivalent to TAGs since the possible adjunctions in a single elementary tree can be precompiled and encoded in the adjunction constraints. However, this transformation might considerably increase the size of the grammar since, for a given elementary tree γ, we need a copy of γ in the TAG for every possible combination of adjunctions in γ. This is the reason why the universal recognition problem for tree-local MCTAG is NP-complete (Søgaard, Lichte, and Maier, 2007; Nesson, Satta, and Shieber, 2008), i.e., recognition in the size of the grammar is NP-complete.

More recent proposals of MCTAG variants that are equivalent to TAG are k-TT-MCTAG (Kallmeyer and Parmentier, 2008) and tree-local MCTAG with flexible composition and k-delayed tree-local MCTAG (Joshi, Kallmeyer, and Romero, 2003; Chiang and Scheffler, 2008). Kallmeyer (2009) presents an extensive overview of different types of MCTAGs.

4.2.2 Linear Indexed Grammars

Indexed grammars were introduced by Aho (1968). An indexed grammar looks like a CFG except that the non-terminals are equipped with stacks of indices.

Definition 4.18 (Indexed grammar).
An indexed grammar *is a tuple* $\langle N, T, I, P, S \rangle$ *where*

- *N, T and I are pairwise disjoint alphabets, non-terminals, terminals and indices,*
- *P is a finite set of productions that are of the form*
  - $A \to \alpha$ *or*
  - $A \to Bf$ *or*
  - $Af \to \alpha$

  with $A, B \in N, f \in I, \alpha \in (N \cup T)^*$,
- *$S \in N$ is the start symbol.*

In a derived sentential form x, non-terminals can be equipped with stacks of indices, i.e., $x \in (NI^* \cup T)^*$. The first kind of production works like context-free productions while copying the stack of A to all non-terminals in α. The second kind of production adds a symbol to the stack of A while replacing A with B. The third kind of production deletes a symbol f from the stack of A and then works like the first kind of production.

An indexed grammar is called a *linear indexed grammar (LIG)* (Gazdar, 1988; Vijay-Shanker, 1987) if in a production $A \to \alpha$ or $Af \to \alpha$ the stack of A is copied only to one non-terminal in α.

We write the productions in a LIG as follows:

- $A[\ldots] \to X_1 \ldots X_i[\ldots] \ldots X_n$ with $X_j \in N \cup T$ for $j \neq i$, $X_i \in N$.
- $A[\ldots] \to B[f \ldots]$
- $A[f \ldots] \to X_1 \ldots X_i[\ldots] \ldots X_n$ with $X_j \in N \cup T$ for $j \neq i$, $X_i \in N$.

The intuition behind the equivalence of TAG and LIG is that, whenever we perform an adjunction in a TAG, we have to keep track of the adjunction site while traversing the adjoined tree since this is the node we have to go back to after having passed the foot node. This keeping track can be done on a stack. Since this stack needs to be available only at the foot node, it is enough to pass it along the spine of the auxiliary tree (the path from root to foot node). This can be modelled with a LIG where the single node in a right-hand side that inherits the stack corresponds to the node on the spine.

4.2.3 Combinatory Categorial Grammars

Besides being shown to be equivalent to LIG, TAG has also been shown to be equivalent to certain variants of *Combinatory Categorial Grammar* (CCG) (Steedman, 2000). A CCG consists of a lexicon that maps terminal symbols to categories of the form A/B or $A\backslash B$. Depending on the categories, adjacent constituents can be combined in certain ways. The possible type of combinations are specified by a set of combinatory rules.

Definition 4.19 (Combinatory Categorial Grammar).
A Combinatory Categorial Grammar is a tuple $\langle N, T, f, R, S \rangle$ where

- *N and T are pairwise disjoint alphabets, the non-terminals (atomic categories) and the terminals (lexical items),*
- *R is a finite set of combinatory rules (see below),*
- *f is a function that maps elements of $T \cup \{\varepsilon\}$ to finite subsets of $C(N)$, the set of categories where*
  - *$N \subseteq C(N)$, and*
  - *if $c_1, c_2 \in C(N)$, then $(c_1/c_2) \in C(N)$ and $(c_1 \backslash c_2) \in C(N)$.*
- *$S \in N$ is the start category.*

Depending on which types of combinatory rules are allowed, we obtain different types of categorial grammars. The version that is weakly equivalent to TAG allows for four types of combinatory rules. Let $x, y, z_1, \ldots$ be variables over $C(N)$ and $|_i$ a variable over $\{/, \backslash\}$. Then the four rules are defined as follows:

1. *Forward application*:
$$(x/y)y \longrightarrow x$$

2. *Backward application*:
$$y(x\backslash y) \longrightarrow x$$

3. *Generalized forward composition*: for some $n \geq 1$,
$$(x/y)(\ldots(y|_1 z_1)|_2 \ldots |_n z_n) \longrightarrow (\ldots(x|_1 z_1)|_2 \ldots |_n z_n)$$

4. *Generalized backward composition*: for some $n \geq 1$,
$$(\ldots(y|_1 z_1)|_2 \ldots |_n z_n)(x\backslash y) \longrightarrow (\ldots(x|_1 z_1)|_2 \ldots |_n z_n)$$

There are two possibilities to restrict these rules in a specific CCG: The initial category possible for values of x can be restricted and the entire category to which y is instantiated can be restricted.

The language of a CCG is the set of strings such that, starting from the start symbol S, it is possible to derive a sequence of categories of the string symbols:
$$L(G) = \{a_1 \ldots a_n \mid S \xrightarrow{*} c_1 \ldots c_n, c_i \in f(a_i), a_i \in T \cup \{\varepsilon\}, 1 \leq i \leq n\}.$$

The crucial observation for the construction of a LIG for a given CCG is that CCG categories can be seen as non-terminals equipped with a stack. Function application amounts to pushing items on a stack while function composition is a combination of pushing and popping.

The weak equivalence between TAG, LIG and CCG has been shown in (Vijay-Shanker and Weir, 1994). See also (Jäger and Michaelis, 2004) for an overview of the relevant literature.

4.3 Summary

In this chapter, we have seen Tree Adjoining Grammar (TAG), an extension of CFG that is mildly context-sensitive. TAGs have been extensively used to model natural languages, and large-coverage implementations such as the XTAG grammar have shown that many natural language phenomena can be adequately modelled with TAG.

TAGs are tree-rewriting grammars. In contrast to CFGs, TAGs allow for larger elementary structures and they allow not only for substitution but also for adjunction. We have shown that TAGs have a range of nice formal properties; they are in particular a substitution-closed Full AFL and their languages satisfy a pumping lemma. From a linguistic point of view, a crucial property of TAG is their extended domain of locality which enables a local description of unbounded dependencies.

Problems

4.1. $L_3 := \{a^n b^n c^n \mid n \geq 0\}$

1. Give a TAG (with adjunction constraints) that generates L_3.
2. Show that TAG without adjunction constraints cannot generate L_3.
   (Hint: Any elementary tree must contain equal numbers of as, bs and cs. And each auxiliary tree can be adjoined at its own root.)

4.2. Show that $\{a^n b^n c^n a^m b^m c^m \mid n, m \geq 0\}$ is a TAL.
Hint: The language $L_3 = \{a^n b^n c^n \mid n \geq 0\}$ is a TAL.

4.3. Show that $\{a^i b^j a^i b^j \mid i, j \geq 0\}$ is a TAL.
Hint: The copy language is a TAL.

4.4. Show that $L := \{a^{2^n} \mid n \geq 0\}$ is not a TAL using the (weak) pumping lemma.

4.5. $L_4 := \{a^n b^n c^n d^n \mid n \geq 0\}$, $L_5 := \{a^n b^n c^n d^n e^n \mid n \geq 0\}$

1. Give a TAG generating L_4.
2. Show that L_5 is not a TAL using the weak pumping lemma.
   Hint: Consider the word $w = a^{c+1} b^{c+1} c^{c+1} d^{c+1} e^{c+1}$ with c being the constant from the pumping lemma.

4.6. Propose elementary trees for the following sentences:

(30) John saw a man with a telescope

(31) Mary took a decision

4.7. Consider sentential subjects as in

(32) That John wins perplexes Bill

Do you prefer adding them by substitution or adding the matrix verb to the sentential subject by adjunction (similarly to sentential complements)? (Note that extraction out of sentential subjects is not allowed.) Give the elementary tree for *perplexes* that you would choose.

4.8. Give the derivation trees for

(33) John obviously is likely to win

(34) Who do you think Bill says will win the race?

4.9. Give a LIG that generates the language $L = \{a^n b^n c^n d^n \mid n \geq 0\}$.

5
Parsing Tree Adjoining Grammars

This chapter treats different parsing techniques for TAG. We will extend the standard algorithms for CFG, i.e., present a CYK parser, different types of Earley algorithms and LR parsing for TAG.

5.1 A CYK Parser for TAG

5.1.1 The Recognizer

As we have seen in Chapter 3, a CYK algorithm is a non-directional bottom-up parser. The first CYK parser for TAG was proposed in (Vijay-Shanker and Joshi, 1985). Here, we present a formulation of this algorithm using deduction rules, similar to the one given in (Kallmeyer and Satta, 2009).

To simplify the deduction rules needed for our CYK algorithm, we assume that the trees in our TAG are such that each node has at most two daughters. Every TAG can be easily transformed into a TAG satisfying this condition, similarly to the transformation into Chomsky Normal Form for CFG. This way, instead of processing the daughters one after the other (as in a CYK with dotted productions), we can move immediately from the set of all daughters to their mother.

The algorithm simulates a bottom-up traversal of the derived tree. At each moment, we are in a specific node in an elementary tree and we have already traversed the part below. In particular, we know about the yield of this part. In a TAG, either the subtree below a node contains a foot node, in which case its yield is separated into two parts, the part on the left and the part on the right of the foot node, or there is no foot node below, in which case the yield is a single substring of the input. Furthermore, we need to keep track of whether we have already adjoined at the node or not since at most one adjunction per node can occur. For this, we can distinguish between a bottom and a top position for the dot on a node. Bottom signifies that we have not performed an adjunction. We can reach the top position either after having performed

L. Kallmeyer, *Parsing Beyond Context-Free Grammars*, Cognitive Technologies,
DOI 10.1007/978-3-642-14846-0_5, © Springer-Verlag Berlin Heidelberg 2010

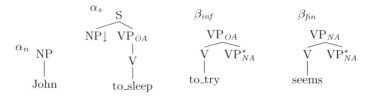

Fig. 5.1. The LTAG $G_{raising}$ for raising constructions

an adjunction or, if the node has no OA constraint, by moving upwards from the bottom position.

In order to capture the relevant information about the current node and the yield of the subtree below, our items have the following form:

$$[\gamma, p_t, i, f_1, f_2, j]$$

where

- $\gamma \in I \cup A$,
- p is the address of a node in γ,
- subscript $t \in \{\top, \bot\}$ specifies whether substitution or adjunction has already taken place ($\top$) or not ($\bot$) at p, and
- $0 \leq i \leq f_1 \leq f_2 \leq j \leq n$ are indices with i, j indicating the left and right boundaries of the yield of the subtree at position p and f_1, f_2 indicating the yield of a gap in case a foot node is dominated by p. We write $f_1 = f_2 = -$ if no gap is involved.

For combining indices, we use the operator $f' \oplus f'' = f$ where $f = f'$ if $f'' = -$, $f = f''$ if $f' = -$, and f is undefined otherwise.

The algorithm walks bottom-up on the derivation tree. As an example let us consider the trace for parsing (35) with the TAG $G_{raising}$ from Fig. 4.1, repeated in Fig. 5.1. The trace is given in Fig. 5.2. It contains only the successful items. While explaining the different rules of the CYK algorithm, we will refer to this trace.

(35) John seems to sleep

We need two rules to process leaf nodes while scanning their labels, depending on whether they have terminal labels or labels ε. These two cases are covered by the two rules **lex-scan** and **eps-scan**. In both cases, the position of the dot is the top since adjunction is not possible at these leaves.

Lex-scan: $\dfrac{}{[\gamma, p_\top, i, -, -, i+1]}$ $\quad l(\gamma, p) = w_{i+1}$

Eps-scan: $\dfrac{}{[\gamma, p_\top, i, -, -, i]}$ $\quad l(\gamma, p) = \varepsilon$

5.1 A CYK Parser for TAG

	Item	Rule
1.	$[\alpha_n, 1_\top, 0, -, -, 1]$	lex-scan (*John*)
2.	$[\beta_{fin}, 11_\top, 1, -, -, 2]$	lex-scan (*seems*)
3.	$[\alpha_s, 211_\top, 2, -, -, 3]$	lex-scan (*to_sleep*)
4.	$[\beta_{fin}, 2_\top, 2, 2, 3, 3]$	foot-predict
5.	$[\alpha_n, \varepsilon_\bot, 0, -, -, 1]$	move-unary from 1.
6.	$[\beta_{fin}, 1_\bot, 1, -, -, 2]$	move-unary from 2.
7.	$[\alpha_s, 21_\bot, 2, -, -, 3]$	move-unary from 3.
8.	$[\alpha_n, \varepsilon_\top, 0, -, -, 1]$	null-adjoin from 5.
9.	$[\beta_{fin}, 1_\top, 1, -, -, 2]$	null-adjoin from 6.
10.	$[\alpha_s, 21_\top, 2, -, -, 3]$	null-adjoin from 7.
11.	$[\alpha_s, 2_\bot, 2, -, -, 3]$	move-unary from 10.
12.	$[\beta_{fin}, \varepsilon_\bot, 1, 2, 3, 3]$	move-binary from 4. and 9.
13.	$[\alpha_s, 1_\top, 0, -, -, 1]$	substitute 8.
14.	$[\beta_{fin}, \varepsilon_\top, 1, 2, 3, 3]$	null-adjoin from 12.
15.	$[\alpha_s, 2_\top, 1, -, -, 3]$	adjoin 14. into 11.
16.	$[\alpha_s, \varepsilon_\bot, 0, -, -, 3]$	move-binary from 13. and 15.
17.	$[\alpha_s, \varepsilon_\top, 0, -, -, 3]$	null-adjoin from 16.

Fig. 5.2. Trace for CYK parsing of (35) with $G_{raising}$

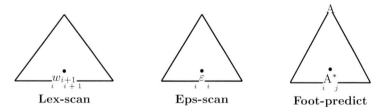

Fig. 5.3. Rules **lex-scan**, **eps-scan** and **foot-predict**

Our sample TAG $G_{raising}$ does not have leaves labelled ε; therefore **eps-scan** is not applied here. The first three items in the trace in Fig. 5.2 result from applications of **lex-scan**.

The rule **foot-predict** processes the foot node of auxiliary trees $\beta \in A$ by guessing the yield below the foot node, i.e., the portion of w spanned by the gap. We use immediately the top position $p_\top$ in the consequent item in order to block adjunction at foot nodes, as usually required in TAG.

Foot-predict: $\dfrac{}{[\beta, p_\top, i, i, j, j]}$ $\beta \in A, p$ foot node address in $\beta, i \leq j$

The fourth item in our sample trace results from applying this rule. Note that, besides this item, all other possibilities for the span of the gap below the foot node (delimited by positions i and j) are guessed as well. We left them out in the trace since they are not successful.

The first three rules are the rules that introduce axioms, i.e., their antecedent set is empty. They are depicted in Fig. 5.3.

When moving up inside a single elementary tree, we either move from only one daughter to its mother, if this is the only daughter, or move from the set of both daughters to the mother node. In the latter case, the two yields must be adjacent. These two moves are performed by means of the operations **move-unary** and **move-binary**:

Move-unary: $\dfrac{[\gamma, (p \cdot 1)_\top, i, f_1, f_2, j]}{[\gamma, p_\bot, i, f_1, f_2, j]}$ node address $p \cdot 2$ does not exist in γ

Move-binary: $\dfrac{[\gamma, (p \cdot 1)_\top, i, f_1, f_2, k], [\gamma, (p \cdot 2)_\top, k, f'_1, f'_2, j]}{[\gamma, p_\bot, i, f_1 \oplus f'_1, f_2 \oplus f'_2, j]}$

The two rules for moving up in the tree are depicted in Fig. 5.4. If we want to generalize this to TAGs with an arbitrary number of daughters per node, we have to replace these two rules with a single new rule that moves from the set of all completed daughter items to the mother node (see the solution of Problem 5.1). Alternatively, we can of course introduce active items and add the daughters one after another to the already completed part of a subtree (see the solution of Problem 5.2).

Examples for such moves are the items 5–7 in our sample trace that are obtained from unary moves, i.e., from moving from a unary daughter to its mother. In the case of a unary move, the information about a gap below a foot node is passed to the mother node. In the case of a binary move, either none of the daughters contains a gap or one of them does and it needs to be passed to the mother. This is obtained by using the operator $\oplus$ defined above for combining the gap information from the two antecedent items. An example for a binary move is item 12, resulting from combining item 9 (first daughter of the root of β_{fin}) and item 4 (second daughter of the root of β_{fin}).

For nodes that do not require adjunction, we can move from the bottom position of the node to its top position. This is done by the rule **null-adjoin**:

Null-adjoin: $\dfrac{[\gamma, p_\bot, i, f_1, f_2, j]}{[\gamma, p_\top, i, f_1, f_2, j]}$ $f_{OA}(\gamma, p) = 0$

Examples for this are items 8–10 in Fig. 5.2

The following rule **substitute** performs a substitution. I.e., it is applied when reaching the root of an initial tree that can be substituted at position p in some elementary tree γ.

Substitute: $\dfrac{[\alpha, \varepsilon_\top, i, -, -, j]}{[\gamma, p_\top, i, -, -, j]}$ $l(\alpha, \varepsilon) = l(\gamma, p), \gamma(p)$ a substitution node

Move-unary:

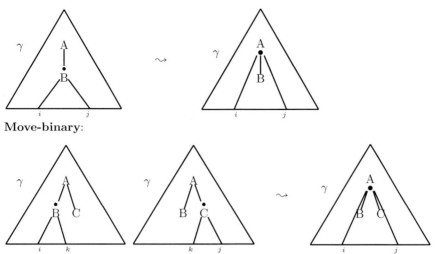

Move-binary:

Fig. 5.4. Rules **move-unary** and **move-binary**

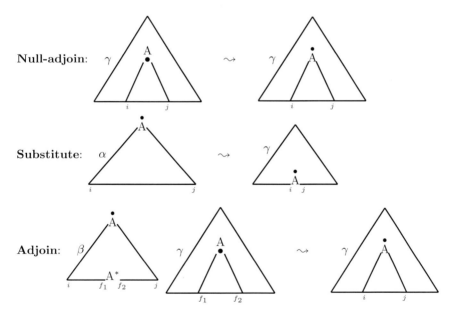

Fig. 5.5. Rules **null-adjoin**, **substitute** and **adjoin**

An example is item 13 that results from substituting the completed α_n tree (item 8) into the node at position 1 in the tree α_s.

Similarly, the rule **adjoin** adjoins an auxiliary tree β at p in γ, under the precondition that the adjunction of β at p in γ is allowed. This rule is applied when reaching the root node of β, i.e., once β has been completely recognized.

Adjoin: $\dfrac{[\beta, \varepsilon_\top, i, f_1, f_2, j], [\gamma, p_\bot, f_1, f'_1, f'_2, f_2]}{[\gamma, p_\top, i, f'_1, f'_2, j]} \quad \beta \in f_{SA}(\gamma, p)$

An example for **adjoin** is item 15., obtained form adjoining the tree β_{fin} (item 14) to the VP node (address 2) of the α_s tree, item 11.

The goal items are all $[\alpha, \varepsilon_\top, 0, -, -, n]$ where $\alpha \in I$ with $l(\alpha, \varepsilon) = S$. In other words, the algorithm aims at finding an initial tree with root label S that spans the entire input.

5.1.2 Complexity

In order to determine the complexity of this algorithm, we have to give an upper bound for the number of applications of the **adjoin** operation. We have $|A|$ possibilities for β, $|A \cup I|$ for γ and m for p where m is the maximal number of internal nodes in an elementary tree. The six indices $i, f_1, f'_1, f'_2, f_2, j$ range from 0 to n. Consequently, **adjoin** can be applied at most $|A||A \cup I|m(n+1)^6$ times and therefore, the time complexity of this algorithm is $\mathcal{O}(n^6)$.

A problem of the CYK algorithm is that it does not use any prediction to restrict the number of parse trees obtained bottom-up. As a consequence, as argued in (Joshi and Schabes, 1997), not only the worst-case but also the best-case complexity is $\mathcal{O}(n^6)$.

5.2 An Earley Parser for TAG

5.2.1 Introduction

As mentioned above, the CYK algorithm has worst-case and best-case time complexity $\mathcal{O}(n^6)$. The reason for this is that, just as in the CFG version of the CYK algorithm, too many partial trees are produced that are not pertinent to the final parse tree. This is due to the pure bottom-up approach. No predictive information is used to restrict the search space during parsing. In order to avoid this problem, we now add a predict operation. The technique is the same as in the case of the Earley algorithm for CFG.

The overall idea of Earley parsing is to perform a left-to-right scanning of the input string while building partial parse trees in a bottom-up fashion and using top-down predictions to restrict the set of possible parse trees. The first proposal of an Earley parsing algorithm for TAG is (Schabes and Joshi, 1988). In the following, we present the algorithm from (Joshi and Schabes, 1997).

Recall that in the case of CFG, we distinguish between predicted and completed categories in the right-hand side of a production. Therefore, we need a dot that marks the position up to which we have already recognized a right-hand side: Everything to the left of the dot has been completed while everything to the right of the dot has been predicted. A dotted production S → NP • VP for instance signifies that we have predicted an S consisting of an NP and a VP and, so far, we have already seen the NP. In order to complete the S, we still need to find an adjacent VP.

In the case of TAG, we also use a dot that is positioned to the left or right of some node in an elementary tree. Now, everything that is to the left and, if the dot is already on the right, also everything that is below the node in question has been completed while the rest of the elementary tree has been predicted. However, in addition to being left or right of a node, we need to keep track of whether we have performed an adjunction or not. Therefore, just like in the CYK algorithm for TAG, we need to distinguish between top and bottom and we end up with four different positions around a node: left above (la), left below (lb), right above (ra) and right below (rb).

Let us for the moment assume a TAG without substitution nodes. Later, we will extend the algorithm to deal with substitution. The parser starts with predicting every initial tree with root symbol S. In the beginning, since nothing has been recognized, we are in position la of the root node. The general idea of how to traverse the derived tree during parsing and how to move from one elementary tree γ to an adjoined tree β and back again is the following: Whenever we are left above a node (position la), we can predict an adjunction and start the traversal of the adjoined tree. Whenever we are left below a foot node, we can move back to the adjunction site and traverse the tree below it. Whenever we are right below an adjunction site, we continue the traversal of the adjoined tree at the right of its foot node. Finally, whenever we are right above the root of an auxiliary tree, we can move back to the right of the adjunction site. This is depicted in Fig. 5.6.

5.2.2 Items

Partial results in our parsing algorithm consist of positions of dots in elementary trees plus the span of the part of the tree that we have already recognized. Therefore, in our items we need to record the name of an elementary tree, a node address in this tree, the position of the dot (la, lb, ra or lb) with respect to this node, the indices delimiting the span of the part of the tree that we have already seen and a flag telling us whether we have already adjoined something to this node. This flag is only relevant when going back from an adjoined auxiliary tree to the attachment site in the original tree. It makes sure the corresponding operation can be performed only once per adjunction site.

Our items have the form

$$[\gamma, p, pos, i, j, k, l, adj]$$

where

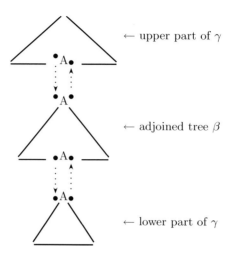

Fig. 5.6. Simulation of adjunction in the Earley algorithm

- $\gamma \in I \cup A$ is an elementary tree,
- p is the Gorn address of a node in γ,
- $pos \in \{la, lb, rb, ra\}$ is the position of the dot on this node,
- i, j, k, l are indices on the input string, where $i, l \in \{0, \ldots, n\}$, $j, k \in \{0, \ldots, n\} \cup \{-\}$, $n = |w|$. As in the CYK case, i is the position preceding the leftmost element in the span of our item and l the position following the rightmost element. The indices j, k characterize the gap below a foot node if there is such a gap. Otherwise, their values are $-$.
- $adj \in \{0, 1\}$ is a flag. It prevents multiple adjunctions at a single node. A value $adj = 1$ signifies that something has already been adjoined to the dotted node.

The different positions of a dot on a node tell us about the part of the tree that has been recognized: An item of the form $[\gamma, p, la, i, j, k, l, 0]$ signifies that in the tree γ, we have recognized the part on the left of the dotted node and that the yield of the sisters of the dotted node to its left ranges from i to l. If γ is an auxiliary tree, the gap in the yield of γ caused by the foot node ranges from j to k. If an item has the form $[\gamma, p, lb, i, -, -, i, 0]$, then this means that the yield of the subtree of γ that is below the dotted node starts at position i. An item of the form $[\gamma, p, rb, i, j, k, l, adj]$ tells us that we have recognized the part below the dotted node (except maybe for some adjunction at the node itself) and the yield of this part ranges from i to l with, if applicable, a gap between positions j and k. Furthermore, if $adj = 0$, nothing has been adjoined so far to the dotted node, while if $adj = 1$, an adjunction has already taken place. If an item has the form $[\gamma, p, ra, i, j, k, l, 0]$, then we have completely recognized the part below the dotted node, including any adjunction at the

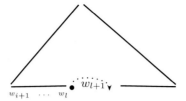

Fig. 5.7. Operation **ScanTerm** of the Earley algorithm

node itself. In γ, the part including the sisters to the left of the dotted node and everything below it spans the part of the input that is characterized by the indices i, j, k, l.

Note that within these items there is no information about the start index of the entire tree γ. In positions above, we only know the yield of the node and its sisters to the left.

5.2.3 Inference Rules

As a notation, in the following, for every tree γ and every node v in γ with node address p, $l(\gamma, p) = l(v)$ is the label of v and $\gamma(p)$ denotes v. Similarly, $f_{SA}(\gamma, p) = f_{SA}(v)$ and $f_{OA}(\gamma, p) = f_{OA}(v)$.

We start by predicting all initial trees with root symbol S. The dot is on the root (node address ε) in the position left above (la).

Initialize: $\dfrac{}{[\alpha, \varepsilon, la, 0, -, -, 0, 0]}$ $\quad \alpha \in I, l(\alpha, \varepsilon) = S$

As in the CFG case, we have rules that predict, rules that scan and rules that complete. Let us first consider the scanning rules that apply whenever we are on the left of a leaf that might be scanned. If the label of the leaf is a terminal, we can apply the operation **scanTerm** and if it is ε, we can apply **scan-ε**. The operation **scanTerm** is depicted in Fig. 5.7.

ScanTerm: $\dfrac{[\gamma, p, la, i, j, k, l, 0]}{[\gamma, p, ra, i, j, k, l+1, 0]}$ $\quad l(\gamma, p) = w_{l+1}$

Scan-ε: $\dfrac{[\gamma, p, la, i, j, k, l, 0]}{[\gamma, p, ra, i, j, k, l, 0]}$ $\quad l(\gamma, p) = \varepsilon$

There are different types of predictions in this algorithm. The first prediction operation occurs when being left above a node that allows for adjunction. Then we can predict the corresponding auxiliary trees. This is done by the operation **predictAdjoinable**, which is depicted in Fig. 5.8.

Fig. 5.8. Operation **PredictAdjoinable** of the Earley algorithm

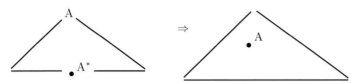

Fig. 5.9. Operation **PredictAdjoined** of the Earley algorithm

PredictAdjoinable: $\dfrac{[\gamma, p, la, i, j, k, l, 0]}{[\beta, 0, la, l, -, -, l, 0]}$ $\beta \in f_{SA}(\gamma, p)$

For nodes that do not require adjunction, we can also predict that no adjunction occurs. In this case, we move simply from position left above to position left below:

PredictNoAdj: $\dfrac{[\gamma, p, la, i, j, k, l, 0]}{[\gamma, p, lb, l, -, -, l, 0]}$ $f_{OA}(\gamma, p) = 0$

After having predicted an adjoined auxiliary tree β, we traverse β until we reach the position left below its foot node. Then we have to predict the tree γ in which the adjunction of β has taken place. Note that this prediction is done without checking whether a matching γ-item exists that allowed previously for the prediction of β. In other words, it can happen that we predict going back to a node that we actually have not seen yet. This is why, as we will explain later, this algorithm is not prefix valid.

The prediction of the possible adjunction site when reaching a foot node is performed by the **predictAdjoined** operation that is depicted in Fig. 5.9.

PredictAdjoined: $\dfrac{[\beta, p_f, lb, l, -, -, l, 0]}{[\gamma, p, lb, l, -, -, l, 0]}$ p_f foot node address in β, $\beta \in f_{SA}(\gamma, p)$

Once we have finished the recognition of the subtree below an adjunction site, we combine this with the item of the adjoined auxiliary tree where everything to the left of the foot node has been processed. This is the first complete operation since here, we are not predicting anything. Instead, we can move the dot over a foot node since we have finished the recognition of the subtree below it. We call this operation **completeFoot**; it is depicted in Fig. 5.10.

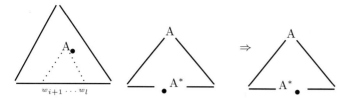

Fig. 5.10. Operation **CompleteFoot** of the Earley algorithm

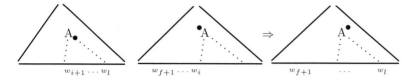

Fig. 5.11. Operation **CompleteNode** of the Earley algorithm

CompleteFoot :
$$\frac{[\gamma, p, rb, i, j, k, l, 0], [\beta, p_f, lb, i, -, -, i, 0]}{[\beta, p_f, rb, i, i, l, l, 0]} \quad \begin{array}{l} p_f \text{ foot node address in } \beta \\ \beta \in f_{SA}(\gamma, p) \end{array}$$

The second complete operation, **completeNode**, combines the part to the left of a node with the part below the node. As a result, we obtain an item with the dot right above the node. If there is a gap in one of the two items because of a foot node, this gap is passed to the new item by using the combination operation $\oplus$ from the CYK algorithm. **CompleteNode** is depicted in Fig. 5.11.

CompleteNode:
$$\frac{[\gamma, p, la, f, g, h, i, 0], [\gamma, p, rb, i, j, k, l, adj]}{[\gamma, p, ra, f, g \oplus j, h \oplus k, l, 0]} \quad l(\beta, p) \in N$$

Once we have finished the traversal of an auxiliary tree, i.e., we have completely recognized the tree and the dot is right above the root node, we continue in the tree where this auxiliary tree has been adjoined. This is done by the **adjoin** operation, depicted in Fig. 5.12.

Adjoin:
$$\frac{[\beta, \varepsilon, ra, i, j, k, l, 0], [\gamma, p, rb, j, g, h, k, 0]}{[\gamma, p, rb, i, g, h, l, 1]} \quad \beta \in f_{SA}(\gamma, p)$$

Note that, contrary to what one might expect, we remain in the position right below the adjunction site. This is why we need the flag *adj* to prevent multiple adjunctions. This flag is required to be 0 in the antecedent γ-item and it is set to 1 in the consequent item. The combination with material to the left, i.e., the move to the position right above, is done by a subsequent application of **completeNode**.

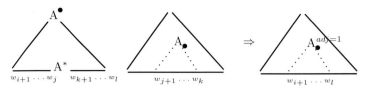

$adj = 1$ prevents the new item from being reused in another adjoin operation.

Fig. 5.12. Operation **Adjoin** of the Earley algorithm

Besides these, we need four operations to move from a dotted node to the leftmost daughter or to the next sister on the right or to the mother node.

MoveDown: $\dfrac{[\gamma, p, lb, i, j, k, l, 0]}{[\gamma, p \cdot 1, la, i, j, k, l, 0]}$ $\gamma(p \cdot 1)$ is defined

MoveRight: $\dfrac{[\gamma, p, ra, i, j, k, l, 0]}{[\gamma, p + 1, la, i, j, k, l, 0]}$ $\gamma(p + 1)$ is defined

MoveUp: $\dfrac{[\gamma, p \cdot m, ra, i, j, k, l, 0]}{[\gamma, p, rb, i, j, k, l, 0]}$ $\gamma(p \cdot m + 1)$ is not defined

Goal items are all items of the form $[\alpha, 0, ra, 0, -, -, n, 0]$, $\alpha \in I, l(\alpha, \varepsilon) = S$. In other words, parsing is successful if we manage to obtain an item where the dot is right above the root of an initial tree, this root node has label S, and the tree spans the entire input.

For illustration, let us consider the example in Fig. 5.13, assuming a grammar that contains the two trees in (36).

(36) α: S—c β: S → a S*

The first column of the table shows the item, the second depicts the dotted tree of this item, i.e., the elementary tree with the dot at the position given by the item, and the third column gives the rule that has led to the creation of this item.

5.2.4 Extending the Algorithm to Substitution

At least for natural languages, we need the substitution operation. Otherwise, it is not possible to respect the principle of elementary tree minimality that excludes the existence of more than one lexical predicate in a single elementary tree.

In the following, we will extend the above algorithm to cover substitution as well. For this, we need an operation that predicts a substitution whenever

5.2 An Earley Parser for TAG

Item	dotted tree	rule
$[\alpha, \varepsilon, la, 0, -, -, 0, 0]$	•S — c	Initialize
$[\beta, \varepsilon, la, 0, -, -, 0, 0]$	•S / a S*	PredictAdjoinable
$[\beta, \varepsilon, lb, 0, -, -, 0, 0]$	S• / a S*	PredictNoAdj
$[\beta, 1, la, 0, -, -, 0, 0]$	S / •a S*	MoveDown
$[\beta, 1, ra, 0, -, -, 1, 0]$	S / a• S*	ScanTerm
$[\beta, 2, la, 0, -, -, 1, 0]$	S / a •S*	MoveRight
$[\beta, 2, lb, 1, -, -, 1, 0]$	S / a •S*	PredictNoAdj
$[\alpha, \varepsilon, lb, 1, -, -, 1, 0]$	•S — c	PredictAdjoined
$[\alpha, 1, la, 1, -, -, 1, 0]$	S — •c	MoveDown
$[\alpha, 1, ra, 1, -, -, 2, 0]$	S — c•	ScanTerm
$[\alpha, \varepsilon, rb, 1, -, -, 2, 0]$	S• — c	MoveUp
$[\beta, 2, rb, 1, 1, 2, 2, 0]$	S / a S*•	CompleteFoot
$[\beta, 2, ra, 0, 1, 2, 2, 0]$	S / a S*•	CompleteNode
$[\beta, \varepsilon, rb, 0, 1, 2, 2, 0]$	S• / a S*	MoveUp
$[\beta, \varepsilon, ra, 0, 1, 2, 2, 0]$	S• / a S*	CompleteNode
$[\alpha, \varepsilon, rb, 0, -, -, 2, 1]$	S• — c	Adjoin
$[\alpha, \varepsilon, ra, 0, -, -, 2, 0]$	S• — c	CompleteNode

Fig. 5.13. Sample Earley parse for input ac (only successful items)

we are left of a substitution node and we need another operation that completes a substitution whenever we arrive at the right of the root node of the substituted initial tree. Joshi and Schabes (1997) trigger the first operation when being left above a substitution node and, once the substitution gets completed, they reach the position right above the substitution node. However, since in our definition of a TAG, adjunction is not allowed for substitution nodes anyway, we can just as well first move to the position left below the substitution node, applying the rule **predictNoAdj**, and predict substitution from here. The advantage is that there are less indices to consider and, in the completion operation, we have even less antecedent items. When completing the substitution, we move to the position right below the substitution node, and then, using **completeNode**, the dot ends up right above the substitution node.

The two additional rules for prediction and completion of substitutions are **predictSubst** and **substitute**:

PredictSubst: $\dfrac{[\gamma, p, lb, i, -, -, i, 0]}{[\alpha, \varepsilon, la, i, -, -, i, 0]}$ $\gamma(p)$ a substitution node, $\alpha \in I, l(\gamma, p) = l(\alpha, \varepsilon)$

Substitute: $\dfrac{[\alpha, \varepsilon, ra, i, -, -, j, 0]}{[\gamma, p, rb, i, -, -, j, 0]}$ $\gamma(p)$ a substitution node, $\alpha \in I, l(\gamma, p) = l(\alpha, \varepsilon)$

Note that the **substitute** operation does not check whether a corresponding γ-item which had triggered the prediction of α exists. This is why it is actually not a true complete operation and we therefore call it **substitute**. The check whether a corresponding γ-item exists is done in the next step, when applying **completeNode** in order to combine the part to the left of the substitution node with the part below it. If no appropriate part to the left exists, we cannot generate more items from the result of our **substitute**.

We chose to define **substitute** this way because it follows the strategy adopted in the case of adjunction where **adjoin** yields an item with position right below the adjunction site and only the following **completeNode** moves up and combines the part below with material to the left. This allows for a higher degree of factorization in our parsing operations.

In contrast to this, in (Joshi and Schabes, 1997), the complete operation for substitution is a true complete operation. It has two antecedent items since it depends also on the γ-item with position left above the substitution node that has triggered the substitution.

Now let us consider as a further example the TAG $G_{raising}$ from Fig. 5.1. We take again the sentence (35), repeated here as (37).

(37) John seems to sleep

The CYK trace for parsing this sentence was shown in Fig. 5.2. The Earley trace can be found in Fig. 5.14. Some of the items are left out. The items 3–12 show how substitution is done: In the substitution node, we first move to the

	Item	Rule
1.	$[\alpha_s, \varepsilon, la, 0, -, -, 0, 0]$	initialize
2.	$[\alpha_s, \varepsilon, lb, 0, -, -, 0, 0]$	predictNoAdj from 1.
3.	$[\alpha_s, 1, la, 0, -, -, 0, 0]$	moveDown from 2.
4.	$[\alpha_s, 1, lb, 0, -, -, 0, 0]$	predictNoAdj from 3.
5.	$[\alpha_n, \varepsilon, la, 0, -, -, 0, 0]$	predictSubst from 4.
6.	$[\alpha_n, \varepsilon, lb, 0, -, -, 0, 0]$	predictNoAdj from 5.
7.	$[\alpha_n, 1, la, 0, -, -, 0, 0]$	moveDown from 6.
8.	$[\alpha_n, 1, ra, 0, -, -, 1, 0]$	scanTerm from 7.
9.	$[\alpha_n, \varepsilon, rb, 0, -, -, 1, 0]$	moveUp from 8.
10.	$[\alpha_n, \varepsilon, ra, 0, -, -, 1, 0]$	completeNode from 9. and 7.
11.	$[\alpha_s, 1, rb, 0, -, -, 1, 0]$	substitute from 10.
12.	$[\alpha_s, 1, ra, 0, -, -, 1, 0]$	completeNode from 11. and 3.
13.	$[\alpha_s, 2, la, 0, -, -, 1, 0]$	moveRight from 12.
	...	
14.	$[\beta_{fin}, 0, ra, 1, 1, 2, 3, 0]$	...
15.	$[\alpha_s, 2, rb, 1, -, -, 3, 1]$	adjoin
16.	$[\alpha_s, 2, ra, 0, -, -, 3, 0]$	completeNode from 15. and 13.
	...	
17.	$[\alpha_s, \varepsilon, ra, 0, -, -, 3, 0]$	moveUp, completeNode

Fig. 5.14. Trace for Earley parsing of (37) with $G_{raising}$

position left below (with **predictNoAdj**), then we predict the substituted tree α_n, traverse it, and when reaching the position right above the root of α_n, we substitute this into an appropriate substitution node (here position 1 in α_s) without checking whether the prediction was done from this node. Only in the next step with **completeNode** do we combine this item with the one where we were in position left above the substitution node.

5.2.5 The Parser

So far, we have seen an Earley-type recognition algorithm for TAG. We can extend the recognizer to a parser by storing each new item together with pointers to the antecedent items that lead to the creation of this item. In the case of the complete operations and adjoin, we have two antecedent items, i.e., we have to store a pair of pointers. In all other cases we have one antecedent item.

Note that it is possible that the same item can be obtained in different ways. In this case, we store the item only once but for every new rule application leading to this item, we add a new pointer/pair of pointers. Consequently, we actually equip our items in the chart with sets (or lists) of sets of pointers.

The chart together with these pointers can be seen as a compact representation of the parse trees. Starting from the goal items and following the pointers, one can read off the single parse trees.

5.2.6 Properties of the Algorithm

Complexity

The worst-case complexity can be reached by the **adjoin** operation:

$$\frac{[\beta, \varepsilon, ra, i, j, k, l, 0], [\gamma, p, rb, j, g, h, k, 0]}{[\gamma, p, rb, i, g, h, l, 1]} \quad \beta \in f_{SA}(\gamma, p)$$

This rule can be applied at most $|A||A \cup I|m(n+1)^6$ times where m is the maximal number of internal nodes per elementary tree. This is because we have at most $|A|$ different possibilities for β, at most $|A \cup I|$ different possibilities for γ and at most m different possibilities for p. The six different indices i, j, g, h, k, l range from 0 to n, i.e., have $n+1$ possible values.

Consequently, the algorithm has an upper time bound of $\mathcal{O}(n^6)$.

However, Joshi and Schabes (1997) report that the average complexity of the parser is better. With unambiguous TAGs, the algorithm runs in time $\mathcal{O}(n^4)$, and on a large class of TAGs it takes even only linear time.

Valid Prefix Property

From the examples and from the explanations of what the algorithm does, it can be seen that we obtain a goal item if and only if there is a successful parse. More precisely, we obtain a goal item $[\alpha, \varepsilon, ra, 0, -, -, n, 0]$ if and only if we can derive a tree γ from α such that $\gamma \in T(G)$ and our input w is the yield of γ.

However, it does not hold for every item in our chart that it is part of a derivation starting from an initial α with root S such that the span of the derived tree up to the dotted node is a prefix of a word in the language. More concretely, we can have items $[\gamma, p, rb, i, j, k, l, 0]$ such that there is no derivation of a saturated derived tree α' from an initial α involving γ where the following holds: Let v' be either the node v at position p in γ (if no adjunction or substitution has occurred at v) or the root of the derived tree that v has been replaced with (by adjunction or substitution). Then the yield of α' is such that the part to the left of v' is between positions 0 and i, and the part below v' is between i and l.

The reason why this is so is that neither **predictAdjoined** nor **adjoin** check for the existence of an item that has triggered the prediction of this adjunction, i.e., the antecedent of the **predictAjoinable** rule that has first introduced the auxiliary tree in question.

As a consequence, this Earley algorithm does not have the Valid Prefix Property, i.e., we can have items $[\gamma, p, pos, i, j, k, l, adj]$ such that there is no word w' in the string language of G with a prefix $w_1 \ldots w_l$.

As an example, consider the TAG in Fig. 5.15 and the items for parsing $bccc$ given in this figure. None of the prefixes of $bccc$ is a prefix of a word in the string language since every word in the language has to start with a

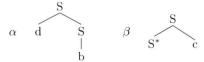

Every word in the language starts with d.
Input bcc leads (among others) to the following items:

Item	Rule
1. $[\alpha, \varepsilon, la, 0, -, -, 0, 0]$	initialize
2. $[\beta, \varepsilon, la, 0, -, -, 0, 0]$	predictAdjoinable from 1.
...	
3. $[\beta, 1, lb, 0, -, -, 0, 0]$	
4. $[\alpha, 2, lb, 0, -, -, 0, 0]$	predictAdjoined from 3.
...	
5. $[\alpha, 2, rb, 0, -, -, 1, 0]$	
6. $[\beta, 1, rb, 0, 0, 1, 1, 0]$	completeFoot form 3. and 5.
...	
7. $[\beta, \varepsilon, ra, 0, 0, 3, 4, 0]$	(after repeated adjunctions of β)
8. $[\alpha, 2, rb, 0, -, -, 4, 1]$	adjoin from 7. and 4.

Fig. 5.15. Non-prefix validity of the Earley parser

d. Therefore all items with an end position > 0, in particular the items 5–8, violate the condition of prefix validity. Only after having processed the entire input do we realize that the resulting parse tree must be a subtree of a larger tree including a preceding d. The problem arises with the first application of **predictAdjoined**, resulting in item 4. Here we predict that the adjunction takes place at the lower S node (address 2) in the tree α, which was actually not the case since the adjoinable tree β was predicted from the root (address ε) of α.

5.2.7 Prefix Valid Earley Parsing

As illustrated with the example in Fig. 5.15, the interest of the valid prefix property lies in the resulting capability of a left to right parser to detect errors as soon as possible. However, ensuring this property for TAG might be costly. Schabes and Joshi (1988) present a prefix valid Earley algorithm for TAG. Essentially, the operation **predictAdjoined** and **adjoin** are defined as complete operations, i.e., they check for the existence of the item that has triggered the adjunction. Furthermore, **adjoin** moves immediately to the position right above the adjunction site. In order to check for the existence of the item triggering the adjunction, one needs to keep track not only of the start of the yield of the sisters to the left but also of the yield of the entire elementary tree. Schabes and Joshi (1988) report a complexity of $\mathcal{O}(n^9)$ for this Earley algorithm.

Nederhof (1997; 1999) presents the first prefix valid Earley parser for TAG with an $\mathcal{O}(n^6)$ time bound. In his algorithm, Nederhof has deduction rules with more than six different indices in the input. However, he argues that some of these positions are not relevant for the application of the rule, i.e., the application of the rule does not depend on their value, they only occur in one of the antecedents and therefore do not need to be compared to other parts of the antecedent or copied to the consequent item. Consequently, these indices do not increase the complexity of the algorithm. They can actually be factored out since they are so-called *don't cares*, and therefore this algorithm has complexity $\mathcal{O}(n^6)$.

In the following, inspired by (Nederhof, 1997; Nederhof, 1999), we modify the above Earley parser such that the resulting algorithm is prefix valid while still being of complexity $\mathcal{O}(n^6)$. We need to introduce additional antecedents in the rules **predictAdjoined**, **completeFoot** and **adjoin**. In all three rules we have to check for the presence of the γ-item that has triggered the first **predictAdjoinable**. For this check to be possible, it is not enough to know about the start position of the span of a node and its sisters to the left, which is what we currently encode as start position in items with position la. In addition, we need to know the start position of the entire elementary tree. For this reason, we add an additional index i_γ to our items.

In order to factor out indices that are not relevant, we introduce values $\sim$ for "don't care". As a result, our item form is now

$$[\gamma, p, pos, i_\gamma, i, f_1, f_2, j, adj]$$

with

- $\gamma \in I \cup A$, p a node position in γ;
- $pos \in \{la, lb, rb, ra\}$ ($i_\gamma =\sim$ if $pos = rb$);
- $i_\gamma, i, f_1, f_2, j \in \{0, \ldots, |w|\} \cup \{-, \sim\}$ indices;
- $adj \in \{0, 1\}$ the adjunction flag.

As before, the index "−" indicates "undefined/not applicable" while an index "$\sim$" indicates "don't care". For the prefix valid algorithm, we extend the deduction rules as mentioned above and, in addition, we introduce new convert rules that factor out some of the indices, i.e., that replace them with the value $\sim$ for "don't care".

The resulting deduction rules are listed in Fig. 5.16. The goal items are all items of the form $[\alpha, 0, ra, 0, 0, -, -, n, 0]$, $\alpha \in I, l(\alpha, \varepsilon) = S$.

The only rule with more than six indices is **completeNode**. However, in all applications of this rule, we have either $g = -$ and $h = -$ or $j = -$ and $k = -$; consequently there are never more than six indices involved. Therefore, the time complexity of this algorithm is $\mathcal{O}(n^6)$.

Note that it is crucial that, as in the non-prefix valid algorithm, after having performed the adjunction, we are still in position right below the adjunction site. Only in the next complete step do we combine this with the

5.2 An Earley Parser for TAG

Initialize: $\dfrac{}{[\alpha, \varepsilon, la, 0, 0, -, -, 0, 0]} \quad \alpha \in I, l(\alpha, \varepsilon) = S$

ScanTerm: $\dfrac{[\gamma, p, la, i_\gamma, i, j, k, l, 0]}{[\gamma, p, ra, i_0, i, j, k, l+1, 0]} \quad l(\gamma, p_\gamma \cdot p) = w_{l+1}$

Scan-ε: $\dfrac{[\gamma, p, la, i_\gamma, i, j, k, l, 0]}{[\gamma, p, ra, i_\gamma, i, j, k, l, 0]} \quad l(\gamma, p_\gamma \cdot p) = \varepsilon$

Convert-rb: $\dfrac{[\gamma, p, rb, \sim, i, j, k, l, 0]}{[\gamma, p, rb, \sim, i, \sim, \sim, l, 0]}$ **Convert-la I:** $\dfrac{[\gamma, p, la, i_\gamma, i, j, k, l, 0]}{[\gamma, p, la, i_\gamma, \sim, \sim, \sim, l, 0]}$

Convert-la II: $\dfrac{[\gamma, p, la, i_\gamma, i, j, k, l, 0]}{[\gamma, p, la, \sim, \sim, \sim, \sim, l, 0]}$

PredictNoAdj: $\dfrac{[\gamma, p, la, i_\gamma, i, j, k, l, 0]}{[\gamma, p, lb, i_\gamma, i, j, k, l, 0]} \quad f_{OA}(\gamma, p) = 0$

PredictAdjoinable: $\dfrac{[\gamma, p, la, \sim, \sim, \sim, \sim, l, 0]}{[\beta, \varepsilon, la, l, l, -, -, l, 0]} \quad \beta \in f_{SA}(\gamma, p)$

PredictAdjoined: $\dfrac{[\beta, p_f, la, i_\beta, i, -, -, m, 0], \quad \beta(p_f) \text{ foot node,}}{[\gamma, p, la, i_\gamma, \sim, \sim, \sim, i_\beta, 0]} \quad \beta \in f_{SA}(\gamma, p)$
$\dfrac{}{[\gamma, p, lb, i_\gamma, m, -, -, m, 0]}$

CompleteFoot: $\dfrac{[\gamma, p, rb, \sim, i, \sim, \sim, l, 0], \quad [\beta, p_f, la, i_\beta, m, -, -, i, 0], \quad \beta(p_f) \text{ foot node,}}{[\gamma, p, la, \sim, \sim, \sim, \sim, i_\beta, 0] \quad \beta \in f_{SA}(\gamma, p)}$
$\dfrac{}{[\beta, p_f, rb, \sim, m, i, l, l, 0]}$

Adjoin: $\dfrac{[\beta, \varepsilon, ra, i_\beta, i_\beta, j, k, l, 0], \quad [\gamma, p, rb, \sim, j, g, h, k, 0], \quad [\gamma, p, la, \sim, \sim, \sim, \sim, i_\beta, 0]}{[\gamma, p, rb, \sim, i_\beta, g, h, l, 1]} \quad \beta \in f_{SA}(\gamma, p)$

CompleteNode: $\dfrac{[\gamma, p, la, i_\gamma, f, g, h, i, 0], [\gamma, p, rb, \sim, i, j, k, l, adj]}{[\gamma, p, ra, i_\gamma, f, g \oplus j, h \oplus k, l, 0]} \quad l(\beta, p) \in N$

MoveDown: $\dfrac{[\gamma, p, lb, i_\gamma, i, j, k, l, 0]}{[\gamma, p \cdot 1, la, i_\gamma, i, j, k, l, 0]}$ **MoveRight:** $\dfrac{[\gamma, p, ra, i_\gamma, i, j, k, l, 0]}{[\gamma, p+1, la, i_\gamma, i, j, k, l, 0]}$

MoveUp: $\dfrac{[\gamma, p \cdot m, ra, i_\gamma, i, j, k, l, 0]}{[\gamma, p, rb, \sim, i, j, k, l, 0]} \quad \gamma(p \cdot m + 1) \text{ is not defined}$

Fig. 5.16. Deduction rules for prefix valid Earley parsing in $\mathcal{O}(n^6)$

part to the left and move to position right above. This is why in **adjoin**, all indices except the end position i_β of the γ-item with the position left above the adjunction site (the one that has triggered the adjunction) can be factored out. The algorithm in (Schabes and Joshi, 1988) moves immediately to the position right above an adjunction site when finishing the adjunction. Therefore, this algorithm has complexity $\mathcal{O}(n^9)$.

As an example, Fig. 5.17 gives the trace of parsing $aaaa$ with the TAG for the copy language (only the successful items are listed). The trees in the TAG for the copy language are repeated in (38):

(38) $\alpha \begin{array}{c} S \\ | \\ \varepsilon \end{array}$ $\beta_a \begin{array}{c} S_{NA} \\ \diagup \; | \\ a \; S \\ \; | \; \diagdown \\ S^*_{NA} \; a \end{array}$ $\beta_b \begin{array}{c} S_{NA} \\ \diagup \; | \\ b \; S \\ \; | \; \diagdown \\ S^*_{NA} \; b \end{array}$

Nederhof (1997; 1999) presents a slightly different Earley algorithm. But he also keeps track of the start position of the yield of an entire elementary tree and he argues in the same way that in his algorithm some of the indices in the deduction rules can be factored out, since they are *don't cares*, and therefore his algorithm has complexity $\mathcal{O}(n^6)$.

The prefix valid Earley algorithm presented here can be easily extended to handle substitution as well (see the solution of Problem 5.4).

5.3 An LR Parser for TAG

5.3.1 Introduction

In the previous section, we have seen an Earley parser for TAG. The idea of Earley is to restrict a bottom-up parser by top-down predictions. If we look more closely at the different operations of the parser, we can see that only some of the operations depend on the actual input. In particular, the top-down predictions are made independently from the input. This observation (which holds for the CFG case as well) leads to the idea to precompile predictions, i.e., to compute them off-line, which results in LR parsing.

The acronym LR signifies the following: L stands for *Left*-to-right scanning of the input while R stands for *R*ight-to-left reduction. In other words, while processing the input from left to right, we produce a rightmost derivation.

The bottom-up parsing technique used in an LR parser is a shift-reduce parser: In the context-free case, we have a stack containing sentential forms and the remaining input. There are two possible operations, an operation *shift* that scans the next input symbol and pushes it onto the stack, and an operation *reduce* that replaces the right-hand side of a production that can be popped in reverse order from the stack by its left-hand side.

In an LR parser, we precompile predictions into states. Each state is a set of dotted productions closed under prediction. The productions in a state tell

5.3 An LR Parser for TAG

	Item	Operation
1	$[\alpha, \varepsilon, la, 0, 0, -, -, 0, 0]$	Initialize
1-1	$[\alpha, \varepsilon, la, 0, \sim, \sim, \sim, 0, 0]$	Convert-la I
1-2	$[\alpha, \varepsilon, la, \sim, \sim, \sim, \sim, 0, 0]$	Convert-la II
	move into first β_a	
2	$[\beta_a, \varepsilon, la, 0, 0, -, -, 0, 0]$	PredictAdjoinable from 1-2
	...	
6	$[\beta_a, 2, la, 0, 0, -, -, 1, 0]$	PredictNoAdj, MoveDown, Scan, MoveRight
6-1	$[\beta_a, 2, la, 0, \sim, \sim, \sim, 1, 0]$	Convert-la I
6-2	$[\beta_a, 2, la, \sim, \sim, \sim, \sim, 1, 0]$	Convert-la II
	move into second β_a	
7	$[\beta_a, \varepsilon, la, 1, 1, -, -, 1, 0]$	PredictAdjoinable from 6-2
	...	
11	$[\beta_a, 2, la, 1, 1, -, -, 2, 0]$	PredictNoAdj, MoveDown, Scan, MoveRight
12	$[\beta_a, 2, lb, 1, 2, -, -, 2, 0]$	PredictNoAdj
13	$[\beta_a, 21, la, 1, 2, -, -, 2, 0]$	MoveDown
	move back into lower part of first β_a	
14	$[\beta_a, 2, lb, 0, 2, -, -, 2, 0]$	PredictAdjoined from 13 and 6-1
15	$[\beta_a, 21, la, 0, 2, -, -, 2, 0]$	MoveDown
	move back into lower part of α	
16	$[\alpha, \varepsilon, lb, 2, -, -, 2, 0]$	PredictAdjoined from 15 and 1-1
	...	
19	$[\alpha, \varepsilon, rb, \sim, 2, -, -, 2, 0]$	MoveDown, Scan-ε, MoveUp
19-1	$[\alpha, \varepsilon, rb, \sim, 2, \sim, \sim, 2, 0]$	Convert-rb
	move back into right part of first β_a	
20	$[\beta_a, 21, rb, \sim, 2, 2, 2, 2, 0]$	CompleteFoot from 19-1, 15 and 1-2
21	$[\beta_a, 21, ra, 0, 2, 2, 2, 2, 0]$	CompleteNode from 20 and 15
	...	
24	$[\beta_a, 2, rb, \sim, 2, 2, 2, 3, 0]$	MoveRight, Scan, MoveUp
24-1	$[\beta_a, 2, rb, \sim, 2, \sim, \sim, 3, 0]$	Convert-rb
	move back into right part of second β_a	
25	$[\beta_a, 21, rb, \sim, 2, 2, 3, 3, 0]$	CompleteFoot from 24-1, 13, 6-2
26	$[\beta_a, 21, ra, 1, 2, 2, 3, 3, 0]$	CompleteFoot from 25, 13
	...	
29	$[\beta_a, 2, rb, \sim, 2, 2, 3, 4, 0]$	MoveRight, Scan, MoveUp
30	$[\beta_a, 2, ra, 1, 1, 2, 3, 4, 0]$	CompleteNode 29, 11
31	$[\beta_a, \varepsilon, rb, 1, 1, 2, 3, 4, 0]$	MoveUp
32	$[\beta_a, \varepsilon, ra, 1, 1, 2, 3, 4, 0]$	CompleteNode 31, 7
	second β_a finished, back to first	
33	$[\beta_a, 2, rb, \sim, 1, 2, 2, 4, 1]$	Adjoin with 32, 24, 6-2
34	$[\beta_a, 2, ra, 0, 0, 2, 2, 4, 0]$	CompleteNode 33,6
35	$[\beta_a, \varepsilon, \sim, rb, 0, 2, 2, 4, 0]$	Move Up
36	$[\beta_a, \varepsilon, ra, 0, 0, 2, 2, 4, 0]$	CompleteNode 35, 2
	first β_a finished, back to α	
37	$[\alpha, \varepsilon, rb, \sim, 0, -, -, 4, 1]$	Adjoin with 36, 19, 1-2
38	$[\alpha, \varepsilon, ra, 0, 0, -, -, 4, 0]$	CompleteNode 37, 1

Fig. 5.17. Sample trace for prefix valid Earley parsing of input word *aaaa*

Productions: 1. S → a S b,   2. S → c

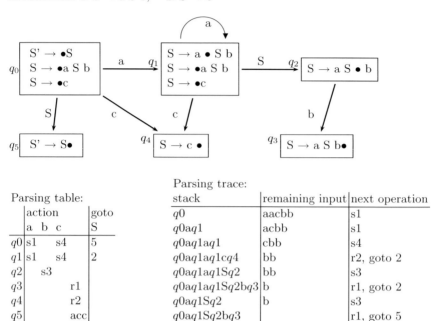

Parsing table:

	action			goto
	a	b	c	S
q0	s1		s4	5
q1	s1		s4	2
q2		s3		
q3		r1		
q4		r2		
q5		acc		

Parsing trace:

stack	remaining input	next operation
q0	aacbb	s1
q0aq1	acbb	s1
q0aq1aq1	cbb	s4
q0aq1aq1cq4	bb	r2, goto 2
q0aq1aq1Sq2	bb	s3
q0aq1aq1Sq2bq3	b	r1, goto 2
q0aq1Sq2	b	s3
q0aq1Sq2bq3		r1, goto 5
q0Sq5		accept

Fig. 5.18. A sample LR(0) automaton and parse table for a CFG

us whether reductions can be performed and the transitions between states tell us about the shift operations and about the new states to move to after a possible shift or reduce.

In the context-free case, we often use a lookahead to make LR parsing more deterministic. For TAG, we present an LR parsing algorithm without lookaheads.

To illustrate the idea of LR parsing, consider the LR(0) parser (zero lookaheads) for a CFG in Fig. 5.18. The states of the automaton are sets of dotted productions closed under prediction. The transitions correspond to moving the dot over the next symbol of a right-hand side. The table is read off the automaton as follows: whenever we have a transition with terminal a, there is a corresponding shift operation si in the table where i is the number of the new state. Whenever a state contains a dotted production with the dot at the end of the right-hand side, we can reduce with this production and the table contains an entry ri where i is the number of the production. Whenever there is a transition with a non-terminal label, there is a corresponding entry in the right part of the table (the *goto* table).

The sample parse trace for aacbb shows how this table is used to determine the different shift and reduce operations during parsing: we start with a stack containing the start state $q0$. If, given the current state and the next input symbol, a shift is possible according to the table, then we push the new terminal followed by the state indicated in the *action* table onto the stack. If a reduction is possible, then we reduce using the production indicated in the *action* table. We pop its right-hand side (in reverse order) and push its left-hand side. The new state is the *goto* value of 1. the state preceding the right-hand side of this production on the stack and 2. the left-hand side category of the production.

This LR parsing algorithm is extended to TAG in (Nederhof, 1998). Nederhof's algorithm is based on an LR parse automaton and it allows for three different operations: an operation *shift* that scans the next input symbol and two reduction operations, *reduce_subtree* and *reduce_aux_tree*, which are performed after having completed the tree below an adjunction site (the gap) and after having completed an auxiliary tree respectively.

We assume that our TAG does not have substitution nodes and does not contain empty words as node labels.

In order to formulate our algorithm, we extend the elementary tree with artificial new nodes: For each $t \in I \cup A$, we add a unique node $\top$ immediately dominating the root of t and for each $t \in A$, we add a unique node $\bot$ immediately dominated by the foot of t.

We use the following notations:

- $\mathcal{N}(t)$ is the set of nodes of a tree t, R_t is the root node of t and F_t the foot node (if it exists).
- $children(N)$ is the list of the children of a node N, given in linear precedence order.
- For a $t \in I \cup A$, (t, N) denotes the subtree of t rooted in N. $\mathcal{T} = I \cup A \cup \{(t, N) | t \in I \cup A, N \in \mathcal{N}(t)\}$ is the set of all subtrees of elementary trees, including the elementary trees themselves.

5.3.2 Construction of the Automaton

Now we can start constructing our automaton. The states of the automaton are sets of items and the transitions are labeled with terminals or nonterminals. Each item represents a subtree of height 1 (mother node N and its daughters) in one of the trees $\tau \in \mathcal{T}$ together with a dot $\bullet$ that specifies up to which daughter the subtree has been recognized. This subtree is notated as a dotted production $N \to \alpha \bullet \beta$ where N is the root and $\alpha\beta$ is the list of the children.

Items therefore have the form $[\tau, N \to \alpha \bullet \beta]$, where

- $\tau \in \mathcal{T}$,
- $N \in \mathcal{N}(\tau)$, and
- $\alpha\beta = children(N)$ are the daughters of N.

We call an item *completed* if is has the form $[t, \top \to R_t\bullet]$, with $t \in I \cup A$, or $[(t, N), N \to \alpha\bullet]$. In other words, a completed item indicates either that we

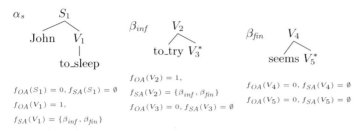

Fig. 5.19. A sample TAG $G'_{raising}$

have completely recognized an entire elementary tree and therefore our dot is to the right of its root or that we have completely recognized a subtree below a node N. In this latter case, there might be adjunctions at N that we have not completed yet. In other words, the completed subtree can be the filler of a foot node gap.

The construction of the set of states of the automaton starts with an initial LR state $q_{in} = \{[t, \top \to \bullet R_t] | t \in I, l(t, \varepsilon) = S\}$. For each state, we compute its closure under prediction and under moving down or up in an elementary tree. Furthermore, from a given state, new states can be computed using functions $goto$ and $goto_\perp$.

As a running example consider the TAG $G'_{raising}$ in Fig. 5.19 that is obtained from our TAG $G_{raising}$ by precompiling substitution and removing some nodes that are not foot nodes and do not allow for adjunctions.

Let us first define the *closure(q)* of a state q. The intuition is that the closure contains all items that can be obtained from an item $[\tau, \ldots]$ in q by moving down in τ or predicting an adjunction or predicting the part below a foot node. The closure of a state q where q is a set of items can be described with the deduction rules in Fig. 5.20. As a first example, consider the initial state of the TAG in Fig. 5.19. It contains the items $[\alpha_s, \top \to \bullet S_1]$ and $[\alpha_s, S_1 \to \bullet John\ V_1]$ where the second item is obtained by moving down. Adjunctions are not predicted since there are no trees that can be adjoined at S_1.

New states are obtained from existing ones by moving the dot over a nonterminal or a terminal node or over a foot node daughter $\perp$. The first two cases are covered by the $goto$ function while the third case is covered by the $goto_\perp$ function. These functions are defined as follows.

Let q be a set of items and M be a node with either $l(M) \in T$ or $f_{SA} \neq \emptyset$. For q and M, we define

$$goto(q, M) = \{[\tau, N \to \alpha M \bullet \beta] | [\tau, N \to \alpha \bullet M\beta] \in closure(q)\}$$

and

$$goto_\perp(q, M) = \{[\tau, F_t \to \perp \bullet] | [\tau, F_t \to \bullet \perp] \in closure(q) \wedge t \in Adj(M)\}.$$

$$\frac{}{\overline{x}} \quad x \in q$$

$$\frac{[\tau, N \to \alpha \bullet M\beta]}{[\tau, M \to \bullet\gamma]} \quad f_{OA}(M) = 0, children(M) = \gamma \quad \text{(move down)}$$

$$\frac{[\tau, N \to \alpha \bullet M\beta]}{[t, \top \to \bullet R_t]} \quad t \in f_{SA}(M) \quad \text{(prediction of adjunction)}$$

$$\frac{[\tau, F_t \to \bullet\bot]}{[(t', N), N \to \bullet\gamma]} \quad \tau \in f_{SA}(N), children(N) = \gamma \quad \text{(prediction of adjoined)}$$

$$\frac{[\tau, M \to \gamma\bullet]}{[\tau, N \to \alpha M \bullet \beta]} \quad [\tau, N \to \alpha M \bullet \beta] \text{ a possible item} \quad \text{(move up)}$$

Fig. 5.20. Definition of the closure of an item set q

With these definitions of the two *goto* functions, we can define the entire set of states of our LR automaton. We start with the closure of the initial state and repeatedly apply *goto* and $goto_\bot$ and build the closure of the new states. We continue this process until no more new states can be found:

The set Q of states is defined as follows:

- $closure(q_{in}) \in Q$.
- For all $q \in Q$ and every node M, if $q' = closure(goto(q, M)) \neq \emptyset$, then $q' \in Q$.
- For all $q \in Q$ and every node M, if $q' = closure(goto_\bot(q, M)) \neq \emptyset$, then $q' \in Q$.
- These are all states in Q.

Note that in (Nederhof, 1998), the states contain only the items obtained from the *goto* function, not the ones obtained from the *closure* functions. The two definitions amount to the same, since the *goto* function are in both cases computed with respect to the closures of the states.

Parsing is successful if we have finished the recognition of an intial tree with root symbol S. Whenever a state contains a completed item for some initial tree with root label S, this is a possible final state. We call the set of final states Q_{fin}:

$$Q_{fin} = \{q \in Q | q \cap \{[t, \top \to R_t\bullet] | t \in I, l(t, \varepsilon) = S\} \neq \emptyset\}.$$

Figure 5.21 shows the states of the LR automaton for the TAG from Fig. 5.19 with the transitions corresponding to the *goto* functions. If a new state q' is the value of $goto(q, M)$, then there is a transition from q to q' labeled M. If a new state q' is the value of $goto_\bot(q, M)$, then there is a transition from q to q' labeled $\bot(M)$.

5.3.3 The Recognizer

For the definition of the recognizer, we need the notion of *reductions*(q) for a given state q. Roughly, reductions are defined as follows: If the state q contains

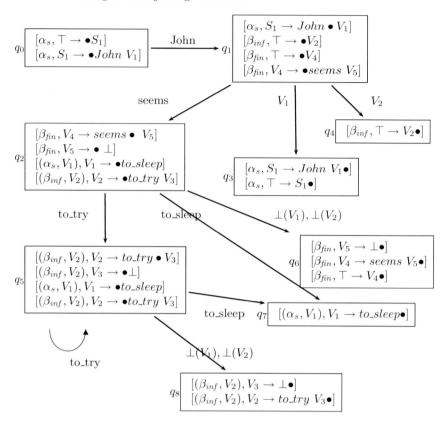

Fig. 5.21. LR automaton for the TAG $G'_{raising}$

a completed item, then either the left-hand side node of its dotted production or, if this is a $\top$ in an auxiliary tree, the whole tree is part of the reductions of q. The reductions of q_7 for example are V_1 while the set of reductions of q_4 contains β_{inf}. The set $reductions(q)$ is needed for the two reduce operations, $reduce\_subtree$ and $reduce\_aux\_tree$: If a node N is in this set, then this means that, in q, we have finished the subtree below N and we can move into the right part of an auxiliary tree β that was adjoined at N. If an auxiliary tree β is in this set, then this means that we have finished the entire auxiliary tree β and we can move back to the node N to which β was adjoined.

We define the set $reductions(q)$ for a given state q as follows:

$$reductions(q) = \{t \in A | [t, \top \to R_t \bullet] \in q\} \cup \\ \{N \in \mathcal{N} | [(t, N), N \to \alpha \bullet] \in q\}.$$

Furthermore, we need the definition of cross-sections through a tree rooted in some node N. Here, the intuition is that the sequences on the stack that can be reduced, i.e., that correspond roughly to the right-hand side of some completed dotted production, are cross-sections. A cross-section of a node N is either the node N or a sequence of cross-sections of the daughters of N in linear precedence order. In addition, nodes in cross-sections that dominate foot nodes are paired with a stack of nodes (indicating where subsequent adjunctions took place).

This leads to the following definition of cross-sections $CS(N)$ of a node N:

We define $\mathcal{M} := \mathcal{N} \cup (\mathcal{N} \times \mathcal{N}^*)$. Then, for a given node N,

- $N \in CS(N)$ if N does not dominate a foot node,
- $(N, L) \in CS(N)$ for each $L \in \mathcal{N}^*$ if N dominates a foot node,
- $x_1 \ldots x_m \in CS(N)$ if $children(N) = M_1 \ldots M_m$ and $x_i \in CS(M_i)$ for $1 \leq i \leq m$.

Furthermore, $CS^+(N) := CS(N) \setminus (\{N\} \cup \{(N, L) \mid L \in \mathcal{N}^*\})$ (the cross-sections without the node itself).

As an example, consider again the trees from our TAG $G'_{raising}$ in Fig. 5.19. We obtain
$CS(S_1) = \{S_1, John\ V_1, John\ to\_sleep\}$ and
$CS(V_3) = \{(V_3, L) \mid L \in \mathcal{N}^*\} \cup \{(\bot, L) \mid L \in \mathcal{N}^*\}$.

During parsing, we use a stack Δ (as in the CFG case) that contains states and symbols. The latter are either terminal nodes or non-terminal nodes equipped with a stack. A configuration (Δ, w) of the parser consists of a stack and the remaining part of the input string.

Parsing starts with the initial state (q_0 in our example) on the stack and w being the entire input. The parser changes from one configuration to another by applying either a shift or a reduce. There is one shift operation and two different reduce operations, *reduce_subtree* and *reduce_aux_tree*, depending on whether we have completed the part below a foot node (the gap) or an adjoined auxiliary tree. We will now define the three different operations.

The operation *shift* pushes the next input symbol followed by a new state on the stack. The new state depends on the *goto* function, i.e., if we are in state q, the next input symbol is a, and q' is the value of $goto(q, a)$, then we push first a and then q' on the stack while reducing the remaining input. We notate the transition from one configuration to another using $\vdash$. The definition of the *shift* operation is as follows.

For all $a \in T, w \in T^*$ and $q, q' \in Q$,

$$(\Delta q, aw) \vdash (\Delta q a q', w) \text{ if } q' = goto(q, a) \neq \emptyset.$$

If we look at the difference between the states q and q', then an operation *shift* amounts to moving the dot over a terminal. This is depicted in Fig. 5.22.

For sample *shift* operations, see the first four steps in the parse in Fig. 5.23, which is based on the automaton from Fig. 5.21.

Fig. 5.22. Shift operation of the LR parser for TAG

Stack	remaining input	operation
q_0	John seems to_try to_sleep	
q_0 John q_1	seems to_try to_sleep	shift
q_0 John q_1 seems q_2	to_try to_sleep	shift
q_0 John q_1 seems q_2 to_try q_5	to_sleep	shift
q_0 John q_1 seems q_2 to_try q_5 to_sleep q_7		shift
q_0 John q_1 seems q_2 to_try q_5 $\perp[V_1]$ q_8		red._subtree
q_0 John q_1 seems q_2 $\perp[V_2\ V_1]$ q_6		red._subtree
q_0 John q_1 $V_2[V_1]$ q_4		red._aux_tree
q_0 John q_1 V_1 q_3		red._aux_tree

Fig. 5.23. Sample LR parse trace with the TAG $G'_{raising}$

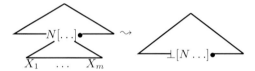

Fig. 5.24. Reduce_subtree operation of the LR parser for TAG

The reduce operation *reduce_subtree* is applied when having completed a subtree rooted in N such that an adjunction occurs at N. In other words, it recognizes the part below a foot node. This is depicted in Fig. 5.24. For this operation to apply, the node N must be in the set of reductions of the current state and the stack must contain a cross-section of N. This tells us that the subtree below N has been completely recognized. We can then remove this cross-section from the stack and push the foot node $\perp$ with a stack containing N followed by a state that depends on the state preceding the cross-section and on N. This is very much as in the CFG case, except that we use cross-sections since the tree below N might have a height > 1. In addition, if the cross-section contained a foot node, then the stack of this foot node is appended to N on the stack of the foot node. We use the function $goto_\perp$ to determine the new state since the recognition of the subtree below a foot node (the gap) enables us to move the dot over a foot node.

The operation *reduce_subtree* is defined as follows.

$$(\Delta q_0 X_1 q_1 \ldots X_m q_m, w) \vdash (\Delta q_0(\perp, [NL])q', w)$$

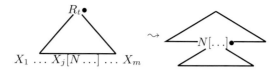

Fig. 5.25. Reduce_aux_tree operation of the LR parser for TAG

if

- $N \in reductions(q_m), X_1 \ldots X_m \in CS^+(N), q' = goto_\perp(q_0, N) \neq \emptyset$, and
- L is defined as follows: if some X_j is of the form (M, L), then this provides L; otherwise $L = [\,]$.

The step following the first shifts in Fig. 5.23 is a *reduce_subtree* step: V_1 is in the reductions of q_7, one of its cross-sections is on the stack and $goto_\perp(q_5, V_1) = q_8$.

The second reduce operation, *reduce_aux_tree*, is applied once an auxiliary tree has been recognized. We then go back to the node where the adjunction occurred, as depicted in Fig. 5.25. For this operation to apply, we must be in a state q where there is an auxiliary tree β in the reductions of this state with one of its cross-sections being on top of the stack. Then, among the elements of the cross-sections, there will be a node equipped with a stack. The top of this stack gives the node N that we will move to. The rest of the stack is passed to N. We remove the cross-section from the stack, push N with its new stack and push a state q' that is obtained from q by following the N transition ($goto(q, N)$).

The operation *reduce_aux_tree* is defined as follows.

$$(\Delta q_0 X_1 q_1 \ldots X_m q_m, w) \vdash (\Delta q_0 X q', w)$$

if

- there is a $\beta \in A$ with $\beta \in reductions(q_m)$ and $X_1 \ldots X_m \in CS^+(R_t)$,
- $q' = goto(q_0, N) \neq \emptyset$ where N is obtained from the unique X_j of the form $M[NL]$, and
- if $L = [\,]$, then $X = N$; otherwise $X = N[L]$.

For an example see the last two steps in Fig. 5.23.

We start by initializing the stack with the initial state q_{in}. The stack always contains an alternation of states $q \in Q$ and nodes or nodes with stacks $X \in \mathcal{M}$.

A parse is successful if, in a sequence of transitions (i.e., applications of *shift*, *reduce_subtree* and *reduce_aux_tree*), the input is completely consumed and the automaton reaches a final state:

Some input w is recognized if $(q_{in}, w) \vdash^* (q_{in} \Delta q, \varepsilon)$ such that $q \in Q_{fin}$.

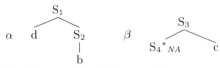

The language is $\{dbc^n \mid n \geq 0\}$.
Some states and transitions of the corresponding LR automaton:

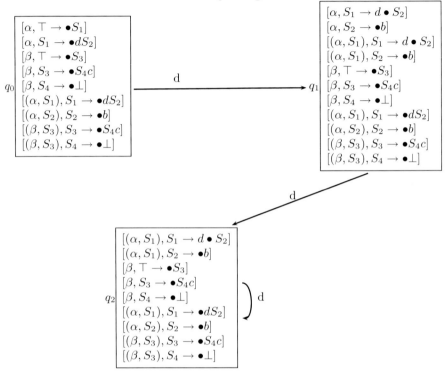

Fig. 5.26. Non-prefix validity of the LR parser from (Nederhof, 1998)

In our example, we end up in state q_3 with the remaining input being empty. q_3 is a final state, so parsing is successful.

As we have seen in this section, Nederhof (1998) shows how to apply LR parsing techniques to TAG. We obtain a shift-reduce parser guided by a precompiled automaton. The overall idea is to precompile predictions and moves that are independent from the actual input into states.

The problem with LR parsing is always that the automata get very large. This holds also for TAG. However, Nederhof (1998) mentions an implementation of the parser generator that suggests that LR automaton generation for a large grammar such as the XTAG grammar is feasible. Prolo (2000) proposes a more efficient version of Nederhof's LR parser with a much smaller size of the parse table.

5.3.4 Valid Prefix Property

As observed in (Prolo, 2000; Prolo, 2003), the LR parser we have seen here does not have the valid prefix property. This holds also for the algorithm in (Prolo, 2000).

The lack of prefix validity is again due to the blind prediction of the subtrees below foot nodes. To see this, we consider the TAG from Fig. 5.15, repeated in Fig. 5.26. We construct the initial state q_0 and two states $q_1 = goto(q_0, d)$ and $q_2 = goto(q_1, d)$. $goto(q_2, d)$ yields again q_2. We obtain the three states given in Fig. 5.26. With these states, for an input of the form ddw, we can reach a configuration $\langle q_0 d q_1 d q_2, w \rangle$. In other words, we are able to process the input up to position 2 (i.e., to recognize the first two input symbols) even though there is no word in the language with dd as a prefix. We can even process any sequence d^k, $k \geq 1$ as a potential prefix of a word in the language. Only later, when trying to reduce, the recognizer would fail because the elements on the stack would not match the required cross-sections.

Prolo (2003) proposes a variant of Nederhof's algorithm that is more restrictive.

5.4 Summary

In this chapter, we have seen how the standard parsing algorithms for CFG can be extended to TAG. We have presented CYK and Earley parsers for TAG and also an LR parser. A crucial difference with CFG is that, because of the adjunction, the yield of a node can consist of two different non-adjacent portions of the input string. This is the case for all nodes dominating foot nodes since the part to the left of the spine of an auxiliary tree is separated from the part to the right of the spine. This leads to an increase of the parsing complexity, compared to CFG. The algorithms we have seen have a time complexity $\mathcal{O}(n^6)$ (compared to $\mathcal{O}(n^3)$ for CFG).

Problems

5.1. Generalize the CYK algorithm in order to make it work for a TAG which has elementary trees with more than two daughters per node. To achieve this, replace the two deduction rules MoveUnary and MoveBinary with a single new rule.

5.2. Generalize the CYK algorithm with dotted items that allows arbitrary numbers of daughters while requiring only rules with maximally two antecedent items. Introduce new dotted items with a left-corner prediction.

5.3. Assume the following definitions:

In a tree γ, a node n_1 with address p_1 *linearly precedes* a node n_2 with address p_2 (notation $n_1 \prec n_2$) iff there are prefixes pi and pj of p_1 and p_2 respectively ($p \in \mathbb{N}^*, i, j \in \mathbb{N}$) such that $i < j$.

Let us call an auxiliary tree β a *left auxiliary tree* iff there is no node in β that is linearly preceded by the foot node.

Now define a *left-auxiliary TAG* as a TAG where all auxiliary trees are left auxiliary trees.

Obviously, in a *left-auxiliary TAG*, the yield of an auxiliary tree comprises only one substring of the input string. (Not two, as is the case in general in TAG.) This makes parsing less complex.

Modify the Earley algorithm from Section 5.2 under the assumption that we have a *left-auxiliary TAG*. (Give the modified deduction rules.)

5.4. Extend the prefix valid Earley algorithm for TAG from Fig. 5.16 to substitution.

5.5. How does the LR parsing algorithm for TAG prevent multiple adjunction loops?

More precisely: What condition for applying the two reduce operations ensures that the following holds? Starting from some subtree below a node N, after 1) recognizing this tree as the tree below the foot node of some β (application of *reduce_subtree*) and, later, when β is completed, 2) going back to the node N where β was adjoined (application of *reduce_aux_tree*), we cannot start once again the same application of *reduce_subtree*, recognizing the subtree below N as the subtree below the foot of β.

5.6. Consider the following TAG:

1. Give the states and closures of states of the LR automaton for this grammar, together with the transitions labelled with the corresponding symbols (if the transition from one state q to another is via an application of $goto(q, M)$, then the label is M; if it is via an application of $goto_\perp(q, M)$, the label is $\perp(M)$).
2. Give the trace of a sample parse using this automaton. The input word is $aacbb$.

6

Multiple Context-Free Grammars and Linear Context-Free Rewriting Systems

6.1 Introduction to MCFG, LCFRS and Simple RCG

Multiple Context-Free Grammars (MCFGs) have been introduced by Seki et al. (1991) while the equivalent *Linear Context-Free Rewriting Systems (LCFRSs)* were independently proposed by Vijay-Shanker, Weir, and Joshi (1987). The central idea is to extend CFGs such that non-terminal symbols can span a tuple of strings that need not be adjacent in the input string. In other words, the yield of a non-terminal symbol can be discontinuous. The grammar contains productions of the form $A_0 \to f[A_1, \ldots, A_q]$ where $A_0, \ldots, A_q$ are non-terminals and f is a function describing how to compute the yield of A_0 (a string tuple) from the yields of $A_1, \ldots, A_q$.

The definition of LCFRS is slightly more restrictive than the one of MCFG concerning the conditions for the functions describing the computations of yields. However, Seki et al. (1991) have shown that the two formalisms are equivalent.

Since discontinuities occur frequently in natural languages, MCFG and LCFRS are interesting formalisms for natural language processing. Furthermore, as we will see, MCFG and LCFRS are equivalent to a range of formalisms used for natural languages, among others, set-local multicomponent TAG (MCTAG) (Joshi, Levy, and Takahashi, 1975; Joshi, 1985; Weir, 1988) and minimalist grammar (MG) (Stabler, 1997; Michaelis, 1998).

As a running example, consider an MCFG for the double copy language where each copy contains as and bs. This MCFG is shown in Fig. 6.1.

One can think of the non-terminals as predicates that are true for certain string tuples. Each non-terminal has a fixed dimension that determines the number of discontinuous substrings in its yield. The start symbol S has always dimension 1.

In our example in Fig. 6.1, the non-terminal A has dimension 3 and its yield contains all triples of non-empty copies w over $\{a, b\}$. The last two rewriting rules, together with the definitions of f_4 and f_5, signify that A yields $\langle a, a, a \rangle$ and $\langle b, b, b \rangle$. The second and third rules together with the definitions of f_2 and

L. Kallmeyer, *Parsing Beyond Context-Free Grammars*, Cognitive Technologies,
DOI 10.1007/978-3-642-14846-0_6, © Springer-Verlag Berlin Heidelberg 2010

Rewriting rules:

$$S \to f_1[A] \quad A \to f_2[A] \quad A \to f_3[A] \quad A \to f_4[\,] \quad A \to f_5[\,]$$

Operations:

$$f_1[\langle X,Y,Z\rangle] = \langle XYZ\rangle \quad f_2[\langle X,Y,Z\rangle] = \langle aX,aY,aZ\rangle \quad f_4[\,] = \langle a,a,a\rangle$$
$$f_3[\langle X,Y,Z\rangle] = \langle bX,bY,bZ\rangle \quad f_5[\,] = \langle b,b,b\rangle$$

Fig. 6.1. An MCFG for $\{www \mid w \in \{a,b\}^+\}$

f_3 specify that from a given triple that satisfies A, we can obtain a new one by either concatenating an a to the left of all copies or concatenating a b to the left of all three copies. Finally, the first rule together with the definition of f_1 signifies that we can obtain a word in the language (satisfying our start symbol predicate S) from a triple in A by concatenating the three elements of the triple.

Another formalism that is equivalent to MCFG and LCFRS and that is based on the same idea of discontinuous yields of non-terminal symbols is *simple Range Concatenation Grammar (SRCG)* (Boullier, 2000b). SRCGs present a syntactic variant of LCFRS. Therefore, any algorithm for parsing MCFG or LCFRS can be easily transferred to simple RCG and vice versa. The CYK parsers presented in Section 7.1 are formulated in terms of MCFG and LCFRS while in Section 7.3, we notate the MCFG as a simple RCG since the incremental Earley parser presented there was developed with this notation.

6.1.1 MCFG and LCFRS

Definition of MCFG

An MCFG (Seki et al., 1991; Seki and Kato, 2008) consists of non-terminals, terminals, functions and rewriting rules of the form described above. The function are so-called *mcf-functions* that we will define below.

Definition 6.1 (Multiple Context-Free Grammar).
A multiple context-free grammar (MCFG) is a 5-tuple $\langle N,T,F,P,S\rangle$ where

- *N is a finite set of non-terminals (predicates), and each $A \in N$ has a dimension $dim(A) \geq 1, dim(A) \in \mathbb{N}$;*
- *T is a finite set of terminals;*
- *F is a finite set of mcf-functions;*
- *P is a finite set of rules of the form $A_0 \to f[A_1,\ldots,A_k]$ with $k \geq 0, f \in F$ such that $f : (T^*)^{dim(A_1)} \times \ldots \times (T^*)^{dim(A_k)} \to (T^*)^{dim(A_0)}$;*
- *$S \in N$ is the start symbol with $dim(S) = 1$.*

An MCFG with maximal predicate dimension k is called a k-MCFG.

6.1 Introduction to MCFG, LCFRS and Simple RCG

The mcf-functions are such that each component of the value of f is a concatenation of some constant strings and some components of its arguments. Furthermore, each component of the right-hand side arguments of a rule is not allowed to appear in the value of f more than once.

Definition 6.2 (mcf-function).
f *is an mcf-function if there is a* $k \geq 0$ *and there are* $d_i > 0$ *for* $0 \leq i \leq k$ *such that* f *is a total function from* $(T^*)^{d_1} \times \ldots \times (T^*)^{d_k}$ *to* $(T^*)^{d_0}$ *such that*

- *the components of* $f(\mathbf{x_1}, \ldots, \mathbf{x_k})$ *are concatenations of a limited number of terminal symbols and the components* x_{ij} *of the* $\mathbf{x_i}$ *(*$1 \leq i \leq k, 1 \leq j \leq d_i$*), and*
- *the components* x_{ij} *of the* $\mathbf{x_i}$ *are used at most once in the components of* $f(\mathbf{x_1}, \ldots, \mathbf{x_k})$.

We can understand an MCFG as a generative device that specifies the yields of the non-terminals. The language of an MCFG is then the yield of the start symbol S.

Definition 6.3 (Language of an MCFG).
Let $G = \langle N, T, F, P, S \rangle$ *be an MCFG.*

1. *For every* $A \in N$:
   - *For every* $A \to f[\,] \in P$, $f(\,) \in yield(A)$.
   - *For every* $A \to f[A_1, \ldots, A_k] \in P$ *with* $k \geq 1$ *and all tuples* $\tau_1 \in yield(A_1), \ldots, \tau_k \in yield(A_k)$, $f(\tau_1, \ldots, \tau_k) \in yield(A)$.
   - *Nothing else is in* $yield(A)$.
2. *The string language of* G *is* $L(G) = \{w \mid \langle w \rangle \in yield(S)\}$.

Linear Context-Free Rewriting Systems (LCFRSs) were introduced in (Vijay-Shanker, Weir, and Joshi, 1987). Their definition is almost the same as the one of MCFGs except that the conditions on mcf-functions are stricter. In LCFRS, the mcf-functions f are required to use every component x_{ij} of the $\mathbf{x_i}$ *exactly* once (instead of at most once) in the components of $f(\mathbf{x_1}, \ldots, \mathbf{x_k})$. However, this stronger condition does not change the generative capacity of the grammars. Seki et al. (1991) show that for every k-MCFG, there is an equivalent k-LCFRS.

Simple RCG

A formalism that is not only equivalent to MCFG and LCFRS but also represents a useful syntactic variant is *simple Range Concatenation Grammar*. We will introduce *Range Concatenation Grammars* (RCGs) (Boullier, 2000b) in Chapter 8. So-called *simple* RCGs (SRCGs) are a restricted form of RCG. We can notate an MCFG as an SRCG if we encode the computation of the mcf-functions inside the rules. To see how this can be done, consider again our sample grammar from Fig. 6.1. In an RCG, the non-terminals are written as predicates with the components of the yields being their arguments. We use variables $X, Y, \ldots$ from a specific set V for the components of the right-hand side predicates of a rule. Writing our sample MCFG as an RCG leads to the grammar in Fig. 6.2. The right-hand side arguments are single pairwise different variables while the arguments of the left-hand side are concatenations of the variables from the right-hand side and of a limited number of new terminals. These concatenations describe how to obtain the yield of the left-hand side predicate from the yields of the right-hand side predicate.

$$S(XYZ) \to A(X,Y,Z)$$
$$A(aX, aY, aZ) \to A(X,Y,Z)$$
$$A(bX, bY, bZ) \to A(X,Y,Z)$$
$$A(a,a,a) \to \varepsilon$$
$$A(b,b,b) \to \varepsilon$$

Fig. 6.2. The MCFG from Fig. 6.1 written as a simple RCG

Definition 6.4 (Simple RCG).

1. A simple RCG (SRCG) is a tuple $G = (N, T, V, P, S)$ where
   a) N is a finite set of predicate names with an arity function dim: $N \to \mathbb{N}$,
   b) T and V are disjoint finite sets of terminals and variables,
   c) P is a finite set of clauses of the form
   $$A(\alpha_1, \ldots, \alpha_{dim(A)})$$
   $$\to A_1(X_1^{(1)}, \ldots, X_{dim(A_1)}^{(1)}) \cdots A_m(X_1^{(m)}, \ldots, X_{dim(A_m)}^{(m)})$$
   for $m \geq 0$ where $A, A_1, \ldots, A_m \in N$, $X_j^{(i)} \in V$ for $1 \leq i \leq m, 1 \leq j \leq dim(A_i)$, and $\alpha_i \in (T \cup V)^*$ for $1 \leq i \leq dim(A)$, and
   d) $S \in N$ is the start predicate name with $dim(S) = 1$.
   As a condition, for all $c \in P$, it holds that every variable $X \in V$ occurring in c occurs exactly once in the left-hand side and exactly once in the right-hand side.
2. A simple RCG $G = (N, T, V, P, S)$ is a simple k-RCG if for all $A \in N, dim(A) \leq k$.

Because of the condition at the end of 1., in a simple RCG, the components of right-hand side arguments are used exactly once in the left-hand side. This amounts to the LCFRS condition on mcf-functions. The equivalence between LCFRS and simple RCG has been shown in (Boullier, 2000b).

The way the string languages of SRCGs are defined is different from that of MCFGs and LCFRSs. In SRCGs, the components of the arguments of predicates are taken to denote portions of a given input string w, denoted by ranges. However, both definitions are equivalent. Only when dropping the linearity constraint are the two definitions of string languages no longer equivalent, as we will see in Chapter 8.

Definition of Ranges

When doing parsing, we are faced with a given input string w and we want to determine which of the non-terminals $A \in N$ is true for which vector of substrings of w. For this, the definitions of ranges and of clause instantiations in SRCGs is useful. We therefore introduce it here.

In order to relate non-terminals A to portions of the input string, we must distinguish between different substrings of the input containing the same terminal symbols. For illustration, consider the input word $w = ababab$ of our double copy language from Fig. 6.1. For a successful analysis of w, we obtain $A(_1b_{2,3}\,b_{4,5}\,b_6)$, $A(_0ab_{2,2}\,ab_{4,4}\,ab_6)$ and $S(_0ababab_6)$ where the subscripts indicate the start and end positions of the substring in w.

In order to formalize these substrings, we introduce *ranges*. A range over a given input string w is a pair $\langle i, j \rangle$ of a start and an end position of a substring in w.

Definition 6.5 (Range).
Let $w \in T^*$ be a word with $w = w_1 \ldots w_n$ where $w_i \in T$ for $1 \leq i \leq n$.

- $Pos(w) := \{0, \ldots, n\}$.
- We call a pair $\langle l, r \rangle \in Pos(w) \times Pos(w)$ with $l \leq r$ a range *in* w. Its yield $\langle l, r \rangle(w)$ is the substring $w_{l+1} \ldots w_r$.
- For two ranges $\rho_1 = \langle l_1, r_1 \rangle, \rho_2 = \langle l_2, r_2 \rangle$, if $r_1 = l_2$, then the concatenation of ρ_1 and ρ_2 is $\rho_1 \cdot \rho_2 = \langle l_1, r_2 \rangle$; otherwise $\rho_1 \cdot \rho_2$ is undefined.
- Two ranges $\langle l_1, r_1 \rangle, \langle l_2, r_2 \rangle$ are overlapping *if*
  1. either $l_1 \leq l_2 < r_1$ and $l_1 < r_2$
  2. or $l_1 < r_2 \leq r_1$ and $l_2 < r_1$.

  For every $a \in T$, we define $ranges(a, w) = \{\langle i-1, i \rangle \mid 1 \geq i \geq n, \langle i-1, i \rangle(w) = a\}$.

In the context of MCFG, given a specific input w, the yields of the non-terminals that might lead to a parse of w are tuples of ranges over w. Furthermore, since our mcf-functions are concatenations of these ranges and new terminals, the ranges are necessarily pairwise non-overlapping.[1]

Definition 6.6 (Range vector).
Let $w \in T^*$.

- A $\rho \in (Pos(w) \times Pos(w))^k$ is a k-dimensional range vector *for* w iff $\rho = \langle \langle l_1, r_1 \rangle, \ldots, \langle l_k, r_k \rangle \rangle$ where $\langle l_i, r_i \rangle$ is a range in w for $1 \leq i \leq k$.

---

[1] This will be different when dealing with Range Concatenation Grammars in Chapter 8 where the different non-terminals of a right-hand side can have overlapping yields.

- For a k-dimensional range vector $\boldsymbol{\rho}$ for w we define the denotation of $\boldsymbol{\rho}$ as
  $\boldsymbol{\rho}(w) := \langle\langle l_1, r_1\rangle(w), \ldots, \langle l_k, r_k\rangle(w)\rangle$.

A range vector $\boldsymbol{\rho}$ is called simple iff its elements are pairwise non-overlapping.

Now we can define the range vectors in the yield of a given predicate A with respect to w, notated as $r\text{-}yield(A)$. For this, we have to apply the functions f directly to the range vectors while mapping the terminals to appropriate ranges of length 1. This way, f is no longer a function and it is no longer defined for all range vectors. (In some cases, it might yield undefined concatenations of ranges.) We call the function that corresponds to f but applies to range vectors f_r. $f_r(\boldsymbol{\rho_1}, \ldots, \boldsymbol{\rho_m})$ concatenates the ranges of its arguments with appropriate ranges from $ranges(a, w)$ for every a occurring in the concatenation specified in f. Here, "appropriate" means that the concatenation of the ranges should be defined. Empty arguments ε in the result of f are replaced with empty ranges $\langle i, i\rangle$, $0 \leq i \leq n$.

Definition 6.7 (r-yield).
Let $G = \langle N, T, F, P, S\rangle$ be an MCFG.

1. For every $A \in N$:
   - For every $A \to f[\,] \in P$ and every simple range vector $\boldsymbol{\rho}$ such that $\boldsymbol{\rho}(w) = f[\,]$, $\boldsymbol{\rho} \in r\text{-}yield(A)$.
   - For every $A \to f[A_1, \ldots, A_k] \in P$ with $k \geq 1$ such that $\boldsymbol{\rho_i} \in r\text{-}yield(A_i)$ for $1 \leq i \leq k$, and for all $\boldsymbol{\rho} \in f_r(\boldsymbol{\rho_1}, \ldots, \boldsymbol{\rho_k})$, $\boldsymbol{\rho} \in r\text{-}yield(A)$.
   - Nothing else is in $r\text{-}yield(A)$.
2. The string language of an MCFG G is $\{w \in T^* \mid \langle\langle 0, n\rangle\rangle \in r\text{-}yield(S) \text{ wrt. } w)\}$.

As a notation, we write $A(\boldsymbol{\rho})$ for $\boldsymbol{\rho} \in r\text{-}yield(A)$.

As an example, consider again our MCFG from Fig. 6.1. Assume that our input is $w = abaabaaba$, which is in the language. w is in the language because with respect to w, we obtain $A(\langle\langle 2, 3\rangle, \langle 5, 6\rangle, \langle 8, 9\rangle\rangle)$ since $f_4(\,) = \langle b, b, b\rangle$. Furthermore, $\langle\langle 1, 3\rangle, \langle 4, 6\rangle, \langle 7, 9\rangle\rangle \in f_{3r}(\langle\langle 2, 3\rangle, \langle 5, 6\rangle, \langle 8, 9\rangle\rangle)$ and therefore $A(\langle\langle 1, 3\rangle, \langle 4, 6\rangle, \langle 7, 9\rangle\rangle)$. With $\langle\langle 0, 3\rangle, \langle 3, 6\rangle, \langle 6, 9\rangle\rangle \in f_{2r}(\langle\langle 1, 3\rangle, \langle 4, 6\rangle, \langle 7, 9\rangle\rangle)$ we have $A(\langle\langle 0, 3\rangle, \langle 3, 6\rangle, \langle 6, 9\rangle\rangle)$. Finally, $\langle\langle 0, 9\rangle\rangle \in f_{1r}(\langle\langle 0, 3\rangle, \langle 3, 6\rangle, \langle 6, 9\rangle\rangle)$ and therefore $S(\langle\langle 0, 9\rangle\rangle)$.

Note that the range vectors in the yield of the predicates are not necessarily ordered. Therefore we also have for instance $A(\langle\langle 5, 6\rangle, \langle 2, 3\rangle, \langle 8, 9\rangle\rangle)$.

In contrast to MCFG/LCFRS, the definition of RCGs is such that they do not have the generative perspective that is present in the definition of MCFGs. I.e., their rules are not taken to describe how to compute the (larger) yield of a left-hand side predicate from the yields of the right-hand side predicates. Rather, the rules describe how to check whether a given tuple is in the yield of a predicate. Consider Fig. 6.2. The first rule tells us that a tuple with a single component satisfies the predicate S if we can separate it into three parts such that the triple of the three parts satisfies A. The second rule tells us that a triple of three substrings (or, rather, ranges) satisfies A if, after having removed an a to the left of each of the components, we obtain a triple that again satisfies A. Rules with empty right-hand sides describe the terminals that satisfy a predicate without further conditions. The last rule for instance signifies that every simple 3-dimensional range vector with yield $\langle b, b, b \rangle$ satisfies A.

In order to formalize this (Boullier, 2000b), we introduce the concept of *instantiation* of a rule. Roughly, an *instantiated* rule is a rule in which variables and arguments are consistently replaced by ranges; its components are *instantiated predicates*. For example $A(\langle g, h \rangle) \to B(\langle g+1, h \rangle)$ is an instantiation of the clause $A(aX_1) \to B(X_1)$ if the target string is such that $w_{g+1} = a$.

Definition 6.8 (Clause instantiation).
Let $G = (N, T, V, P, S)$ be a simple RCG. For a given clause $A(\boldsymbol{\alpha}) \to A_1(\boldsymbol{\alpha_1}) \cdots A_m(\boldsymbol{\alpha_m}) \in P$ $(0 \leq m)$,

1. an instantiation *with respect to a string* $w = t_1 \ldots t_n$ *consists of a function* $f : \{t' \mid t' \text{ is an occurrence of some } t \in T \text{ in the clause}\} \cup V \cup \{Eps_i \mid 1 \leq i \leq dim(A), \boldsymbol{\alpha}(i) = \varepsilon\} \to \{\langle i, j \rangle \mid i \leq j, i, j \in \mathbb{N}\}$ *such that*
   a) *for all occurrences* t' *of a* $t \in T$ *in* $\boldsymbol{\alpha}$, $f(t')(w) = t$,
   b) *for all* $X \in V$, $f(X) = \langle j, k \rangle$ *for some* $0 \leq j \leq k \leq n$,
   c) *for all* x, y *adjacent in one of the elements of* $\boldsymbol{\alpha}$ *there are* i, j, k *with* $f(x) = \langle i, j \rangle, f(y) = \langle j, k \rangle$; *we define then* $f(xy) = \langle i, k \rangle$,
   d) *for all* $Eps \in \{Eps_i \mid 1 \leq i \leq dim(A), \boldsymbol{\alpha}(i) = \varepsilon\}$, *there is a* j, $0 \leq j \leq n$ *with* $f(Eps) = \langle j, j \rangle$; *we define then for every* ε-*argument* $\boldsymbol{\alpha}(i)$ *that* $f(\boldsymbol{\alpha}(i)) = f(Eps_i)$;
2. *if* f *is an instantiation of* c, *then* $A(f(\boldsymbol{\alpha})) \to A_1(f(\boldsymbol{\alpha_1})) \cdots A_m(f(\boldsymbol{\alpha_m}))$ *is an* instantiated clause *where* $f(\langle x_1, \ldots, x_k \rangle) = \langle f(x_1), \ldots, f(x_k) \rangle$.

We can then define that in each SRCG derivation step, we replace the left-hand side of an instantiated clause with its right-hand side. The string language of a simple RCG is the set $\{w \mid S(\langle 0, |w| \rangle) \stackrel{*}{\Rightarrow} \varepsilon\}$.

Derivation Trees

For a given input word w and a given SRCG, the set of instantiated clauses with respect to w is a CFG whose non-terminals are the instantiated predicates, whose set of terminals is empty and whose productions are the instantiated clauses. The start symbol is $S(\langle 0, |w| \rangle)$. The question whether w is part of the language amounts to deciding whether $S(\langle 0, |w| \rangle) \stackrel{*}{\Rightarrow} \varepsilon$. Based on this observation, Boullier (1998a) defines the parse forest of ε in this CFG as the parse forest of w in the SRCG. In other words, for a given w, every derivation tree of ε in the CFG of instantiated clauses with respect to w is an SRCG derivation tree of w.

Simple RCG for $\{wcwc \,|\, w \in \{a,b\}^*\}$:

$$S(XY) \to T(X,Y)$$
$$T(aY, aU) \to T(Y,U)$$
$$T(bY, bU) \to T(Y,U)$$
$$T(c,c) \to \varepsilon$$

Derivation tree (our definition) for $aacaac$:

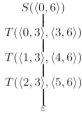

Derivation tree (Boullier's definition) for $aacaac$:

$$S(\langle 0,6 \rangle)$$
$$|$$
$$T(\langle 0,3 \rangle, \langle 3,6 \rangle)$$
$$|$$
$$T(\langle 1,3 \rangle, \langle 4,6 \rangle)$$
$$|$$
$$T(\langle 2,3 \rangle, \langle 5,6 \rangle)$$
$$|$$
$$\varepsilon$$

Fig. 6.3. A sample derivation tree in a simple RCG

Alternatively, one can also define the SRCG derivation trees as trees whose leaves are labelled with the terminals of the input and whose internal nodes are labelled with predicate names. An edge between internal nodes tells us about a rewrite relation while an edge between an internal node and a leaf tells us that the leaf was used to compute one of the components of the yield of the internal node. In the following, we will formalize this notion of SRCG derivation trees. Note that the information we encode in these derivation trees is also implicitly available in the derivation trees defined in (Boullier, 1998a).

The derivation trees are partially ordered; more particularly, only the leaf nodes are ordered. The internal nodes are labelled with non-terminals and the leaves are labelled with ranges that refer to terminals in a specific string w. All internal nodes are licensed by rules in the grammar.

See Fig. 6.3 for a derivation tree in a simple RCG. As a convention, we depict the leaves in the order of their labels, i.e., a leaf with label $\langle i,j \rangle$ precedes a leaf with label $\langle j,k \rangle$. Furthermore, sister nodes are depicted in the order of the left boundaries of the leftmost leaf that they dominate. This is why the nodes labelled T are always depicted as the middle daughters in Fig. 6.3.

Definition 6.9 (Derivation tree of a simple RCG).
Let $G = \langle N, T, V_G, P, S \rangle$ be a simple RCG (i.e., an LCFRS).

1. Let $w = a_1 \ldots a_n$ with $a_i \in T, 1 \leq i \leq n$.
   Let $D = \langle V, E, r \rangle$ be a tree such that there are n pairwise different leaves $u_1, \ldots, u_n$ in D with $l(u_i) = \langle i-1, i \rangle$ $(1 \leq i \leq n)$ and all other leaves have a label $\langle i,i \rangle$ for some i with $0 \leq i \leq n$.
   a) We define $r\text{-}yield(u) = \{l(u)\}$ for every leaf u.

Clauses:
$S(XY) \to A(X,Y)$
$A(aa,a) \to \varepsilon$
$A(a,aa) \to \varepsilon$

derivation tree:

```
      S
      |
      A
    / | \
   a  a  a
```

r-yield of the A-node:
$\{(\langle 0,1\rangle, \langle 1,3\rangle),$
$(\langle 0,2\rangle, \langle 2,3\rangle)\}$

Fig. 6.4. An example where a derivation tree node yields more than one range vector

b) For every internal node $v_0 \in V$, for every order $v_1,\ldots,v_k$ of the pairwise different daughters of v_0 that are internal nodes such that $l(v_i) = A_i$ for $0 \leq i \leq k$, and for every rule $A_0(\boldsymbol{\alpha_0}) \to A_1(\boldsymbol{\alpha_1}),\ldots,A_k(\boldsymbol{\alpha_k})$, if there is an instantiation $A_0(\boldsymbol{\rho_0}) \to A_1(\boldsymbol{\rho_1}),\ldots,A_k(\boldsymbol{\rho_k})$ of this rule wrt w such that
  i. $\boldsymbol{\rho_i} \in r\text{-}yield(v_i)$, $1 \leq i \leq k$, and
  ii. there is a daughter u of v_0 that is a leaf iff either one of the terminals in $\boldsymbol{\alpha_0}$ or an ε-argument in $\boldsymbol{\alpha_0}$ is mapped to $l(u)$ by this instantiation,
then $\boldsymbol{\rho_0} \in r\text{-}yield(v_0)$.
Nothing else is in $r\text{-}yield(v_0)$.

D is a derivation tree of w in G iff $(\langle 0,n\rangle) \in r\text{-}yield(r)$ and $l(r) = S$.

2. The tree language of G is

$$L_T(G) = \{D \mid D \text{ is a derivation tree of some } w \in T \text{ in } G\}.$$

The reason why there can be more than one possibility for the r-yield of a node v is that adjacent terminals can belong to the same or to different arguments as exemplified in Fig. 6.4.

A further example of an SRCG/LCFRS derivation tree can be found in the solution of Problem 6.6.

Before we proceed, let us add a remark on how the three formalisms LCFRS, MCFG and SRCG differ in their respective terminologies. In LCFRS terminology, the dimension of a non-terminal and of a grammar is sometimes called *fan-out* while, in the context of SRCG, we encounter the term *arity* for the same concept. Furthermore, *productions* or *rules* in LCFRS and MCFG are called *clauses* when dealing with SRCG. Finally, the *non-terminals* in MCFG and LCFRS are called *predicates* in SRCG.

6.1.2 Formal Properties

String Languages

We will now list some important properties of the string languages generated by MCFG and the equivalent LCFRS and SRCG.

Seki et al. (1991) show the following pumping lemma for k-MCFLs, the class of languages generated by k-MCFGs.

Lemma 6.10 (Pumping Lemma for k-MCFLs).
For any k-MCFL L, if L is an infinite set then there exist some $u_j \in T^*$ $(1 \leq j \leq k+1)$, $v_j, w_j, s_j \in T^* (1 \leq j \leq k)$, which satisfy the following conditions:

1. $\Sigma_{j=1}^{k} |v_j s_j| > 0$, and
2. for any $i \geq 0$,

$$z_i = u_1 v_1^i w_1 s_1^i u_2 v_2^i w_2 s_2^i \ldots u_k v_k^i w_k s_k^i u_{k+1} \in L.$$

With this pumping lemma, one can show that k-MCFG can generate the counting languages only up to $2k$:

Lemma 6.11. $L_{2k+1} = \{a_1^n a_2^n \ldots a_{2k+1}^n \,|\, n \geq 1, a_i \in T \text{ for } 1 \leq i \leq 2k+1\}$ is not a k-MCFL.

Since it is possible to find a $(k+1)$-MCFG for L_{2k+1}, we can conclude that the class of k-MCFLs is a proper subset of the class of $(k+1)$-MCFLs.

Note that the pumping lemma from (Seki et al., 1991) is only a weak pumping lemma since it is existential. This means that it only tells us that there *exists* a string in the language that is of a limited length and that contains substrings that can be iterated. In contrast to this, the CFG pumping lemma for instance is universal since it says that within *every* string of sufficient length we find two pumpable substrings of a limited distance. Kanazawa (2009) proves a stronger pumping lemma for a restricted class of k-MCFLs, so-called *well-nested k-MCFLs*.

Since LCFRSs have a context-free backbone, the construction of a letter-equivalent CFG for a given LCFRS is rather straightforward. This means that, with Parikh's theorem (see p. 25), MCFLs are semilinear and, consequently, satisfy the constant growth property (Vijay-Shanker, Weir, and Joshi, 1987). Furthermore, since every CFL is a 1-MCFL, they contain all context-free languages. When introducing different parsing algorithms for MCFG, we will see that the languages generated by MCFG are polynomially parsable. Finally, MCFGs can generate the copy language (see the MCFG for the double copy language given in Fig. 6.1) and therefore describe cross-serial dependencies. Consequently, we have the following result:

Lemma 6.12.
The class of MCFL (LCFRL/SRCL) is mildly context-sensitive.

In fact, so far, no mildly context-sensitive language class has been identified that contains languages that are not MCFLs. Therefore, without an actual proof, MCFG and equivalent formalisms such as LCFRS and simple RCG are taken to provide the best characterization of mildly context-sensitive language classes. However, Kallmeyer and Satta (2009) suggest that there might be other formalisms generating mildly context-sensitive languages as well that are not comparable to MCFG. The grammar formalism they are investigating is TT-MCTAG, a certain type of multicomponent TAG introduced in (Lichte, 2007). TT-MCTAGs generate polynomial languages, as shown in (Kallmeyer and Satta, 2009); they are more powerful than TAG and therefore can describe cross-serial dependencies and include CFLs. Whether they generate only semilinear languages is an open question and also their relation to MCFG is not clear yet. They can describe the type of permutations occurring in German scrambling constructions. These phenomena have been argued to be beyond the power of MCFG and LCFRS (Becker, Rambow, and Niv, 1992). On the other hand, Kallmeyer and Satta (2009) suggest that TT-MCTAG might not be able to generate the double copy language from Fig. 6.1. If this can be shown and if the languages of TT-MCTAG are semilinear, then MCFLs would no longer be the only mildly context-sensitive class for which we do not have a larger class that is still mildly context-sensitive.

MCFLs have the following closure properties (Seki et al., 1991):

Lemma 6.13 (Closure Properties of MCFL).
For every $k \geq 1$,

1. *the class k-MCFL is closed under substitution.*
2. *the class k-MCFL is closed under union, concatenation, Kleene closure and ε-free Kleene closure.*
3. *the class k-MCFL is closed under intersection with regular languages.*

k-MCFLs being closed under substitution means that if L is a k-MCFL over the terminal alphabet T and f assigns a k-MCFL to every $t \in T$, then the language $f(L) = \{w_1 \ldots w_n \mid$ there is a $t_1 \ldots t_n \in L$ with $w_i \in f(t_i)$ for $1 \leq i \leq n\}$ is also a k-MCFL. The k-MCFG for $f(L)$ can be obtained from the one for L and the ones for $f(t)$, $t \in T$, as follows. Without loss of generality we assume the sets of variables and non-terminals in the different grammars to be pairwise disjoint. We then take the grammar for L and replace every terminal a in a left-hand side (where the grammar is in RCG-style syntax) with a new variable X_a and add $S_a(X_a)$ to the right-hand side, where S_a is the start symbol of the grammar of $f(a)$.

For two k-MCFLs L_1, L_2 generated by the k-MCFGs G_1, G_2 with start symbols S_1, S_2 respectively (and, again, without loss of generality disjoint sets of non-terminals), the k-MCFGs for the union and concatenation can be obtained in the following way. The union, $L_1 \cup L_2$ is generated by the grammar with the rules from G_1 and G_2 and additional rules $S(X) \to S_1(X)$, $S(X) \to S_2(X)$ where S is a new start symbol. The concatenation $\{w_1 w_2 \mid w_1 \in L_1, w_2 \in L_2\}$ is generated by the grammar with the rules from G_1 and G_2 and an additional rule $S(XY) \to S_1(X)S_2(Y)$ where S is a new start symbol.

Concerning the Kleene closure, for a k-MCFL L generated by the k-MCFG G, if we add the rules $S'(XY) \to S(X)S'(Y)$ and $S'(\varepsilon) \to \varepsilon$ to G where S' is a new start symbol, we obtain a k-MCFG that generates the Kleene closure L^* of L. If we add the rules $S'(XY) \to S(X)S'(Y)$ and $S'(X) \to S(X)$ to G

2-MCFG generating the copy language:
$S(XY) \to A(X,Y)$ $A(aX, aY) \to A(X,Y)$ $A(bX, bY) \to A(X,Y)$ $A(\varepsilon, \varepsilon) \to \varepsilon$

Intersect with $a^*b^*a^*b^*$, generated by a DFA with $Q = F = \{q_0, q_1, q_2, q_3\}$, initial state q_0 and
$\delta(q_0, a) = q_0$ $\delta(q_0, b) = q_1$ $\delta(q_1, b) = q_1$ $\delta(q_1, a) = q_2$
$\delta(q_2, a) = q_2$ $\delta(q_2, b) = q_3$ $\delta(q_3, b) = q_3$

Resulting k-MCFG: The new start symbol is S'.
S'-rules:
$S'(X) \to S[q_0, q_0](X)$
$S'(X) \to S[q_0, q_1](X)$
$S'(X) \to S[q_0, q_3](X)$
Words from a^*:
$S[q_0, q_0](XY) \to A[q_0, q_0, q_0, q_0](X,Y)$
$A[q_0, q_0, q_0, q_0](aX, aY) \to A[q_0, q_0, q_0, q_0](X,Y)$
$A[q_0, q_0, q_0, q_0](\varepsilon, \varepsilon) \to \varepsilon$
Words from b^+:
$S[q_0, q_1](XY) \to A[q_0, q_1, q_1, q_1](X,Y)$
$A[q_0, q_1, q_1, q_1](bX, bY) \to A[q_1, q_1, q_1, q_1](X,Y)$
$A[q_1, q_1, q_1, q_1](bX, bY) \to A[q_1, q_1, q_1, q_1](X,Y)$
$A[q_1, q_1, q_1, q_1](\varepsilon, \varepsilon) \to \varepsilon$
Words from $a^+b^+a^+b^+$:
$S[q_0, q_3](XY) \to A[q_0, q_1, q_1, q_3](X,Y)$
$A[q_0, q_1, q_1, q_3](aX, aY) \to A[q_0, q_1, q_2, q_3](X,Y)$
$A[q_0, q_1, q_2, q_3](aX, aY) \to A[q_0, q_1, q_2, q_3](X,Y)$
$A[q_0, q_1, q_2, q_3](bX, bY) \to A[q_1, q_1, q_3, q_3](X,Y)$
$A[q_1, q_1, q_3, q_3](bX, bY) \to A[q_1, q_1, q_3, q_3](X,Y)$
$A[q_1, q_1, q_3, q_3](\varepsilon, \varepsilon) \to \varepsilon$

Fig. 6.5. Intersecting an MCFL with a regular language

where S' is again a new start symbol, we obtain a k-MCFG that generates ε-free Kleene closure L^+ of L.

Finally, for the intersection of a k-MCFL L with a regular language, we take the DFA that accepts the regular language and we enrich the non-terminals $A \in N$ in the k-MCFG of L with lists of states $q_1, q'_1, \ldots, q_{dim(A)}, q'_{dim(A)}$ from the DFA. The path from q_i to q'_i is the path traversed while processing the ith component of A. An example is given in Fig. 6.5.

There are languages that are polynomial and of constant growth and that cannot be generated by LCFRS/SRCG:

Lemma 6.14. $L = \{(a^m b^m)^n \mid m, n \geq 1\}$ *is not an MCFL.*

Proof. In order to show the lemma, we assume that there is a fixed k such that there is a k-MCFG generating L.

We now intersect L with the regular language $(a^+b^+)^{k+1}$, which yields the language $L' = \{(a^m b^m)^{k+1} \mid m \geq 1\}$. This language does not satisfy the pumping lemma for k-MCFL since the iterated parts in the pumping lemma must each consist of either as or bs (otherwise we would increase the number

of substrings a^m and b^m when iterating). Furthermore, if we have at most $2k$ iterated parts, the iterations necessarily lead to words where the a^m and b^m parts no longer have all the same exponent. Consequently, L' and therefore also L are not k-MCFLs. Since this holds for any k, L is not an MCFL.
□

The language from Lemma 6.14 is definitely of constant growth since all words $(ab)^n$ are in the language, i.e., all words containing the same numbers of as and bs. We will see in Chapter 8 an RCG for the language from Lemma 6.14 which proves that this language is polynomial.

Tree Languages

Borrowing notions from dependency grammar, Maier and Lichte (2009) define different characteristic properties of trees with crossing branches. Since these definitions can be applied immediately to the derivation trees of SRCG/LCFRS, we list them here.

We can distinguish different types of LCFRS/SRCG derivation trees depending on the number of discontinuities and the type of nesting described by these trees. The types of trees we encounter in an SRCG tree language have direct consequences for parsing.

Maier and Lichte (2009) redefine notions such as *gap degree* and *well-nestedness* that have been introduced for dependency structures in a more general way for syntactic structures such that they apply to both, dependency trees and constituency trees.

In order to formulate the definitions of gap degree and well-nestedness, we introduce the notion of *projection* of a node v in a derivation tree as $\pi(v) = \{j \mid 1 \leq j \leq n$ and there is an m such that $r\text{-}yield(v)(m) = \langle i, k \rangle$ with $i < j \leq k\}$. Intuitively, the projection is the set of indices of all terminals that are in the r-yield of a node.

Then, following (Maier and Lichte, 2009), we can define the *gap degree* of a derivation tree as follows:

Definition 6.15 (Gap degree).
   Let $G = \langle N, T, V_G, P, S \rangle$ be a simple RCG (i.e., a LCFRS).

- Let $D = \langle V, E, r \rangle$ be a derivation tree for a string $w = a_1 \ldots a_n$ with $a_i \in T, 1 \leq i \leq n$.
    1. *For every node $v \in V$, we define that $\langle i, j \rangle$ is a* gap *in $\pi(v)$ if $i, j \in \pi(v)$, $i + 1 < j$ and there is no $k \in \pi(v)$ with $i < k < j$.*
       The gap degree *of v is defined as the number of gaps in $\pi(v)$.*
    2. *The* gap degree *of D is the maximal gap degree of any of its nodes.*
- *The* gap degree *of G is the maximal gap degree of any of the trees in $L_T(G)$.*

Fig. 6.6. A derivation tree with crossing branches that has gap degree 0

Note that this definition depends only on input symbols in the yield. It does not take empty components into account. This is because Maier and Lichte (2009) consider only constituent trees that do not have leaves with label ε. In the case of ε-leaves, i.e., leaves labelled with a range $\langle i, i \rangle$, we can have crossing branches that do not lead to a gap. See Fig. 6.6 for an example.

Besides considering gap degree, Maier and Lichte (2009) also transfer the dependency-based notion of well-nestedness to syntactic structures. This amounts to the following definition:

Definition 6.16 (Well-nestedness).
Let $G = \langle N, T, V_G, P, S \rangle$ be a simple RCG.

- A derivation tree $D = \langle V, E, r \rangle \in L_T(G)$ is well-nested if there are no nodes $v_1, v_2 \in V$ with $\pi(v_1) \cap \pi(v_2) = \emptyset$ such that there are $i_1, i_2 \in \pi(v_1)$ and $j_1, j_2 \in \pi(v_2)$ with $i_1 < j_1 < i_2 < j_2$.
- G is well-nested if all trees in $L_T(G)$ are well-nested.

Maier and Lichte (2009) are dealing only with SRCG derivation trees where all leaves are labelled $\langle i, i+1 \rangle$ for some $0 \leq i < n$ (no ε-leaves) and, furthermore, for any node v in a derivation tree and any k, $1 \leq k < |yield(v)|$, we have that the end position of the range $\rho(k)$ is lower than the start position of $\rho(k+1)$. In other words, whenever we have different arguments, there is actually a gap in between.

In grammars G where the derivation trees satisfy these conditions, it holds that the gap degree of the grammar plus 1 is its arity. Furthermore, such a grammar is ill-nested iff it contains clauses with variables X_1, X_2, X_3, X_4 that occur in this order in the left-hand side such that X_1 and X_3 are arguments of some right-hand side predicate A and X_2 and X_4 are arguments of a different right-hand side predicate B. This corresponds to the definition of *well-nested LCFRS* given in (Kanazawa, 2009).

6.1.3 Applications

Biological Structures

Formal grammars have been proposed for RNA secondary structure prediction techniques. For example, *stem loop* structures can be represented using CFGs, and recognition (or *secondary structure prediction*) can be achieved in

$\mathcal{O}(n^3)$ where n is the length of the input sequence (or *primary structure*). For the modelling of *pseudoknot* structures (see Fig. 6.7), which cannot be represented using CFG due to the crossing dependencies, among other formalisms, stochastic MCFG has been proposed in (Kato, Seki, and Kasami, 2006).

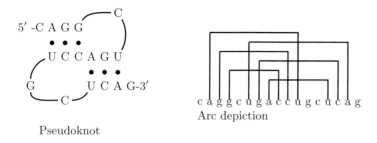

Fig. 6.7. RNA secondary structure

Constituency Treebanks with Discontinuities

While most treebank annotation schemes rely on an annotation backbone based on context-free grammar, in the German NeGra treebank, discontinuous phrases are annotated directly using crossing branches. Figure 6.8 shows an example tree from NeGra, involving two discontinuous VPs.

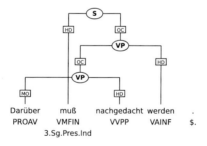

Fig. 6.8. A tree from NeGra

Maier and Søgaard present in (Maier and Søgaard, 2008) an algorithm for the extraction of SRCGs from such treebanks, interpreting the trees as SRCG derivation trees. This is almost immediate, except for the arity of the non-terminal categories: In the treebank, we can have the same non-terminal with different arities, for instance a VP without a gap (arity 1), a VP with a single gap (arity 2), and so on. In the corresponding SRCG, we have to distinguish these non-terminals by mapping them to different predicates.

The algorithm first creates a so-called lexical clause $P(a) \to \varepsilon$ for each pre-terminal P dominating some terminal a. Then for all other non-terminals A_0 with the children $A_1 \cdots A_m$, a clause $A_0 \to A_1 \cdots A_m$ is created. The arguments of the $A_1 \cdots A_m$ are single variables where the number of arguments is the number of discontinuous parts in the yield of a predicate. The arguments of A_0 are concatenations of these variables that describe how the discontinuous parts of the yield of A_0 are obtained from the yields of its daughters.

More precisely, the non-terminals (predicates) in our simple RCG are all A_k where A is a non-terminal label in the treebank and k is a possible arity for A. For a given treebank tree $\langle V, E, r \rangle$, the algorithm constructs the following clauses. Let us assume that $w_1, \ldots, w_n$ are the terminal labels of the leaves in $\langle V, E, r \rangle$ with $w_i \prec w_j$ for $1 \leq i < j \leq n$. We introduce a variable X_i for every w_i, $1 \leq i \leq n$.

- For every pair of nodes $v_1, v_2 \in V$ with $\langle v_2, v_2 \rangle \in E$, $l(v_2) \in T$, we add $l(v_1)(l(v_2)) \to \varepsilon$ to the grammar. (We omit the arity subscript here since pre-terminals are always of arity 1.)
- For every node $v \in V$ with $l(v) = A_0 \notin T$ such that there are exactly m nodes $v_1, \ldots, v_m \in V$ ($m \geq 1$) with $\langle v, v_i \rangle \in E$ and $l(v_i) = A_i \notin T$ for all $1 \leq i \leq m$, we now create a clause

$$A_0(\mathbf{x}_1^{(0)}, \ldots, \mathbf{x}_{\dim(A_0)}^{(0)})$$
$$\to A_1(\mathbf{x}_1^{(1)}, \ldots, \mathbf{x}_{\dim(A_1)}^{(1)}) \cdots A_m(\mathbf{x}_1^{(m)}, \ldots, \mathbf{x}_{\dim(A_m)}^{(m)})$$

where for the predicate A_i, $0 \leq i \leq m$, the following must hold:

1. The concatenation of all arguments of A_i is the concatenation of all $X \in \{X_i \mid \langle v_i, v_i' \rangle \in E^*$ with $l(v_i') = w_i\}$ such that X_i precedes X_j if $i < j$, and
2. a variable X_j with $1 \leq j < n$ is the right boundary of an argument of A_i if and only if $X_{j+1} \notin \{X_i \mid \langle v_i, v_i' \rangle \in E^*$ with $l(v_i') = w_i\}$, i.e., an argument boundary is introduced at each discontinuity.

As a further step, in our new clause, all right-hand side arguments of length > 1 are replaced in both sides of the clause with a single new variable.

Finally, all predicates A in the clause are equipped with an additional subscript $dim(A)$ which gives us the final predicate in our simple RCG.

For the tree in Fig. 6.8, the algorithm produces for instance the following clauses:

$$\text{PROAV}(\text{Darüber}) \to \varepsilon$$
$$\text{VMFIN}(\text{muß}) \to \varepsilon$$
$$\text{VVPP}(\text{nachgedacht}) \to \varepsilon$$
$$\text{VAINF}(\text{werden}) \to \varepsilon$$
$$S_1(X_1 X_2 X_3) \to \text{VP}_2(X_1, X_3) \text{ VMFIN}(X_2)$$
$$\text{VP}_2(X_1, X_2 X_3) \to \text{VP}_2(X_1, X_2) \text{ VAINF}(X_3)$$
$$\text{VP}_2(X_1, X_2) \to \text{PROAV}(X_1) \text{ VVPP}(X_2)$$

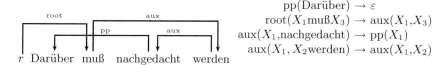

Fig. 6.9. Clauses extracted from a dependency tree

Dependencies and LCFRSs

A similar algorithm has been proposed for the extraction of LCFRS from dependency treebanks (Kuhlmann, 2007; Kuhlmann and Satta, 2009). Here, the non-terminals of the RCG are the labels of the edges. Each clause is lexicalized where the lexical item is the label of the node to which the corresponding edge is directed. See Fig. 6.9 for an example.

Maier and Lichte (2009) give a general formulation of both algorithms, the one for constituency treebank grammar extraction and the one for dependency treebank grammar extraction.

6.2 Equivalent Formalisms

LCFRS, MCFG and SRCG are important formalisms for natural language processing, not only because they allow us to describe discontinuity phenomena but also because they are equivalent to several other grammar formalisms that have been motivated by linguistic considerations.

6.2.1 Set-Local Multicomponent TAG

In Chapter 4, we have introduced MCTAG, a special type of TAG where the elementary trees are grouped into tree sets. Depending on the restrictions we impose on the underlying TAG derivation trees, we obtain different types of MCTAGs. *Set-local* MCTAGs are defined by the condition that, whenever a tree set from the grammar is used, the trees from this set must adjoin to (or substitute) nodes belonging to trees from a single tree set that has been added previously. See Fig. 2.16, p. 34 for a sample set-local MCTAG. In order to formulate this condition on the derivation tree, we require a partition of the nodes into sets V_i $(1 \leq i \leq n)$ such that the labels of each V_i form a tree set from the grammar. A derivation is set-local if for each such set V_i, the set of nodes immediately dominating nodes from V_i is contained in a single other set V_j.

Definition 6.17 (Set-locality condition).
Let $G = \langle N, T, S, I, A, \mathcal{A} \rangle$ be an MCTAG. Let $D = \langle V, E, r \rangle$ be the derivation tree of a saturated derived initial tree in G_{TAG}.

D is set-local *iff*

(SL) *there is a partition $V_1, \ldots, V_n$ of V such that for each V_i ($1 \le i \le n$): $\Gamma_i := \{\gamma \mid l(v) = \gamma \text{ for some } v \in V_i\} \in \mathcal{A}$, $|V_i| = |\Gamma_i|$, and for all V_i ($1 \le i \le n$), either $V_i = \{l(r)\}$ or there is a V_j ($1 \le j \le n$) such that for every $v \in V_i$ there is a $v' \in V_j$ with $\langle v', v \rangle \in E$.*

Note that in the literature, the term MCTAG is sometimes used as meaning set-local MCTAG.

The equivalence between LCFRS and set-local MCTAG has been shown in (Weir, 1988).

6.2.2 Minimalist Grammars

Minimalist Grammars (MGs) were proposed by Stabler (1997) as a formalization of Chomsky's Minimalist Program (Chomsky, 1995). Roughly, MGs consist of a set of trees together with two operations, *merge* and *move*, that allow us to transform these trees. Michaelis (2001a; 2001b) shows that MGs are equivalent to LCFRS.

An MG consists of a set *Lex* of finite ordered binary trees $\tau = \langle V, E, r \rangle$, so-called *expressions*. In such expressions τ, there is an additional relation of *projection* defined among sisters. For every $v_1 \ne v_2$ such that there exists a v with $\langle v, v_1 \rangle, \langle v, v_2 \rangle \in E$, either v_1 projects over v_2 or vice versa. Furthermore, all leaves in τ are labeled with a finite sequence of features.

A node $v \in V$ in an expression $\tau = \langle V, E, r \rangle$ is called a *maximal projection* if either $v = r$ or its sister projects over v. The *head* of a node $v \in V$ is the leaf $h(v)$ such that $\{v' \mid \langle v, v' \rangle \in E^+, \langle v', h(v) \rangle \in E^*\}$ does not contain maximal projections, i.e., the path from v to its head contains only nodes that project over their sisters.

In addition to the set *Lex* of expressions in the grammar, MG provides two operations, *merge* and *move* to create new expressions. *Merge* builds a new tree from two existing ones by considering them the two subtrees dominated by a new root node. Its application depends on the head features of the two trees and it modifies these features. *Move* transforms a single tree into a new one. Roughly, it consists of extracting a subtree, replacing it with a trace ε or deleting its phonetic material in the original place. The extracted subtree and the result of deleting it in the original tree become sisters with a new root node as mother.

For more details, see (Stabler, 1997).

6.2.3 Finite-Copying LFG

Lexical Functional Grammar (LFG) (Kaplan and Bresnan, 1982) is a grammar formalism that distinguishes between different structural levels. For a sentence, we have a *constituent structure (c-structure)* that is a non-transformational context-free derivation tree. In addition, the grammar defines a second level of description, the *functional structure (f-structure)* that represents grammatical functions and predicate-argument relations. F-structures are represented with feature structures. Each node in the c-structure is linked to exactly one f-structure. See Fig. 6.10 for an example. In order to depict the link between c- and f-structures, every node in the c-structure carries the name of its f-structure as a subscript.

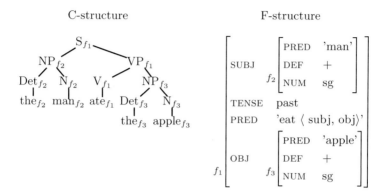

Fig. 6.10. C-structure and f-structure in LFG

In the grammar, c-structures are described with standard phrase structure rules, i.e., with context-free rewriting rules, such as S → NP VP and NP → Det N. These rules are equipped with information about how the mother node (left-hand side) f-structure and the f-structures of the daughter nodes (right-hand side) are related. For a given node, the symbols ↑ and ↓ refer to the f-structures of the mother node and of the node itself. Figure 6.11 shows some LFG rewriting rules equipped with f-structure equations that yield structures as in Fig. 6.10.

$$S \rightarrow \underset{(\uparrow \text{SUBJ}) = \downarrow}{\text{NP}} \quad \underset{\uparrow = \downarrow}{\text{VP}}$$

$$NP \rightarrow \underset{\uparrow = \downarrow}{\text{Det}} \quad \underset{\uparrow = \downarrow}{\text{N}}$$

$$VP \rightarrow \underset{\uparrow = \downarrow}{\text{V}} \quad \underset{(\uparrow \text{OBJ}) = \downarrow}{\text{NP}}$$

Fig. 6.11. Linking of c-structure and f-structure in LFG

Depending on the type of f-structure equations in a grammar, one obtains more or less restricted types of LFG. Seki et al. (1993) define *finite-copying* LFGs as grammars where, roughly, in a single derivation tree, only a limited number of nodes can be linked to the same f-structure where the limit is given by a grammar constant. Seki et al. (1993) show that finite-copying LFG and MCFG are weakly equivalent.

6.3 Summary

This chapter has introduced MCFG and the equivalent LCFRS and SRCG. The underlying idea, in comparison to CFG, is to allow the yields of non-terminals to be tuples of strings instead of single strings. The rewriting rules specify how to compute the yield of the left-hand side non-terminal from the yields of the right-hand side non-terminals. Depending on the number of discontinuities we allow (i.e., depending on the arity or fan-out), we obtain a hierarchy of grammar formalisms.

MCFGs are particularly interesting since their string language class is the largest set of mildly context-sensitive string languages characterized by a grammar formalism that we know of so far. MCFG have been shown to be equivalent to set-local MCTAG, minimalist grammar and finite-copying LFG, formalisms that have been motivated by the need for certain types of linguistic descriptions in order to capture the syntax of natural languages. Furthermore, dependency treebanks and constituency treebanks with crossing branches allow us in a very natural way to extract MCFGs.

Problems

6.1. Give an MCFG for the counting language $L_4 = \{a^k b^k c^k d^k \mid k \geq 1\}$.

6.2. Consider the MCFG given by the following clauses (in SRCG notation):
$S(XYZ) \to A(Y)B(X,Z)$
$A(aX) \to A(X)$ $A(a) \to \varepsilon$
$B(bX, bYb) \to B(X,Y)$ $B(\varepsilon, \varepsilon) \to \varepsilon$

1. Give the sets $yield(A)$ and $yield(B)$.
2. What is the string language generated by the grammar?
3. Given a word $w = abbb$, what is the set $r\text{-}yield(B)$ with respect to w?

6.3. What are the languages generated by the following LCFRSs/simple RCGs?

1. $N = \{S, A, B\}$, start symbol S, $T = \{a, b, c, d\}$ and rules
$S(XYZU) \to A(X,Z)B(Y,U)$ $A(aXb, aYb) \to A(X,Y)$ $A(\varepsilon, \varepsilon) \to \varepsilon$
$B(cXd, cYd) \to B(X,Y)$ $B(\varepsilon, \varepsilon) \to \varepsilon$
2. $N = \{S, A\}$, start symbol S, $T = \{a, b\}$ and rules
$S(XY) \to A(XY)$ $A(aX, bY) \to A(X,Y)$
$A(X,Y) \to A(Y,X)$ $A(\varepsilon, \varepsilon) \to \varepsilon$

6.4. Consider again the second simple RCG from Problem 6.3. Take the input word $w = abba$.

1. What are the instantiations of $A(aX, bY) \to A(X, Y)$ with respect to w under the assumption that the two components of A are never overlapping and have equal length?
2. Give the simple RCG derivation of w, i.e., the derivation $S(\langle 0, 4\rangle) \overset{*}{\Rightarrow} \varepsilon$ where each step consists of replacing the lhs of an instantiated clause with its rhs.

6.5. Show that for every $k > 0$, the language $\{w^{2k+1} \,|\, w \in \{a, b\}^*\}$ is not a k-MCFL.

6.6. Give the language generated by the following simple RCG and give the derivation tree for a string of length 9.
S-REL(XYZ) →VP-REL(X, Z)N-SUBJ(Y)
VP-REL(X, YZ) →NP-REL(X, Z)V(Y)
NP-REL(X,a copy of Y) →NP-REL(X, Y)
NP-REL(X,a picture of Y) →NP-REL(X, Y)
N-SUBJ(Peter) → ε
V(painted) → ε
NP-REL(whom, ε) → ε

7
Parsing MCFG, LCFRS and Simple RCG

7.1 CYK Parsing of MCFG

In this section, we present different non-directional bottom-up parsing algorithms for MCFG. The algorithms are described in (Seki et al., 1991; Ljunglöf, 2004; Burden and Ljunglöf, 2005).

7.1.1 The Basic Algorithm

We start with the basic CYK algorithm presented in (Seki et al., 1991). The idea is roughly that once all predicates in the right-hand side of a rule have been found, we can complete a left-hand side. We process the input from left to right while, for every index i reached so far (i.e., we have seen the input up to position i), we compute all tuples in the yield of any predicate A whose rightmost component ends at position i. For the computation of these tuples, we start with the terminating rules and obtain then further predicates and yields by moving from completed right-hand sides to completed left-hand sides. The input word w is in the language if and only if S with range vector $\langle\langle 0, n \rangle\rangle$ is in the final set of parsing results.

We can describe this algorithm using deduction rules. Seki et al. (1991) give only a pseudo-code representation that shows also the order in which to compute the different yields of the predicates.

Our items describe a predicate with its yield. Therefore they have the form

$$[A, \rho]$$

with $A \in N$; ρ is a $dim(A)$-dimensional simple range vector in w.

While explaining the algorithm, we will illustrate the different steps with the trace for parsing *ababab* with the grammar from Fig. 6.1, repeated in Fig. 7.1. This trace is shown in Fig. 7.2.

The initial items are obtained from the terminating rules, i.e., the rules with no predicates in the right-hand side. For a rule $A \to f[\,]$, if we can find a

Rewriting rules:

$$S \to f_1[A] \quad A \to f_2[A] \quad A \to f_3[A] \quad A \to f_4[\,] \quad A \to f_5[\,]$$

Operations:

$$f_1[\langle X,Y,Z\rangle] = \langle XYZ\rangle \quad f_2[\langle X,Y,Z\rangle] = \langle aX,aY,aZ\rangle \quad f_4[\,] = \langle a,a,a\rangle$$
$$f_3[\langle X,Y,Z\rangle] = \langle bX,bY,bZ\rangle \quad f_5[\,] = \langle b,b,b\rangle$$

Fig. 7.1. An MCFG for $\{www \,|\, w \in \{a,b\}^+\}$

simple range vector ρ over the input w such that the denotation of this vector in w (i.e., the vector of substrings of w corresponding to the ranges) is $f()$, then this range vector is in the yield of A.

Axioms: $\dfrac{}{[A,\rho]} \quad A \to f[\,], f() = \rho(w)$

For an example, see the first five items in the trace in Fig. 7.2. Looking at these items, we can already see an inconvenience of the definition of MCFGs, namely that they are not ordered, i.e., that the order of the components of a tuple is not necessarily their order in the input string. Of course, from looking at our sample grammar, we can see that A is an ordered predicate. Based on this knowledge, we could exclude the second and third items. We will see later that the property to be ordered does not restrict the expressive power, i.e., for a given MCFG, we can find an equivalent ordered MCFG. However, for this section, we will follow the literature and present the algorithms for unordered MCFG.

The second rule we need, **complete**, applies whenever, for a given rule, we have found appropriate range vectors for all predicates of the right-hand side. Appropriate means that their combination according to the function specified in the rule is defined, i.e., all required concatenations are possible. Then we can compute a range vector in the yield of the left-hand side predicate.

Complete: $\dfrac{[A_1,\rho_1],\ldots,[A_m,\rho_m]}{[A,\rho]} \quad \begin{array}{l} A \to f[A_1,\ldots,A_m], \\ \rho \in f[\rho_1,\ldots,\rho_m] \end{array}$

As an example for the application of **complete**, see the items 6–8 in Fig. 7.2.

The goal item is $[S, \langle\langle 0,n\rangle\rangle]$. Item 8 in our example is a goal item.

As in the CFG CYK case, we can compute the items in the order of the rightmost yield position while, each time, starting with the application of the rule **axiom** and then doing all possible **complete** operations. We define the rightmost position of a range vector $\rho = \langle\langle l_1,r_1\rangle,\ldots,\langle l_k,r_k\rangle\rangle$ as $max\{r_1,\ldots,r_k\}$.

7.1 CYK Parsing of MCFG   133

	Item	Rule
1	$[A, \langle\langle 0,1\rangle, \langle 2,3\rangle, \langle 4,5\rangle\rangle]$	axiom with $A \to f_4[\,]$
2	$[A, \langle\langle 0,1\rangle, \langle 4,5\rangle, \langle 2,3\rangle\rangle]$	axiom with $A \to f_4[\,]$
3	$[A, \langle\langle 2,3\rangle, \langle 0,1\rangle, \langle 4,5\rangle\rangle]$	axiom with $A \to f_4[\,]$
	...	
4	$[A, \langle\langle 1,2\rangle, \langle 3,4\rangle, \langle 5,6\rangle\rangle]$	axiom with $A \to f_5[\,]$
5	$[A, \langle\langle 1,2\rangle, \langle 5,6\rangle, \langle 3,4\rangle\rangle]$	axiom with $A \to f_5[\,]$
	...	
6	$[A, \langle\langle 0,2\rangle, \langle 2,4\rangle, \langle 4,6\rangle\rangle]$	complete, with 4 and $A \to f_2[A]$
7	$[A, \langle\langle 0,2\rangle, \langle 4,6\rangle, \langle 2,4\rangle\rangle]$	complete, with 5 and $A \to f_2[A]$
	...	
8	$[S, \langle\langle 0,6\rangle\rangle]$	complete, with 6 and $S \to f_1[A]$

Fig. 7.2. Parse of the input *ababab* with the basic CYK algorithm

for all $i = 0$ **to** n **do**
    apply all axiom rules with rightmost position i and add the new items to $\mathcal{C}$ and $\mathcal{A}$
    repeat
        for every item x in $\mathcal{A}$ **do**
            for every complete step with x and items from $\mathcal{C}$ as antecedent items and y as consequent **do**
                if $y \notin \mathcal{C}$ **then**
                    add y to $\mathcal{C}$ and $\mathcal{A}$
                end if
            end for
            remove x from $\mathcal{A}$
        end for
    until $\mathcal{A} = \emptyset$
    if $[S, \langle\langle 0, n\rangle\rangle] \in \mathcal{C}$ **then**
        return true
    end if
end for

Fig. 7.3. Pseudo-code of the basic CYK algorithm

We can then implement the parser using a chart $\mathcal{C}$ and an agenda $\mathcal{A}$. When processing position i, the agenda contains all new items with rightmost index i that still need to be processed for possible applications of **complete**. This algorithm is sketched in Fig. 7.3.

The algorithm in Fig. 7.3 is a recognizer. As usual, we can extend it to a parser by adding backpointers to the items we store in the chart: In every **complete** step, we add a pointer from the consequent item to the set of antecedent items. Then the final chart together with these backpointers represents the parse forest. The single parse trees can be obtained by following the backpointers, starting from the goal item. In case of ambiguities there might be more than one backpointer for a given item.

$$S \to f_1[A] := \langle A^{(1)} A^{(2)} A^{(3)} \rangle$$
$$A \to f_2[A] := \langle aA^{(1)}, aA^{(2)}, aA^{(3)} \rangle$$
$$A \to f_3[A] := \langle bA^{(1)}, bA^{(2)}, bA^{(3)} \rangle$$
$$A \to f_4[\,] := \langle a, a, a \rangle$$
$$A \to f_5[\,] := \langle b, b, b \rangle$$

Fig. 7.4. The MCFG from Fig. 7.1 with range constraint vectors

An obvious disadvantage of this basic CYK algorithm is that, in order to perform a **complete**, one has to find items for all arguments of a right-hand side of a rule at the same time.

7.1.2 The Naïve Algorithm

As a first strategy for binarization of the CYK algorithm, Burden and Ljunglöf (2005) propose moving a dot through the right-hand side of the rules. They call this the *naïve algorithm* since it is rather immediate when applying the techniques known from CFGs to MCFG parsing. But, as we will see, there are more efficient ways of binarizing the parsing operations.

The items of this algorithm have to encode dotted rules and all range vectors for the already recognized predicates of the right-hand side.

We know that the arguments of the right-hand side predicates are taken as single components of the arguments of the left-hand side. We refer to the kth component of the ith element of the right-hand side as $A_i^{(k)}$. Then we can pair the rewriting rules with an explicit recipe of how to compute the yield of the left-hand side from the yields of the right-hand side predicates as follows:

$$A_0 \to f[A_1, \ldots, A_n] := \langle x_1, \ldots, x_k \rangle$$

where $k = dim(A_0)$, $x_i \in (T \cup \{A^{(m)} \mid A \in \{A_1, \ldots, A_n\}, 1 \leq m \leq dim(A)\})^*$. The vector $\mathbf{x} = \langle x_1, \ldots, x_k \rangle$ is called a *range constraint vector*.

As an example, consider again the MCFG for the double copy language from Fig. 7.1. With the encoding of the mcf-functions as a range constraint vector, we obtain the rules in Fig. 7.4. The second rule for example tells us that when applying f_2 to a triple in the yield of A, we obtain a new triple in the yield of A whose ith component ($1 \leq i \leq 3$) is a terminal a concatenated with the ith component of the first triple.

The naïve algorithm starts by guessing the ranges corresponding to the terminals in the range constraint vector of a rule. Later, when completing the right-hand side predicates one by one, the ranges corresponding to the component symbols $A^{(i)}$ will be found as well.

We now define the possible guesses for the terminals of a range constraint vector. Given a w, we can map the terminal symbols to appropriate ranges in w. Appropriate means that the yield of the range contains the terminal and that all concatenations are well defined.

7.1 CYK Parsing of MCFG

	Item	Rule
1	$[S \to f_1[\bullet A] := \langle A^{(1)} A^{(2)} A^{(3)}\rangle]]$	predict
2	$[A \to f_2[\bullet A] := \langle \langle 0,1\rangle A^{(1)}, \langle 2,3\rangle A^{(2)}, \langle 4,5\rangle A^{(3)}\rangle]$	predict
3	$[A \to f_2[\bullet A] := \langle \langle 0,1\rangle A^{(1)}, \langle 4,5\rangle A^{(2)}, \langle 2,3\rangle A^{(3)}\rangle]$	predict
	...	
4	$[A \to f_3[\bullet A] := \langle \langle 1,2\rangle A^{(1)}, \langle 3,4\rangle A^{(2)}, \langle 5,6\rangle A^{(3)}\rangle]$	predict
	...	
5	$[A \to f_5[\bullet] := \langle \langle 1,2\rangle, \langle 3,4\rangle, \langle 5,6\rangle\rangle]$	predict
6	$[A, \langle\langle 1,2\rangle, \langle 3,4\rangle, \langle 5,6\rangle\rangle]$	convert 5
7	$[A \to f_2[A\bullet] := \langle\langle 0,2\rangle, \langle 2,4\rangle, \langle 4,6\rangle\rangle]$	complete 2 with 6
8	$[A, \langle\langle 0,2\rangle, \langle 2,4\rangle, \langle 4,6\rangle\rangle]$	convert 7
9	$[S \to f_1[A\bullet] := \langle\langle 0,6\rangle\rangle]]$	complete 1 with 8
10	$[S, \langle\langle 0,6\rangle\rangle]]$	convert 9

Fig. 7.5. Parse of the input *ababab* with the naïve CYK algorithm

Definition 7.1. *Let* **x** *be a range constraint vector and x be a component of* **x***. We define* $\mathbf{x}^w$ *as follows:*

- *if* $x \in T^*$, *then* $\langle x \rangle^w = \{\langle l, r\rangle \mid \langle l, r\rangle(w) = x\}$
- *if* $x = yVz$ *with* $V = A^{(m)}$, *then* $\langle x \rangle^w = \{\alpha_1 A^{(m)} \alpha_2 \mid \alpha_1 \in \langle y \rangle^w, \alpha_2 \in \langle z \rangle^w\}$.

$\mathbf{x}^w$ *is then obtained by applying this to all components of* **x** *such that the ranges occurring in the result are all pairwise non-overlapping.*

We use two different types of items in our algorithm, namely active items containing a dotted rule and passive items. The latter have the same form $[A, \rho]$ as the items from the basic CYK algorithm. They can be obtained once an entire right-hand side has been recognized.

The active items have the form

$$[A_0 \to f[\mathbf{A} \bullet \mathbf{A}']; \phi]$$

where the components of ϕ are concatenations of ranges and variables $A^{(i)}$.

As already explained, we start by predicting possible ranges for the terminals in the range constraint vectors of the rules of our grammar. This is a completely blind prediction; any rule is predicted as being potentially used.

Predict: $\dfrac{}{[A \to f[\bullet\mathbf{B}]; \phi]}$ $A \to f[\mathbf{B}] := \mathbf{x}$ and $\phi \in \mathbf{x}^w$

As an example consider the items 1–5 in Fig. 7.5. The trace shows only a part of the items generated by the **predict** rule. It is obvious from this example that a large number of items is predicted that never will be used. One reason for this is again that in general, MCFGs are not ordered. Therefore items such as 3 are predicted as well where the second component starts at position 4 while the third component starts at position 2. The second reason is of course the completely unconstrained prediction strategy. All rules where we can find ranges for the terminals occurring in the rule are predicted as being potentially used. This can be ameliorated with more intelligent prediction strategies such as top-down prediction (Earley) or left-corner prediction. We will come back to this issue in Section 7.1.5.

The rule **convert** turns a completely recognized active item into a passive item.

Convert: $\dfrac{[A \to f[\mathbf{B}\bullet]; \phi]}{[A; \phi]}$

An example is item 6 in our trace that is obtained from the completely recognized item 5.

The **complete** rule moves the dot over a non-terminal if a corresponding passive item exists. Corresponding means that the variables $A^{(i)}$ can be replaced with the ranges from the passive items and the ranges in the result are all well defined and pairwise non-overlapping.

Complete: $\dfrac{[A \to f[\mathbf{B} \bullet B_k \mathbf{B}']; \phi], [B_k; \psi]}{[A \to f[\mathbf{B} B_k \bullet \mathbf{B}']; \phi']}$ $\quad \phi' = \phi[B_k/\psi]$

Here, $\phi[B_k/\psi]$ means replacing every occurrence of $B_k^{(i)}$ in ϕ with $\psi(i)$ for all i, $1 \leq i \leq dim(B_k)$.

An example is item 7 in Fig.7.5, which is obtained by moving the dot in item 1 over the A predicate. This operation is licensed by the existence of the passive item 6.

This algorithm is better than the basic one since in its **complete** operations, it combines only one completed predicate with an active item. However, the completed predicate has $dim(B_k)$ ranges. Therefore, even this more binarized complete operation combines $2dim(B_k)$ range boundaries (for the $dim(B_k)$ arguments of the passive items) with the active item, each of the boundaries having a value between 0 and n. This can only be avoided if we do not combine all the components of a passive items at once with an active item. The active algorithm presented in the next section is a first strategy in this direction.

7.1.3 The Active Algorithm

The idea of the *active algorithm* from Burden and Ljunglöf (2005) is to use the dot to traverse the range constraint vector ϕ. This means that we process the different parts of the components of the yield of the left-hand side from left to right. Moving the dot over a terminal means scanning the next input symbol. Moving the dot over a variable $A^{(i)}$ means that there is an A-predicate whose ith component licenses this move. While moving the dot through the range constraint vector, we replace terminals and component variables $A^{(i)}$ with appropriate ranges.

The passive items are of the form $[A, \rho]$ as before. The active items contain a rule with its dotted range constraint vector. Furthermore, every terminal and every component variable to the left of the dot has been replaced with its range. Finally, we have to keep track of the ranges found for the component variables since, when finding further components of a predicate, we have to check whether they match with the components we have already seen. Therefore active items have the form

$$[A \to f[\mathbf{B}]; (\phi, \rho \bullet x, \psi); \Gamma]$$

where ϕ is a list of ranges, ρ is a range, x contains terminals and component variables, and ψ is a vector of words of terminals and component variables. Γ encodes the bindings already found for the component variables of the clause; it contains range vectors for the predicates in $\mathbf{B}$ if these are found; otherwise it contains the variables $B_k^{(i)}$ for these ranges.

Such an active item indicates that the first arguments of A have been recognized yielding the ranges ϕ and the next argument is recognized up to the position marked by the dot so far yielding ρ. The rest of this argument (range constraints x) and the following arguments (range constraints ψ) are still waiting for completion.

The operation **predict** introduces a new rule with the dot on the left of its range constraint vector.

Predict: $\dfrac{}{[A \to f[\mathbf{B}]; (\bullet x, \Psi); \Gamma_\mathbf{B}]}$ $\quad A \to f[\mathbf{B}] := (x, \Psi)$

We define that $\Gamma_\mathbf{B}$ contains the range variables for the vector $\mathbf{B}$.

See the first 5 items in Fig. 7.6 for examples of **predict**. Note that, in contrast to the naïve algorithm, we do not guess the ranges corresponding to the terminals during prediction. Instead, they are determined by the **scan** operation that moves the dot over a terminal while replacing the terminal with its range.

Scan: $\dfrac{[A \to f[\mathbf{B}]; (\Phi, \alpha \bullet ax, \Psi); \Gamma]}{[A \to f[\mathbf{B}]; \Phi, \alpha \cdot \langle l, r \rangle \bullet x, \Psi); \Gamma]}$ $\quad \langle l, r \rangle(w) = a$

Examples are the items 6 and 7 in Fig. 7.6, which are both obtained by scanning an a.

Once the dot has reached the end of a component of the left-hand side yield, we can move the dot to the next component. This is done by the **complete** operation.

Complete: $\dfrac{[A \to f[\mathbf{B}]; (\Phi, \alpha \bullet, x, \Psi); \Gamma]}{[A \to f[\mathbf{B}]; (\Phi, \alpha, \bullet x, \Psi); \Gamma]}$

Examples of items obtained from **complete** are for instance the items 9 and 12 in Fig. 7.6.

	Item	Rule
1	$[S \to f_1[A] := \langle \bullet A^{(1)} A^{(2)} A^{(3)} \rangle, \langle \langle A^{(1)}, A^{(2)}, A^{(3)} \rangle \rangle]$	predict
2	$[A \to f_2[A] := \langle \bullet a A^{(1)}, a A^{(2)}, a A^{(3)} \rangle, \langle \langle A^{(1)}, A^{(2)}, A^{(3)} \rangle \rangle]$	predict
3	$[A \to f_3[A] := \langle \bullet b A^{(1)}, b A^{(2)}, b A^{(3)} \rangle, \langle \langle A^{(1)}, A^{(2)}, A^{(3)} \rangle \rangle]$	predict
4	$[A \to f_4[\,] := \langle \bullet a, a, a \rangle, \langle\,\rangle]$	predict
5	$[A \to f_5[\,] := \langle \bullet b, b, b \rangle, \langle\,\rangle]$	predict
6	$[A \to f_2[A] := \langle \langle 0,1 \rangle \bullet A^{(1)}, a A^{(2)}, a A^{(3)} \rangle, \langle \langle A^{(1)}, A^{(2)}, A^{(3)} \rangle \rangle]$	scan a from 2
7	$[A \to f_2[A] := \langle \langle 2,3 \rangle \bullet A^{(1)}, a A^{(2)}, a A^{(3)} \rangle, \langle \langle A^{(1)}, A^{(2)}, A^{(3)} \rangle \rangle]$	scan a from 2
	...	
8	$[A \to f_4[\,] := \langle \langle 0,1 \rangle \bullet, a, a \rangle, \langle\,\rangle]$	scan a from 4
	...	
9	$[A \to f_4[\,] := \langle \langle 0,1 \rangle, \bullet a, a \rangle, \langle\,\rangle]$	compl. 8
10	$[A \to f_4[\,] := \langle \langle 0,1 \rangle, \langle 2,3 \rangle \bullet, a \rangle, \langle\,\rangle]$	scan from 9
	...	
11	$[A \to f_5[\,] := \langle \langle 1,2 \rangle \bullet, b, b \rangle, \langle\,\rangle]$	scan from 5
12	$[A \to f_5[\,] := \langle \langle 1,2 \rangle, \bullet b, b \rangle, \langle\,\rangle]$	compl. 11
	...	
13	$[A \to f_5[\,] := \langle \langle 1,2 \rangle, \langle 3,4 \rangle, \langle 5,6 \rangle \bullet \rangle, \langle\,\rangle]$	...
14	$[A, \langle \langle 1,2 \rangle, \langle 3,4 \rangle, \langle 5,6 \rangle \rangle]$	convert 13
15	$[A \to f_2[A] := \langle \langle 0,2 \rangle \bullet, a A^{(2)}, a A^{(3)} \rangle, \langle \langle \langle 1,2 \rangle, A^{(2)}, A^{(3)} \rangle \rangle]$	combine 6 with 14
	...	
16	$[A \to f_2[A] := \langle \langle 0,2 \rangle, \langle 2,3 \rangle \bullet A^{(2)}, a A^{(3)} \rangle, \langle \langle \langle 1,2 \rangle, A^{(2)}, A^{(3)} \rangle \rangle]$	...
17	$[A \to f_2[A] := \langle \langle 0,2 \rangle, \langle 2,4 \rangle \bullet, a A^{(3)} \rangle, \langle \langle \langle 1,2 \rangle, \langle 3,4 \rangle, A^{(3)} \rangle \rangle]$	combine 16 with 14
	...	
18	$[A, \langle \langle 0,2 \rangle, \langle 2,4 \rangle, \langle 4,6 \rangle \rangle]$	
19	$[S \to f_1[A] := \langle \langle 0,2 \rangle \bullet A^{(2)} A^{(3)} \rangle, \langle \langle \langle 0,2 \rangle, A^{(2)}, A^{(3)} \rangle \rangle]$	compl. 1 with 18
20	$[S \to f_1[A] := \langle \langle 0,4 \rangle \bullet A^{(3)} \rangle, \langle \langle \langle 0,2 \rangle, \langle 2,4 \rangle, A^{(3)} \rangle \rangle]$	compl. 19 with 18
21	$[S \to f_1[A] := \langle \langle 0,6 \rangle \bullet \rangle, \langle \langle \langle 0,2 \rangle, \langle 2,4 \rangle, \langle 4,6 \rangle \rangle \rangle]$	compl. 20 with 18
22	$[S, \langle \langle 0,6 \rangle \rangle]$	convert 21

Fig. 7.6. Parse of the input *ababab* with the active CYK algorithm

Once we reach the end of the last component of the left-hand side yield, we can turn our active item into a passive one by applying the operation **convert**.

Convert: $\dfrac{[A \to f[\mathbf{B}]; (\Phi, \alpha \bullet), \mathbf{\Gamma}]}{[A; (\Phi, \alpha)]}$

This leads for example to item 14 in our sample trace.

The most important operation in this algorithm is the **combine** operation that moves the dot over a component variable if a corresponding passive item has been found. In this case, the range of the component variable is stored in the vector Γ. Furthermore, as a side condition, the components of the right-hand side predicate whose ranges have been found in previous steps (i.e., who are already present in Γ) must be the same ranges as the corresponding components of the passive item.

Combine: $\dfrac{[A \to f[\mathbf{B}]; (\Phi, \alpha \bullet B_k^{(i)} x, \Psi), \mathbf{\Gamma}], [B_k; \boldsymbol{\rho}]}{[A \to f[\mathbf{B}]; (\Phi, \alpha \cdot \boldsymbol{\rho}(i) \bullet x, \Psi); \mathbf{\Gamma'}]}$ $\quad \mathbf{\Gamma}(k)$ compatible with $\boldsymbol{\rho}, \mathbf{\Gamma'} = \mathbf{\Gamma}(k, i := \boldsymbol{\rho}(i))$

Here the term *compatible* means that for every $1 \leq i \leq dim(B_k)$, either $\mathbf{\Gamma}(k)(i) = \boldsymbol{\rho}(i)$ or $\mathbf{\Gamma}(k)(i) = B_k^{(i)}$.

The item 15 is a first example for applying this operation.

The goal item is again $[S, \langle\langle 0, n \rangle\rangle]$, which is item 22 in our trace.

A problem with this algorithm is that, even though in the combine operation we are moving the dot only over component variables $B_k^{(i)}$, in order to do so, we need an entirely recognized B_k predicate. However, since we need only the ith component of this daughter predicate, we could just as well use an active B_k item with a completed ith component to license the combination. This idea leads to the incremental algorithm in (Burden and Ljunglöf, 2005) that will be described in the next section.

7.1.4 The Incremental Algorithm

The idea of the incremental algorithm is to process the input from left to right while, for every input position i, calculating all possible active and passive items that span a part of the input with end position i. In particular, instead of entirely completing a predicate before combining it with a higher predicate, we can use its jth component as soon as it is finished without having to wait for all the other components.

In the sample trace for the active item, we need for instance item 18 (which ends at position 6) in order to obtain item 19 (which ends at position 2). This is no longer the case in the incremental algorithm. As soon as we have seen the first component of the daughter A predicate (this was the case in item 15), we can use it to move the dot in the mother predicate, i.e., with item 15, we can immediately obtain item 19.

A difficulty with the general MCFG definition is, as already mentioned, that these grammars are not ordered. Consequently, for a range vector $\boldsymbol{\rho} = \langle\langle l_1, r_1\rangle, \ldots, \langle l_k, r_k\rangle\rangle$ in the yield of a predicate A it is not necessarily the case that $r_i \leq l_{i+1}$ for all $1 \leq i < k$. Therefore, when processing the components of a left-hand side predicate from left to right with respect to the input w, we do not necessarily process them from left to right with respect to the order in the rule.

In order to be able to process the left-hand side components in an order different from the one in the rule, we now use explicit features $R_1, \ldots, R_{dim(A)}$ for the range constraints of the $dim(A)$ ranges of a predicate A. This way, the argument index is no longer given by the position in the range constraint vector and we can process the arguments in any order.

For the incremental algorithm we use only active items of the form

$$[A \to f[\mathbf{B}]; (\phi, R_i = \rho \bullet x, \psi); \mathbf{\Gamma}]$$

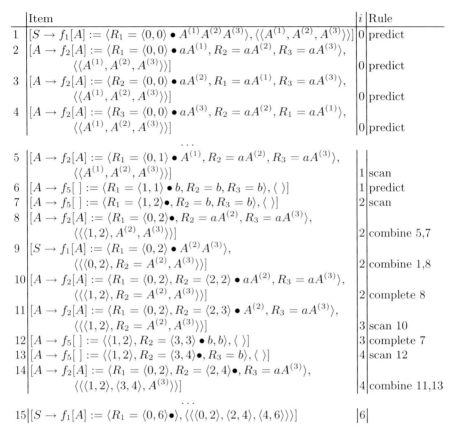

Fig. 7.7. Parse of the input *ababab* with the incremental CYK algorithm

that are defined as in the active algorithm except for the explicit names R_i of the component range constraints. Furthermore, the order in the range constraint vectors need not be the same as in the original rule in the grammar.

As before, the **predict** operation introduces a new rule with the dot on the left of one of the components of the left-hand side. In contrast to the active algorithm, we now guess the starting index of this component by having the dot preceded by a corresponding range.

Predict: $\dfrac{}{[A \to f[\mathbf{B}]; (R_i = \langle k, k \rangle \bullet x, \Psi_1, \Psi_2); \mathbf{\Gamma_B}]}$ $\begin{array}{l} A \to f[\mathbf{B}'] := (\Psi_1, x, \Psi_2) \\ \text{with } x \text{ the } i\text{th element,} \\ 1 \leq i \leq dim(A), \\ 1 \leq k \leq n \end{array}$

Here, $\mathbf{\Gamma_B}$ contains again the range variables for the vector $\mathbf{B}$.

A sample parse with this algorithm is shown in Fig. 7.7 (*i* gives the current input position). We restrict ourselves to the successful items. The first four items arise from the **predict** operation. Here, again, the disadvantage of having a potentially unordered MCFG is visible: Any of the three components of A could be the one starting at position 0.

Scan moves the dot over a terminal. A result of this operation is for example item 3 in Fig. 7.7.

Scan: $\dfrac{[A \to f[\mathbf{B}]; (\Phi, R_i = \langle l, r \rangle \bullet ax, \Psi); \Gamma]}{[A \to f[\mathbf{B}]; (\Phi, R_i = \langle l, r+1 \rangle \bullet x, \Psi); \Gamma]}$ $\quad \langle r, r+1 \rangle(w) = a$

The **combine** operation moves the dot over a component variable $B_k^{(i)}$ if there is an active B_k item whose ith component has been completed and whose other completed components are compatible with the components seen so far in the item with B_k in the right-hand side.

Combine: $\dfrac{[A \to f[\mathbf{B}]; (\Phi_1, R_j = \alpha \bullet B_k^{(i)} x, \Psi_1), \Gamma]\quad [B_k \to g[\mathbf{C}]; (\Phi_2, R_i = \beta\bullet, \Psi_2), \Gamma_\mathbf{C}]}{[A \to f[\mathbf{B}]; (\Phi_1, R_j = \alpha \cdot \beta \bullet x, \Psi_1); \Gamma(k, i := \beta)]}$ $\quad \begin{array}{l}\Gamma(k) \text{ compatible}\\ \text{with } (\Phi_2)\end{array}$

Here, the term "compatible" means that for every $1 \leq h \leq dim(B_k)$, if $R_h = \alpha_h \in (\Phi_2)$, then $\Gamma(k)(h) = \alpha_h$.

The first application of **combine** in our trace in Fig. 7.7 leads to item 8.

The **complete** operation, as before, moves a dot that is at the end of a component to another component. Again, as in the **predict** operation, it guesses the starting position of this other component.

Complete: $\dfrac{[A \to f[\mathbf{B}]; (\Phi, R_i = \langle l_i, r_i \rangle\bullet, \Psi_1, R_j = x, \Psi_2); \Gamma]}{[A \to f[\mathbf{B}]; (\Phi, R_i = \alpha, r_j = \langle k, k \rangle \bullet x, \Psi_1, \Psi_2); \Gamma]}$ $\quad r_i \leq k \leq n$

An application of **complete** leads for example to item 10.

Every item of the form $[S \to f[\mathbf{A}] := \langle R_1 = \langle 0, n \rangle\bullet\rangle, \Gamma]$ is a goal item. In our example, item 15 is a goal item.

7.1.5 Prediction Strategies

A problem of these algorithms is that, as in the CYK case for CFG, the predictions are blind and consequently, we predict and then compute a lot of partial results that are actually not reachable given the predicates we are looking for and the predicates we have already found.

As mentioned in (Burden and Ljunglöf, 2005), this problem can be avoided by replacing the unrestricted prediction with a restricted prediction that takes the parsing context into account. There are mainly two possibilities, namely a top-down restricted prediction which amounts to an Earley parsing strategy, or a left-corner restricted prediction.

More concretely, in the first case, a $A \to f[\mathbf{B}]$ with a dot left of $R_i = \alpha$ is only predicted (by **predict** or **complete**) if there is another item looking for $A^{(i)}$. This leads to an Earley variant of the incremental parser. See the solution of Problem 7.1 for the modified deduction rules.

The second strategy amounts to checking the existence of a left corner when predicting, i.e., $A \to f[\mathbf{B}]$ with a dot left of $R_i = \alpha$ is only predicted if either the first symbol in α is the next terminal in the input or there is an item that has found the first symbol in α.

Besides the extension of the incremental algorithm to an Earley parser (solution of Problem 7.1), another technique to do Earley parsing for MCFG has been proposed in (Kanazawa, 2008). Kanazawa considers the MCFG as a Datalog program and uses magic-sets rewriting to obtain a prefix valid Earley parser.

7.2 Simplifying Simple RCGs

So far, we have assumed unconstrained MCFGs. However, as in the case of CFGs, before parsing, we can eliminate useless symbols and empty arguments. Furthermore, we can order the grammar and even binarize the rules, i.e., transform the MCFG into some kind of Chomsky Normal Form. This section explains the different transformations. We will notate the grammars as SRCGs since we have the impression that this notation is easier to read. Furthermore, some of the transformations given below have been introduced for simple RCGs.

7.2.1 Eliminating Useless Rules

Boullier (1998b) shows a range of useful properties of simple RCG that can help to make parsing easier. First, Boullier defines rules that cannot be used in reductions $S(\langle 0, n \rangle) \overset{*}{\Rightarrow} \varepsilon$ for any $w \in T^*$ as *useless*. For a simple RCG, there exists an equivalent simple RCG that does not contain useless rules.

The removal of the useless rules can be done in the same way as in the CFG case (Hopcroft and Ullman, 1979):

1. All rules need to be eliminated that cannot lead to a terminal sequence. This can be done recursively: Starting from the terminating rules and following the rules from right to left, the set of all non-terminals leading to terminals can be computed recursively.
   We can characterize this set N_T with the following deduction rules:

$$\frac{}{[A]} \; A(\boldsymbol{\alpha}) \to \varepsilon \in P \qquad \frac{[A_1], \ldots, [A_m]}{[A]} \; A(\boldsymbol{\alpha}) \to A_1(\boldsymbol{\alpha_1}) \ldots A_m(\boldsymbol{\alpha_m}) \in P$$

   All rules that contain non-terminals in their right-hand side that are not in this set are eliminated.

Original simple RCG rules:
$S(XY) \to A(X,Y)$, $A(a, \varepsilon) \to \varepsilon$, $A(\varepsilon, a) \to \varepsilon$, $A(a, b) \to \varepsilon$

Set of pairs characterizing possibilities for ε-components:
$N_\varepsilon = \{(S, 1), (A, 10), (A, 01), (A, 11)\}$

Rules after ε-elimination:
$S'(X) \to S^1(X)$,
$S^1(X) \to A^{10}(X)$, $A^{10}(a) \to \varepsilon$,
$S^1(X) \to A^{01}(X)$, $A^{01}(b) \to \varepsilon$,
$S^1(XY) \to A^{11}(X, Y)$, $A^{11}(a, b) \to \varepsilon$

Fig. 7.8. Elimination of ε-rules in a simple RCG

2. In the resulting simple RCG, the unreachable rules need to be eliminated. This is done starting from all S-rules and moving from left-hand sides to right-hand sides. If the right-hand side contains a predicate A, then all A-rules are reachable. Each time, the rules for the predicates in a right-hand side are added.
We can characterize the set N_S of non-terminals reachable from S with the following deduction rules:

$$\frac{}{[S]} \qquad \frac{[A]}{[A_1], \ldots, [A_m]} \quad A(\boldsymbol{\alpha}) \to A_1(\boldsymbol{\alpha_1}) \ldots A_m(\boldsymbol{\alpha_m}) \in P$$

Rules whose left-hand side predicate is not in this set are eliminated.

7.2.2 Eliminating ε-Rules

A second useful transformation given in (Boullier, 1998b) and already mentioned in (Seki et al., 1991) is the elimination of ε-rules that is possible in a way similar to CFG. We define that a rule is an ε-rule (or ε-clause) if one of the arguments of the left-hand side is the empty string ε.

A simple RCG is ε-free if it either contains no ε-rules or there is exactly one rule $S(\varepsilon) \to \varepsilon$ and S does not appear in any of the right-hand sides of the rules in the grammar.

First, we have to compute for all predicates A, all ways to have empty ranges among the components of the yields. For this, we introduce vectors $\iota \in \{0, 1\}^{dim(A)}$ and we generate a set N_ε of pairs (A, ι) where ι signifies that it is possible for A to have a tuple τ in its yield with $\tau(i) = \varepsilon$ if $\iota(i) = 0$ and $\tau(i) \neq \varepsilon$ if $\iota(i) \neq 0$. A pair (A, ι) is written A^ι.

Take, for instance, an RCG with the rules in Fig. 7.8. In this RCG, the yield of S cannot be empty. For A, either none of the components is empty or only the first one or only the second one is empty. This would therefore lead to a set N_ε given in the figure.

The set N_ε is constructed recursively:

1. $N_\varepsilon = \emptyset$.
2. For every rule $A(x_1, \ldots, x_{dim(A)}) \to \varepsilon$, add (A, ι) to N_ε with, for all $1 \leq i \leq dim(A)$, $\iota(i) = 0$ if $x_i = \varepsilon$, else $\iota(i) = 1$.
3. Repeat until N_ε does not change any more:
   For every rule $A(x_1, \ldots, x_{dim(A)}) \to A_1(\alpha_1) \ldots A_k(\alpha_k)$ and all (A_1, ι_1), $\ldots$, $(A_k, \iota_k) \in N_\varepsilon$:
   Calculate a vector $(x'_1, \ldots, x'_{dim(A)})$ from $(x_1, \ldots, x_{dim(A)})$ by replacing every variable that is the jth variable of A_m in the right-hand side such that $\iota_m(j) = 0$ with ε.
   Then add (A, ι) to N_ε with, for all $1 \leq i \leq dim(A)$, $\iota(i) = 0$ if $x'_i = \varepsilon$, else $\iota(i) = 1$.

Now that we have the set N_ε we can obtain reduced rules from the ones in the grammar where ε-arguments are left out. Consider again our sample grammar in Fig. 7.8. The new predicate S' is mainly for the case of ε being in the language, which does not apply here. The new predicates A^{01} and A^{10} represent the former predicate A reduced to only the non-empty component. A^{11} encodes the case where none of the components is empty.

To obtain this grammar, we roughly add to the new grammar for every rule in the original grammar all reductions of that rule where components that might be empty get deleted. For example, the rule $S(XY) \to A(X, Y)$ of the original grammar together with $(A, 10) \in N_\varepsilon$ leads to the rule $S^1(X) \to A^{10}(X)$ which covers the case where the second component of A is empty and is therefore deleted. We must make sure that we do not add any $A^{0 \ldots 0}$-rules. Such predicates get entirely deleted in the right-hand sides.

More precisely, to obtain the new set of rules P_ε, we proceed as follows.

1. $P_\varepsilon = \emptyset$
2. We pick a new start symbol $S' \notin N_\varepsilon$.
   If $S^0 \in N_\varepsilon$ (i.e., $\varepsilon \in L(G)$), we add $S'(\varepsilon) \to \varepsilon$ to P_ε.
   If $S^1 \in N_\varepsilon$, we add $S'(X) \to S^1(X)$ to P_ε.
3. For every rule $A(\alpha) \to A_1(\mathbf{x}_1) \ldots A_k(\mathbf{x}_k) \in P$: add all ε-reductions of this rule to P_ε.

   The ε-reductions of $A(\alpha) \to A_1(\mathbf{x}_1) \ldots A_k(\mathbf{x}_k)$ are obtained as follows: For all combinations of $\iota_1, \ldots, \iota_k$ such that $A_i^{\iota_i} \in N_\varepsilon$ for $1 \leq i \leq k$,

(i) for all i, $1 \leq i \leq k$, replace A_i in the right-hand side with $A_i^{\iota_i}$, and for all j, $1 \leq j \leq dim(A_i)$: if $\iota_i(j) = 0$, then remove the jth component of $A_i^{\iota_i}$ from the right-hand side and delete the variable $\mathbf{x}_i(j)$ in the left-hand side. Furthermore, if $\iota_i \in 0^+$, then remove A_i with its arguments from the right-hand side.
(ii) Let $\iota \in \{0, 1\}^{dim(A)}$ be the vector with $\iota(i) = 0$ iff the ith component of A (in the left-hand side) is empty in the rule obtained from (i). If $\iota \notin 0^+$, then remove all ε-components in the left-hand side and replace A with A^ι. Add the resulting rule to the set of ε-reductions of $A(\alpha) \to A_1(\mathbf{x}_1) \ldots A_k(\mathbf{x}_k)$.

7.2.3 Ordered Simple RCG

As pointed out above, the fact that MCFGs in general are not ordered complicates parsing considerably since when using a rule in parsing, the order of the yield components of its left-hand side in the input is not necessarily the order of the components in the rule.

Villemonte de la Clergerie (2002) mentions that every simple RCG (hence, every MCFG) can be transformed into an equivalent ordered simple RCG. A proof for LCFRS, where this property is called *monotone*, is given in (Kracht, 2003). First, let us think more closely about what ordered as a grammar property means. To obtain that the order of the components of the left-hand side predicate of a rule corresponds always to their order in the input, it is enough to make sure that for every rule and every single right-hand side predicate, the order of the variables for the components of this predicate in the rule is the same as the order of these variables in the arguments of the left-hand side predicate.

Definition 7.2 (Ordered simple RCG).
A simple RCG is ordered if for every rule $A(\boldsymbol{\alpha}) \to A_1(\boldsymbol{\alpha_1}) \dots A_k(\boldsymbol{\alpha_k})$ and every $A_i(\boldsymbol{\alpha_i}) = A_i(Y_1, \dots, Y_{dim(A_i)})$ $(1 \leq i \leq k)$, the order of the components of $\boldsymbol{\alpha_i}$ in $\boldsymbol{\alpha}$ is $Y_1, \dots, Y_{dim(A_i)}$.

In the literature, the fact that for every simple RCG, there is an equivalent ordered simple RCG is taken to be obvious (Villemonte de la Clergerie, 2002). However, we will sketch the construction here. It is roughly as follows: We check for every rule whether the component order in one of the right-hand side predicates A does not correspond to the one in the left-hand side. If so, we add a new predicate that differs from A only with respect to the order of the components. We replace A in the rule with the new predicate with reordered components. Furthermore, we add a copy of every A-rule with A replaced in the left-hand side by the new predicate and reordering of the components.

For the construction, we notate the permutations of components as vectors where the ith element is the image of i. For a predicate A, id is the vector $\langle 1, 2, \dots, \dim(A) \rangle$. The vector $\langle 2, 1, 3 \rangle$ for instance specifies a permutation of three elements such that the first becomes the second, the second the first, and the third remains the third. For two such permutations p_1, p_2 of the same dimension (i.e., $|p_1| = |p_2|$), $p_1 \cdot p_2$ is defined as the vector p with $p(i) = p_2(p_1(i))$ for $1 \leq i \leq |p_1|$. p is the composition of p_1 and p_2.

We construct the set P' of new rules that is initialized as the original set P. The algorithm is shown in Fig. 7.9.

Note that in general, this transformation algorithm is exponential in the size of the original grammar, since for a given predicate it could be the case that we need all predicates A^p where p is a permutation of the arguments. Then, for each of these, we have to add copies of all the original A-clauses with a modified left-hand side order. As a small example see Fig. 7.10.

$P' := P$ with all predicates A replaced with A^{id};
$N' := \{A^{id} \mid A \in N\}$;
repeat
  for all rules $r = A^p(\alpha) \to A_1^{p_1}(\alpha_1) \ldots A_k^{p_k}(\alpha_k)$ in P' **do**
    for all $i = 1$ **to** k **do**
      if $A_i^{p_i}(\alpha_i) = A_i^{p_i}(Y_1, \ldots, Y_{dim(A_i)})$ and the order of the $Y_1, \ldots, Y_{dim(A_i)}$
      in α is $p(Y_1, \ldots, Y_{dim(A_i)})$ where p is not the identity **then**
        introduce a predicate $A_i^{p_i'}$ with $p_i' = p_i \circ p$
        replace $A_i^{p_i}(\alpha_i)$ in r with $A_i^{p_i'}(p(\alpha_i))$
        if $A_i^{p_i'} \notin N'$ **then**
          add $A_i^{p_i'}$ to N'
          for every $A_i^{p_i}$-rule $A_i^{p_i}(\gamma) \to \Gamma \in P'$ **do**
            add a new rule $A_i^{p_i'}(p(\gamma)) \to \Gamma$ to P'
          end for
        end if
      end if
    end for
  end for
until P' does not change any more

Fig. 7.9. Algorithm for transforming a simple RCG into an ordered simple RCG

Original clauses:
$S(XY) \to A(X,Y) \quad A(X,Y) \to A(Y,X) \quad A(aX,bY) \to A(X,Y) \quad A(a,b) \to \varepsilon$

Clauses after transformation into ordered RCG:
$S^{\langle 1 \rangle}(XY) \to A^{\langle 1,2 \rangle}(X,Y)$
$A^{\langle 1,2 \rangle}(X,Y) \to A^{\langle 2,1 \rangle}(X,Y) \qquad A^{\langle 2,1 \rangle}(X,Y) \to A^{\langle 1,2 \rangle}(X,Y)$
$A^{\langle 1,2 \rangle}(aX,bY) \to A^{\langle 1,2 \rangle}(X,Y) \quad A^{\langle 2,1 \rangle}(bX,aY) \to A^{\langle 2,1 \rangle}(X,Y)$
$A^{\langle 1,2 \rangle}(a,b) \to \varepsilon \qquad\qquad\qquad A^{\langle 2,1 \rangle}(b,a) \to \varepsilon$

Fig. 7.10. Example for transforming a simple RCG into an ordered simple RCG

In many applications this transformation is not needed since we are encountering only ordered simple RCGs, for instance when extracting simple RCGs from treebanks, as described in Section 6.1.3. The extraction algorithm from (Maier and Søgaard, 2008) algorithm produces ε-free ordered SRCGs. The ε-freeness results from the fact that there are no traces in Negra, while the ordering property is ensured by the ascending numbering of the variables. Furthermore, since there are no empty words, whenever there is a gap, i.e., a separation between two arguments, this gap contains at least one input symbol. All these properties are useful for parsing.

A further example that shows the whole chain of 1. ordering the clauses, 2. removing useless clauses and 3. removing ε-clauses is given in the solution of Problem 7.2.

for all rules $r = A(\boldsymbol{\alpha}) \to A_0(\boldsymbol{\alpha_0}) \ldots A_m(\boldsymbol{\alpha_m})$ in P with $m > 1$ **do**
  remove r from P
  $R := \emptyset$
  pick new predicate names $C_1, \ldots, C_{m-1}$
  add the rule $A(\boldsymbol{\alpha}) \to A_0(\boldsymbol{\alpha_0})C_1(\boldsymbol{\gamma_1})$ to R where $\boldsymbol{\gamma_1}$ is obtained by reducing $\boldsymbol{\alpha}$ with $\boldsymbol{\alpha_0}$
  for all $i = 1$ **to** $m - 2$ **do**
    add the rule $C_i(\boldsymbol{\gamma_i}) \to A_i(\boldsymbol{\alpha_i})C_{i+1}(\boldsymbol{\gamma_{i+1}})$ to R where $\boldsymbol{\gamma_{i+1}}$ is obtained by reducing $\boldsymbol{\gamma_i}$ with $\boldsymbol{\alpha_i}$
  end for
  add the rule $C_{m-1}(\boldsymbol{\gamma_{m-2}}) \to A_{m-1}(\boldsymbol{\alpha_{m-1}})A_m(\boldsymbol{\alpha_m})$ to R
  for every rule $r' \in R$ **do**
    replace right-hand side arguments of length > 1 with new variables (in both sides) and add the result to P
  end for
end for

Fig. 7.11. Algorithm for binarizing a simple ordered RCG

7.2.4 Binarization of the Rules

An additional transformation that might be useful for parsing is a binarization of the parse trees, i.e., a transformation into some kind of *Chomsky Normal Form (CNF)* where the rules contain at most two predicates in their right-hand side. In LCFRS terminology, the length of the right-hand side of a production is called its *rank*. The *rank* of an LCFRS is given by the maximal rank of its productions. If the maximal dimension of the grammar is k, then the binarization limits the maximal number of variables per rule to $2k$ and, consequently, the maximal number of range boundaries to $4k$.

The transformation can be performed similarly to the CNF transformation for CFG (Hopcroft and Ullman, 1979; Grune and Jacobs, 2008).

We define the reduction of a vector $\boldsymbol{\alpha_1} \in [(T \cup V)^*]^{k_1}$ by a vector $\boldsymbol{\alpha_2} \in (V^*)^{k_2}$ where all variables in $\boldsymbol{\alpha_2}$ occur in $\boldsymbol{\alpha_1}$ as follows: take all variables from $\boldsymbol{\alpha_1}$ (in their order) that are not in $\boldsymbol{\alpha_2}$ while starting a new element in the resulting vector whenever a variable is, in $\boldsymbol{\alpha_1}$, in a different element than the preceding variable in the result or in the same element but not adjacent to it. For instance, $\langle aX_1, X_2, bX_3 \rangle$ reduced with $\langle X_2 \rangle$ yields $\langle X_1, X_3 \rangle$ and $\langle aX_1X_2bX_3 \rangle$ reduced with $\langle X_2 \rangle$ yields $\langle X_1, X_3 \rangle$ as well.

The transformation is like the one for CFGs in the sense that for right-hand sides longer than 2, we introduce a new non-terminal (i.e., a new predicate) that covers the right-hand side without the first element. The algorithm is given in Fig. 7.11, while Fig. 7.12 shows an example. In this example, there is only one rule with a right-hand side longer than 2. In a first step, we introduce the new predicates and rules that binarize the right-hand side. This leads to the set R. In a second step, before adding the rules from R to the grammar, whenever a right-hand side argument contains several variables, these are collapsed into a single new variable.

Original simple RCG:
$S(XYZUVW) \to A(X,U)B(Y,V)C(Z,W)$
$A(aX, aY) \to A(X,Y) \qquad A(a,a) \to \varepsilon$
$B(bX, bY) \to B(X,Y) \qquad B(b,b) \to \varepsilon$
$C(cX, cY) \to C(X,Y) \qquad C(c,c) \to \varepsilon$

Transformation to CNF:
Rule with right-hand side of length > 2: $S(XYZUVW) \to A(X,U)B(Y,V)C(Z,W)$
For this rule, we obtain
$R = \{S(XYZUVW) \to A(X,U)C_1(YZ,VW), C_1(YZ,VW) \to B(Y,V)C(Z,W)\}$

Equivalent CNF RCG:
$S(XPUQ) \to A(X,U)C_1(P,Q) \qquad C_1(YZ,VW) \to B(Y,V)C(Z,W)$
$A(aX, aY) \to A(X,Y) \qquad A(a,a) \to \varepsilon$
$B(bX, bY) \to B(X,Y) \qquad B(b,b) \to \varepsilon$
$C(cX, cY) \to C(X,Y) \qquad C(c,c) \to \varepsilon$

Fig. 7.12. Sample transformation of an ordered simple RCG to CNF

Note however that in principle there are different ways to binarize a given simple RCG rule. We could choose every partition of the right-hand side predicates into two sets and then introduce new predicates for each element of the partition. The arities of the new predicates depend on the partitions we choose.

To illustrate this, consider the clause

$$A(aXY, cZ, dU) \to B(X)C(Y,Z)D(U).$$

There are three possibilities for binarization:

1. We can partition the right-hand side into $B(X)$ and $C(Y,Z)D(U)$. This leads to a new clause with maximal right-hand side arity 3 and four variables:

   $$A(aXY, cZ, dU) \to B(X)E1(Y,Z,U), \quad E1(Y,Z,U) \to C(Y,Z)D(U).$$

2. We can partition the right-hand side into $C(Y,Z)$ and $B(X)D(U)$. This leads to a new clause with maximal right-hand side arity 2 and four variables:

   $$A(aXY, cZ, dU) \to E2(X,U)C(Y,Z), \quad E2(X,U) \to B(X)D(U).$$

3. We can partition the right-hand side into $D(U)$ and $B(X)C(Y,Z)$. This leads to a new clause with maximal right-hand side arity 2 and three variables:

   $$A(aV, cZ, dU) \to E3(V,Z)D(U), \quad E3(XY,Z) \to B(X)C(Y,Z).$$

The third possibility is the best one since it gives us a minimal arity and a minimal variable number per clause.

Gómez-Rodríguez et al. (2009) have shown how to obtain an optimal binarization for a given LCFRS. In the following, we will adapt their ideas to our simple RCG notation. We assume that we are only considering partitions of right-hand sides where one of the sets contains only a single predicate. The extension to the general case is left to the reader.

For a given clause $c = A_0(\mathbf{x_0}) \to A_1(\mathbf{x_1}) \ldots A_k(\mathbf{x_k})$, we define the *characteristic string* $s(c, A_i)$ of the A_i-reduction of c as follows: Concatenate the elements of $\mathbf{x_0}$, separated with new additional symbols \$ while replacing every component from $\mathbf{x_i}$ with a \$. We then define the arity of the characteristic string, $dim(s(c, A_i))$, as the number of maximal substrings $x \in V^+$ in $s(A_i)$.

Our binarization algorithm (see Fig. 7.13) first checks for a given clause c with right-hand side length > 2 on all right-hand side predicates B for the maximal arity (given by $dim(s(c,B))$) and the number of variables $(dim(s(c,B)) + dim(B))$ we would obtain when binarizing with this predicate. This check provides the optimal candidate. In a second step we then perform the same binarization as before, except that we use the optimal candidate now instead of the first element of the right-hand side.

The fact that we have this binarization allows us a more efficient use of the basic CYK algorithm from (Seki et al., 1991). We repeat the deduction rules here using the simple RCG notation for LCFRS. Items have the form $[A, \boldsymbol{\rho}]$ where $A \in N$; $\boldsymbol{\rho}$ is a simple range vector of dimension $dim(A)$.

Then the two deduction rules are

Scan $\dfrac{}{[A, \boldsymbol{\rho}]} \quad A(\boldsymbol{\rho}(w)) \to \varepsilon \in P$

Complete: $\dfrac{[B, \boldsymbol{\rho_B}], [C, \boldsymbol{\rho_C}]}{[A, \boldsymbol{\rho_A}]} \quad \begin{array}{l} A(\boldsymbol{\rho_A}) \to B(\boldsymbol{\rho_B})C(\boldsymbol{\rho_C}) \\ \text{is an instantiation of a } c \in P \text{ wrt. } w \end{array}$

The complexity of this parsing algorithm depends on the arity of the simple RCG (see the solution of Problem 7.3 for the complexity). This confirms that it is crucial to keep the arity (the fan-out in LCFRS terminology) as low as possible while binarizing a given simple RCG.

7.3 An Incremental Earley Parser for Simple RCG

7.3.1 The Algorithm

For this algorithm, we assume that our simple RCGs are ordered and ε-free. As a consequence, we can perform an incremental parsing while traversing the arguments of left-hand side predicates from left to right.

The algorithm is a modification of the incremental CYK from (Burden and Ljunglöf, 2005) and is very close to the strategy adopted by Thread Automata

repeat
    for all rules $r = A(\boldsymbol{\alpha}) \to A_0(\boldsymbol{\alpha_0}) \ldots A_m(\boldsymbol{\alpha_m})$ in P with $m > 1$ **do**
        $cand = 0$
        $arity = $ number of variables in r
        $vars = $ number of variables in r
        for all $i = 0$ **to** m **do**
            $cand\text{-}arity = dim(s(r, A_i))$;
            if $cand\text{-}arity < arity$ and $dim(A_i) < arity$ **then**
                $arity = max(\{cand\text{-}arity, dim(A_i)\})$;
                $vars = cand\text{-}arity + dim(A_i)$;
                $cand = i$;
            else if $cand\text{-}arity \leq arity$, $dim(A_i) \leq arity$ and $cand\text{-}arity + dim(A_i) < vars$ **then**
                $arity = max(\{cand\text{-}arity, dim(A_i)\})$;
                $vars = cand\text{-}arity + dim(A_i)$;
                $cand = i$
            end if
        end for
        remove r from P
        $R := \emptyset$
        add the rule $A(\boldsymbol{\alpha}) \to A_i(\boldsymbol{\alpha_i})C(\boldsymbol{\gamma})$ to R where $\boldsymbol{\gamma}$ is obtained by reducing $\boldsymbol{\alpha}$ with $\boldsymbol{\alpha_i}$
        add the rule $C(\boldsymbol{\gamma}) \to A_0(\boldsymbol{\alpha_0}) \ldots A_{i-1}(\boldsymbol{\alpha_{i-1}}) A_{i+1}(\boldsymbol{\alpha_{i+1}}) \ldots A_m(\boldsymbol{\alpha_m})$ to R
        for every rule $r' \in R$ **do**
            replace right-hand side arguments of length > 1 with new variables (in both sides) and add the result to P
        end for
    end for
until P does not change any more

Fig. 7.13. Algorithm for binarizing a simple ordered RCG – optimized version

in (Villemonte de la Clergerie, 2002). It is given in (Kallmeyer and Maier, 2009; Kallmeyer, 2009) and has been implemented in the TuLiPA (Tübingen Linguistic Parsing Architecture) framework.[1]

The general strategy is as follows: We process the arguments of the left-hand sides of rules incrementally, starting from an S-rule. Whenever we reach a variable, we move into the rule of the corresponding rhs predicate (**predict** or **resume**). Whenever we reach the end of an argument, we **suspend** this rule and move into the parent rule that has called the current one. In addition, we treat the case where we reach the end of the last argument and move into the parent as a special case. Here, we first **convert** the item into a passive one and then **complete** the parent item with this passive item. This allows for some additional factorization.

---

[1] http://sourcesup.cru.fr/tulipa/

7.3 An Incremental Earley Parser for Simple RCG

In our SRCG, without loss of generality, we use variables $\{X_1, X_2, \ldots\}$ and assume that each rule contains occurrences of all variables $\{X_1, X_2, \ldots, X_k\}$ for some k.

Passive items have again the form $[A, \rho]$ where A is a predicate of some dimension k, and ρ is a simple range vector of arity k.

Active items contain rules with a dot in the left-hand side. The position of this dot is given by a pair $\langle i, j \rangle$. Active items have the form

$$[A(\phi) \to A_1(\phi_1) \ldots A_m(\phi_m), pos, \langle i, j \rangle, \rho]$$

where

- $A(\phi) \to A_1(\phi_1) \ldots A_m(\phi_m) \in P$;
- $pos \in \{0, \ldots, n\}$ is the position up to which we have processed the input;
- $\langle i, j \rangle \in \mathbb{N}^2$ marks the position of our dot in the arguments of the predicate A; $\langle i, j \rangle$ indicates that we have processed the arguments up to the jth element of the ith argument;
- ρ is a range vector containing the bindings of the variables and terminals occurring in the left-hand side of the rule. ($\rho(i)$ is the range the ith element is bound to.) When first predicting a rule, it is initialized with a vector containing only symbols "?" for "unknown". We call such a vector (of appropriate arity) ρ_{init}.

As notations, we write $\rho(X)$ for the range bound to the variable X in ρ; furthermore, we write $\rho(\langle i, j \rangle)$ for the range bound to the jth element in the ith argument of the rule left-hand side.

Applying a range vector ρ containing variable bindings for a given rule c to the argument vector of the left-hand side of c means mapping the ith element in the arguments to $\rho(i)$ and concatenating adjacent ranges. The result is defined iff every argument is thereby mapped to a range.

We start by predicting the S-predicate:

Initialize: $\dfrac{}{[S(\phi) \to \Phi, 0, \langle 1, 0 \rangle, \rho_{init}]} \quad S(\phi) \to \Phi \in P$

Whenever the next symbol after the dot is the next terminal in the input, we can scan it.

Scan: $\dfrac{[A(\phi) \to \Phi, pos, \langle i, j \rangle, \rho]}{[A(\phi) \to \Phi, pos+1, \langle i, j+1 \rangle, \rho']} \quad \phi(i, j+1) = w_{pos+1}$

where ρ' is ρ updated with $\rho(i, j+1) = \langle pos, pos+1 \rangle$.

Whenever our dot is left of a variable that is the first argument of some rhs predicate B, we predict new B-rules:

Predict: $\dfrac{[A(\phi) \to \ldots B(X, \ldots) \ldots, pos, \langle i, j \rangle, \rho_A]}{[B(\psi) \to \Psi, pos, \langle 1, 0 \rangle, \rho_{init}]} \quad \begin{array}{l}\phi(i, j+1) = X, \\ B(\psi) \to \Psi \in P\end{array}$

Whenever we arrive at the end of an argument that is not the last argument, we suspend the processing of this rule and we go back to the item that was used to predict it.

Suspend: $$\frac{[B(\boldsymbol{\psi}) \to \boldsymbol{\Psi}, pos', \langle i,j \rangle, \boldsymbol{\rho}_B], \ [A(\boldsymbol{\phi}) \to \ldots B(\boldsymbol{\xi}) \ldots, pos, \langle k,l \rangle, \boldsymbol{\rho}_A]}{[A(\boldsymbol{\phi}) \to \ldots B(\boldsymbol{\xi}) \ldots, pos', \langle k, l+1 \rangle, \boldsymbol{\rho}]}$$

where

- the dot in the antecedent A-item precedes the variable $\boldsymbol{\xi}(i)$,
- $|\boldsymbol{\psi}(i)| = j$ (the ith argument has length j and has therefore been completely processed),
- $|\boldsymbol{\psi}| < i$ (the ith argument is not the last argument of B),
- $\boldsymbol{\rho}_B(\boldsymbol{\psi}(i)) = \langle pos, pos' \rangle$, and
- for all $1 \leq m < i$, $\boldsymbol{\rho}_B(\boldsymbol{\psi}(m)) = \boldsymbol{\rho}_A(\boldsymbol{\xi}(m))$.

$\boldsymbol{\rho}$ is $\boldsymbol{\rho}_A$ updated with $\boldsymbol{\rho}_A(\boldsymbol{\xi}(i)) = \langle pos, pos' \rangle$.

Whenever we arrive at the end of the last argument, we convert the item into a passive one:

Convert: $$\frac{[B(\boldsymbol{\psi}) \to \boldsymbol{\Psi}, pos, \langle i,j \rangle, \boldsymbol{\rho}_B]}{[B, \boldsymbol{\rho}]} \qquad |\boldsymbol{\psi}(i)| = j, |\boldsymbol{\psi}| = i, \boldsymbol{\rho}_B(\boldsymbol{\psi}) = \boldsymbol{\rho}$$

Whenever we have a passive B item we can use it to move the dot over the variable of the last argument of B in a parent A-rule that was used to predict it.

Complete: $$\frac{[B, \boldsymbol{\rho}_B], \ [A(\boldsymbol{\phi}) \to \ldots B(\boldsymbol{\xi}) \ldots, pos, \langle k,l \rangle, \boldsymbol{\rho}_A]}{[A(\boldsymbol{\phi}) \to \ldots B(\boldsymbol{\xi}) \ldots, pos', \langle k, l+1 \rangle, \boldsymbol{\rho}]}$$

where

- the dot in the antecedent A-item precedes the variable $\boldsymbol{\xi}(|\boldsymbol{\rho}_B|)$,
- the last range in $\boldsymbol{\rho}_B$ is $\langle pos, pos' \rangle$, and
- for all $1 \leq m < |\boldsymbol{\rho}_B|$, $\boldsymbol{\rho}_B(m) = \boldsymbol{\rho}_A(\boldsymbol{\xi}(m))$.

$\boldsymbol{\rho}$ is $\boldsymbol{\rho}_A$ updated with $\boldsymbol{\rho}_A(\boldsymbol{\xi}(|\boldsymbol{\rho}_B|)) = \langle pos, pos' \rangle$.

Whenever we are left of a variable that is not the first argument of one of the rhs predicates, we resume the rule of the rhs predicate.

Resume: $$\frac{[A(\boldsymbol{\phi}) \to \ldots B(\boldsymbol{\xi}) \ldots, pos, \langle i,j \rangle, \boldsymbol{\rho}_A], \ [B(\boldsymbol{\psi}) \to \boldsymbol{\Psi}, pos', \langle k-1, l \rangle, \boldsymbol{\rho}_B]}{[B(\boldsymbol{\psi}) \to \boldsymbol{\Psi}, pos, \langle k, 0 \rangle, \boldsymbol{\rho}_B]}$$

where

- $\boldsymbol{\phi}(i)(j+1) = \boldsymbol{\xi}(k), k > 1$ (the next element is a variable that is the kth element in $\boldsymbol{\xi}$, i.e., the kth argument of B),

7.3 An Incremental Earley Parser for Simple RCG

$L = \{a^n b^n \mid n > 0\}$. An ordered simple ε-free RCG for L:
$S(X_1 X_2) \longrightarrow A(X_1, X_2) \qquad A(aX_1, bX_2) \longrightarrow A(X_1, X_2) \qquad A(a, b) \longrightarrow \varepsilon$

Parsing Trace for input $w = aabb$:

	pos	item	ρ	action
1	0	$S(\bullet X_1 X_2) \longrightarrow A(X_1, X_2)$	$(?, ?)$	axiom
2	0	$A(\bullet aX_1, bX_2) \longrightarrow A(X_1, X_2)$	$(?, ?, ?, ?)$	predict from 1
3	0	$A(\bullet a, b) \longrightarrow \varepsilon$	$(?, ?)$	predict from 1
4	1	$A(a \bullet X_1, bX_2) \longrightarrow A(X_1, X_2)$	$(\langle 0, 1 \rangle, ?, ?, ?)$	scan from 2
5	1	$A(a\bullet, b) \longrightarrow \varepsilon$	$(\langle 0, 1 \rangle, ?)$	scan from 3
6	1	$A(\bullet aX_1, bX_2) \longrightarrow A(X_1, X_2)$	$(?, ?, ?, ?)$	predict from 4
7	1	$A(\bullet a, b) \longrightarrow \varepsilon$	$(?, ?)$	predict from 4
8	1	$S(X_1 \bullet X_2) \longrightarrow A(X_1, X_2)$	$(\langle 0, 1 \rangle, ?)$	susp. 5, back to 1
9	1	$A(a, \bullet b) \longrightarrow \varepsilon$	$(\langle 0, 1 \rangle, ?)$	resume 5, from 8
10	2	$A(a \bullet X_1, bX_2) \longrightarrow A(X_1, X_2)$	$(\langle 1, 2 \rangle, ?, ?, ?)$	scan from 6
11	2	$A(a\bullet, b) \longrightarrow \varepsilon$	$(\langle 1, 2 \rangle, ?)$	scan from 7
12	2	$A(\bullet aX_1, bX_2) \longrightarrow A(X_1, X_2)$	$(?, ?, ?, ?)$	predict from 10
13	2	$A(\bullet a, b) \longrightarrow \varepsilon$	$(?, ?)$	predict from 10
14	2	$A(aX_1 \bullet, bX_2) \longrightarrow A(X_1, X_2)$	$(\langle 0, 1 \rangle, \langle 1, 2 \rangle, ?, ?)$	susp. 11, back to 4
15	2	$S(X_1 \bullet X_2) \longrightarrow A(X_1, X_2)$	$(\langle 0, 2 \rangle, ?)$	susp. 14, back to 1
16	2	$A(aX_1, \bullet bX_2) \longrightarrow A(X_1, X_2)$	$(\langle 0, 1 \rangle, \langle 1, 2 \rangle, ?, ?)$	resume 14, from 15
17	3	$A(aX_1, b \bullet X_2) \longrightarrow A(X_1, X_2)$	$(\langle 0, 1 \rangle, \langle 1, 2 \rangle, \langle 2, 3 \rangle, ?)$	scan 16
18	3	$A(a, \bullet b) \longrightarrow \varepsilon$	$(\langle 1, 2 \rangle, ?)$	resume 11, from 17
19	4	$A(a, b\bullet) \longrightarrow \varepsilon$	$(\langle 1, 2 \rangle, \langle 3, 4 \rangle)$	scan 18
20	4	$A(\langle 1, 2 \rangle, \langle 3, 4 \rangle)$		convert 19
21	4	$A(aX_1, bX_2 \bullet) \longrightarrow A(X_1, X_2)$	$(\langle 0, 1 \rangle, \langle 1, 2 \rangle, \langle 2, 3 \rangle, \langle 3, 4 \rangle)$	compl. 17, from 20
22	4	$A(\langle 0, 2 \rangle, \langle 2, 4 \rangle)$		convert 21
23	4	$S(X_1 X_2 \bullet) \longrightarrow A(X_1, X_2)$	$(\langle 0, 2 \rangle, \langle 2, 4 \rangle)$	compl. 15, from 22
24	4	$S(\langle 0, 4 \rangle)$		convert 23

Fig. 7.14. Sample parse with the incremental Earley algorithm for ordered SRCG

- $|\psi(k-1)| = l$, and
- $\rho_A(\xi(m)) = \rho_B(\psi)(m)$ for all $1 \leq m \leq k-1$.

The goal items have the form $[S(\phi) \rightarrow \Phi, n, \langle 1, j \rangle, \psi]$ with $|\phi(1)| = j$ (i.e., a dot at the end of lhs argument).

Extending this algorithm to grammars that are not ε-free requires the following changes: The vectors ρ that record the ranges bound to variables and occurrences of terminals have to record also the ranges bound to ε-arguments in the left-hand side. In other words, empty arguments are treated as arguments containing special variables that require to be bound to ε. The bindings are found through an additional rule **scan-ε** that moves the dot over such a special ε-variable while updating the range vector with $\langle pos, pos \rangle$ as the range this ε is bound to.

7.3.2 Filters

Depending on what the grammar looks like, a range of filters can be applied to decrease the number of items in the chart. A filter is an additional condition on the form of items. For instance, in a ε-free grammar, the number of variables in the part of the left-hand side arguments of a rule that has not been processed yet must be less than or equal to the length of the remaining input.

We will discuss in the following some filters that are particularly useful when dealing with natural languages.

Remaining Input Length Filter

If we are dealing with ε-free grammars, then we know that each variable must cover at least one input symbol. Then, in a situation where we have i input symbols left, it does not make sense to predict a clause with more than i variables or terminals in the left-hand side since there is no way to instantiate this clause with the remaining input. This idea to filter out items that predict material that is longer than the remainig input goes back to (Kuno, 1965).

We obtain as an additional filtering condition on the validity of an active item that the length of the remaining input must be greater than or equal to the number of variables and terminal occurrences to the right of the dot in the left-hand side of the clause. More formally, an active item $[A(\phi) \to A_1(\phi_1) \ldots A_m(\phi_m), pos, \langle i, j \rangle, \rho]$ satisfies the **length filter** iff

$$(n - pos) \geq (|\phi(i)| - j) + \Sigma_{k=i+1}^{dim(A)} |\phi(k)|.$$

The length filter is applied to results of **predict**, **resume**, **suspend** and **complete**. Especially in cases where we have very large grammars, such a condition avoids a considerable number of items.

The simple RCGs extracted from treebanks with crossing branches such as Tiger and Negra are ε-free since they do not contain traces. Therefore, for these grammars, the remaining input length filter can be applied.

Terminal Filter

A second filter, used for instance in (Langer, 1998; Klein and Manning, 2003), checks for the presence of required pre-terminals. Assume that pre-terminals are treated as terminals, so this filter amounts to checking for the presence of all terminals in the predicted part of a clause (the part to the right of the dot) in the remaining input. Furthermore, we check that the terminals appear in the predicted order and that the distance between two of them is at least the number of variables/terminals in between. In other words, an active item

$[A(\phi) \to A_1(\phi_1)\ldots A_m(\phi_m), pos, \langle i,j\rangle, \rho]$ satisfies the **terminal filter** iff we can find an injective mapping $f_T : Term = \{\langle k,l\rangle \mid \phi(k)(l) \in T$ and either $k > i$ or $(k = i$ and $l > j)\} \to \{pos+1,\ldots,n\}$ such that

1. $w_{f_T(\langle k,l\rangle)} = \phi(k)(l)$ for all $\langle k,l\rangle \in Term$;
2. for all $\langle k_1,l_1\rangle, \langle k_2,l_2\rangle \in Term$ with $k_1 = k_2$ and $l_1 < l_2$, $f_T(\langle k_2,l_2\rangle) \geq f_T(\langle k_1,l_1\rangle) + (l_2 - l_1)$;
3. for all $\langle k_1,l_1\rangle, \langle k_2,l_2\rangle \in Term$ with $k_1 < k_2$, $f_T(\langle k_2,l_2\rangle) \geq f_T(\langle k_1,l_1\rangle) + (|\phi(k_1)| - l_1) + \Sigma_{k=k_1+1}^{k_2-1}|\phi(k)| + l_2$.

Checking this filtering condition amounts to a linear traversal of the part of the left-hand side of the clause that is to the right of the dot. We start with index $i = pos + 1$; for every variable or gap we increment i by 1. For every terminal a, we search the next a in the input, starting at position i. If it occurs at position j, then we set $i = j$ and continue our traversal of the remaining parts of the left-hand side of the clause.

7.4 Summary

This chapter has presented various parsing algorithms for MCFG and the equivalent LCFRS and SRCG. Since MCFG is a straightforward extension of CFG, the adaptation of CFG parsing algorithms is possible for this formalism. However, the fact that we deal with discontinuities, increases considerably the number of yield boundaries to consider in single parsing steps. We have presented several ways to transform a given SRCG into an equivalent one that satisfies some normal form condition such as orderedness, ε-freeness or binary branching of rewriting rules. We have seen different CYK and Earley algorithms where the transformation into grammars satisfying some of these constraints helped to decrease the complexity of parsing.

Recently, LCFRS/SRCGs have started to get used in the context of data-driven parsing as well (Levy, 1999; Kallmeyer and Maier, 2009; Kallmeyer and Maier, 2010; Maier, 2010; Maier and Kallmeyer, 2010).

Problems

7.1. Give the deduction rules for the incremental CYK for MCFG with a top-down prediction (i.e., for an Earley algorithm).

7.2. Consider the simple RCG with the following clauses:
$S(XYZU) \to A(X,Z)B(U,Y)$ $S(XYZ) \to A(X,Z)C(Y)$
$A(aX, aZ) \to A(X,Z)$ $A(\varepsilon, c) \to \varepsilon$
$B(Xb, Yb) \to B(X,Y)$ $B(\varepsilon, c) \to \varepsilon$
$C(aXY) \to D(X)C(Y)$ $D(d) \to \varepsilon$

1. Perform the following transformations on this simple RCG while obtaining always weakly equivalent simple RCGs:
   a) Transform the grammar into an ordered simple RCG.
   b) Remove useless rules.
   c) Remove ε-rules.
2. What is the string language generated by this grammar?

7.3. Take the CYK for binarized simple RCG given at the end of section 7.2.4. Assume that we have a simple binary k-RCG. What is the time complexity of this algorithm?

7.4. A deduction rule does not specify an order in which its antecedent items must appear or its side conditions must be fulfilled. However, being able to make such assumptions can be beneficial for an actual implementation.

Consider the incremental Earley parser from section 7.3. If we assume an ε-free grammar, what assumption can we make with respect to the antecedent items in the **Suspend** operation?

8
Range Concatenation Grammars

8.1 Introduction to Range Concatenation Grammars

8.1.1 Definition of RCG

In this chapter, we turn to *Range Concatenation Grammars* (RCGs) (Boullier, 1998a; Boullier, 1999b; Boullier, 2000b), the most powerful formalism treated in this book.

In the previous chapter, we have already seen *simple* RCG, a syntactic variant of LCFRS. As already mentioned, in a simple RCG, we can understand non-terminals as predicates that are satisfied by all the string tuples that are in their yields. A rewriting rule (*clause*) with left-hand side predicate A is then the specification of a sufficient condition for a string tuple to satisfy the predicate A.

Consider for example the clause $A(aXa, Y, bZb) \to B(X, Z)C(Y)$. It tells us that a sufficient condition for a string triple $\langle w_1, w_2, w_3 \rangle$ to satisfy the predicate A is that a) w_1 has the form $aw'_1 a$, b) w_3 has the form $bw'_3 b$, c) the pair $\langle w'_1, w'_3 \rangle$ satisfies the predicate B, and d) $\langle w_2 \rangle$ satisfies the predicate C.

In the case of simple RCG, we require for each clause that the right-hand side arguments are single variables and that every variable in the left-hand side occurs exactly once in the right-hand side and vice versa. If we drop these requirements, we obtain general RCGs. We can keep the same perspective of the clauses formulating sufficient conditions for a string tuple for satisfying the left-hand side predicate.

RCGs in general allow us for instance clauses of the following forms:

1. $A(aX, bY) \to B(X)$ that tells us that a pair $\langle w_1, w_2 \rangle$ satisfies A if a) w_1 has the form aw'_1, b) w_2 has the form bw'_2, and c) w'_1 satisfies the predicate B.

   We say that clauses where the left-hand side contains variables that do not occur in the right-hand side or vice versa are *erasing* clauses.

L. Kallmeyer, *Parsing Beyond Context-Free Grammars*, Cognitive Technologies, DOI 10.1007/978-3-642-14846-0_8, © Springer-Verlag Berlin Heidelberg 2010

Clauses:
$S(XY) \to S(X)eq(X,Y)$
$S(a) \to \varepsilon$
$eq(aX, aY) \to eq(X, Y)$
$eq(a, a) \to \varepsilon$

Fig. 8.1. An RCG for $\{a^{2^n} \mid n \geq 0\}$

Clauses:
$S(XYZU) \to S_2(X,U)\text{Coord}(Y)S_2(Z,U)$
$S_2(XY, Z) \to N(X)VP(Y, Z)$
$VP(X, Y) \to V(X)N(Y)$
$V(\text{likes}) \to \varepsilon \quad V(\text{hates}) \to \varepsilon$
$N(\text{John}) \to \varepsilon \quad N(\text{Mary}) \to \varepsilon$
$N(\text{Bill}) \to \varepsilon \quad \text{Coord}(\text{and}) \to \varepsilon$
$L = \{xy \text{ and } zuv \mid y, u \in \{\text{likes}, \text{hates}\}, x, z, v \in \{\text{John}, \text{Mary}, \text{Bill}\}\}$

Derived structure for *John likes and Bill hates Mary*:

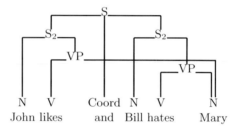

Fig. 8.2. An RCG for gapping constructions

2. $A(aXa) \to A(X)B(X)$ that tells us that $\langle w_1 \rangle$ satisfies A if a) w_1 has the form $aw'_1 a$, b) $\langle w'_1 \rangle$ satisfies the predicate A and c) $\langle w'_1 \rangle$ satisfies also the predicate B.

Clauses where either the left-hand side or the right-hand side contains more than one occurrence of the same variable are called *non-linear* clauses. Non-linear clauses allow to check more than one condition (predicate) for a single string.

As an example for the use of non-linear clauses in RCGs, see the RCG in Fig. 8.1 that generates the string language $\{a^{2^n} \mid n \geq 0\}$. The first clause tells us that for a string that contains not just a single a to be in the language, it must be possible to separate the string into two parts such that the first part is also in the language and the two parts satisfy the predicate *eq*. *eq* yields all pairs of equal non-empty strings containing only as. Note that $\{a^{2^n} \mid n \geq 0\}$ is a non-semilinear language, i.e., it is an example of a Range Concatenation Language (RCL) that is not of constant growth.

As a further example consider the RCG in Fig. 8.2 for gapping constructions. Here, we use material twice in the right-hand side of the first clause since the noun at the end of the sentence is supposed to fill the gap in the first sentence of the coordination. Therefore it is part of two different VPs (and of two different sentences).

Furthermore, besides the additional possibility of copying or erasing variables in one side of a clause, we are even allowed to have right-hand side arguments that are sequences of terminals and variables, not just single variables. We call such clauses *combinatorial*. The sequences denote concatenations. We take terminals and variables to denote ranges in an input string. A concatenation xy denotes then the concatenation of the ranges corresponding to x and y.

Take for instance a combinatorial clause such as $A(X,Y) \to B(XY)$ which would be allowed in an RCG. This clause signifies in terms of ranges over a given input string that a pair of ranges $\langle \langle l_1, r_1 \rangle, \langle l_2, r_2 \rangle \rangle$ satisfies A if a) the two ranges can be concatenated, i.e., are adjacent ($r_1 = l_2$) and b) their concatenation $\langle l_1, r_2 \rangle$ satisfies B.

The addition of combinatorial clauses does not give any extra expressive power; as shown in (Boullier, 1998a), for any RCG there is an equivalent non-combinatorial RCG.

We will now define RCGs (Boullier, 1998a; Boullier, 1999b; Boullier, 2000b).

Definition 8.1 (Positive Range Concatenation Grammar).
A positive Range Concatenation Grammar (PRCG) is a tuple $G = \langle N, T, V, S, P \rangle$ *such that*

- *N is a finite set of predicates, each with a fixed arity;*
- *T and V are disjoint alphabets of terminals and of variables;*
- *$S \in N$ is the start predicate, a predicate of arity 1;*
- *P is a finite set of* clauses

$$A_0(x_{01}, \ldots, x_{0a_0}) \to \varepsilon$$

or

$$A_0(x_{01}, \ldots, x_{0a_0}) \to A_1(x_{11}, \ldots, x_{1a_1}) \ldots A_n(x_{n1}, \ldots, x_{na_n}) \text{ with } n \geq 1$$

where $A_i \in N, x_{ij} \in (T \cup V)^*$ and a_i the arity of A_i.

Besides the positive predicates occurring in PRCGs, Boullier (2000b) also defines so-called *negative RCGs* (NRCGs). The negative variant allows for negative predicate calls of the form $\overline{A(\alpha_1, \ldots, \alpha_n)}$. Such a predicate is meant to recognize the complement language of its positive counterpart.

Definition 8.2 (Negative Range Concatenation Grammar).
A negative Range Concatenation Grammar (NRCG) is a tuple $G = \langle N, T, V, S, P \rangle$ *like a PRCG except that some predicates in the right-hand sides of clauses can have the form* $\overline{A(\alpha_1, \ldots, \alpha_n)}$ *where $A(\alpha_1, \ldots, \alpha_n)$ is as in the definition of positive RCG clauses.*

An RCG with maximal predicate arity k is called an RCG of arity k (k-RCG for short).

Throughout the book, we consider only PRCGs. Therefore, whenever we use the term "RCG", we actually mean "PRCG".

When applying a clause with respect to a string $w = t_1 \ldots t_n$, the arguments of the predicates are instantiated with substrings of w, more precisely with the corresponding ranges. Ranges have been introduced in Chapter 6. A range $\langle i, j \rangle$ with $0 \leq i < j \leq n$ corresponds to the substring between positions i and j, i.e., to the substring $t_{i+1} \ldots t_j$.

The definition of a clause instantiation introduced in Chapter 6 is now extended to RCGs in general:

Definition 8.3 (Clause instantiation).
Let $G = (N, T, V, P, S)$ be a RCG. For a given clause $c = A_0(\boldsymbol{\alpha_0}) \to A_1(\boldsymbol{\alpha_1}) \cdots A_m(\boldsymbol{\alpha_m})$ $(0 \leq m)$ and a string $w = t_1 \ldots t_n$,

1. an instantiation of c with respect to w consists of a function $f : \{t' \mid t'$ is an occurrence of some $t \in T$ in the clause$\} \cup V \cup \{Eps_{i,j} \mid 1 \leq i \leq m, 1 \leq j \leq dim(A_i), \boldsymbol{\alpha_i}(j) = \varepsilon\} \to \{\langle i, j \rangle \mid i \leq j, i, j \in \mathbb{N}\}$ such that
    a) for all occurrences t' of a $t \in T$ in the clause, $f(t') := \langle i, i+1 \rangle$ for some $i, 0 \leq i < n$ such that $t_i = t$,
    b) for all $X \in V$, $f(X) = \langle j, k \rangle$ for some $0 \leq j \leq k \leq n$,
    c) for all x, y adjacent in one of the elements of $\boldsymbol{\alpha_i}$ $(0 \leq i \leq m)$, there are l, j, r with $f(x) = \langle l, j \rangle, f(y) = \langle j, r \rangle$; we then define $f(xy) = \langle l, r \rangle$,
    d) for all $Eps \in \{Eps_{i,j} \mid 1 \leq i \leq m, 1 \leq j \leq dim(A_i), \boldsymbol{\alpha_i}(j) = \varepsilon\}$, there is a k, $0 \leq k \leq n$ with $f(Eps) = \langle k, k \rangle$; we then define for every ε-argument $\boldsymbol{\alpha_i}(j)$ that $f(\boldsymbol{\alpha_i}(j)) = f(Eps_{i,j})$,
2. if f is an instantiation of c with respect to w, then $A_0(f(\boldsymbol{\alpha_0})) \to A_1(f(\boldsymbol{\alpha_1})) \cdots A_m(f(\boldsymbol{\alpha_m}))$ is an instantiated clause where $f(\langle x_1, \ldots, x_k \rangle) = \langle f(x_1), \ldots, f(x_k) \rangle$.

Take for instance the clause $S(aXYb) \to B(X, X)C(cZ)$. Then a possible instantiation of this clause with respect to some string $w = acb$ is a function $f : \{a^{(1)}, X, Y, b^{(1)}, c^{(1)}, Z\} \to \{\langle l, r \rangle \mid 0 \leq l \leq r \leq 3\}$ where the superscripts mark the number of the occurrence, i.e., $c^{(1)}$ is for example the first c occurring in the clause. f in this case must be defined as follows: $f(a^{(1)}) = \langle 0, 1 \rangle$, $f(b^{(1)}) = \langle 1, 2 \rangle$, $f(c^{(1)}) = \langle 2, 3 \rangle$. Furthermore, either $f(X) = \langle 1, 1 \rangle$ and $f(Y) = \langle 1, 2 \rangle$ or $f(X) = \langle 1, 2 \rangle$ and $f(Y) = \langle 2, 2 \rangle$. Finally, $f(Z) = \langle 3, 3 \rangle$. The corresponding instantiated clauses are $S(\langle 0, 2 \rangle) \to B(\langle 1, 1 \rangle, \langle 1, 1 \rangle)C(\langle 2, 3 \rangle)$ and $S(\langle 0, 2 \rangle) \to B(\langle 1, 2 \rangle, \langle 1, 2 \rangle)C(\langle 2, 3 \rangle)$.

In each RCG derivation step, the left-hand side of an instantiated clause is replaced by its right-hand side. The derivation relation is defined as follows:

8.1 Introduction to Range Concatenation Grammars

$G = \langle \{S, A, B\}, \{a, b\}, \{X, Y, Z\}, S, P \rangle$ with clauses
$S(X\,Y\,Z) \to A(X, Z)\,B(Y)$
$A(a\,X, a\,Y) \to A(X, Y)$
$B(b\,X) \to B(X)$
$A(\varepsilon, \varepsilon) \to \varepsilon$
$B(\varepsilon) \to \varepsilon$

First we apply the following clause instantiation:
$S(X \quad Y \quad Z) \to A(X, \quad Z) \quad B(Y)$
$\quad \downarrow \quad \downarrow \quad \downarrow \qquad \downarrow \quad \downarrow \qquad \downarrow$
$\langle 0,2 \rangle \langle 2,3 \rangle \langle 3,5 \rangle \quad \langle 0,2 \rangle \langle 3,5 \rangle \quad \langle 2,3 \rangle$
$\quad aa \quad\ b \quad\ aa \qquad aa \quad\ aa \qquad b$

With this instantiation, $S(\langle 0,5 \rangle) \Rightarrow A(\langle 0,2 \rangle, \langle 3,5 \rangle) B(\langle 2,3 \rangle)$. Then
$B(b \quad X) \to B(X)$
$\quad \downarrow \quad \downarrow \qquad \downarrow$
$\langle 2,3 \rangle \langle 3,3 \rangle \quad \langle 3,3 \rangle$ and $B(\varepsilon) \to \varepsilon$
$\quad b \quad \varepsilon \qquad \varepsilon$

lead to $A(\langle 0,2 \rangle, \langle 3,5 \rangle) B(\langle 2,3 \rangle) \Rightarrow A(\langle 0,2 \rangle, \langle 3,5 \rangle) B(\langle 3,3 \rangle) \Rightarrow A(\langle 0,2 \rangle, \langle 3,5 \rangle)$.
$A(a \quad X \quad a \quad Y) \to A(X, \quad Y)$
$\quad \downarrow \quad \downarrow \quad \downarrow \quad \downarrow \qquad \downarrow \quad \downarrow$
$\langle 0,1 \rangle \langle 1,2 \rangle \langle 3,4 \rangle \langle 4,5 \rangle \quad \langle 1,2 \rangle \langle 4,5 \rangle$
$\quad a \quad a \quad a \quad a \qquad a \quad a$

leads to $A(\langle 0,2 \rangle, \langle 3,5 \rangle) \Rightarrow A(\langle 1,2 \rangle, \langle 4,5 \rangle)$. Then
$A(a \quad X \quad a \quad Y) \to A(X, \quad Y)$
$\quad \downarrow \quad \downarrow \quad \downarrow \quad \downarrow \qquad \downarrow \quad \downarrow$
$\langle 1,2 \rangle \langle 2,2 \rangle \langle 4,5 \rangle \langle 5,5 \rangle \quad \langle 2,2 \rangle \langle 5,5 \rangle$ and $A(\varepsilon, \varepsilon) \to \varepsilon$
$\quad a \quad \varepsilon \quad a \quad \varepsilon \qquad \varepsilon \quad \varepsilon$

lead to $A(\langle 1,2 \rangle, \langle 4,5 \rangle) \Rightarrow A(\langle 2,2 \rangle, \langle 5,5 \rangle) \Rightarrow \varepsilon$

Fig. 8.3. A sample RCG derivation for the input $w = aabaa$

Definition 8.4 (RCG derivation).

- For an $A \in N$ with arity k and ranges $\langle i_1, j_1 \rangle, \ldots, \langle i_k, j_k \rangle$ with respect to a given w, if there is an instantiated clause with respect to w whose left-hand side is $A(\langle i_1, j_1 \rangle, \ldots, \langle i_k, j_k \rangle)$, then in one derivation step (notated $\ldots \Rightarrow_{G,w} \ldots$) $A(\langle i_1, j_1 \rangle, \ldots, \langle i_i, j_k \rangle)$ can be replaced with the right-hand side of this instantiated clause.
- $\overset{*}{\Rightarrow}_{G,w}$ is the reflexive transitive closure of $\Rightarrow_{G,w}$.

For illustration, consider the RCG derivation in Fig. 8.3. This grammar is a simple RCG whose string language is $L(G) = \{a^n b^k a^n \mid k, n \in \mathbb{N}\}$.

We can define the yields of predicates as sets of string tuples or sets of range vectors, both with respect to a given string w (Boullier, 1998a). The first is the *string language*, the second the *range language* of the predicate. The string language is defined via the range language.

Definition 8.5 (Range language and string language).

- The range language of an $A \in N$ with $dim(A) = k$ for some $w \in T^*$ is

Clauses:
$S(X) \to M(X,X,X)$
$M(bX,Y,Z) \to M(X,Y,Z)$ $M(cX,Y,Z) \to M(X,Y,Z)$
$M(X,aY,Z) \to M(X,Y,Z)$ $M(X,cY,Z) \to M(X,Y,Z)$
$M(X,Y,aZ) \to M(X,Y,Z)$ $M(X,Y,bZ) \to M(X,Y,Z)$
$M(aX,bY,cZ) \to M(X,Y,Z)$ $M(\varepsilon,\varepsilon,\varepsilon) \to \varepsilon$

$L(G) = MIX = \{w \mid w \in \{a,b,c\}^*, |w|_a = |w|_b = |w|_c\}$

Fig. 8.4. A sample RCG for the MIX language

$$R(A,w) = \{\boldsymbol{\rho} \mid \boldsymbol{\rho} \text{ is a } k\text{-dimensional range vector, and } A(\boldsymbol{\rho}) \stackrel{*}{\Rightarrow}_{G,w} \varepsilon\}.$$

- The string language *of an* $A \in N$ *with* $dim(A) = k$ *for some* $w \in T^*$ *is*

$$L(A,w) = \{\boldsymbol{\rho}(w) \mid \boldsymbol{\rho} \in R(A,w)\}.$$

- The string language *of an RCG G is*

$$L(G) = \{w \in T^* \mid \langle\langle 0, |w|\rangle\rangle \in R(S,w)\}.$$

As a further example consider the RCG given in Fig. 8.4 (adapted from Boullier (1999b)) that generates the so-called MIX language. MIX is a puzzling language, since it is not clear which language class it belongs to. It has been suggested that it cannot be generated by indexed grammars (Boullier, 1999b) and there is a general suspicion that it is not in the class of LCFRL though nobody has proven this so far. The RCG in Fig. 8.4 does the following: it takes three copies of the input and goes through them while skipping all bs and cs in the first copy, all as and cs in the second and all as and bs in the third. Whenever we reach an a in the first copy, a b in the second and a c in the third, these are taken to belong together and they are deleted. This way, the three copies are entirely traversed while connecting the ith a in the first copy with the ith b in the second and the ith c in the third for $1 \leq i \leq |w|_a$. If it is possible to cover all as, bs and cs in the input in this way, then the word is in the language.

Definition 8.6 (Simple Range Concatenation Grammar).
An RCG is

- non-combinatorial *if for every clause* $c \in P$, *all the arguments in the right-hand side of c are single variables.*
- bottom-up linear *if for every clause* $c \in P$, *no variable appears more than once in the left-hand side of c.*
- top-down linear *if for every clause* $c \in P$, *no variable appears more than once in the right-hand side of c.*
- linear *if it is top-down and bottom-up linear.*
- bottom-up non-erasing *if for every clause* $c \in P$, *each variable occurring in the right-hand side of c occurs also in its left-hand side.*

8.1 Introduction to Range Concatenation Grammars

Clauses:
$S(X) \to A(X)$ $S(XYZ) \to A(X)eq(X,Y)S(YZ)$
$A(aXb) \to A(X)$ $A(ab) \to \varepsilon$
$eq(aX, aY) \to eq(X, Y)$ $eq(bX, bY) \to eq(X, Y)$ $eq(\varepsilon, \varepsilon) \to \varepsilon$

$L(G)\{(a^m b^m)^n \mid m, n \geq 1\}$

Fig. 8.5. RCG for a non-MCFL of constant growth

- top-down non-erasing *if for every clause $c \in P$, each variable occurring in the left-hand side of c occurs also in its right-hand side.*
- non-erasing *if it is top-down and bottom-up non-erasing.*
- simple *if it is non-combinatorial, linear and non-erasing.*

Boullier (1998a) shows the following facts concerning equivalences between the different types of RCG one obtains when imposing some of the above-mentioned properties:

Lemma 8.7.

1. *For any RCG, there is an equivalent non-combinatorial RCG.*
2. *For any non-combinatorial bottom-up erasing RCG, there is an equivalent non-combinatorial bottom-up non-erasing RCG.*
3. *For any non-combinatorial bottom-up non-erasing top-down erasing RCG, there is an equivalent non-combinatorial non-erasing RCG.*

In other words, the possibilities of combinatorial clauses and erasing clauses do not increase the generative capacity of the grammar. For every RCG, there is an equivalent non-combinatorial non-erasing RCG. The crucial property for RCG's being more powerful than simple RCG is the possible non-linearity of the clauses.

As already mentioned in Chapter 6, simple RCGs and Linear Context-Free Rewriting Systems (LCFRSs) (Vijay-Shanker, Weir, and Joshi, 1987) are equivalent (see Boullier (1998b)). Consequently, simple RCGs are mildly context-sensitive (Joshi, 1985).

There are languages that are of constant growth and that cannot be generated by simple RCG. An example is $L = \{(a^m b^m)^n \mid m, n \geq 1\}$ for which we have shown in Chapter 6 that it is not an MCFL. The RCG generating this language is given in Fig. 8.5. The grammar works as follows: The predicate A yields all words $a^m b^m$. For a word to be in the language it must either have the form $a^m b^m$ (first clause $S(X) \to A(X)$) or the form $w_1 w_2 w_3$ such that w_1 is of the form $a^m b^m$, w_2 is equal to w_1 and $w_2 w_3$ is also a word in the language (second clause $S(XYZ) \to A(X)eq(X,Y)S(YZ)$).

RCGs in general have been shown to generate the entire class PTIME (Bertsch and Nederhof, 2001), i.e., the class of all languages L such that the problem whether $w \in L$ for a given $w \in T^*$ can be decided in an amount of time polynomial in the length $n = |w|$ of w.

Lemma 8.8. *The set of string languages generated by RCGs is exactly the class of all polynomial languages (Bertsch and Nederhof, 2001).*

The fact that every language generated by an RCG is polynomial is confirmed by the existence of polynomial parsing algorithms (see Chapter 9).

The other direction, i.e., the inclusion of all polynomial languages in the set of RCG string languages is shown in Appendix A of (Bertsch and Nederhof, 2001) by constructing an equivalent RCG for a given two-way alternating finite automaton with k heads. It is known that two-way alternating finite automata recognize exactly the class PTIME. The idea of the construction is roughly as follows: Such an automaton is non-deterministic and alternates between existential branching states (only one possibility needs to be successful) and universal branching states (all possibilities must be successful). In the corresponding RCG, the former is modelled by a set of different clauses while the latter is modelled by single clauses with the predicates corresponding to all possibilities in the right-hand side.

8.1.2 Applications

Phenomena Beyond LCFRS

A phenomenon in natural languages that LCFRS cannot deal with in a general way is unbounded scrambling as found in German and other free word order languages. As an example consider (39):

(39) a. ... dass er den Kühlschrank seinem Freund zu reparieren
        ... that he the fridge$_{acc}$ his friend$_{dat}$ to repair

    zu versprechen versucht
    to promise   tries
    '... that he tries to promise his friend to repair the fridge'

  b. ... dass er seinem Freund den Kühlschrank zu reparieren
        ... that he his friend$_{dat}$ the fridge$_{acc}$ to repair

    zu versprechen versucht
    to promise   tries
    '... that he tries to promise his friend to repair the fridge'

Under the assumption that we consider only infinite verbs with a single argument, we get a general configuration where k noun phrases are followed by k verbs, each noun phrase depending on a single verb, and while having the order of the verbs fixed, we allow for all permutations of the noun phrases.

As a formal language that captures this, the language of all strings $\pi(n^{[1]} \ldots n^{[m]}) v^{[1]} \ldots v^{[m]}$ with $m \geq 1$, π a permutation, and $n^{[i]} = n$ a nominal argument of $v^{[i]} = v$ for $1 \leq i \leq m$ has been proposed; nominal argument is taken to imply that both come from the same element in the grammar. Such a language cannot be generated by an LCFRS (Becker, Rambow, and Niv, 1992; Rambow, 1994).

Boullier (1999b) gives an RCG for this language that is a negative RCG. Something similar can be done, though, also with only positive predicates in the right-hand sides. The clauses roughly do the following with the input string: First they separate it into two components, the nominal elements and the verbal elements. Then, for each n in the first component, the clauses search through the verbal elements until having found the head of this noun. Similarly, for each v, the clauses search through the nominal components until having found the appropriate argument. Note that this works only if there is function that tells us for a given noun whether a given verb is its head. Boullier (1999b) assumes this function to be previously defined. In general, this function is however what we want to compute during parsing. It is not unique, i.e., there can be more than one such function for a given string.

As mentioned earlier, there are also examples of natural language phenomena that have been argued to be non-semilinear. These are Chinese number names (Radzinski, 1991) and case stacking in Old Georgian (Michaelis and Kracht, 1997). For the first, Chinese number names, Boullier (1999b) gives an RCG that describes them.

Multiple Aspects of Linguistic Structure

RCGs allow us to describe different linguistic aspects of strings in a single system (Sagot, 2005). This is due to the fact that RCGs are closed under intersection. One can for example require that a sentence be syntactically well formed and semantically well formed and describe the two conditions within a single system, using syntactic predicates and semantic predicates. Relations between the two can be captured as well since they are part of a single grammar.

To see how the description of different linguistic layers within a single RCG can be achieved, consider the following sample clause that captures constituent structure and syntactic functions:

$$S(XZU) \to NP(X)\ VP(ZU)\ \text{Head}(Z,ZU)\ \text{Subject}(X,Z).$$

RCG as a Pivot Formalism

Since the class of string languages of RCGs is the entire class PTIME, there is a large range of formalisms that can be transformed into equivalent RCGs. Examples are TAG (for which we will see the transformation to RCG as proposed in (Boullier, 1999b) in the next section), tree-local and set-local MC-TAG (Kallmeyer (2009) gives the transformation to RCG), a restricted form of *tree-local MCTAG with shared nodes (SN-MCTAG)* (see (Kallmeyer, 2005) for the transformation to RCG), and k-TT-MCTAG (the transformation can be found in (Kallmeyer and Parmentier, 2008)). Note that all these examples use only simple RCG, i.e., the sub-class of RCG that is equivalent to LCFRS.

$$S(X,Y) \to S_0(X,Y)S_0'(X,Y)$$
$$S_0(XY,Z) \to S_1(X,Z)D(Y)$$
$$S_1(aXc,abY) \to S_1(X,Y)$$
$$S_1(X,Y) \to B(X)CD(Y)$$
$$S_0'(XY,Z) \to S_1'(Y,Z)A(X)$$
$$S_1'(bXd,Ycd) \to S_1'(X,Y)$$
$$S_1'(X,Y) \to C(X)AB(Y)$$
$$A(aX) \to A(X),\ A(\varepsilon) \to \varepsilon$$
$$B(bX) \to B(X),\ B(\varepsilon) \to \varepsilon$$
$$C(cX) \to C(X),\ C(\varepsilon) \to \varepsilon$$
$$D(dX) \to D(X),\ D(\varepsilon) \to \varepsilon$$
$$CD(cdX) \to CD(X),\ CD(\varepsilon) \to \varepsilon$$
$$AB(abX) \to AB(X),\ AB(\varepsilon) \to \varepsilon$$
$$L(G) = \{\langle a^n b^m c^n d^m, (ab)^n (cd)^m \rangle \mid n, m \geq 0\}$$

Fig. 8.6. A $(2,2)$-BRCG for text alignment

Examples of formalisms that can be transformed into non-simple RCGs are *agreement grammar* and *right-linear unification grammar* (Søgaard, 2007). Here, again, the ability of RCG to describe different features and relations for the same parts of the input within a single clause is crucial for the transformation.

Machine Translation

Søgaard (2008) proposes using RCGs to model the alignment between texts in the context of machine translation. He uses RCGs with binary start predicate names where the two arguments present the two strings whose alignment is to be modelled. The maximal arity in general is 2. Furthermore, an argument in the left-hand side of a clause contains at most two variables and the grammars are bottom-up non-erasing, i.e., every variable in the left-hand side of some clause occurs also in its right-hand side. Such RCGs are called $(2,2)$-*BRCG*.

The fact that Søgaard uses non-simple RCGs, in particular non-linear rules, allows to derive different alignment patterns for the same pair of strings in parallel. The overall alignment structure is then the union of the single alignments or, in other words, the different languages obtained according to the single alignments are intersected.

Take for instance the language of pairs $\langle a^n b^m c^n d^m, (ab)^n (cd)^m \rangle$ where the as and cs from the first string are aligned with the abs from the second string while the bs and ds from the first are aligned with the cds from the second. This can be achieved by the $(2,2)$-BRCG in Fig. 8.6 that generates the first alignment via the S_0 predicate and the second via the S_0' predicate.

Søgaard (2008) shows that in a similar way, inside-out alignments can be obtained which is a type of alignment that occurs in about 5% of the sentence

$$S(XYZUV) :- N(Y)V_{inf}(U)Object(U,Y)S(XZV)$$
$$S(XY) :- N(X)V_{fin}(Y)Subject(Y,X)$$

Fig. 8.7. LMG for scrambling constructions

pairs in a Chinese-English parallel corpus. The example from Fig. 8.6 is a cross-serial alignment structure. Such structures occur frequently in aligned corpora, for instance for language pairs such as English-Spanish and English-Portuguese (see the overview in (Søgaard, 2008)). Both types of structure are problematic for most formalisms proposed previously for machine translation.

8.2 Relations to Other Formalisms

8.2.1 Literal Movement Grammars

A formalism that is closely related to RCG is *Literal Movement Grammar (LMG)* (Groenink, 1995; Groenink, 1996; Groenink, 1997) (see also (Kracht, 2003) for an introduction to LMG). Groenink's work is actually the starting point for defining RCGs in (Boullier, 1998a). The definition of LMG is exactly the same as the one of RCG except that the predicates do not have a fixed arity. This difference is not relevant for the generative capacity as long as the set of clauses and therefore the set of arities for a non-terminal $A \in N$ is finite. Just like RCGs, LMGs consider non-terminals as predicates and their clauses have the same syntax as the clauses of an RCG. They are written $A(\boldsymbol{\alpha}) :- A_1(\boldsymbol{\alpha_1}) \ldots A_m(\boldsymbol{\alpha_m})$ instead of $A(\boldsymbol{\alpha}) \to A_1(\boldsymbol{\alpha_1}) \ldots A_m(\boldsymbol{\alpha_m})$.

The difference lies in the way clauses are instantiated. As we have seen, in an RCG, all occurrences of terminals, variables and empty arguments are mapped to ranges in a given string w. This is different in LMG. Here, all variables are mapped to sequences of terminals. This means that 1. different occurrences of the same variable X can be mapped to different occurrences of the same string, 2. a clause can contain terminals that are not present in the input string, and 3. concatenations of strings not adjacent in the input are allowed.

As an example, see the LMG in Fig. 8.7 for scrambling constructions. This LMG picks in its first clause an arbitrary noun from the input and an arbitrary verb such that the verb follows the noun in the string. If the noun is a possible object of the verb, then it is considered to depend on it and the two are deleted. The process continues with the concatenation of the remaining parts. In the end, we are left with a last noun and a last verb such that the noun is a possible subject of the verb. Note that this grammar does not require all nouns to precede all verbs; the nouns only have to precede the verbs they depend on. This is actually more close to what we find in natural languages.

According to what we have just seen, the instantiations of LMG clauses are defined as mappings from variables to terminal strings, not to ranges:

Definition 8.9 (LMG clause instantiation).
Let $G = \langle N, T, V, S, P \rangle$ be a LMG.
For a clause $c = A(\boldsymbol{\alpha}) \coloneq A_1(\boldsymbol{\alpha_1}) \ldots A_m(\boldsymbol{\alpha_m}) \in P$, every function $f : \{x \mid x \in V, x \text{ occurs in } c\} \to T^*$ is an instantiation of c.
We call $A(f(\boldsymbol{\alpha})) \coloneq A_1(f(\boldsymbol{\alpha_1})) \ldots A_m(f(\boldsymbol{\alpha_m}))$ then an instantiated clause where f is extended as follows:

1. $f(\varepsilon) = \varepsilon$;
2. $f(t) = t$ for all $t \in T$;
3. $f(xy) = f(x)f(y)$ for all $x, y \in T^*$;
4. $f(\langle \alpha_1, \ldots, \alpha_m \rangle) = (\langle f(\alpha_1), \ldots, f(\alpha_m) \rangle)$ for all $(\langle \alpha_1, \ldots, \alpha_m \rangle) \in [(T \cup V)^*]^m$, $m \geq 1$.

The language is, as in the case of RCG, the set of all strings w such that $S(w)$ can be reduced to ε by subsequently replacing left-hand sides of instantiated clauses by right-hand sides. Groenink (1996) formulates this adopting a deductive perspective.

Definition 8.10 (LMG string language).
Let $G = \langle N, T, V, S, P \rangle$ be a LMG.

1. The set $L_{pred}(G)$ of instantiated predicates $A(\boldsymbol{\tau})$ where $A \in N$ and $\boldsymbol{\tau} \in (T^*)^k$ for some $k \geq 1$ is defined by the following deduction rules:

   - $\dfrac{}{A(\boldsymbol{\tau})}$ $\quad A(\boldsymbol{\tau}) \coloneq \varepsilon$ is an instantiated clause
   - $\dfrac{A_1(\boldsymbol{\tau_1}) \ldots A_m(\boldsymbol{\tau_m})}{A(\boldsymbol{\tau})}$ $\quad A(\boldsymbol{\tau}) \coloneq A_1(\boldsymbol{\tau_1}) \ldots A_m(\boldsymbol{\tau_m})$ is an instantiated clause

2. The string language of G is

$$\{w \in T^* \mid S(w) \in L_{pred}(G)\}.$$

The crucial difference with RCG is that, in the derivation (or, rather deduction) for a string w, the string vectors we obtain in instantiated clauses need not be part of w. In other words, from an automaton perspective, we can not only read the input but even write on it. Furthermore, different occurrences of the same variable can be mapped to different occurrences of the same string. This is why LMGs are more powerful than RCGs.

To illustrate the difference, consider the two sample grammars in Fig. 8.8. Depending on whether we consider them as RCGs or LMGs, they yield different string languages. In grammar 1, the crucial difference is that in the RCG, because of XX being an argument in the first clause, X must necessarily be mapped to an empty range $\langle i, i \rangle$; otherwise it is not possible to concatenate it with itself. In the LMG, X is mapped to a string and two occurrences of this string can be concatenated. In grammar 2, because of Xb being an argument in the right-hand side of the first clause, in an RCG, we require the Y concatenated with X in the left-hand side to be mapped to a range starting with a b. In the LMG, the b need not be part of the input string.

Grammar 1	Grammar 2
RCG clauses:	RCG clauses:
$S(aXb) \to B(XX)$	$S(XY) \to A(Xb)C(Y)$
$B(bX) \to B(X)$	$A(ab) \to \varepsilon$
$B(\varepsilon) \to \varepsilon$	$C(b) \to \varepsilon$
	$C(c) \to \varepsilon$
String language of the RCG: $\{ab\}$	
	String language of the RCG: $\{ab\}$
String language of the LMG with the same clauses: $\{ab^k \mid k \geq 1\}$	String language of the LMG with the same clauses: $\{ab, ac\}$

Fig. 8.8. String languages of RCG versus LMG

The definitions of *bottom-up* and *top-down linear* and *non-erasing* and of *non-combinatorial* given above for RCGs can be applied to LMGs as well. In fact, these terms were introduced first in (Groenink, 1996) for LMGs.

The class of string languages generated by LMGs that are linear, non-erasing and non-combinatorial is exactly the class generated by simple RCGs and LCFRSs. Groenink (1996) identifies another important sub-class of LMG, so-called *simple LMG*. In a simple LMG, the right-hand side arguments are single variables and each variable occuring in the right-hand side of a clause occurs exactly once in its left-hand side. Groenink shows that these grammars generate exactly the class of all polynomial languages. Consequently, simple LMGs are equivalent to RCGs.

Definition 8.11 (Simple LMG).
An LMG is simple *if it is non-combinatorial, bottom-up non-erasing and bottom-up linear.*

Lemma 8.12. *For every RCG G there exists a simple LMG G' such that $L(G) = L(G')$ and vice versa.*

If, instead of bottom-up non-erasing and bottom-up linearity as in simple LMG, we require the grammar to be top-down non-erasing and top-down linear, we obtain *parallel multiple context-free grammars (PMCFGs)* (Seki et al., 1991; Seki et al., 1993).

Definition 8.13 (PMCFG).
An LMG is a parallel multiple context-free grammar *(PMCFG) if it is non-combinatorial, top-down non-erasing and top-down linear.*

In other words, in a PMCFG, the right-hand side argumets of the clauses are single variables and every variable occurring in the left-hand side of some clause occurs exactly once in its right-hand side. This allows for clauses where

$$S(XXX) :\!\!- A(X)$$
$$A(aX) :\!\!- A(X)$$
$$A(bX) :\!\!- A(X)$$
$$A(\varepsilon) :\!\!- A(\varepsilon)$$

Fig. 8.9. PMCFG for $\{w^3 \mid w \in \{a,b\}^*\}$

variables appear more than once in the left-hand side. A first example is given in Fig. 8.9.

The class of languages generated by PMCFG is larger than the one generated by LCFRS, MCFG and simple RCG. Obviously, each MCFG is a PMCFG; therefore the class of MCFL is contained in the class of string languages generated by PMCFG. Figure 8.10 gives an example from (Seki et al., 1991) of a PMCFG generating a language that is not an MCFL.

$$S(a) :\!\!- \varepsilon$$
$$S(XX) :\!\!- S(X)$$

Fig. 8.10. PMCFG for $\{a^{2^n} \mid n \geq 0\}$

Lemma 8.14.

- *For every MCFG G, there is a PMCFG G' such that $L(G) = L(G')$.*
- *There exists a PMCFG G such that there is no MCFG G with $L(G) = L(G')$.*

PMCFGs are less powerful than simple LMGs and RCGs (Boullier, 1998a). Ljunglöf (2005) extends PMCFG with intersection, which leads to a formalism equivalent to LMG and RCG.

Lemma 8.15.

- *For every PMCFG G, there is a simple LMG G' such that $L(G) = L(G')$.*
- *There exists a simple LMG G such that there is no PMCFG G with $L(G) = L(G')$.*

8.2.2 CFG, TAG and MCFG

It is immediate that every CFG is a simple 1-RCG and vice versa (Boullier, 2000a). All we need to do is to write a CFG production $A \to X_1 \ldots X_k$ as an RCG clause $\overline{A}(Y_1 \ldots Y_k) \to \gamma$ (and vice versa) where for all $1 \leq i \leq k$, $Y_i = X_i$, and γ is the concatenation of all $\overline{X_i}(X_i)$ where $1 \leq i \leq k$ and $X_i \in N$. The start predicate is $\overline{S}$. An example is given in Fig. 8.11.

CFG:
$S \to aSb$
$S \to \varepsilon$

Equivalent simple 1-RCG:
$\overline{S}(aSb) \to \overline{S}(S)$
$\overline{S}(\varepsilon) \to \varepsilon$

Fig. 8.11. A CFG and the equivalent simple 1-RCG

Lemma 8.16. *For a language L there is a CFG G with $L = L(G)$ iff there is a simple 1-RCG G' with $L = L(G')$.*

This does not hold for 1-RCGs in general. Since we can have more than one right-hand side predicate for the same argument(s), it follows immediately that k-RCGs are closed under intersection.

Lemma 8.17. *For every $k \geq 1$, the class of string languages of k-RCGs is closed under intersection.*

For the proof, assume that we have two RCGs with start symbols S_1 and S_2. Then we can construct an RCG for the intersection of the two string languages by taking the union of the two clause sets plus an additional clause $S(X) \to S_1(X) S_2(X)$ where S is the new start symbol.

With this property, we obtain for instance that the non-context-free language $\{a^n b^n c^n \mid n \geq 1\} = \{a^n b^n c^k \mid n, k \geq 1\} \cap \{a^k b^n c^n \mid n \geq 1\}$ is generated by a 1-RCG since it is the intersection of two context-free languages. This leads to the following lemma:

Lemma 8.18. *The class of string languages of 1-RCG properly contains the class of context-free languages.*

Tree Adjoining Languages are contained in the set of languages of simple 2-RCGs (Boullier, 1999b). The two language classes are not equal, i.e., there are simple 2-RCGs that generate languages that are not TALs (Seki et al., 1991; Boullier and Sagot, 2009).

Lemma 8.19. *The set of string languages of TAG is properly contained in the set of string languages of simple 2-RCG:*

1. *For every TAG G there is a simple 2-RCG G' such that $L(G) = L(G')$.*
2. *There is a simple 2-RCG G such that there is not TAG G' with $L(G) = L(G')$.*

In order to show the first part of the lemma, we give the transformation from TAG to simple RCG, following Boullier (1998a; 1999b): The RCG contains predicates $\langle \alpha \rangle(X)$ and $\langle \beta \rangle(L, R)$ for initial and auxiliary trees respectively. X covers the yield of α and all trees added to α by adjunction or substitution, while L and R cover those parts of the yield of β (including all trees added to β by adjunction or substitution) that are to the left and the right of the foot node of β. The clauses in the RCGs reduce the arguments of these predicates by identifying those parts that come from the elementary tree α/β itself and those parts that come from one of the elementary trees added by substitution or adjunction. A sample TAG with an equivalent RCG is shown in Fig. 8.12.

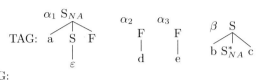

Equivalent RCG:

- $S(X) \to \langle \alpha_1 \rangle(X)$ (every word in the language is the yield of a tree derived from α_1)
- $\langle \alpha_1 \rangle(aF) \to \langle \alpha_2 \rangle(F) \mid \langle \alpha_3 \rangle(F)$ (either the yield of α_1 is a followed by the yield of tree that substitutes at F)
- $\langle \alpha_1 \rangle(aB_1B_2F) \to \langle \beta \rangle(B_1, B_2)\langle \alpha_2 \rangle(F) \mid \langle \beta \rangle(B_1, B_2)\langle \alpha_3 \rangle(F)$ (or β adjoins to S in α; then the yield is a followed by the left part of β, the right part of β and the tree substituted at F)
- $\langle \beta \rangle(B_1 b, cB_2) \to \langle \beta \rangle(B_1, B_2)$ (β can adjoin to its root; then the left part is the left part of the adjoined β follwed by b; the right part is c followed by the right part of the adjoined β)
- $\langle \alpha_2 \rangle(d) \to \varepsilon \quad \langle \alpha_3 \rangle(e) \to \varepsilon \quad \langle \beta \rangle(b, c) \to \varepsilon$ (the yields of α_2, α_3 and β can be d, e and the pair b (left) and c (right) resp.)

Fig. 8.12. A sample TAG and an equivalent RCG

In order to make the choice of an adjoined/substituted tree locally for every node and not at once for the entire elementary tree, Boullier introduces additional so-called *branching predicates* $\langle adj, \gamma, p \rangle$ and $\langle subst, \gamma, p \rangle$ that correspond to the edges in derivation trees. E.g., in the example in Fig. 8.12, the clauses $\langle \alpha_1 \rangle(aB_1B_2F) \to \langle \beta \rangle(B_1, B_2)\langle \alpha_2 \rangle(F) \mid \langle \beta \rangle(B_1, B_2)\langle \alpha_3 \rangle(F)$ would be replaced with the clauses $\langle \alpha_1 \rangle(aB_1B_2F) \to \langle adj, \alpha_1, 2 \rangle(B_1, B_2)\langle sub, \alpha_1, 3 \rangle(F)$, $\langle adj, \alpha_1, 2 \rangle(X, Y) \to \langle \beta \rangle(X, Y)$ and $\langle sub, \alpha_1, 3 \rangle(X) \to \langle \alpha_2 \rangle(X) \mid \langle \alpha_3 \rangle(X)$.

Since the yields of initial trees require unary predicates while the yields of auxiliary trees require binary predicates, the maximal predicate arity in the resulting simple RCG is 2. Furthermore, since we encode the yields of elementary trees always from left to right, we obtain an ordered simple 2-RCG.

More precisely, the construction goes as follows:

We define the decoration string σ_γ of an elementary tree γ as in (Boullier, 1999b): each internal node has two variables L and R and each substitution node has one variable X (L and R represent the left and right parts of the yield of the adjoined tree and X represents the yield of a substituted tree). In a top-down left-to-right traversal the left variables are collected during the top-down traversal, the terminals and variables of substitution nodes are collected while visiting the leaves and the right variables are collected during bottom-up traversal. Furthermore, while visiting a foot node, a separating "," is inserted. The string obtained in this way is the decoration string.

1. We add a start predicate S and clauses $S(X) \to \langle \alpha \rangle(X)$ for all $\alpha \in I$ with root label S.
2. For every $\gamma \in I \cup A$, let L_p, R_p be the left and right symbols in σ_γ for the node at position p if this is not a substitution node; let X_p be the symbol for the node at position p if this is a substitution node.
   We assume that $p_1, \ldots, p_k$ are the possible adjunction sites, and $p_{k+1}, \ldots, p_l$ are the substitution sites in γ. Then the RCG contains all clauses

$$\langle \gamma \rangle(\sigma_\gamma) \to \langle adj, \gamma, p_1 \rangle(L_{p_1}, R_{p_1}) \ldots \langle adj, \gamma, p_k \rangle(L_{p_k}, R_{p_k}) \\ \langle sub, \gamma, p_{k+1} \rangle(X_{p_{k+1}}) \ldots \langle sub, \gamma, p_l \rangle(X_{p_l}).$$

3. For all predicates $\langle adj, \gamma, p \rangle$, the RCG contains all clauses

$$\langle adj, \gamma, p \rangle(L, R) \to \langle \gamma' \rangle(L, R)$$

such that γ' can be adjoined at position p in γ.

4. For all predicates $\langle adj, \gamma, p \rangle$ where $f_{OA}(node(\gamma, p)) = 0$ (adjunction not obligatory), the RCG contains a clause

$$\langle adj, \gamma, p \rangle(\varepsilon, \varepsilon) \to \varepsilon.$$

5. For all predicates $\langle sub, \gamma, p \rangle$ and all γ' that can be substituted into position p in γ, the RCG contains a clause

$$\langle sub, \gamma, p \rangle(X) \to \langle \gamma' \rangle(X).$$

This construction yields a simple RCG whose predicates describe the nodes and edges of TAG derivation trees. Therefore constructing such a simple RCG for a given TAG and then uing the RCG for parsing amounts to doing TAG parsing on the derivation tree. This can have advantages in particular for parsing TAG variants where additional conditions on the derivation trees are imposed, such as different types of multicomponent TAGs (Kallmeyer, 2009). Following the same idea, Kallmeyer and Parmentier (2008) extend this construction to TT-MCTAG (Lichte, 2007) and use the resulting RCG for parsing.

As already mentioned, the equivalence between k-LCFRS and simple k-RCG is immediate (Boullier, 2000b).

Lemma 8.20. *For a language L there is a k-LCFRS G with $L = L(G)$ iff there is a simple k-RCG G' with $L = L(G')$.*

8.3 Summary

In this chapter, we have introduced Range Concatenation Grammars, a grammar formalism that can be seen as an extension of LCFRS and MCFG that

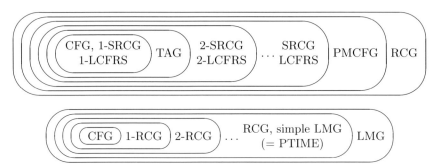

Fig. 8.13. Hierarchy of different types of RCG and LMG string languages

drops the non-erasingness and linearity constraints. Crucially, the productions (clauses) of an RCG are instantiated with substrings of the input w, determined by ranges. Because of this, RCGs are more limited than Literal Movement Grammars, which look similar but do not require the instantiations of arguments and variables in clauses to be part of the input string w.

Figure 8.13 summarizes the hierarchies of string languages for the different formalisms considered in this chapter. Only for the inclusions $k\text{-}RCL \subseteq (k+1)\text{-}RCL$ $(1 \leq k)$ has it not been shown so far that these are proper inclusions, although it seems plausible. All other inclusions are proper inclusions. The entire class of string languages generated by RCGs is particularly interesting since it contains all polynomial languages.

Problems

8.1. Consider the RCG with the following clauses:
$$S(XY) \rightarrow A(X,Y)B(X,Y)$$
$$A(aX, aY) \rightarrow A(X, Y) \qquad B(bX, bY) \rightarrow B(X, Y)$$
$$A(bX, Y) \rightarrow A(X, Y) \qquad B(aX, Y) \rightarrow B(X, Y)$$
$$A(X, bY) \rightarrow A(X, Y) \qquad B(X, aY) \rightarrow B(X, Y)$$
$$A(\varepsilon, \varepsilon) \rightarrow \varepsilon \qquad B(\varepsilon, \varepsilon) \rightarrow \varepsilon$$
The language generated by this grammar is

$$\{w_1 w_2 \mid w_1, w_2 \in \{a, b\}^*, |w_1|_a = |w_2|_a, |w_1|_b = |w_2|_b\}.$$

Give the derivation of $w = abba$ with all clause instantiations using this RCG.

8.2. Consider the following RCGs G_1 and G_2:

- $G_1 = \langle \{S, A, B\}, \{a, b\}, \{X, Y, Z, U, V\}, S, P \rangle$ with P the following set of clauses:

$$S(cXYcZUcV) \to A(X,Z,V)B(Y,U)$$
$$A(aXa,aYa,aZa) \to A(X,Y,Z)$$
$$A(aa,aa,aa) \to \varepsilon$$
$$B(bX,bY) \to B(X,Y)$$
$$B(\varepsilon,\varepsilon) \to \varepsilon$$

- $G_2 = \langle \{S,S_1,S_2,A,B,C,D,E\}, \{a,b,c\}, \{X,Y\}, S, P \rangle$ with P the following set of clauses:

$$S(X) \to S_1(X)S_2(X) \quad S_1(XY) \to D(X)C(Y) \quad S_2(XY) \to A(X)E(Y)$$
$$D(aXb) \to D(X) \quad\quad A(aX) \to A(X)$$
$$D(\varepsilon) \to \varepsilon \quad\quad A(a) \to \varepsilon$$
$$C(cX) \to C(X) \quad\quad E(bYc) \to E(Y)$$
$$C(c) \to \varepsilon \quad\quad E(\varepsilon) \to \varepsilon$$

Determine for each of G_1 and G_2

1. whether it is simple, and
2. what the string language is that it generates.

8.3. Give RCGs for the following string languages:

1. $L_1 = \{w^4 \mid w \in \{c,d\}^*\}$;
2. $L_2 = \{a^{3^n} \mid n \geq 0\}$.

8.4. Give LMGs for the string languages from Problem 8.3.

8.5. Consider the following TAG:

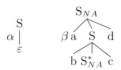

Give the equivalent simple 2-RCG following the construction from Section 8.2.2.

9

Parsing Range Concatenation Grammars

9.1 Basic RCG Parsing

In the following, we will see different parsing algorithms for RCGs. Let us consider a variant of the RCG for the MIX language from Fig. 8.4 as a running example. This variant is given in Fig. 9.1.

Clauses:

$S(XYZ) \to A(X,Z)M(Y,Y)$ $M(cX,Y) \to M(X,Y)$ $A(aX,aY) \to A(X,Y)$
$M(bX,cY) \to M(X,Y)$ $M(X,bY) \to M(X,Y)$ $A(\varepsilon,\varepsilon) \to \varepsilon$
$M(\varepsilon,\varepsilon) \to \varepsilon$

$L(G) = \{a^n w a^n \mid n \geq 0, w \in \{b,c\}^*, |w|_b = |w|_c\}$

Fig. 9.1. RCG for a variant of MIX

The predicate M in this grammar takes two copies of a word w. It processes both copies from left to right while ignoring (deleting) all cs in the first and bs in the second and matching every b in the first with a c in the second copy. This way, M checks whether w contains equal numbers of bs and cs.

We will first consider a basic CYK parser that passes from completely recognized right-hand sides of clauses to completed left-hand sides. Then we will see two basic Earley parsing algorithms, i.e., algorithms that have a top-down prediction and a bottom-up completion. They have in common that at prediction time they compute all instantiations of possible clauses.

All the three algorithms presented in this section are such that within the items we only have to keep track of predicates/clauses whose instantiations are fully determined.

L. Kallmeyer, *Parsing Beyond Context-Free Grammars*, Cognitive Technologies,
DOI 10.1007/978-3-642-14846-0_9,

9.1.1 CYK Parsing with Passive Items

CYK (Cocke, Younger, Kasami) parsing is a non-directional bottom-up parsing technique. As in the case of TAG and LCFRS/SRCG, it is also possible to apply this technique to RCG since, again, we are dealing with grammars containing rewriting rules where a derivation step consists of replacing the left-hand side of a rule with its right-hand side. Following the derivation in reverse order amounts to CYK parsing.

We use only passive items, i.e., items consisting of a non-terminal and its span. The items have therefore the form

$$[A, \boldsymbol{\rho}]$$

where A is a predicate and $\boldsymbol{\rho}$ is a range vector of dimension $dim(A)$ (containing the ranges that the arguments of A are instantiated with). In contrast to MCFG and SRCG, the range vector need not be non-overlapping since the grammar can be non-linear.

Since we are proceeding bottom-up, we start with the rules that have an empty right-hand side: The **scan** operation deduces an instantiated predicate from these rules.

Scan: $\dfrac{}{[A, \boldsymbol{\rho}]}$ $A(\boldsymbol{\rho}) \to \varepsilon$ an instantiated clause

Moving from the set of instantiated right-hand side predicates to the left-hand side of a clause is done by the **complete** rule:

Complete: $\dfrac{[A_1, \boldsymbol{\rho}_1] \ldots [A_k, \boldsymbol{\rho}_k]}{[A_0, \boldsymbol{\rho}]}$ $A_0(\boldsymbol{\rho}_0) \to A_1(\boldsymbol{\rho}_1) \cdots A_k(\boldsymbol{\rho}_k)$ an instantiated clause

The **goal** item is $[S, (\langle 0, n \rangle)]$ since we want to be able to deduce an S predicate spanning the entire input.

Concerning our example grammar from Fig. 9.1, for an input word $w = acbbca$, we would (among others) deduce for instance the items in Fig. 9.2. Instead of $\langle i, j \rangle$, we write $_i x_j$ where $x = w_{i+1} \cdots w_j$ for better readability.

Note that this way of CYK parsing using instantiated clauses can be understood as a two-step process: First we compute the set of instantiated clauses for the input w from the grammar. The result is a CFG whose non-terminals are instantiated predicates and whose terminal alphabet is empty. The start symbol is $S(\langle 0, |w| \rangle)$. In a second step, we perform a CFG CYK parsing for the input ε, using this CFG.[1]

The computation of the CFG consisting of instantiated clauses with respect to w is polynomial in the length n of w since for each of the $|P|$ clauses, we have to try for each range boundary in the clause (limited by a constant), all possible values from 0 to n. For each of these combinations of values, we

---

[1] Of course, in an efficient implementation, we would not compute all instantiated clauses first but rather compute them only when needed.

9.1 Basic RCG Parsing   179

Trace (only successful items listed):

item	op.	inst. clause	clause
$[M, (_5\varepsilon_5, {_5}\varepsilon_5)]$	scan	$M(_5\varepsilon_5, {_5}\varepsilon_5) \to \varepsilon$	$M(\varepsilon, \varepsilon) \to \varepsilon$
$[A, (_1\varepsilon_1, {_6}\varepsilon_6)]$	scan	$A(_1\varepsilon_1, {_6}\varepsilon_6) \to \varepsilon$	$A(\varepsilon, \varepsilon) \to \varepsilon$
$[A, (_0a_1, {_5}a_6)]$	compl.	$A(_0a_1, {_5}a_6) \to A(_1\varepsilon_1, {_6}\varepsilon_6)$	$A(aX, aY) \to A(X, Y)$
$[M, (_4c_5, {_5}\varepsilon_5)]$	compl.	$M(_4c_5, {_5}\varepsilon_5) \to M(_5\varepsilon_5, {_5}\varepsilon_5)$	$M(cX, Y) \to M(X, Y)$
$[M, (_3bc_5, {_4}c_5)]$	compl.	$M(_3bc_5, {_4}c_5) \to M(_4c_5, {_5}\varepsilon_5)$	$M(bX, cY) \to M(X, Y)$
...			
$[M, (_1cbbc_5, {_1}cbbc_5)]$	compl.	$M(_1cbbc_5, {_1}cbbc_5)$ $\to M(_2bbc_5, {_1}cbbc_5)$	$M(cX, Y) \to M(X, Y)$
$[S, (_0acbbca_6)]$	compl.	$S(_0acbbca_6)$ $\to A(_0a_1, {_5}a_6)$ $M(_1cbbc_5, {_1}cbbc_5)$	$S(XYZ)$ $\to A(X, Z)M(Y, Y)$

Fig. 9.2. Basic CYK parsing of $w = acbbca$

need to check whether the instantiation is valid in the sense of mapping adjacent elements to adjacent ranges and terminals to corresponding ranges. This check can be done in constant time. Consequently, the fixed recognition problem for RCGs can be solved in polynomial time (Bertsch and Nederhof, 2001). CYK parsing with the resulting grammar and $w = \varepsilon$ amounts actually to removing all non-terminals that cannot yield a string in T^*, i.e., to removing all useless symbols. The CFG non-terminals (instantiated predicates) X in the chart are exactly those that allow us to derive ε, i.e., $X \overset{*}{\Rightarrow} \varepsilon$ and $\{\varepsilon\} = T^*$. If $S(\langle 0, n \rangle)$ is among the useful symbols, i.e., $S(\langle 0, n \rangle) \overset{*}{\Rightarrow} \varepsilon$, then w is in the language.

In contrast to RCGs, in the case of LMGs, the number of possible instantiations of a rewriting rule, given an input string w, is not polynomial in the length of w since it is actually independent from w. There are in general infinitely many possible instantiations.

9.1.2 Non-directional Top-Down Parsing

We now add a prediction operation to the basic CYK and then, in the third algorithm in this section, we extend the algorithm further to an algorithm with active items where we move a dot through the right-hand sides of instantiated clauses.

The idea of top-down parsing is to instantiate the start predicate with the entire string and to recursively check if there is a way to reduce all right-hand side predicates to ε. Roughly, for each instantiated predicate, we compute all instantiated clauses with this predicate being its left-hand side, and we then predict all right-hand side elements of this clause. Once we have completed all right-hand side elements of an instantiated clause, we can complete its left-hand side element.

We use only passive items, i.e., items consisting of a non-terminal, its span and a flag that marks whether the item is predicted or completed. The items have therefore the form

$$[A, \boldsymbol{\rho}, \mathit{flag}]$$

where A is a predicate, $\boldsymbol{\rho}$ is a range vector of dimension $dim(A)$ (containing, as before, the ranges that the arguments of A are instantiated with) and $\mathit{flag} \in \{c, p\}$ indicates if the item has been completed (value c) or predicted (value p).

As an axiom, we predict S ranging over the entire input. Therefore, the **initialize** rule is as follows:

$$\textbf{Initialize:}\ \frac{}{[S, (\langle 0, n \rangle), p]}$$

The **predict** operation predicts new items for previously predicted items.

$$\textbf{Predict:}\ \frac{[A_0, \boldsymbol{\rho}_0, p]}{[A_1, \boldsymbol{\rho}_1, p] \ldots [A_k, \boldsymbol{\rho}_k, p]}\quad \begin{array}{l} A_0(\boldsymbol{\rho}_0) \to A_1(\boldsymbol{\rho}_1) \cdots A_k(\boldsymbol{\rho}_k) \\ \text{an instantiated clause} \end{array}$$

The **scan** operation switches the flag on an item describing a predicted predicate to completed, given that there is a corresponding ε-clause:

$$\textbf{Scan:}\ \frac{[A, \boldsymbol{\rho}, p]}{[A, \boldsymbol{\rho}, c]}\quad A(\boldsymbol{\rho}) \to \varepsilon \text{ an instantiated clause}$$

The **complete** rule sets the flag on a completed left-hand side predicate to completed.

$$\textbf{Complete:}\ \frac{[A_0, \boldsymbol{\rho}, p], [A_1, \boldsymbol{\rho}_1, c] \ldots [A_k, \boldsymbol{\rho}_k, c]}{[A_0, \boldsymbol{\rho}, c]}\quad \begin{array}{l} A_0(\boldsymbol{\rho}_0) \to A_1(\boldsymbol{\rho}_1) \cdots A_k(\boldsymbol{\rho}_k) \\ \text{an instantiated clause} \end{array}$$

Recognition is successful if there is a way to declare the start predicate completed. Consequently, the **goal** item is $[S, (\langle 0, n \rangle), c]$.

Figure 9.3 lists some of the successful items one obtains with this algorithm parsing $w = acbbca$ with the RCG from Fig. 9.1. Of course, besides the successful predictions, a lot of instantiated predicates are predicted that do not lead to a parse. In order to do a more efficient RCG Earley parsing, we have to find ways to reduce the number of predicted items.

9.1.3 Directional Top-Down Parsing

The above algorithm can be improved by completing right-hand side predicates from left to right and stopping further completion once a predicate fails. This variant corresponds to the algorithm presented in (Boullier, 2000b).

For the directional top-down parsing algorithm, we need to distinguish between *passive items* and *active items*. Passive items have the same form and meaning as the items of the non-directional top-down parsing algorithm. Active items allow us to move a dot through the right-hand side of an instantiated clause. They have the form

9.1 Basic RCG Parsing   181

Some of the successful items:		
item	op.	clause
$[S,(_0acbbca_6),p]$	initial.	
$[A,(_0a_1,\ _5a_6),p]$	pred.	$S(XYZ) \to A(X,Z)M(Y,Y)$
$[M,(_1cbbc_5,\ _1cbbc_5),p]$		
...		
$[M,(_5\varepsilon_5,\ _5\varepsilon_5),p]$		
$[M,(_5\varepsilon_5,\ _5\varepsilon_5),c]$	scan	$M(\varepsilon,\varepsilon) \to \varepsilon$
...		
$[A,(_0a_1,\ _5a_6),c]$		
$[M,(_1cbbc_5,\ _1cbbc_5),c]$		
$[S,(_0acbbca_6),c]$	compl.	$S(XYZ) \to A(X,Z)M(Y,Y)$

Fig. 9.3. Non-directional top-down parsing of $w = acbbca$

$$[A(\boldsymbol{\rho}) \to \Phi \bullet \Psi]$$

where $A(\boldsymbol{\rho}) \to \Phi\Psi$ is an instantiated clause.

The axiom is the prediction of the start predicate ranging over the entire input. The **initialize** rule is the same as in the non-directional top-down case.

We have two predict operations. The first one, **predict-rule**, predicts active items with the dot on the left of the right-hand side for a given predicted passive item.

$$\textbf{Predict-rule:} \quad \frac{[A,\boldsymbol{\rho},p]}{[A(\boldsymbol{\rho}) \to \bullet\Psi]} \quad A(\boldsymbol{\rho}) \to \Psi \text{ an instantiated clause}$$

Predict-pred predicts a passive item for the predicate following the dot in an active item:

$$\textbf{Predict-pred:} \quad \frac{[A(\boldsymbol{\rho}) \to \Phi \bullet B(\boldsymbol{\rho_B})\Psi]}{[B,\boldsymbol{\rho_B},p]}$$

The **scan** operation is the same as in the non-directional case, i.e., it allows us to turn a predicted instantiated predicate into a completed one if there is a corresponding ε-clause.

Complete moves the dot over a predicate in the right-hand side of an active item if the corresponding passive item has been completed.

$$\textbf{Complete:} \quad \frac{[B,\boldsymbol{\rho_B},c],[A(\boldsymbol{\rho}) \to \Phi \bullet B(\boldsymbol{\rho_B})\Psi]}{[A(\boldsymbol{\rho}) \to \Phi B(\boldsymbol{\rho_B}) \bullet \Psi]}$$

Once the dot has reached the right end of a clause, we can **convert** the active item into a *completed* passive item:

$$\textbf{Convert:} \quad \frac{[A(\boldsymbol{\rho}) \to \Phi\bullet]}{[A,\boldsymbol{\rho},c]}$$

182   9 Parsing Range Concatenation Grammars

The **goal** item is again $[S, (\langle 0, n \rangle), c]$.

This algorithm performs a classical Earley parsing using the CFG of instantiated clauses obtained from the RCG with respect to the specific input w. It amounts to computing all instantiated predicates that are 1. reachable from the start symbol $S(\langle 0, n \rangle)$ and 2. useful in the sense that they allow us to derive a string of terminals (the only possible terminal string is ε). The completed passive items in the chart are exactly these predicates. Again, if $S(\langle 0, n \rangle)$ is among them, then w is in the language.

For illustration, see the items given in Fig. 9.4 that are some of the items one obtains when parsing $w = acbbca$ with the grammar from Fig. 9.1.

Some of the successful items:

item	operation
$[S, (_0 acbbca_6), p]$	initialize
$[S(_0 acbbca_6) \to \bullet A(_0 a_1, {_5} a_6) M(_1 cbbc_5, {_1} cbbc_5)]$	pred.-rule
$[A, (_0 a_1, {_5} a_6), p]$	pred.-pred
$[A(_0 a_1, {_5} a_6) \to \bullet A(_1 \varepsilon_1, {_6} \varepsilon_6)]$	pred.-rule
$[A, (_1 \varepsilon_1, {_6} \varepsilon_6), p]$	pred.-pred
$[A, (_1 \varepsilon_1, {_6} \varepsilon_6), c]$	scan
$[A(_0 a_1, {_5} a_6) \to A(_1 \varepsilon_1, {_6} \varepsilon_6) \bullet]$	complete
$[A, (_0 a_1, {_5} a_6), c]$	convert
$[S(_0 acbbca_6) \to A(_0 a_1, {_5} a_6) \bullet M(_1 cbbc_5, {_1} cbbc_5)]$	complete
$[M, (_1 cbbc_5, {_1} cbbc_5), p]$	pred.-pred

. . .

Fig. 9.4. Directional top-down parsing of $w = acbbca$

An obvious problem of the top-down algorithms seen in this section is that they compute all possible instantiations of A-clauses, given the prediction of an instantiated A-predicate. Take again our sample RCG from Fig. 9.1 and the input word $w = acbbca$. Starting from the first prediction of $[S, (\langle 0, 6 \rangle), p]$, **predict-rule** would predict all active items $[S(\langle 0, 6 \rangle) \to \bullet A(\langle 0, i \rangle, \langle j, 6 \rangle) M(\langle i, j \rangle, \langle i, j \rangle)]$ for all $0 \leq i \leq j \leq n$.

The computation of all possible instantiations is very costly and will be avoided in the algorithms that we present in Section 9.2. There, we will use sets of constraints on range boundaries (instead of range vectors) and predict in the Earley algorithm only one active item $[S(XYZ) \to \bullet A(X, Z)M(Y, Y), \{0 = X_l, X_l \leq X_r, X_r = Y_l, Y_l \leq Y_r, Y_r = Z_l, Z_l \leq Z_r, 6 = Z_r\}]$. (In the constraints, for variable v, v_l stands for the left and v_r for the right boundary of its range.)

9.1.4 Optimizations

Filters

A closer look at an RCG can sometimes tell us something about the way the arguments of certain predicates have to be instantiated. This knowledge can be used to restrict the number of predicted clause instantiations.

Precompiled restrictions that can be useful concern information about argument lengths, information about relations between range boundaries and information about terminals occurring in the yields of certain predicates. Let us consider some examples. We stay with our sample RCG from Fig. 9.1. For this RCG, we can deduce the following constraints on instantiations from the grammar:

1. **Length constraints**
   Concerning the predicate A, the only clauses we have are $A(aX, aY) \to A(X, Y)$ and $A(\varepsilon, \varepsilon) \to \varepsilon$. From these clauses, it is obvious, that every range vector $(\langle l_1, r_1 \rangle, \langle l_2, r_2 \rangle)$ in the yield of A, no matter what the input w is, has to be such that $r_2 - l_2 = r_1 - l_1$.

2. **Boundary relations**
   For the predicate A, in its first appearance in a right-hand side, in the clause $S(XYZ) \to A(X, Z)\ldots$, its first argument precedes the second one in the input. Since the A-clauses only remove material to the left of the two argument, the arguments never get longer. Therefore, every range vector $(\langle l_1, r_1 \rangle, \langle l_2, r_2 \rangle)$ in the yield of A, independently from the input w, has to be such that $r_1 \leq l_2$.
   For the predicate M, we have the following clauses: $M(cX, Y) \to M(X, Y)$, $M(bX, cY) \to M(X, Y)$, $M(X, bY) \to M(X, Y)$, $M(\varepsilon, \varepsilon) \to \varepsilon$. Given that the first appearance of M is as $M(Y, Y)$ in a right-hand side and that all M-clauses remove material on the left of their arguments, we can deduce that every range vector $(\langle l_1, r_1 \rangle, \langle l_2, r_2 \rangle)$ in the yield of M, no matter what the input w is, has to be such that $r_1 = r_2$.

3. **Terminal constraints**
   Given the clauses in the RCG, it is obvious that the strings in the yield of A, independently from w, can only contain terminals a and no bs or cs. For M it holds that it yields only bs and cs and no as.

Given these constraints, we would for instance for the input $w = acbbca$ immediately guess the correct instantiation of the first S clause.

Some of these constraints are proposed in (Boullier, 1998a): Boullier proposes the definition of the sets $First$ and $Last$ for every predicate $A \in N$ that can be used to check on the terminals at the beginning and the end of a range vector.

Definition 9.1 (First and Last).
Let $G = (N, T, V, P, S)$ be an RCG. For every $A \in N$ and k, $1 \leq k \leq dim(A)$, we define

1. $First(A,k) = \{t \mid S(\langle 0,n\rangle) \stackrel{*}{\Rightarrow}_{G,w} \Gamma_1 A(\rho_1,\ldots,\rho_k,\ldots,\rho_{dim(A)})\Gamma_2 \stackrel{*}{\Rightarrow}_{G,w} \varepsilon$ for some $w \in T^*$ such that either $t \in T$ and $\rho_k(w) = tv$ for some $v \in T^*$ or $t = \varepsilon$ and $\rho_k(w) = \varepsilon\}$.
2. $Last(A,k) = \{t \mid S(\langle 0,n\rangle) \stackrel{*}{\Rightarrow}_{G,w} \Gamma_1 A(\rho_1,\ldots,\rho_k,\ldots,\rho_{dim(A)})\Gamma_2 \stackrel{*}{\Rightarrow}_{G,w} \varepsilon$ for some $w \in T^*$ such that either $t \in T$ and $\rho_k(w) = vt$ for some $v \in T^*$ or $t = \varepsilon$ and $\rho_k(w) = \varepsilon\}$.

See (Boullier, 1998a) for more details on the computation of the sets $First$ and $Last$. These sets can be used to constrain the possible instantiated clauses that are predicted. For instance, for our sample grammar and the predicate A, we obtain $First(A,1) = First(A,2) = Last(A,1) = Last(A,2) = \{\varepsilon, a\}$. Therefore we predict only instantiations where the arguments of the predicate A are either ε or start and end with an a.

Furthermore, Boullier also proposes precompiling length constraints for the different arguments of a predicate. In our sample grammar, this would tell us for instance that for the A-predicate, the argument lengths must always be equal.

Reordering Right-Hand Sides

In contrast to CFG, in an RCG, the order of the right-hand side predicates is not relevant. However, if we move a dot through the right-hand side, we fix an order in which we process the elements of the right-hand side. A reordering of the right-hand sides of clauses does not affect the language that is generated and it might lead to a better parsing behavior in the sense that right-hand side predicates about whose range vectors we know more are perhaps processed earlier.

In his implementation of the directional top-down parser (2000b), Boullier performs a dynamic reordering of right-hand sides, depending on which predicate yields we know more about. This is one of the reasons why his parser is actually very efficient.

Take for instance the following clause $S(aXbYcZd) \to A(X,Y)B(Z)$ and assume an input string $w = aaaabbbbcdd$. Then, given this input string, in an instantiation of this clause where S yields the entire string w (i.e., the left-hand side is $S(\langle 0, |w|\rangle)$), we necessarily have Z mapped to $_9d_{10}$; this is the only possibility. Therefore, after having predicted this clause, one should first check the B predicate whose range vector is uniquely specified.

9.2 Parsing with Constraint Propagation

As we have seen, the algorithms presented in Section 9.1 have in common that even in predicted items, instantiations are fully specified. In other words, at prediction time, all possible instantiations of all possible clauses have to be computed. The computation of these instantiations is a constraint satisfaction problem that is very costly to solve (Parmentier and Maier, 2008). Furthermore, this strategy of early instantiation computation leads to a high number of items which, in turn, leads to an increased number of parsing operations that do not contribute to a successful parse.

Kallmeyer, Maier, and Parmentier (2009b; 2009a) propose to avoid this adopting a lazy computation of range boundaries: The computation of instantiations is done only at completion time while at prediction time, only the available constraints on the instantiations are accumulated. In other words, as long as we predict, we use some kind of underspecified instantiations (sets of constraints on range boundaries). Only in the **scan** and **convert** steps are these constraints solved and the concrete range boundaries computed.

In the following, we first present a CYK algorithm with active items that moves a dot through the right-hand sides of the clauses. This algorithm uses range boundary constraints in order to achieve the desired underspecification. After that, we extend this algorithm with a top-down prediction.

9.2.1 Range Constraints

Before presenting the algorithms, we will introduce the range constraint representation that they use. It consists of a vector or pairs of range boundary variables and a set of constraints on these variables. The syntax of the constraints allows us to express facts about equality (with another variable or a constant), orderedness (with respect to another variable or a constant), exact distance and minimal distance (between variables).

Definition 9.2 (Range constraint vector).
Let $V_r = \{r_1, r_2, \ldots\}$ be a set of range boundary variables.
A *range constraint vector of dimension* k *is a pair* $\langle \mathbf{r}, C \rangle$ *where*

1. $\mathbf{r} \in (V_r^2)^k$; we define $V_r(\mathbf{r})$ as the set of range boundary variables occurring in $\mathbf{r}$.
2. C is a set of constraints c_r that have one of the following forms:
   - $r_1 = r_2$ for $r_1, r_2 \in V_r(\mathbf{r})$,
   - $k = r_1$ for $r_1 \in V_r(\mathbf{r})$ and $k \in \mathbb{N}$,
   - $r_1 + k = r_2$ for $r_1, r_2 \in V_r(\mathbf{r})$ and $k \in \mathbb{N}$,
   - $k \leq r_1$ for $r_1 \in V_r(\mathbf{r})$ and $k \in \mathbb{N}$,
   - $r_1 \leq k$ for $r_1 \in V_r(\mathbf{r})$ and $k \in \mathbb{N}$,
   - $r_1 \leq r_2$ for $r_1, r_2 \in V_r(\mathbf{r})$, or
   - $r_1 + k \leq r_2$ for $r_1, r_2 \in V_r(\mathbf{r})$ and $k \in \mathbb{N}$.

We say that a range vector $\boldsymbol{\rho}$ satisfies a range constraint vector $\langle \mathbf{r}, C \rangle$ iff $\boldsymbol{\rho}$ and $\mathbf{r}$ are of the same dimension k and there is a function $f : V_r \to \mathbb{N}$ that maps $\mathbf{r}(i).l$ to $\boldsymbol{\rho}(i).l$ and $\mathbf{r}(i).r$ to $\boldsymbol{\rho}(i).r$ for all $1 \leq i \leq k$ such that all constraints in C are satisfied. Furthermore, we say that a range constraint vector $\langle \mathbf{r}, C \rangle$ is satisfiable iff there exists a range vector $\boldsymbol{\rho}$ that satisfies it.

The constraints we accumulate during parsing have different origins: Some of them arise from the clauses themselves and are independent from the input while others arise from the input and from already completed predicates. The former can be precompiled as the range constraint vectors of the clauses.

In order to keep track of the constraints found for the range boundaries of variables, occurrences of terminals and ε-arguments, we assume that in a given clause, these elements are equipped with distinct subscript indices, starting with 1 and ordered from left to right (where for variables, only the first occurrence is relevant for this order). We then introduce a function $\varUpsilon : P \to \mathbb{N}$ that gives the maximal index in a clause. Furthermore, we define $\varUpsilon(c, x)$ for a given clause c and x a variable or an occurrence of a terminal or an ε-argument as the index of x in c.

The clause $c_1 = S(XYZ) \to A(X, Z)M(Y, Y)$ for instance has $\varUpsilon(c_1) = 3$ with $\varUpsilon(c_1, X) = 1, \varUpsilon(c_1, Y) = 2, \varUpsilon(c_1, Z) = 3$; the clause $c_2 = A(aX, aY) \to A(X, Y)$ has $\varUpsilon(c_2) = 4$ with $\varUpsilon(c_2, a^{(1)}) = 1$, and so on; and the clause $c_3 = A(\varepsilon, \varepsilon) \to \varepsilon$ has $\varUpsilon(c_3) = 2$.

Definition 9.3 (Range constraint vector of a clause).
For every clause c, we define its range constraint vector $\langle \mathbf{r}, C \rangle$ *as follows:*

1. $\mathbf{r}$ *has dimension $\varUpsilon(c)$ and all range boundary variables in $\mathbf{r}$ are pairwise different.*
2. *For all $\langle r_1, r_2 \rangle \in \mathbf{r}$, $r_1 \leq r_2 \in C$.*
3. *For all occurrences x of terminals in c with $i = \varUpsilon(c, x)$, $\mathbf{r}(i).l + 1 = \mathbf{r}(i).r \in C$.*
4. *For all x, y that are variables or occurrences of terminals in c such that xy is a substring of one of the arguments in c, $\mathbf{r}(\varUpsilon(c, x)).r = \mathbf{r}(\varUpsilon(c, y)).l \in C$.*
5. *For all occurrences x of ε-arguments with $i = \varUpsilon(c, x)$, $\mathbf{r}(i).l = \mathbf{r}(i).r \in C$.*
6. *These are all constraints in C.*

The range constraint vector of a clause c captures all information about boundaries forming a range, ranges containing only a single terminal, and adjacent variables/terminal occurrences in c.

Take for instance the first clause of our sample RCG from Fig. 9.1, $S(XYZ) \to A(X, Z)M(Y, Y)$. As range constraints, we obtain for this clause the range constraint vector $\langle (\langle r_1, r_2 \rangle, \langle r_3, r_4 \rangle, \langle r_5, r_6 \rangle), \{r_1 \leq r_2, r_3 \leq r_4, r_5 \leq r_6, r_2 = r_3, r_4 = r_5\} \rangle$.

We say that an instantiation f of a clause c satisfies a range constraint vector $\langle \mathbf{r}, C \rangle$ of dimension $\varUpsilon(c)$ if the following holds: let ρ be the vector $(\rho_1, \ldots, \rho_{\varUpsilon(c)})$ such that for $1 \leq i \leq \varUpsilon(c)$ and x be the element (variable/terminal occurrence or ε-argument) with $\varUpsilon(c, x) = i$, $\rho_i = f(x)$. Then f satisfies $\langle \mathbf{r}, C \rangle$ iff ρ satisfies $\langle \mathbf{r}, C \rangle$.

9.2.2 CYK Parsing with Active Items

An obvious disadvantage of the basic CYK algorithm is that, in order to perform a *complete* step, all $A_1, \ldots, A_k$ in the right-hand side must be checked for appropriate items. This leads to many indices that need to be checked at the same time.

To avoid this, we can again move a dot through the right-hand side of a clause, as in the case of the previous formalisms seen in this book. Therefore, besides passive items, we also need active items. Passive items are again of the form
$$[A, \boldsymbol{\rho}]$$
where A is a predicate and $\boldsymbol{\rho}$ is a range vector of dimension $dim(A)$. The active items we need are, however, different from the active items used in the directional top-down algorithm seen above since we now use range constraint vectors instead of fully specified instantiations. In the active items, while traversing the right-hand side of the clause, we keep a record of the positions already found for the left and right boundaries of variables and terminal occurrences. This is achieved by subsequently enriching the range constraint vector of the clause.

Active items have the form
$$[A(\boldsymbol{\alpha}) \to \Phi \bullet \Psi, \langle \mathbf{r}, C \rangle]$$
with $A(\boldsymbol{\alpha}) \to \Phi\Psi$ a clause, $\Phi\Psi \neq \varepsilon$, $\Upsilon(A(\boldsymbol{\alpha}) \to \Phi\Psi) = j$ and $\langle \mathbf{r}, C \rangle$ a range constraint vector of dimension j. We require that $\langle \mathbf{r}, C \rangle$ be satisfiable.

Items that are distinguished from each other only by a bijection of the range variables are considered equivalent. I.e., if the application of a rule yields a new item such that an equivalent one has already been generated, this new one is not added to the set of partial results.

The **scan** rule is the same as in the basic algorithm:

Scan: $\dfrac{}{[A, \boldsymbol{\rho}]}\quad A(\boldsymbol{\rho}) \to \varepsilon$ an instantiated clause

In addition, we have an **initialize** rule that introduces clauses with the dot on the left of the right-hand side:

Initialize: $\dfrac{}{[A(\boldsymbol{\alpha}) \to \bullet\Phi, \langle \mathbf{r}, C \rangle]}$

$A(\boldsymbol{\alpha}) \to \Phi$ is a clause with range constraint vector $\langle \mathbf{r}, C' \rangle, \Phi \neq \varepsilon$, and C is obtained from C' by adding $0 \leq r$ for every left boundary variable r and $r \leq n$ for every right boundary variable r.

The **complete** rule moves the dot over a predicate in the right-hand side of an active item provided the corresponding passive item has been completed:

$$\dfrac{[B, \boldsymbol{\rho}_\mathbf{B}], [A(\boldsymbol{\alpha}) \to \Phi \bullet B(x_1...y_1, ..., x_k...y_k)\Psi, \langle \mathbf{r}, C \rangle]}{[A(\boldsymbol{\alpha}) \to \Phi B(x_1...y_1, ..., x_k...y_k) \bullet \Psi, \langle \mathbf{r}, C' \rangle]}$$

where $C' = C \cup \{\boldsymbol{\rho}_\mathbf{B}(j).l = \mathbf{r}(\Upsilon(x_j)).l,\ \boldsymbol{\rho}_\mathbf{B}(j).r = \mathbf{r}(\Upsilon(y_j)).r \mid 1 \leq j \leq k\}$.

Trace (only successful items listed):

	item	operation
1	$[M, (_5\varepsilon_5, {_5\varepsilon_5})]$	scan
2	$[A, (_1\varepsilon_1, {_6\varepsilon_6})]$	scan
3	$[A(aX, aY) \to \bullet A(X,Y), \{a_1.l+1 = a_1.r, a_1.r = X.l, X.l \leq X.r,$ $a_2.l+1 = a_2.r, a_2.r = Y.l, Y.l \leq Y.r\}]$	initialize
4	$[A(aX, aY) \to A(X,Y)\bullet, \{\ldots, 1 = X.l, 1 = X.r, 6 = X.l, 6 = X.r\}]$	compl. 3, 2
5	$[A, (_0a_1, {_5a_6})]$	convert 4
6	$[S(XYZ) \to \bullet A(X,Z)M(Y,Y), \{X.l \leq X.r, Y.l \leq Y.r, Z.l \leq Z.r,$ $X.r = Y.l, Y.r = Z.l, X.r \leq Z.l\}]$	initialize
7	$[S(XYZ) \to A(X,Z) \bullet M(Y,Y), \{\ldots, 0 = X.l, 1 = X.r, ,$ $5 = Z.l, 6 = Z.r\}]$	comp. 5, 6 comp. 5, 6
	...	
8	$[M, (_1cbbc_5, {_1cbbc_5})]$	
9	$[S(XYZ) \to A(X,Z)M(Y,Y)\bullet, \{\ldots, 1 = Y.l, 5 = Y.r\}]$	comp. 7, 8
10	$[S, (_0acbbca_6)]$	convert 9

Fig. 9.5. CYK parsing with active items and constraint propagation, $w = acbbca$

Note that the conditions on the items require the new constraint set for **r** to be satisfiable.

Convert turns an active item with the dot at the end of the right-hand side into a completed passive item:

$$\textbf{Convert:} \quad \frac{[A(\boldsymbol{\alpha}) \to \Psi\bullet, \langle \mathbf{r}, C \rangle]}{[A, \boldsymbol{\rho}]}$$

where there is an instantiation f of $A(\boldsymbol{\alpha}) \to \Psi$ that satisfies $\langle \mathbf{r}, C \rangle$ such that $f(A(\boldsymbol{\alpha})) = A(\boldsymbol{\rho})$.

The **goal** item is $[S, (\langle 0, n \rangle)]$.

A sample parse trace is shown in Fig. 9.5. For the sake of readability, instead of the range boundary variables, we use $X.l$ and $X.r$ respectively for the left and right range boundary of the range associated with X. Furthermore, the constraints $0 \leq X.l$ and $X.r \leq 6$ are left aside.

9.2.3 Earley Parsing

We now add a prediction operation to the CYK algorithm with active items, which leads to an Earley-style algorithm. The passive items are different, depending on whether they are predicted or completed. Predicted passive items contain range constraint vectors since when predicting a category, the left and right boundaries of its arguments might not be known. They therefore have the form $[A, \langle \mathbf{r}, C \rangle]$, where $\langle \mathbf{r}, C \rangle$ is a range constraint vector of dimension $dim(A)$. Completed passive items have the form $[A, \boldsymbol{\rho}]$ where $\boldsymbol{\rho}$ is a range vector of dimension $dim(A)$. The active items are the same as in the CYK case in the preceding section.

9.2 Parsing with Constraint Propagation

Trace (only successful items listed):

	item	operation
1	$[S, \langle(\langle r_1, r_2\rangle), \{0 = r_1, 6 = r_2\}\rangle]$	initialize
2	$[S(XYZ) \to \bullet A(X,Z)M(Y,Y), \{X.l \leq X.r, Y.l \leq Y.r, Z.l \leq Z.r,$ $X.r = Y.l, Y.r = Z.l, 0 = X.l, 6 = Z.r\}]$	pred.-rule
3	$[A, (\langle r_1, r_2\rangle, \langle r_3, r_4\rangle), \{r_1 \leq r_2, r_3 \leq r_4, r_2 \leq r_3, 0 = r_1, 6 = r_4\}]$	pred.-pred
4	$[A(aX, aY) \to \bullet A(X,Y), \{a_1.l + 1 = a_1.r, a_1.r = X.l, X.l \leq X.r,$ $a_2.l + 1 = a_2.r, a_2.r = Y.l, Y.l \leq Y.r, \ldots,$ $0 = a_1.l, 6 = Y.r\}]$	initialize pred.-rule
5	$[A, (\langle r_1, r_2\rangle, \langle r_3, r_4\rangle), \{r_1 \leq r_2, r_3 \leq r_4, r_2 \leq r_3, 1 = r_1, 6 = r_4\}]$	pred.-pred
6	$[A, (_1\varepsilon_1, {}_6\varepsilon_6)]$	scan
7	$[A(aX, aY) \to A(X,Y)\bullet, \{0 = a_1.l, 1 = a_1.r, 1 = X.l, 1 = X.r,$ $5 = a_2.l, 6 = a_2.r, 6 = Y.l, 6 = Y.r\}]$	compl. 4,6
8	$[A, (_0 a_1, {}_5 a_6)]$	convert

$\ldots$

Fig. 9.6. Earley parsing with constraint propagation, $w = acbbca$

The axiom is the prediction of an S ranging over the entire input, i.e., the **initialize** rule is as follows:

$$\textbf{Initialize:} \quad \frac{}{[S, \langle(\langle r_1, r_2\rangle), \{0 = r_1, n = r_2\}\rangle]}$$

We have two predict operations. The first one, **predict-rule**, predicts active items with the dot on the left of the right-hand side for a given predicted passive item:

$$\textbf{Predict-rule:} \quad \frac{[A, \langle \mathbf{r}, C\rangle]}{[A(x_1 \ldots y_1, \ldots, x_k \ldots y_k) \to \bullet \Psi, \langle \mathbf{r}', C'\rangle]}$$

where $\langle \mathbf{r}', C'\rangle$ is obtained from the range constraint vector of the clause $A(x_1 \ldots y_1, \ldots, x_k \ldots y_k) \to \Psi$ by taking all constraints from C, mapping all $\mathbf{r}(i).l$ to $\mathbf{r}'(\Upsilon(x_i)).l$ and all $\mathbf{r}(i).r$ to $\mathbf{r}'(\Upsilon(y_i)).r$, and then adding the resulting constraints to the range constraint vector of the clause.

The second predict operation, **predict-pred**, predicts a passive item for the predicate following the dot in an active item:

$$\textbf{Predict-pred:} \quad \frac{[A(\ldots) \to \Phi \bullet B(x_1 \ldots y_1, \ldots, x_k \ldots y_k)\Psi, \langle \mathbf{r}, C\rangle]}{[B, \langle \mathbf{r}', C'\rangle, p]}$$

where $\mathbf{r}'(i).l = \mathbf{r}(\Upsilon(x_i)).l$, $\mathbf{r}'(i).r = \mathbf{r}(\Upsilon(y_i)).r$ for all $1 \leq i \leq k$ and $C' = \{c \,|\, c \in C, c$ contains only range variables from $\mathbf{r}'\}$.

Note that some (implicit) constraints get lost here since we do not inherit constraints from the transitive closure of C.

The **scan** rule can be applied if a predicted predicate can be derived by an ε-clause:

$$\textbf{Scan:} \quad \frac{[A, \langle \mathbf{r}, C\rangle, p]}{[A, \boldsymbol{\rho}, c]}$$

where there is a clause $A(\boldsymbol{\alpha}) \to \varepsilon$ with a possible instantiation f that satisfies $\langle \mathbf{r}, C \rangle$ such that $f(A(\boldsymbol{\alpha})) = A(\boldsymbol{\rho})$.

Finally, deduction rules for **complete** and **convert** are the ones from the CYK algorithm with active items except that we add flags c to the passive items occurring in these rules.

Again, the **goal** item is $[S, (\langle 0, n \rangle), c]$.

To understand how this algorithm works, consider the example in Fig. 9.6.

The algorithm shows a great similarity to the directional top-down algorithm, both of them being Earley algorithms where a dot is moved through the right-hand side of a clause. The crucial difference is that while in the first algorithm, we are using range vectors to record the variable bindings, in the Earley-style algorithm presented here, we use range constraint vectors. Due to the fact that range constraint vectors allow us to leave range boundaries unspecified, we can compute values of range boundaries in a more incremental fashion since we do not have to guess all clause instantiations at once as in the top-down algorithm. This becomes particularly clear when comparing the **complete** rules of the non-directional top-down algorithm and the Earley-style algorithm. In the former, we check the compatibility of the range vector of the completed item with the range vector of the item which is to be completed as a side condition. In the latter however, we add the information contributed by the range vector of the completed item dynamically to the range constraint vector of the item to be completed.

We can optimize the parsers with constraint propagation similarly to what we have proposed at the end of the section on directional top-down parsing with instantiated clauses. I.e., first we can precompile additional constraints from the grammar that follow from the entire grammar, not only from single clauses as is the case for the range constraint vectors of the clauses. Furthermore, by dynamically reordering the right-hand sides of clauses, we can extend the operation **predict-pred** so as to predict always the predicate from the remaining right-hand side whose yield boundaries are maximally specified.

Obtaining a Parse Forest

So far, we have described recognizers, not parsers. The way to obtain a parse forest from the item set resulting from the Earley recognizer with range boundary constraints is rather obvious. Whenever a convert is done, a fully instantiated clause has been found. By collecting these clauses, we obtain a compact representation of our parse forest. Starting from an S predicate ranging over the entire input and following the clauses for the instantiated predicates in the right-hand sides, we can read off the single parse trees from this forest.

9.3 Summary

We have seen in this chapter that a crucial property of RCGs is that in a derivation, the variables, terminals and empty arguments of clauses must be instantiated with actual substrings (ranges) of the input string. As a consequence, the set of instantiated clauses for a given string w is a finite set. We can consider these instantiated clauses as context-free rewriting rules. In other words, the set of instantiated clauses for a given string w is a context-free grammar, and we can apply CFG parsing techniques to this grammar in order to determine whether ε is in the language generated by this grammar, which is equivalent to w being in the language of the RCG. The first algorithms seen in this chapter perform a CYK and an Earley parsing, using the CFG of instantiated clauses.

Since the computation of clause instantiations is costly, it should be done as late as possible. In the second part of this chapter, we have seen a technique of constraint propagation during RCG parsing that allows a lazy computation of clause instantiations. In the algorithms seen there, in active items, i.e., items where only parts of the right-hand side of a clause have been completed while parts of it have only been predicted, we collect all available constraints on the clause instantiations. Only when reaching the end of a right-hand side do we compute the actual instantiation.

We have seen different ways of optimizing the algorithms seen in this chapter. Firstly, certain constraints on the yields of the predicates in the grammar can be precompiled from the grammar. Secondly, a dynamic reordering of right-hand sides during parsing can help to continue always with the predicate with the maximally specified yield in the predicted part of a right-hand side.

Besides the approaches mentioned in this chapter, Barthélemy et al. (2001) propose obtaining, from a given RCG, a more general 1-RCG that, roughly, treats the different arguments of a predicate as independent from each other. This 1-RCG can be used as a guide for parsing with the original RCG.

In conclusion, one has to admit, though, that a general efficient RCG-parsing is difficult. However, from the different examples and applications that we have seen in the preceding chapter, it becomes clear that there are useful subclasses of RCG that are beyond simple RCG. Examples are the $(2,2)$-BRCGs proposed by Søgaard (2008) for alignment and the non-erasing bottom-up linear RCGs one might use to describe gapping and other elliptical phenomena. Developing efficient parsers for restricted types of RCG might be possible.

Problems

9.1. Consider the basic CYK algorithm seen at the beginning of the chapter. Assume that we are dealing with binarized RCGs, i.e., with RCGs where the right-hand sides of the clauses contain at most two elements. Furthermore, assume that the RCGs are non-combinatorial and that the left-hand side arguments in the clauses have length ≤ 2.

What is the complexity of the CYK algorithm, given these restrictions?

9.2. Give the range constraints for the clause $A(aX, Ya, \varepsilon) \to C(XY)$.

9.3. Consider the RCG G with the following clauses.
$$S(XY) \to A(X, X)B(Y, Y)$$
$$A(aX, bY) \to A(X, Y) \qquad B(cX, dY) \to B(X, Y)$$
$$A(bX, Y) \to A(X, Y) \qquad B(dX, Y) \to B(X, Y)$$
$$A(X, aY) \to A(X, Y) \qquad B(X, cY) \to B(X, Y)$$
$$A(\varepsilon, \varepsilon) \to \varepsilon \qquad B(\varepsilon, \varepsilon) \to \varepsilon$$

1. What is the string language $L(G)$?
2. Compute the sets $First(A, 1)$, $First(A, 2)$, $First(B, 1)$ and $First(B, 2)$.
3. What are possible filters that might help to restrict the computation of clause instantiations during top-down parsing?

10
Automata

We have seen the definitions of Finite State Automata (FSA) and of Push-Down Automata (PDA) in Chapter 1. The former accept all regular languages while the latter accept all context-free languages. In this chapter, we present automaton models for different extensions of CFG, in particular for TAG and LCFRS.

10.1 Embedded Push-Down Automata

Embedded Push-Down Automata (EPDA) have been introduced in (Vijay-Shanker, 1987). EPDA recognize the class of Tree-Adjoining Languages (TALs) and are a natural extension of push-down automata (PDA), the class of automata which recognizes CFG (Hopcroft and Ullman, 1979). The central idea behind EPDA is to replace the single push-down store used in PDA with a stack of non-empty push-down stores as depicted in Fig. 10.1. We can perform some nested rewriting on the top-most stack, i.e., besides treating it as a PDA stack, we can wrap new stacks around it. This is crucial for the extended power of EPDA, compared to PDA. While the single push-down store in a PDA can only handle the nested dependencies of CFL, we will see that the stack of push-down stores can handle the cross-serial dependencies of TAL.

10.1.1 Definition of EPDA

An EPDA consists of a finite state control, a one-way input tape and a stack of non-empty stacks. The finite control sees always the top symbol of the top stack and the current input symbol. Depending on these symbols and the current state of the automaton, it performs a move. Such a move is divided into two parts: In a first operation, the top-most stack Υ is treated as in the PDA case. I.e., its top-most symbol is replaced by a new, possibly empty, sequence of stack symbols. In a second operation, the entire stack (of stacks) is then treated as in the PDA case, i.e., the new top-most stack Υ' that was

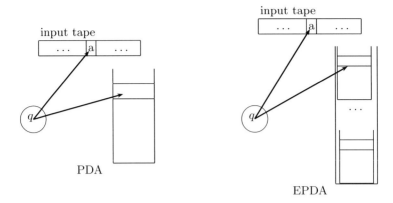

Fig. 10.1. PDA and EPDA

obtained from the first operation is replaced by a sequence of k stacks that includes Υ' ($k \geq 0$).

As in the case of PDA, there are two equivalent ways of defining the acceptance mode of an EPDA. Either an input w is accepted if, after having read the entire input, the automaton finishes with an empty stack, or w is accepted if, after having read the entire w, the automaton ends up in a final state.

Before giving the formal definition, let us consider an example (taken from (Vijay- Shanker, 1987)). An EPDA that accepts the language $L_4 = \{a^n b^n c^n d^n \mid n \geq 0\}$ could work as follows: Assume that each input symbol corresponds to a different state. Then the automaton can use the stacks to keep track of the number of bs, cs and ds that are still required: For each a encountered in the input, a symbol B is pushed on the top-most stack (to ensure that the number of as is equal to the number of bs), and below the top-most stack, an extra stack with a single D is introduced (this ensures that the number of as equals the number of ds). For each b encountered in the input, we have to find a top-most symbol B on the top-most stack which is removed. Furthermore, to make sure we find later a corresponding c, below the top-most stack, an extra stack with a single C is introduced. After having read all as and bs, we have a sequence of stacks; each one contains a single symbol $x \in \{C, D\}$ where the number of C-stacks equals the number of D-stacks (and the number of as encountered earlier) and all C-stacks precede (i.e., are higher than) all D-stacks. Now we process the remaining input while deleting the stacks. For each c encountered in the input, if the top-most symbol of the top-most stack is C, we delete this stack and proceed. For each d encountered in the input, if the top-most symbol of the top-most stack is D, we delete this stack and proceed. We accept if no input symbols are left and the stack is empty.

Definition 10.1 (Embedded Push-Down Automaton).
An Embedded Push-Down Automaton (EPDA) M *is a 7-tuple* $\langle Q, \Sigma, \Gamma, \delta, q_0, Q_F, Z_0 \rangle$, *where*

- Q *is a finite set of states,* $q_0 \in Q$ *is the start state and* $Q_F \subseteq Q$ *is the set of final states.*
- Γ *is the finite set of stack symbols and* $Z_0 \in \Gamma$ *is the initial stack symbol.*
- Σ *is the finite set of input symbols.*
- δ *is the transition function* $Q \times (\Sigma \cup \{\varepsilon\}) \times \Gamma \to P_{fin}(Q \times \Upsilon^* \times \Gamma^* \times \Upsilon^*)$, *where* $\Upsilon = \Gamma^*$ *correspond to push-downs of stack symbols.*

We can give an instantaneous description of an EPDA by a *configuration*. A configuration is of type $Q \times \Upsilon^* \times \Sigma^* \times \Sigma^*$, i.e., it consists of the current state $q \in Q$, the stack of stacks $s \in \Upsilon^*$, the already recognized part of the input $w_1 \in \Sigma^*$ and the part $w_2 \in \Sigma^*$ which is yet to be recognized. Within Υ^*, we mark each start (bottom) of a stack with the symbol $\ddagger$ (assuming without loss of generality that $\ddagger \notin \Gamma$) and, as a convention, the top is the rightmost element. The initial configuration of an EPDA is

$$\langle q_0, \ddagger Z_0, \varepsilon, w \rangle$$

where the automaton is in the start state q_0, there is only one stack on the stack, this single stack contains only the initial stack symbol Z_0 and the entire input is still to be recognized.

Definition 10.2 (EPDA transition).
Let $\langle Q, \Sigma, \Gamma, \delta, q_0, Q_F, Z_0 \rangle$ *be an EPDA,* $\Upsilon = \{\ddagger\gamma \,|\, \gamma \in \Gamma^*\}$.

- *For all* $q_1, q_2 \in Q, a \in (\Sigma \cup \{\varepsilon\}), w_1, w_2 \in \Sigma^*, \alpha, \alpha_1, \alpha_2 \in \Upsilon^*, Z \in \Gamma, \beta, \gamma \in \Gamma^*$,
  a) $\langle q_1, \alpha\ddagger\beta Z, w_1, aw_2 \rangle \vdash \langle q_2, \alpha\alpha_1\ddagger\beta\gamma\alpha_2, w_1 a, w_2 \rangle$
     if $\langle q_2, \alpha_1, \gamma, \alpha_2 \rangle \in \delta(q_1, a, Z)$ *and* $\beta\gamma \neq \varepsilon$.
  b) $\langle q_1, \alpha\ddagger Z, w_1, aw_2 \rangle \vdash \langle q_2, \alpha\alpha_1\alpha_2, w_1 a, w_2 \rangle$
     if $\langle q_2, \alpha_1, \varepsilon, \alpha_2 \rangle \in \delta(q_1, a, Z)$.
- $\stackrel{*}{\vdash}$ *is the reflexive transitive closure of* $\vdash$.

Note that empty transitions are allowed ($a \in (\Sigma \cup \{\varepsilon\})$), i.e., transitions that do not read an input symbol. The case b) covers the special case where the top-most stack is emptied. We then assume that this stack gets deleted and therefore even its bottom-stack symbol $\ddagger$ disappears.

We now define the two modes of acceptance for EPDA:

Definition 10.3 (Language of an EPDA).
Let $M = \langle Q, \Sigma, \Gamma, \delta, q_0, Q_F, Z_0 \rangle$ *be an EPDA.*

1. M *accepts the languages* $L(M)$ *in its final states:*

$$L(M) = \{w \,|\, \langle q_0, \ddagger Z_0, \varepsilon, w \rangle \stackrel{*}{\vdash} \langle q_f, \alpha, w, \varepsilon \rangle \text{ for some } q_f \in Q_F, \alpha \in \Upsilon^*\}.$$

2. M accepts the languages $N(M)$ by empty stack:

$$N(M) = \{w \mid \langle q_0, \ddagger Z_0, \varepsilon, w \rangle \overset{*}{\vdash} \langle q, \varepsilon, w, \varepsilon \rangle \text{ for some } q \in Q\}.$$

Now we can specify the automaton for L_4 as sketched above. It is given in Fig. 10.2 and a sample run of this automaton for the input word $aabbccdd$ is shown in Fig. 10.3. The states $q_0, \ldots, q_3$ serve to distinguish the a-reading phase, b-reading phase and so on. Note however that we do not need all of them; it would be enough to distinguish between a "stack-creating" phase (during which the as are read) and then a "stack-reducing" phase that collapses states $q_1, \ldots, q_3$ into a single state.

EPDA $M = \langle Q, \Sigma, \Gamma, \delta, q_0, Q_F, Z_0 \rangle$ with
$Q = \{q_0, q_1, q_2, q_3\}$, $Q_F = \emptyset$, $Z_0 = \#$, $\Sigma = \{a, b, c, d\}$, $\Gamma = \{\#, B, C, D\}$
Transition function δ:
$\delta(q_0, a, \#) = \{(q_0, \ddagger D, B, \varepsilon)\}$ $\delta(q_0, a, B) = \{(q_0, \ddagger D, BB, \varepsilon)\}$
$\delta(q_0, b, B) = \{(q_1, \ddagger C, \varepsilon, \varepsilon)\}$ $\delta(q_1, b, B) = \{(q_1, \ddagger C, \varepsilon, \varepsilon)\}$
$\delta(q_1, c, C) = \{(q_2, \varepsilon, \varepsilon, \varepsilon)\}$ $\delta(q_2, c, C) = \{(q_2, \varepsilon, \varepsilon, \varepsilon)\}$
$\delta(q_2, d, D) = \{(q_3, \varepsilon, \varepsilon, \varepsilon)\}$ $\delta(q_3, d, D) = \{(q_3, \varepsilon, \varepsilon, \varepsilon)\}$

Fig. 10.2. An EPDA M with $N(M) = L_4 = \{a^n b^n c^n d^n \mid n \geq 0\}$

Recognition of $aabbccdd$ with M:
$(q_0, \ddagger\#, \varepsilon, aabbccdd)$
$\vdash (q_0, \ddagger D \ddagger B, a, abbccdd)$
$\vdash (q_0, \ddagger D \ddagger D \ddagger BB, aa, bbccdd)$
$\vdash (q_1, \ddagger D \ddagger D \ddagger C \ddagger B, aab, bccdd)$
$\vdash (q_1, \ddagger D \ddagger D \ddagger C \ddagger C, aabb, ccdd)$
$\vdash (q_2, \ddagger D \ddagger D \ddagger C, aabbc, cdd)$
$\vdash (q_2, \ddagger D \ddagger D, aabbcc, dd)$
$\vdash (q_3, \ddagger D, aabbccd, d)$
$\vdash (q_3, \varepsilon, aabbccdd, \varepsilon)$

Fig. 10.3. A sample run of the EPDA M from Fig. 10.2

As in the case of PDA, it holds also for EPDA that the set of languages accepted by EPDA with the empty stack is the same as the set of languages accepted by EPDA with a final state. This is shown in (Vijay-Shanker, 1987).

Lemma 10.4.

1. For every EPDA M, there is an EPDA M' such that $L(M) = N(M')$.
2. For every EPDA M, there is an EPDA M' such that $N(M) = L(M')$.

To show the first part, for a given M, we have to add transitions that move into a new "stack-emptying" state q' once we have reached a final state and that then empty the stack. For the second part, we add to M a new initial state and a new initial stack symbol. From these we move to the original initial symbols, perform the run of the automaton M and, once we reach a configuration where only our new stack symbol remains on the stack, move into a new final state. For an example of the latter, see the solution of Problem 10.1.

10.1.2 EPDA and TAG

Vijay- Shanker (1987) shows that EPDA accept exactly the class of all Tree Adjoining Languages (TALs). Vijay-Shanker's proof, however, does not give direct constructions of equivalent TAGs for given EPDA and vice versa. Instead, he shows how to construct an equivalent Modified Head Grammar (MHG) for a given EPDA and vice versa. Since the equivalence between MHG and TAG has been established earlier, this proves the equivalence between TAG and EPDA.

Lemma 10.5. *For every TAG G there is an EPDA M and vice versa such that $L(G) = L(M)$ (Vijay- Shanker, 1987).*

Let us nevertheless sketch the idea of how to construct an equivalent EPDA for a given TAG. We let the moves of the EPDA correspond to the expansion of nodes in a TAG derivation. We assume one stack symbol for each node. The symbol corresponding to the next node to be expanded is the top-most stack symbol of the automaton. When we adjoin to a node, we add the root node symbol of the new auxiliary tree to the current top stack. When moving down in a tree along the spine of an auxiliary tree, we place new stacks above and below the current one. These encode the parts to the left and the right of the spine of the adjoined auxiliary tree. This ensures that when recognizing adjunction, we recognize the left part of the auxiliary tree, the subtree below the node where the adjunction took place (i.e., below the foot node) and the right part of the auxiliary tree. When moving down without being on the spine of some auxiliary tree, we simply replace the mother node symbol by the daughters (in reverse order, i.e., the leftmost daughter on top).

An example is given in Fig. 10.4. In order to separate adjunction from moving to the daughters, we distinguish top and bottom ($\top$ and $\bot$) node names on the stack. For a node N, the symbol $N^\top$ is replaced with $N^\bot$ if no adjunction is predicted and with the symbols $N^\bot R_\beta$ if adjunction of β is predicted and R_β is the root node of β. A sample run for the input *aacbb* is shown in Fig. 10.5.

10.1.3 Bottom-Up Embedded Push-Down Automata

Bottom-up Embedded Push-Down Automata (BEPDA) have been first proposed in (Schabes, 1990; Schabes and Vijay-Shanker, 1990) as the "dual"

TAG:

$$R_\alpha \qquad R_\beta$$
$$| \qquad /|\backslash$$
$$c \qquad a\ F\ b$$

(R_α and R_β allow for adjunction of β.)

Equivalent EPDA:
$M = \langle Q, \Sigma, \Gamma, \delta, q_0, Q_F, Z_0 \rangle$ with
$Q = \{q_0, q_1, q_2, q_3\}$, $Q_F = \emptyset$
$Z_0 = \#$, $\Sigma = \{a, b, c\}$, $\Gamma = \{\#, R_\alpha, R_\beta, F, A, B, C\}$
Transition function δ:

$\langle q, \varepsilon, R_\alpha^\top, \varepsilon \rangle \in \delta(q, \varepsilon, \#)$	start initial tree
$\langle q, \varepsilon, R_\alpha^\perp, \varepsilon \rangle \in \delta(q, \varepsilon, R_\alpha^\top)$	no adjunction at R_α
$\langle q, \varepsilon, C, \varepsilon \rangle \in \delta(q, \varepsilon, R_\alpha^\perp)$	move down
$\langle q, \varepsilon, R_\alpha^\perp R_\beta^\top, \varepsilon \rangle \in \delta(q, \varepsilon, R_\alpha^\top)$	adjunction of β
$\langle q, \varepsilon, R_\beta^\perp R_\beta^\top, \varepsilon \rangle \in \delta(q, \varepsilon, R_\beta^\top)$	adjunction of β
$\langle q, \varepsilon, R_\beta^\perp, \varepsilon \rangle \in \delta(q, \varepsilon, R_\beta^\top)$	no adjunction at R_β
$\langle q, \ddagger B, F, \ddagger A \rangle \in \delta(q, \varepsilon, R_\beta^\perp)$	move down
$\langle q, \varepsilon, \varepsilon, \varepsilon \rangle \in \delta(q, \varepsilon, F)$	no adjunction at F, move back
$\langle q, \varepsilon, \varepsilon, \varepsilon \rangle \in \delta(q, a, A)$	match a with input
$\langle q, \varepsilon, \varepsilon, \varepsilon \rangle \in \delta(q, b, B)$	match b with input
$\langle q, \varepsilon, \varepsilon, \varepsilon \rangle \in \delta(q, c, C)$	match c with input

Acceptance with the empty stack.

Fig. 10.4. TAG and equivalent EPDA

Stacks	remaining input	
$\ddagger \#$	aacbb	
$\ddagger R_\alpha^\top$	aacbb	start traversal of α
$\ddagger R_\alpha^\perp R_\beta^\top$	aacbb	predict adjunction of β
$\ddagger R_\alpha^\perp R_\beta^\perp R_\beta^\top$	aacbb	predict adjunction of β
$\ddagger R_\alpha^\perp R_\beta^\perp R_\beta^\perp$	aacbb	predict no adjunction
$\ddagger B \ddagger R_\alpha^\perp R_\beta^\perp F \ddagger A$	aacbb	move down in β
$\ddagger B \ddagger R_\alpha^\perp R_\beta^\perp F$	acbb	scan a
$\ddagger B \ddagger R_\alpha^\perp R_\beta^\perp$	acbb	leave β
$\ddagger B \ddagger B \ddagger R_\alpha^\perp F \ddagger A$	acbb	move down in β
$\ddagger B \ddagger B \ddagger R_\alpha^\perp F$	cbb	scan a
$\ddagger B \ddagger B \ddagger R_\alpha^\perp$	cbb	leave β
$\ddagger B \ddagger B \ddagger C$	cbb	move down in α
$\ddagger B \ddagger B$	bb	scan c
$\ddagger B$	b	scan b
ε	ε	scan b

Fig. 10.5. A sample run of the EPDA from Fig. 10.4

of EPDA while (Rambow, 1994) gives a formal definition of this automaton model. BEPDA accept all Tree Adjoining Languages. The EPDA we have seen for TALs simulate TAG derivations in a top-down way, i.e., they perform a top-down recognition. This is the only way an EPDA can recognize a TAL.[1] In contrast to this, BEPDA simulate a bottom-up recognition of a TAL.

The idea of BEPDA is the following: In an EPDA, we have two types of moves. The first type consists of manipulating the top-most stack and wrapping new stacks around it. The second (see case b) in the transition definition) applies only when the top-most stack is empty and it consists of deleting (popping) this stack. In a BEPDA, we reverse the two moves, i.e., we have the following two moves: The first one is an operation of unwrapping where sequences of stacks are removed around a designated stack which becomes the new top stack and, furthermore, a sequence of symbols is popped from the new top stack and replaced with a single stack symbol. The second possible move consists of pushing a new empty stack onto the stack of stacks.

The BEPDA for a given TAG first shifts all terminals onto the stack of stacks, each stored in a separate stack. Then it performs bottom-up reductions where, when moving up along the spine of an auxiliary tree, the parts to the left and to the right are stack sequences around the current stack that are unwrapped.

For more details and a formal definition of BEPDA, see (Rambow, 1994).

10.1.4 k-Order EPDA

The concept of EPDA was extended in (Weir, 1988; Weir, 1992) to k-order EPDA. In the first version, (1988), Weir called this automaton model Nested Push-Down Automata (NPDA).

The generalization is as follows: For a given stack symbol alphabet Γ, a simple stack $\gamma \in \Gamma^*$ is called a first-order stack while a stack of first-order stacks is called a second-order stack and so on. In general, a stack of $(k-1)$-order stacks is a k-order stack. Each move in a simple EPDA takes the top-most first-order stack, manipulates it the way it is possible within a PDA and then, on the second-order stack, wraps other first-order stacks around it. This can be extended by defining that a move in a k-order EPDA manipulates a k-order stack by taking its top-most $(k-1)$-order stack, manipulating it the way it is possible in a $(k-1)$-order EPDA and then wrapping other k-order stacks around it.

This definition leads to a hierarchy of automata, the so-called *Weir Hierarchy*. The first class of this hierarchy, 1-order EPDA, are PDA, i.e., generate exactly the context-free languages. The second class, 2-order EPDA, are the EPDA from (Vijay-Shanker, 1987) that generate exactly the Tree Adjoining Languages.

---

[1] This differs from PDA and CFG where, for a given CFG, one can construct a PDA that performs a top-down recognition or a PDA that performs a bottom-up recognition.

10.2 Two-Stack Automata

Two-Stack Automata (2-SA) have been introduced by Becker (1994). They constitute an alternative automaton model for TAG.

10.2.1 General Definition

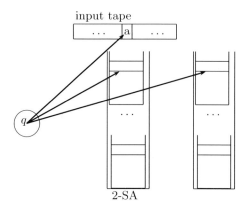

Fig. 10.6. 2-SA

Compared to EPDA, 2-SA have not one but two stacks, both being stacks of stacks (see Fig. 10.6). However, it is not possible to perform nested operations on these stacks as in EPDA where a set of new stacks can be wrapped around the current top-most stack. In a 2-SA, both stacks are accessible and one can freely push symbols onto the top-most stacks. Furthermore, one can pop symbols from the top of stack 1 and, if stack 1 is empty, also pop symbols from the top of stack 2. The restriction that for popping something from stack 2, stack 1 must be empty is crucial for the limited generative capacity of the automata. If we drop this restriction, 2-SA are much more powerful than needed, more precisely, they are Turing complete. This is the case because we can use the two stacks to simulate the moves of a Turing Machine.

In the following, we use again a special symbol that is not in the stack alphabet Γ for the bottom of a stack. In 2-SA, this symbol is explicitly given within the specification of the automaton. As in the EPDA case, if the top stack of a stack is emptied, its bottom symbol gets deleted as well, except if there is no other remaining stack. Then the bottom symbol remains and serves to mark the empty stack. Consequently, we never have the bottom symbol as the current stack symbol except when the entire stack is empty.

Definition 10.6 (Two-Stack Automaton).
A Two-Stack Automaton (2-SA) M is a 7-tuple $\langle Q, q_0, \Sigma, \Gamma, \ddagger, Z_0, \delta \rangle$, where

- Q is a finite set of states; $q_0 \in Q$ is the start state.
- Σ is the finite set of input symbols.
- Γ is the finite set of stack symbols, $\ddagger \notin \Gamma$ is the bottom stack symbol and $Z_0 \in \Gamma$ is the initial stack symbol.
- δ is the transition function, $\delta : Q \times (\Sigma \cup \{\varepsilon\}) \times (\Gamma \cup \{\ddagger\}) \times (\Gamma \cup \{\ddagger\}) \to P_{fin}(Q \times \Xi \times \Xi)$ where $\Xi = \{\ddagger\} \cup \Gamma^* \cup \{\gamma_1 \ddagger \gamma_2 \,|\, \gamma_1, \gamma_2 \in \Gamma^*\}$.
  δ satisfies the following restrictions:
  1. For all $q \in Q, a \in \Sigma \cup \{\varepsilon\}$, $s_1 \in \Gamma$ and $s_2 \in \Gamma \cup \{\ddagger\}$, all elements in $\delta(q, a, s_1, s_2)$ are of the form $\langle q', \xi_1, \xi_2 \rangle$ with $\xi_1, \xi_2 \in \Gamma^* \cup \{\gamma_1 \ddagger \gamma_2 \,|\, \gamma_1, \gamma_2 \in \Gamma^*\}$ (we cannot pop from stack 2).
  2. For all $q \in Q, a \in \Sigma \cup \{\varepsilon\}$, $s_2 \in \Gamma$, all elements in $\delta(q, a, \ddagger, s_2)$ are of the form $\langle q', \ddagger, \gamma \rangle$ with $\gamma \in \Gamma^*$ (if stack 1 is empty, we can pop from stack 2).

An instantaneous description of a 2-SA is given by a tuple $\langle y, s_1, s_2, w_1, w_2 \rangle$ where $q \in Q$ is the current state, $s_i \in \{\ddagger\gamma \,|\, \gamma \in \Gamma^*\}^*$ is the ith stack ($1 \leq i \leq 2$), $w_1 \in T^*$ is the already consumed input and $w_2 \in T^*$ is the remaining part of the input.

Transitions are defined in the same way as for PDA, except that two stacks are manipulated: $\langle q', \xi_1, \xi_2 \rangle \in \delta(q, a, s_1, s_2)$ tells us that, if the automaton is in state q, the next input symbol is a and the top-most stack symbols are s_1 and s_2 respectively, then, while reading input symbol a, we can change to q' and replace s_1 with ξ_1 and s_2 with ξ_2. In addition, top-most symbols $\ddagger$ are ignored, i.e., get deleted.

The language $N(M)$ is defined as the set of words that the automaton accepts with both stacks being empty.

(Becker, 1994) shows that 2-SA accept the same class of languages as EPDA, namely the class of Tree Adjoining Languages.

Let us briefly sketch how to construct an equivalent 2-SA for a given TAG. We simulate a top-down left-to-right traversal of the derivation tree, similarly to what we have done with an EPDA. The top of stack 1 is the next node to be expanded. It is replaced with its daughters if it is not on a spine. If it is on a spine, it is replaced with the left part of its daughters and the next node on the spine while the right part is stored on stack 2 for later processing. Whenever stack 1 is empty, we have reached a point in our traversal where we are to the right of a foot node, i.e., the left part of the auxiliary tree and the part below have been processed. As an example, Fig. 10.7 shows the 2-SA that accepts the language generated by the TAG from Fig. 10.4 and Fig. 10.8 shows a sample run of this automaton.

2-SA can be generalized to n-Stack Automata (n-SA). Depending on how the accessibility of the n stacks is restricted, different types of hierarchies can be obtained.

$M = \langle \{q\}, \{a,b,c\}, \Gamma, \delta, q, \emptyset, \# \rangle$ with $\Gamma = \{\#, R_\alpha, R_\beta, F, A, B, C\}$
Transition function δ:

$$\begin{aligned}
\langle q, R_\alpha^\top, \varepsilon \rangle &\in \delta(q, \varepsilon, \#, \#) && \text{start initial tree} \\
\langle q, R_\alpha^\bot, X \rangle &\in \delta(q, \varepsilon, R_\alpha^\top, X) && \text{no adjunction at } R_\alpha \\
\langle q, C, X \rangle &\in \delta(q, \varepsilon, R_\alpha^\bot, X) && \text{move down} \\
\langle q, R_\alpha^\bot R_\beta^\top, X \rangle &\in \delta(q, \varepsilon, R_\alpha^\top, X) \; \text{adj. of } \beta \text{ at } R_\alpha \\
\langle q, R_\beta^\bot R_\beta^\top, X \rangle &\in \delta(q, \varepsilon, R_\beta^\top, X) \; \text{adj. of } \beta \text{ at } R_\beta \\
\langle q, R_\beta^\bot, X \rangle &\in \delta(q, \varepsilon, R_\beta^\top, X) && \text{no adjunction at } R_\beta \\
\langle q, FA, XB \rangle &\in \delta(q, \varepsilon, R_\beta^\bot, X) && \text{move down} \\
\langle q, \varepsilon, X \rangle &\in \delta(q, \varepsilon, F, X) && \text{no adj. at } F, \text{ move back} \\
\langle q, \varepsilon, X \rangle &\in \delta(q, a, A, X) && \text{match } a \text{ with input} \\
\langle q, \ddagger, \varepsilon \rangle &\in \delta(q, b, \ddagger, B) && \text{match } b \text{ with input} \\
\langle q, \varepsilon, X \rangle &\in \delta(q, c, C, X) && \text{match } c \text{ with input}
\end{aligned}$$

where $X \in \Gamma \cup \{\ddagger\}$

Acceptance with empty stacks.

Fig. 10.7. 2-SA for the TAG from Fig. 10.4

Stack 1	Stack 2	remaining input	
$\ddagger\#$	$\ddagger\#$	aacbb	
$\ddagger R_\alpha^\top$	$\ddagger$	aacbb	start traversal of α
$\ddagger R_\alpha^\bot R_\beta^\top$	$\ddagger$	aacbb	predict adjunction of β
$\ddagger R_\alpha^\bot R_\beta^\bot R_\beta^\top$	$\ddagger$	aacbb	predict adjunction of β
$\ddagger R_\alpha^\bot R_\beta^\bot R_\beta^\bot$	$\ddagger$	aacbb	predict no adjunction
$\ddagger R_\alpha^\bot R_\beta^\bot FA$	$\ddagger B$	aacbb	move down in β
$\ddagger R_\alpha^\bot R_\beta^\bot F$	$\ddagger B$	acbb	scan a
$\ddagger R_\alpha^\bot R_\beta^\bot$	$\ddagger B$	acbb	leave β
$\ddagger R_\alpha^\bot FA$	$\ddagger BB$	acbb	move down in β
$\ddagger R_\alpha^\bot F$	$\ddagger BB$	cbb	scan a
$\ddagger R_\alpha^\bot$	$\ddagger BB$	cbb	leave β
$\ddagger C$	$\ddagger BB$	cbb	move down in α
$\ddagger$	$\ddagger BB$	bb	scan c
$\ddagger$	$\ddagger B$	b	scan b
$\ddagger$	$\ddagger$	ε	scan b

Fig. 10.8. A sample run of the 2-SA from Fig. 10.7

10.2.2 Strongly-Driven Two-Stack Automata

Strongly-driven Two-Stack Automata (SD-2SA) are a variant of 2-SA introduced in (Villemonte de la Clergerie and Pardo, 1998; Alonso Pardo, Nederhof, and Villemonte de la Clergerie, 2000) explicitly aiming at an elegant representation of different parsing strategies (top-down and bottom-up) for TAGs and LIGs.

Let us first take an intuitive look at the working principle of SD-2SA. The central idea is to assign different roles to the two stacks. An SD-2SA uses a *master stack (MS)* for most of its operations and a *auxiliary stack (AS)* for "bookkeeping". Concretely, the AS is a stack of so-called *session stacks*. At every moment, only the top-most stack can be accessed. This behavior is similar to the behavior of EPDA, where at every moment, we can only access the top-most stack in our push-down store of stacks. Furthermore, SD-2SA show a linear behavior, since in every session, we are first in mode "write" where we push elements on the master stack MS. At some point, we switch to mode "erase" and then we start to pop elements form the MS. Once we have done so, in the same session, we cannot go back to mode "write" and restart pushing elements onto the MS. The only way to exit a session is to reach a configuration with mode erase, an empty session stack (on top of the AS) and the MS element that initiated the session. During a session, action marks are pushed onto the MS. These ensure that the erase operations on the session mirror exactly the previously executed writing actions.

An SD-2SA distinguishes the two alphabets for the two stacks and provides an initial and a final stack symbol for the MS.

Definition 10.7 (Strongly-Driven Two-Stack Automata). *A strongly-driven Two-Stack Automaton (SD-2SA) M is a tuple $\langle \Sigma, \mathcal{M}, \mathcal{X}, \$_0, \$_f, \Theta \rangle$ where*

- *Σ denotes a finite set of terminals,*
- *$\mathcal{M}$ denotes the finite set of master stack elements,*
- *$\mathcal{X}$ denotes the finite set of auxiliary stack elements,*
- *$\$_0, \$_f \in \mathcal{M}$ are two distinguished master stack elements, the* initial *and the* final *symbol, and*
- *Θ is a finite set of transitions.*

The master stack consists of elements from $\mathcal{M}$ where each of them is preceded by an action mark. The action marks are $\mathcal{D} = \{\nearrow, \searrow, \rightarrow, \models\}$ where they have the following meaning: $\nearrow$ indicates that an element has been pushed onto the AS, $\searrow$ indicates that an element has been popped from the AS, $\rightarrow$ indicates that no action has been performed on the AS and $\models$ indicates that a new session has been started with a new empty session stack pushed onto the AS. On the AS, new session starts are marked with $\models^w$ or $\models^e$ depending on whether the corresponding session has been started in write or erase mode. In other words, the master stack MS is a word of $(\mathcal{DM})^*$ and the auxiliary stack AS is a word of $(\{\models^w, \models^e\}\mathcal{X}^*)^*$.

A configuration in an SD-2SA is a tuple (m, i, M, A) where $m \in \{w, e\}$ is the current mode, i the current input position, and M and A are the MS and AS respectively. The initial configuration is $(w, 0, \models \$_0, \models^w)$ and the final configuration is $(e, n, \models \$_f, \models^w)$ where n is the length of the input.

The transitions allow us to manipulate the two stacks, respecting the above-mentioned restrictions. For more details see (Villemonte de la Clergerie and Pardo, 1998).

Villemonte de la Clergerie and Pardo (1998) propose a compact representation of sub-derivations using so-called *escaped context-free derivations*. This allows for a tabular implementation of SD-2SA and thereby, they achieve a time complexity of $\mathcal{O}(n^6)$ and a space complexity of $\mathcal{O}(n^5)$.

10.3 Thread Automata

Thread Automata (TA) have been proposed by Villemonte de la Clergerie (2002). They are the most powerful automaton model that we treat in this book. TA accept the class of all LCFRLs. In the following, we will first sketch the idea of TA by explaining how a TA can simulate a top-down recognition of a TAL. Then we give the general definition and, finally, we show how to obtain an equivalent TA for a given TAG and a given ordered simple RCG. The latter amounts roughly to the incremental Earley parsing that we have seen in Section 7.3. TA are non-deterministic and, if all possibilities are pursued independently from each other, they are of exponential complexity. However, in combination with a compact representation of sub-derivations as items and with tabulation techniques, they become polynomial.

10.3.1 Idea

TA were developed in order to specify an automaton model for mildly context-sensitive languages. In fact, they accept all LCFRLs, the largest mildly context-sensitive class of languages we know of. However, as mentioned earlier, there are probably other grammar formalisms that generate also only mildly context-sensitive languages and that generate languages that are outside LCFRL.

The overall idea of TA is as follows: We have a set of threads, one of which is the active thread. Each thread has a unique path that situates it within the tree-shaped thread structure. Whenever a new thread is started, its path is a concatenation of the parent thread path and a new symbol. This way, from a given active thread, we can always find its parent thread (the one that started it) and its daughter threads. The moves of the automaton are the following: We can change the content of the active thread, start a new daughter thread or move into an existing daughter thread, or move into the parent thread while, eventually, terminating the active thread.

Take for instance a TAG. In the corresponding TA, we have a thread for each elementary tree of a derivation. The content of this thread is a single dotted node in this elementary tree. When predicting an adjunction, we start a daughter thread; when reaching the left of the foot node, we suspend the daughter thread and go back to the parent thread. When reaching the right of the part below the adjunction site in the parent thread, we continue the daughter thread of the adjoined tree, which gets terminated once the auxiliary tree is completely traversed. We then go back to the parent thread.

The operations provided in a TA are **SWAP** (changes the content of the active thread while possibly scanning a terminal), **PUSH** (creates a new sub-thread while suspending its parent), **POP** (ends the active thread, returning

10.3 Thread Automata   205

control to its parent), **SPUSH** (resumes a suspended sub-thread), and **SPOP** (resumes the parent of the active thread while changing its content). We write a thread as $p : A$ where p is its thread path (i.e., its address) and A its content.

Figure 10.9 shows the evolution of the thread set when running a TA for the TAG from Fig. 10.4 with the input *aacbb*. The bold thread is always the active one. The final configuration is defined as requiring to contain the thread $1 : ret$, i.e., if the automaton ends up in this configuration after having consumed the entire input, the word is in the language. *ret* is a special symbol that indicates that the elementary tree has been completely processed.

$$\text{Elementary trees:} \quad \begin{array}{c} R_\alpha \\ | \\ c \end{array} \quad \begin{array}{c} R_\beta \\ /|\backslash \\ a\ F\ b \end{array} \quad (R_\alpha \text{ and } R_\beta \text{ allow for adjunction of } \beta.)$$

Sample thread set of corresponding TA:

thread set	operation
$[1 : {}^\bullet R_\alpha]$	
$[1 : {}^\bullet R_\alpha], [11 : {}^\bullet R_\beta]$	PUSH
$[1 : {}^\bullet R_\alpha], [11 : {}^\bullet R_\beta], [111 : {}^\bullet R_\beta]$	PUSH
$[1 : {}^\bullet R_\alpha], [11 : {}^\bullet R_\beta], [111 : {}_\bullet R_\beta]$	SWAP
$[1 : {}^\bullet R_\alpha], [11 : {}^\bullet R_\beta], [111 : {}^\bullet a]$	SWAP
$[1 : {}^\bullet R_\alpha], [11 : {}^\bullet R_\beta], [111 : a^\bullet]$	SWAP (scan a)
$[1 : {}^\bullet R_\alpha], [11 : {}^\bullet R_\beta], [111 : {}^\bullet F]$	SWAP
$[1 : {}^\bullet R_\alpha], [11 : {}_\bullet R_\beta], [111 : {}^\bullet F]$	SPOP
$[1 : {}^\bullet R_\alpha], [11 : {}^\bullet a], [111 : {}^\bullet F]$	SWAP
$[1 : {}^\bullet R_\alpha], [11 : a^\bullet], [111 : {}^\bullet F]$	SWAP (scan a)
$[1 : {}^\bullet R_\alpha], [11 : {}^\bullet F], [111 : {}^\bullet F]$	SWAP
$[1 : {}_\bullet R_\alpha], [11 : {}^\bullet F], [111 : {}^\bullet F]$	SPOP
$[1 : {}^\bullet c], [11 : {}^\bullet F], [111 : {}^\bullet F]$	SWAP
$[1 : c^\bullet], [11 : {}^\bullet F], [111 : {}^\bullet F]$	SWAP (scan c)
$[1 : R_{\alpha\bullet}], [11 : {}^\bullet F], [111 : {}^\bullet F]$	SWAP
$[1 : R_{\alpha\bullet}], [11 : F^\bullet], [111 : {}^\bullet F]$	SPUSH
$[1 : R_{\alpha\bullet}], [11 : {}^\bullet b], [111 : {}^\bullet F]$	SWAP
$[1 : R_{\alpha\bullet}], [11 : b^\bullet], [111 : {}^\bullet F]$	SWAP (scan b)
$[1 : R_{\alpha\bullet}], [11 : R_{\beta\bullet}], [111 : {}^\bullet F]$	SWAP
$[1 : R_{\alpha\bullet}], [11 : R_{\beta\bullet}], [111 : F^\bullet]$	SPUSH
$[1 : R_{\alpha\bullet}], [11 : R_{\beta\bullet}], [111 : {}^\bullet b]$	SWAP
$[1 : R_{\alpha\bullet}], [11 : R_{\beta\bullet}], [111 : b^\bullet]$	SWAP (scan b)
$[1 : R_{\alpha\bullet}], [11 : R_{\beta\bullet}], [111 : R_{\beta\bullet}]$	SWAP
$[1 : R_{\alpha\bullet}], [11 : R_{\beta\bullet}], [111 : R_\beta{}^\bullet]$	SWAP
$[1 : R_{\alpha\bullet}], [11 : R_{\beta\bullet}], [111 : ret]$	SWAP
$[1 : R_{\alpha\bullet}], [11 : R_\beta{}^\bullet]$	POP
$[1 : R_{\alpha\bullet}], [11 : ret]$	SWAP
$[1 : R_\alpha{}^\bullet]$	POP
$[1 : ret]$	SWAP

Fig. 10.9. A sample run with a TA for the TAG from Fig. 10.4

Let us briefly explain the thread sets in Fig. 10.9. We use the position left/right above/below (depicted with a dot) that we know from the TAG Earley parsing. Whenever, in the active thread, we are left above a possible adjunction site, we can predict an adjunction by starting a sub-thread. This happens in the first two steps, the PUSH operations. When reaching the position left above a foot node, we can suspend the thread and resume the parent. This is the case in the SPOP steps. Whenever we arrive right below an adjunction site, we can resume the daughter of the adjoined tree whose content is the foot node (see the SPUSH steps in the example). Whenever we arrive right above the root of an auxiliary tree, we do a POP, i.e., finish this thread and resume the parent. We use a special symbol *ret* to mark the fact that we have completely traversed the elementary tree and we can therefore finish this thread. Besides moving this way from one elementary tree to another, we can move down, move left and move up inside a single elementary tree (while eventually scanning a terminal) using the SWAP operation.

This Thread Automaton simulates a top-down recognition since it performs a top-down left-to-right traversal of the derived tree.

10.3.2 General Definition of TA

We will now give the formal definition of TA.

Definition 10.8 (Thread Automaton).
A Thread Automaton *is a tuple* $\langle N, T, S, F, \kappa, \mathcal{K}, \delta, \mathcal{U}, \Theta \rangle$ *where*

- N *and* T *are non-terminal and terminal alphabets with* $S, F \in N$ *the start and end symbols;*
- κ, *the triggering function, is a partial function from* N *to some finite set* $\mathcal{K}$
- $\mathcal{U}$ *is a finite set of labels used to identify threads.*
- δ *is a partial function from* N *to* $\mathcal{U} \cup \{\bot\}$ *used to specify threads that can be created or resumed at some point.*
- Θ *is a finite set of transitions.*

Every thread has a thread path $p \in \mathcal{U}$ and its content is a non-terminal symbol.

Definition 10.9 (Thread, Configuration).
Let $M = \langle N, T, S, F, \kappa, \mathcal{K}, \delta, \mathcal{U}, \Theta \rangle$ *be a TA.*

- *A* thread *is a pair* $p : A$ *with* $p \in \mathcal{U}^*, A \in N$. p *is the thread path, and* A *is the content of the thread.*
- *A* thread store *is a set of threads whose addresses are closed by prefix.*
- *A* configuration *of* M *is a tuple* $\langle i, p, \mathcal{S} \rangle$ *where* i *is an input position,* $\mathcal{S}$ *is a thread set and* p *is a thread path in* $\mathcal{S}$.

Note that a thread contains only a single non-terminal, not (like a stack in a 2-SA) a sequence of symbols.

The transitions defined within Θ allow us to move from one configuration to another. They implement the operations explained above.

Definition 10.10 (TA Transitions).
Let $M = \langle N, T, S, F, \kappa, \mathcal{K}, \delta, \mathcal{U}, \Theta \rangle$ be a TA. All transitions in Θ have one of the following forms:

- $B \xrightarrow{\alpha} C$ with $B, C \in N, \alpha \in T^*$ *(SWAP operation)*
- $b \to [b]C$ with $b \in \mathcal{K}, C \in N$ *(PUSH operation)*
- $[B]C \to D$ with $B, C, D \in N$ *(POP operation)*
- $b[C] \to [b]D$ with $b \in \mathcal{K}, C, D \in N$ *(SPUSH operation)*
- $[B]c \to D[c]$ with $c \in \mathcal{K}, B, D \in N$ *(SPOP operation)*

These operations allow the following moves: SWAP changes the content of active thread from B to C while scanning α and augmenting input position with $|\alpha|$. PUSH, for an active thread $p : B$, creates a new sub-thread $pu : C$ and suspends the current one. pu has not been used yet and $\kappa(B) = b, \delta(B) = u$. POP ends the active thread $pu : C$ and resumes the parent while replacing B with D in the parent thread. It requires $\delta(c)$ to be $\perp$. SPUSH resumes a suspended sub-thread $pu : C$ of the active thread $p : B$ while replacing C with D. As a condition, it requires that $\kappa(B) = b, \delta(B) = u$. SPOP resumes the parent thread $p : B$ of the active thread $pu : C$ while replacing B with D, under the condition that $\kappa(C) = c, \delta(C) = \perp$.

We can define the set of possible configurations, based on these operations. For this, we use deduction rules. The initial configuration is the active thread $\varepsilon : S$ with input position 0. The final configuration (i.e., the goal item) has input position $|w| = n$ and contains the thread $u : F$ where $u = \delta(S)$ as active thread and the still present initial thread $\varepsilon : S$.

Definition 10.11. *Let $M = \langle N, T, S, F, \kappa, \mathcal{K}, \delta, \mathcal{U}, \Theta \rangle$ be a TA, and $w \in T^*$ be an input word.*

The set of configurations for w, $C(M, w)$, is then defined by the following deduction rules:

- Initial configuration: $\dfrac{}{\langle 0, \varepsilon, \{\varepsilon : S\} \rangle}$

- Swap: $\dfrac{\langle i, p, \mathcal{S} \cup p : B \rangle}{\langle i + |\alpha|, p, \mathcal{S} \cup p : C \rangle}$ $B \xrightarrow{\alpha} C, w_{i+1} \ldots w_{i+|\alpha|} = \alpha$

- Push: $\dfrac{\langle i, p, \mathcal{S} \cup p : B \rangle}{\langle i, pu, \mathcal{S} \cup p : B \cup pu : C \rangle}$ $b \to [b]C, \kappa(B) = b, \delta(B) = u,$ $pu \notin dom(\mathcal{S})$

- **Pop:** $\dfrac{\langle i, pu, \mathcal{S} \cup p : B \cup pu : C\rangle}{\langle i, p, \mathcal{S} \cup p : D\rangle}$ $[B]C \to D, \delta(C) = \bot, pu \notin dom(\mathcal{S})$

- **Spush:** $\dfrac{\langle i, p, \mathcal{S} \cup p : B \cup pu : C\rangle}{\langle i, pu, \mathcal{S} \cup p : B \cup pu : D\rangle}$ $b[C] \to [b]D, \kappa(B) = b, \delta(B) = u$

- **Spop:** $\dfrac{\langle i, pu, \mathcal{S} \cup p : B \cup pu : C\rangle}{\langle i, p, \mathcal{S} \cup p : D \cup pu : C\rangle}$ $[B]c \to D[c], \kappa(C) = c, \delta(C) = \bot$

The language of a TA is the set of words that allow us, starting from the initial thread set $\{\varepsilon : S\}$, to reach the set $\{\varepsilon : S, \delta(S) : F\}$ after having scanned the entire input.

Definition 10.12 (Language).
Let $M = \langle N, T, S, F, \kappa, \mathcal{K}, \delta, \mathcal{U}, \Theta \rangle$ be a TA,
The language of M is defined as follows:

$$L(M) = \{w \mid \langle n, \delta(S), \{\varepsilon : S, \delta(S) : F\}\rangle \in C(M, w)\}.$$

The intuition behind this definition is that, from the initial thread $\varepsilon : S$, we can non-deterministically choose a sub-thread $\delta(S) : A$ to start our recognition. The recognition is successful if we manage to reach the final thread symbol on this start sub-thread after having terminated all further sub-threads. The only threads remaining in our thread set are then $\varepsilon : S$ and $\delta(S) : F$. In the case of TAG, starting from $\varepsilon : S$, we can choose any initial tree and move into a corresponding thread. Once the traversal of this tree is finished, we are done. The thread set is then $\{\varepsilon : S, \delta(S) : ret\}$.

Obviously, a direct application of transitions to configurations would lead to an exponential time complexity and even looping in many cases. In order to obtain an efficient implementation of TA, one has to find some way to tabulate and share computations. For this purpose, Villemonte de la Clergerie (2002) uses a compact representation of certain sub-derivations that can be stored and retrieved for later reuse. This idea goes back to (Villemonte de la Clergerie and Pardo, 1998). For more details, see (Villemonte de la Clergerie, 2002).

10.3.3 Constructing a TA for a TAG

We can now give the TA for the TAG from Fig. 10.4 for which we have already seen a sample run in Fig. 10.9. The TA is shown in Fig. 10.10. There is only one detail that actually differs from the thread sets given in Fig. 10.9: we add an additional symbol S, the start thread is $\varepsilon : S$ and this thread starts a sub-thread $1 : {}^\bullet R_\alpha$. In the final configuration, we then obtain threads $\varepsilon : S, 1 : ret$ as required by the definition of the language of a TA. In other words, to obtain thread sets that correspond to the TA given in Fig. 10.10, one has to add the thread $\varepsilon : S$ to all the thread sets in Fig. 10.9.

The TA $M = \langle N, T, S, ret, \kappa, \mathcal{K}, \delta, \mathcal{U}, \Theta \rangle$ is as follows:

- N contains all symbols $^{\bullet}X, _{\bullet}X, X_{\bullet}, X^{\bullet}$ where X is a node in one of the elementary trees, i.e., $X \in \{R_\alpha, c, R_\beta, a, F, b\}$. Furthermore, N contains a special symbol ret and a special symbol S.
- $T = \{a, b, c\}$.
- S is the initial thread symbol and ret is the final thread symbol.
- $\mathcal{K} = N, \kappa(A) = A$ for all $A \in N$.
- $\mathcal{U} = \{1\}, \delta(X) = 1$ for all $A \in N \setminus \{^{\bullet}F, ret\}, \delta(ret) = \bot, \delta(^{\bullet}F) = \bot$.
- Transitions Θ:

$S \to [S]^{\bullet}R_\alpha$	start initial tree
$^{\bullet}R_\alpha \to {_{\bullet}R_\alpha}, \; ^{\bullet}R_\beta \to {_{\bullet}R_\beta}$	predict no adjunction
$_{\bullet}R_\alpha \to {^{\bullet}c}, \; _{\bullet}R_\beta \to {^{\bullet}a}$	move down
$^{\bullet}c \xrightarrow{c} c^{\bullet}, \; ^{\bullet}a \xrightarrow{a} a^{\bullet}, \; ^{\bullet}b \xrightarrow{b} b^{\bullet}$	scan
$a^{\bullet} \to {^{\bullet}F}, \; F^{\bullet} \to {^{\bullet}b}$	move right
$c^{\bullet} \to R_{\alpha\bullet}, \; b^{\bullet} \to R_{\beta\bullet}$	move up
$R_{\alpha\bullet} \to R_\alpha^{\bullet}, \; R_{\beta\bullet} \to R_\beta^{\bullet}$	move up if no adjunction
$^{\bullet}R_\alpha \to [^{\bullet}R_\alpha]^{\bullet}R_\beta, \; ^{\bullet}R_\beta \to [^{\bullet}R_\beta]^{\bullet}R_\beta$	predict adjoined tree
$[^{\bullet}R_\alpha]^{\bullet}F \to {_{\bullet}R_\alpha}[^{\bullet}F], \; [^{\bullet}R_\beta]^{\bullet}F \to {_{\bullet}R_\beta}[^{\bullet}F]$	back to adjunction site
$R_{\alpha\bullet}[^{\bullet}F] \to [R_{\alpha\bullet}]F^{\bullet}, \; R_{\beta\bullet}[^{\bullet}F] \to [R_{\beta\bullet}]F^{\bullet}$	resume adjoined tree
$R_\alpha^{\bullet} \to ret, \; R_\beta^{\bullet} \to ret$	complete elementary tree
$[R_{\alpha\bullet}]ret \to R_\alpha^{\bullet}, \; [R_{\beta\bullet}]ret \to R_\beta^{\bullet}$	terminate adjunction, go back

Fig. 10.10. A TA for the TAG from Fig. 10.4

Note that the parent thread is always uniquely determined and after having finished the part below a foot node, the thread of the adjoined tree is determined by the δ-value of the adjunction site. Each adjunction site in a tree has to have a unique δ-value. In our case, we have only one adjunction site per tree; therefore we chose 1 as the value. A second adjunction site could have value 2, and so on. Furthermore, every sub-thread started for some adjunction has to be terminated in order to finish with a thread set containing only a single thread. Therefore, this TA traverses only valid derived trees of the tree language of the original TAG and performs a prefix valid Earley recognition.

From this example, the general construction can be inferred. See (Villemonte de la Clergerie, 2002) for more details. We obtain the following theorem for the class of languages recognized by TA:

Lemma 10.13. *For every TAG G, there is a TA M such that $L(G) = L(M)$.*

10.3.4 Constructing a TA for an Ordered SRCG

In this section, we will see how to construct a TA for a given ordered simple RCG. Recall that SRCGs are equivalent to MCFGs and LCFRSs.

The overall idea of the construction is as follows. The TA simulates a top-down left-to-right prefix valid recognition. (It can be seen as some kind of incremental CYK recognizer with top-down prediction.) We have one thread for each clause we process. We start with one of the S-clauses where S is the start predicate of the SRCG. For each newly predicted clause, a thread is started that will eventually traverse the entire left-hand side of the clause. The automaton moves through the left-hand side arguments of the clauses. Whenever it reaches a variable that is the first argument of some right-hand side predicate, it predicts a clause for this predicate, which means that it starts a corresponding new child thread. Whenever an argument has been entirely recognized, the thread can be suspended and its parent thread can be resumed. Whenever the automaton reaches a variable that is the kth argument of some right-hand side predicate with $k \geq 1$, we resume the child thread corresponding to this predicate.

In order to keep track of our position within the left-hand side arguments of some clause c, we introduce new symbols $c_{k,i}$ indicating that we are going to process the $(i+1)$th element of the kth argument in the left-hand side of c. In other words, we have processed everything up to the ith element of the kth left-hand side argument. The non-terminal symbols N of the automaton contain then all the predicate names, a special symbol ret and all the new symbols $c_{k,i}$.

$\mathcal{U} = \{1, \ldots, m\}$ where m is the maximal number of right-hand side predicates in the clauses of the RCG. In other words, the daughter address indicates the right-hand side element corresponding to this daughter thread.

$\mathcal{K}$ and the functions κ and δ are used to indicate, for a given variable in the left-hand side (indicated by its position symbol $c_{k,i}$), which of the right-hand side elements contains this variable as an argument. This determines the daughter thread that processes this variable. Furthermore, when starting a daughter thread for the first time, the function κ indicates the corresponding predicate. Therefore, $\mathcal{K} = N \cup \{void\}$ and

- $\kappa(c_{k,i}) = A$ and $\delta(c_{k,i}) = j$ if A is the jth predicate in the right-hand side of c and $c(k, i+1)$ is its first argument,
- $\kappa(c_{k,i}) = void$ and $\delta(c_{k,i}) = j$ if $c(k, i+1)$ is an argument of the jth predicate in the right-hand side of c but not its first argument,
- $\kappa(c_{k,i}) = void$ and $\delta(c_{k,i}) = \bot$ if $c(k, i+1)$ does not exist, i.e., we have reached the end of the kth argument and, instead of moving into a daughter thread, we have to suspend this thread and resume the parent.

The final thread symbol is again ret with $\delta(ret) = \bot$; the start symbol is a new symbol S' with $\delta(S') = 1$ and therefore the final configuration has to contain the thread set $\{\varepsilon : S', 1 : ret\}$.

Before we explain how to define the transitions Θ of the TA in general, let us have a look at an example. Figure 10.11 shows a small SRCG, the corresponding TA and a sample run of this TA with only the successful configurations listed. Let us go through the TA transitions in this example. From the initial configuration, we predict the start predicate using the first transition. Whenever the dot precedes the variable X in one of the two first clauses,

Clauses of the SRCG:
$\alpha : S(XYZ) \to A(X,Y,Z)$
$\beta : A(aX, aY, aZ) \to A(X,Y,Z)$
$\gamma : A(b,b,b) \to \varepsilon$

Transitions of the corresponding TA (start symbol S'):
Call: $S' \to [S']S$ $\alpha_{1,0} \to [\alpha_{1,0}]A$ $\beta_{1,1} \to [\beta_{1,1}]A$
Predict: $S \to \alpha_{1,0}$ $A \to \beta_{1,0}$ $A \to \gamma_{1,0}$
Scan: $\beta_{1,0} \xrightarrow{a} \beta_{1,1}$ $\beta_{2,0} \xrightarrow{a} \beta_{2,1}$ $\beta_{3,0} \xrightarrow{a} \beta_{3,1}$
           $\gamma_{1,0} \xrightarrow{b} \gamma_{1,1}$ $\gamma_{2,0} \xrightarrow{b} \gamma_{2,1}$ $\gamma_{3,0} \xrightarrow{b} \gamma_{3,1}$
Suspend: $[\alpha_{1,0}]\beta_{1,2} \to \alpha_{1,1}[\beta_{1,2}]$ $[\alpha_{1,1}]\beta_{2,2} \to \alpha_{1,2}[\beta_{2,2}]$ $[\alpha_{1,2}]ret \to \alpha_{1,3}$
         $[\alpha_{1,0}]\gamma_{1,1} \to \alpha_{1,1}[\gamma_{1,1}]$ $[\alpha_{1,1}]\gamma_{2,1} \to \alpha_{1,2}[\gamma_{2,1}]$
         $[\beta_{1,1}]\beta_{1,2} \to \beta_{1,2}[\beta_{1,2}]$ $[\beta_{2,1}]\beta_{2,2} \to \beta_{2,2}[\beta_{2,2}]$ $[\beta_{3,1}]ret \to \beta_{3,2}$
         $[\beta_{1,1}]\gamma_{1,1} \to \beta_{1,2}[\gamma_{1,1}]$ $[\beta_{2,1}]\gamma_{2,1} \to \beta_{2,2}[\gamma_{2,1}]$
Resume $\alpha_{1,1}[\beta_{1,2}] \to [\alpha_{1,1}]\beta_{2,0}$ $\beta_{2,1}[\beta_{1,2}] \to [\beta_{2,1}]\beta_{2,0}$
         $\alpha_{1,1}[\gamma_{1,0}] \to [\alpha_{1,1}]\gamma_{2,0}$ $\beta_{2,1}[\gamma_{1,0}] \to [\beta_{2,1}]\gamma_{2,0}$
         $\alpha_{1,2}[\beta_{2,2}] \to [\alpha_{1,2}]\beta_{3,0}$ $\beta_{2,1}[\beta_{2,2}] \to [\beta_{2,1}]\beta_{3,0}$
         $\alpha_{1,2}[\gamma_{2,0}] \to [\alpha_{1,2}]\gamma_{3,0}$ $\beta_{3,1}[\gamma_{2,0}] \to [\beta_{3,1}]\gamma_{3,0}$
Publish: $\alpha_{1,3} \to ret$ $\beta_{3,2} \to ret$ $\gamma_{3,1} \to ret$

Configurations for $w = ababab$:

thread set	rem. input	
$\varepsilon : S'$	$ababab$	
$\varepsilon : S', \mathbf{1 : S}$	$ababab$	initialize
$\varepsilon : S', \mathbf{1 : \alpha_{1,0}}$	$ababab$	predict
$\varepsilon : S', 1 : \alpha_{1,0}, \mathbf{11 : A}$	$ababab$	call
$\varepsilon : S', 1 : \alpha_{1,0}, \mathbf{11 : \beta_{1,0}}$	$ababab$	predict
$\varepsilon : S', 1 : \alpha_{1,0}, \mathbf{11 : \beta_{1,1}}$	$babab$	scan
$\varepsilon : S', 1 : \alpha_{1,0}, 11 : \beta_{1,1}, \mathbf{111 : A}$	$babab$	call
$\varepsilon : S', 1 : \alpha_{1,0}, 11 : \beta_{1,1}, \mathbf{111 : \gamma_{1,0}}$	$babab$	predict e
$\varepsilon : S', 1 : \alpha_{1,0}, 11 : \beta_{1,1}, \mathbf{111 : \gamma_{1,1}}$	$abab$	scan
$\varepsilon : S', 1 : \alpha_{1,0}, \mathbf{11 : \beta_{1,2}}, 111 : \gamma_{1,1}$	$abab$	suspend
$\varepsilon : S', \mathbf{1 : \alpha_{1,1}}, 11 : \beta_{1,2}, 111 : \gamma_{1,1}$	$abab$	suspend
$\varepsilon : S', 1 : \alpha_{1,1}, \mathbf{11 : \beta_{2,0}}, 111 : \gamma_{1,1}$	$abab$	resume
$\varepsilon : S', 1 : \alpha_{1,1}, \mathbf{11 : \beta_{2,1}}, 111 : \gamma_{1,1}$	bab	scan
$\varepsilon : S', 1 : \alpha_{1,1}, 11 : \beta_{2,1}, \mathbf{111 : \gamma_{2,0}}$	bab	resume
$\varepsilon : S', 1 : \alpha_{1,1}, 11 : \beta_{2,1}, \mathbf{111 : \gamma_{2,1}}$	ab	scan
$\varepsilon : S', 1 : \alpha_{1,1}, \mathbf{11 : \beta_{2,2}}, 111 : \gamma_{2,1}$	ab	suspend
$\varepsilon : S', \mathbf{1 : \alpha_{1,2}}, 11 : \beta_{2,2}, 111 : \gamma_{2,1}$	ab	suspend
$\varepsilon : S', 1 : \alpha_{1,2}, \mathbf{11 : \beta_{3,0}}, 111 : \gamma_{2,1}$	ab	resume
$\varepsilon : S', 1 : \alpha_{1,2}, \mathbf{11 : \beta_{3,1}}, 111 : \gamma_{2,1}$	b	scan
$\varepsilon : S', 1 : \alpha_{1,2}, 11 : \beta_{3,1}, \mathbf{111 : \gamma_{3,0}}$	b	resume
$\varepsilon : S', 1 : \alpha_{1,2}, 11 : \beta_{3,1}, \mathbf{111 : \gamma_{3,1}}$	ε	scan
$\varepsilon : S', 1 : \alpha_{1,2}, 11 : \beta_{3,1}, \mathbf{111 : ret}$	ε	publish
$\varepsilon : S', 1 : \alpha_{1,2}, \mathbf{11 : \beta_{3,2}}$	ε	suspend
$\varepsilon : S', 1 : \alpha_{1,2}, \mathbf{11 : ret}$	ε	publish
$\varepsilon : S', \mathbf{1 : \alpha_{1,3}}$	ε	suspend
$\varepsilon : S', \mathbf{1 : ret}$	ε	publish

Fig. 10.11. A TA for a sample ordered simple RCG

we predict an A (second and third **call** transition). The **predict** transitions predict, based on a given predicate, a clause for this predicate and the traversal of this clause starts at the beginning of the first left-hand side argument. **Scan** applies whenever the dot precedes a terminal. The dot is then moved over this terminal while matching it with the next input symbol. **Suspend** is applied when reaching the end of an argument, for instance after having processed the first two elements of the first left-hand side argument in β (thread content $\beta_{1,2}$). In this case, we return to the parent thread where we can move the dot over a variable. A special case is **suspend** operations where we have finished the clause of a daughter thread (thread content ret). Whenever the dot precedes a variable that is not a first argument in the right-hand side (for instance $\alpha_{1,1}$, which indicates that the dot precedes Y in the first clause), we can **resume** the corresponding daughter thread. Finally, **publish** applies whenever the automaton reaches the end of a left-hand side (for instance $\beta_{3,2}$, which indicates that the dot follows the second element of the first argument in the left-hand side of β). We then change the thread content to ret, which indicates that this thread is ready to be terminated.

In general, in a TA for an ordered simple RCG, we have the following transitions:

- **Call** starts a new thread, either for the start predicate or for a daughter predicate:
  $S' \to [S']S$ (initial call), $\gamma_{k,i} \to [\gamma_{k,i}]A$ if $\kappa(\gamma_{k,i}) = A$.
- **Predict** predicts a new clause for a predicted predicate:
  $A \to \gamma_{1,0}$ for all A-clauses γ.
- **Scan** moves the dot over a terminal in the left-hand side while scanning the next input symbol:
  $\gamma_{k,i} \overset{\gamma(k,i+1)}{\to} \gamma_{k,i+1}$ if $\gamma(k, i + 1)$ is a terminal.
- **Publish** marks the end of a predicate:
  $\gamma_{k,j} \overset{\varepsilon}{\to} ret$ where the arity of the left-hand side predicate in γ is k and the kth argument in the left-hand side has length j.
- **Suspend** suspends a daughter thread and resumes the parent:
  $[\gamma_{k,i}]ret \to \gamma_{k,i+1}$ if $\gamma(k, i + 1)$ is a variable that is the last argument of a right-hand side predicate in γ, and
  $[\gamma_{k,i}]\beta_{l,j} \to \gamma_{k,i+1}[\beta_{l,j}]$ if $\gamma(k, i + 1)$ is a variable X, β is a B-clause and X is the lth argument of B in the right-hand side of γ but not its last argument, and the lth argument of the left-hand side in β has length j.
- **Resume** resumes an already present daughter thread:
  $\gamma_{k,i}[\beta_{l,j}] \to \beta_{l+1,0}$ if $\gamma(k, i+1)$ is a variable X, β is a B-clause and X is the $(l + 1)$th argument of B in the right-hand side of γ, and the lth argument of the left-hand side in β has length j.

This is not exactly the TA proposed in (Villemonte de la Clergerie, 2002) for SRCGs although the overall idea is the same. Our construction corresponds more closely to the incremental Earley parser for ordered simple RCG from Section 7.3.

With this construction, we obtain the following result:

Lemma 10.14. *For every simple RCG G, there is a TA M such that $L(G) = L(M)$.*

Whether there are languages that cannot be generated by simple RCG but that can be recognized by a TA is an open question.

10.4 Summary

In this chapter, we have seen a variety of different automata that have been proposed as extensions of PDA. The first group are automata that assume, compared to PDA, either more than one stack or a stack with a richer structure, namely a stack of stacks. The more restricted versions of these automata such as Embedded Push-Down Automata (EPDA) and 2-Stack Automata (2-SA) are devices that accept exactly the class of Tree Adjoining Languages.

In the last section, Thread Automata (TA) have been presented. TA are able to recognize all Linear Context-Free Rewriting Languages (LCFRLs), i.e., all languages generated by LCFRS or the equivalent simple RCG and MCFG. We have seen how to construct equivalent TA for given TAGs or simple RCGs. In both cases, the automaton simulates a top-down left-to-right traversal of the derived trees, which amounts to an Earley-style recognition. Villemonte de la Clergerie (2002) has presented a polynomial implementation of TA.

Problems

10.1. Consider the EPDA M from Fig. 10.2 with $N(M) = \{a^n b^n c^n d^n \mid n \geq 0\}$. Give an EPDA M' such that $N(M) = L(M')$.

10.2. Give an EPDA M that accepts the copy language $\{ww \mid w \in \{a,b\}^*\}$ with an empty stack, i.e., as $N(M)$.

10.3. Consider the following TA: $M = \langle N, T, S, ret, \kappa, \mathcal{K}, \delta, \mathcal{U}, \Theta \rangle$ with $N = \{S, S', S_A, S_B, A, B, ret\}$, $T = \{a,b\}$, $\mathcal{K} = N$ and κ the identity, $\delta(S) = \delta(A) = \delta(S_A) = \delta(B) = \delta(S_B) = 1$, $\delta(ret) = \bot$ and the following transitions:

$S \to [S]S'$,
$S' \xrightarrow{a} A_2$, $\quad S' \xrightarrow{a} S_A$, $\quad S_A \to [S_A]S'$,
$S' \xrightarrow{b} B_2$, $\quad S' \xrightarrow{b} S_B$, $\quad S_B \to [S_B]S'$,
$A_2 \xrightarrow{a} ret$, $\quad [S_A]ret \to A_2$,
$B_2 \xrightarrow{b} ret$, $\quad [S_B]ret \to B_2$

1. What is the string language accepted by this TA?
2. Choose a word of length 4 in this language and give the thread sets (only successful items) that are generated for this word.

Appendix A: Hierarchy of Grammar Formalisms

The following figure recalls the language hierarchy that we have developed in the course of the book.

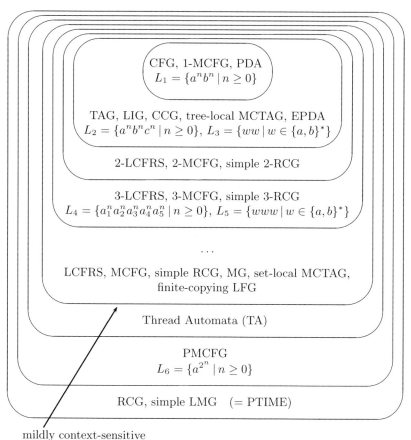

For each class the different formalisms and automata that generate/accept exactly the string languages contained in this class are listed. Furthermore, examples of typical languages for this class are added, i.e., of languages that belong to this class while not belonging to the next smaller class in our hierarchy. The inclusions are all proper inclusions, except for the relation between LCFRS and Thread Automata (TA). Here, we do not know whether the inclusion is a proper one. It is possible that both devices yield the same class of languages.

Appendix B: List of Acronyms

The following table lists all acronyms that occur in this book.

(2,2)-BRCG	Binary bottom-up non-erasing RCG with at most two variables per left-hand side argument
2-SA	Two-Stack Automaton
ACG	Abstract Categorial Grammar
AFL	Abstract Family of Languages
CCG	Combinatory Categorial Grammar
CFG	Context-Free Grammar
CNF	Chomsky Normal Form
EPDA	Extended Push-Down Automaton
FSA	Finite State Automaton
GCFG	Generalized Context-Free Grammar
GNF	Greibach Normal Form
HPSG	Head-Driven Phrase Structure Grammar
IG	Indexed Grammar
LCFRS	Linear Context-Free Rewriting System
LFG	Lexical Functional Grammar
LIG	Linear Indexed Grammar
LTAG	Lexicalized TAG
LMG	Literal Movement Grammar
MCFG	Multiple Context-Free Grammar
MCTAG	Multicomponent Tree Adjoining Grammar
MG	Minimalist Grammar
NRCG	Negative Range Concatenation Grammar
NPDA	Nested Push-Down Automaton
PDA	Push-Down Automaton
PMCFG	Parallel Multiple Context-Free Grammar
PRCG	Positive Range Concatenation Grammar
RCG	Range Concatenation Grammar
SD-2SA	Strongly-Driven Two-Stack Automaton

SNMCTAG	tree-local MCTAG with shared nodes
SRCG	Simple Range Concatenation Grammar
TA	Thread Automaton
TAG	Tree Adjoining Grammar
TSG	Tree Substitution Grammar
TT-MCTAG	Tree-Tuple MCTAG with Shared Nodes
V-TAG	Vector-TAG

Solutions

Problems of Chapter 2

2.1 $L_2 := \{a^n b^n \mid n \geq 0\}$

1. $G = \langle N, T, P, S \rangle$ with $N = \{S\}$, $T = \{a, b\}$, start symbol S and productions $S \to aSb$, $S \to \varepsilon$.
2. Assume that such a CFG exists. Its productions are then all of the form $X \to \alpha a \beta b \gamma$ with $X \in N$, $\alpha, \beta, \gamma \in N^*$ such that if such a production is applied when generating a string $a_1 \ldots a_n b_1 \ldots b_n$, then the a and b of the production necessarily end up at positions i and $n+i$ for some i, $1 \leq i \leq n$. Then replacing each of these productions $X \to \alpha a \beta b \gamma$ with $X \to \alpha a \beta a \gamma$ and $X \to \alpha b \beta b \gamma$ leads to a CFG generating the copy language. This contradicts the fact that the copy language is not context-free. □

2.2 A first homomorphism can the homomorphism f from (Shieber, 1985).

After having applied f to Swiss German, we intersect with the regular language $w\{a,b\}^* x \{c,d\}^* y$, which leads to $\{w v_1 x v_2 y \mid v_1 \in \{a,b\}^*, v_2 \in \{c,d\}^*$ such that $|v_1| = |v_2|$ and for all i, $1 \leq i \leq |v_1|$, if the ith symbol in v_1 is an a (a b), the ith symbol in v_2 is a c (a d)$\}$.

Finally we apply a second homomorphism g to the result of the intersection with $g(w) := g(x) := g(y) := \varepsilon, g(a) := g(c) := a, g(b) := g(d) := b$.

This leads to the copy language.

2.3
There are several possibilities. The simplest one:

Linguistically, this is unsatisfying since the S node comes with the lexical item *John* even though it is the maximal projection of the verb. A lexicalized TSG for the given CFG where the S node comes with the verb is not possible.

2.4

1. The copy language $L := \{ww \,|\, w \in T^*\}$ is letter equivalent to $L' := \{ww^R \,|\, w \in T^*$ and w^R is w in reverse order$\}$, which is a CFL: It is generated by the CFG with productions $S \to \varepsilon$ and $S \to xSx$ for all $x \in T$. Consequently (with Parikh's theorem) L' and also L are semilinear. □
2. Assume that $\{a^{2^n} \,|\, n \geq 0\}$ satisfies the constant growth property with c_0 and C. Then take a $w = a^{2^m}$ with $|w| = 2^m > max(\{c_0\} \cup C)$. Then, according to the definition of constant growth, for $w' = a^{2^{m+1}}$ there must be a $w'' = a^{2^k}$ with $|w'| = |w''| + c$ for some $c \in C$. I.e., $2^{m+1} = 2^k + c$. Consequently (since $k \leq m$) $c \geq 2^m$. Contradiction. □

Problems of Chapter 3

3.1

The items can have the form $[\bullet A, i, -], 0 \leq i \leq n$ (for predicted categories) and $[A\bullet, i, j], 0 \leq i < j \leq n$ (for completed categories). The goal item is $[S\bullet, 0, n]$. We need the following deduction rules:

1. An operation *scan-predict* that, starting from a predicted A-item, predicts a B-item, based on the existence of a production $A \to aB$:
$$\frac{[\bullet A, i, -]}{[\bullet B, i+1, -]} \quad \text{there is a production } A \to aB \in P \text{ with } w_{i+1} = a.$$

2. An operation *scan* that turns a predicted A into a completed A based on the existence of a production $A \to a$:
$$\frac{[\bullet A, i, -]}{[A\bullet, i, i+1]} \quad \text{there is a production } A \to a \in P \text{ with } w_{i+1} = a.$$

3. An operation *complete* that turns a predicted A into a completed A based on the existence of a completed B and a production $A \to aB$:
$$\frac{[\bullet A, i, -][B\bullet, i+1, j]}{[A\bullet, i, j]} \quad \text{there is a production } A \to aB \in P \text{ with } w_{i+1} = a.$$

3.2

To show: If $[A \to \alpha \bullet \beta, i, j]$ then $S \stackrel{*}{\Rightarrow} w_1 \cdots w_i A\gamma \Rightarrow w_1 \cdots w_i \alpha\beta\gamma \stackrel{*}{\Rightarrow} w_1 \cdots w_j \beta\gamma$ for some $\gamma \in (N \cup T)^*$.

We show this by an induction on the deduction rules:

- Axioms: $\dfrac{}{[S \to \bullet\alpha, 0, 0]} \quad S \to \alpha \in P$

  Trivially, if $[S \to \bullet\alpha, 0, 0]$ is obtained by this rule, then $S \stackrel{*}{\Rightarrow} \varepsilon S \Rightarrow \varepsilon\alpha$.

- Predict: $\dfrac{[A \to \alpha \bullet B\beta, i, j]}{[B \to \bullet\gamma, j, j]}$ $B \to \gamma \in P$

  We assume that the claim holds for the antecedent item. We then obtain (because of the production $B \to \gamma$) $S \stackrel{*}{\Rightarrow} w_1 \cdots w_i A\gamma' \Rightarrow w_1 \cdots w_i \alpha B\beta\gamma' \stackrel{*}{\Rightarrow} w_1 \cdots w_j B\beta\gamma' \Rightarrow w_1 \cdots w_j \gamma\gamma'$.

- Scan: $\dfrac{[A \to \alpha \bullet a\beta, i, j]}{[A \to \alpha a \bullet \beta, i, j+1]}$ $w_{j+1} = a$

  Since the claim holds for the antecedent item, with the side condition, it holds immediately for the consequent item.

- Complete: $\dfrac{[A \to \alpha \bullet B\beta, i, j], [B \to \gamma\bullet, j, k]}{[A \to \alpha B \bullet \beta, i, k]}$

  Since the induction claim holds for the antecedent items, we have in particular $B \stackrel{*}{\Rightarrow} w_{j+1} \cdots w_k$. With this and the claim for the antecedent A-item, we obtain $S \stackrel{*}{\Rightarrow} w_1 \cdots w_i A\gamma' \Rightarrow w_1 \cdots w_i \alpha B\beta\gamma' \stackrel{*}{\Rightarrow} w_1 \cdots w_j B\beta\gamma' \Rightarrow w_1 \cdots w_k \beta\gamma'$.

The algorithm is sound since, as a special case, we obtain for the goal items that $[S \to \alpha\bullet, 0, n]$ implies $S \Rightarrow \alpha \stackrel{*}{\Rightarrow} w_1 \cdots w_n$.

3.3

The space complexity of the CYK algorithm is determined by the memory requirement for the chart. Since this is an $|N| \times n \times n$ table, we obtain a space complexity $\mathcal{O}(n^2)$.

3.4

The most complex rule is **complete** with three indices ranging form 0 to n and with $|P|^2$ possible productions and $l_{rhs} = max_{A \to \alpha \in P}(|\alpha| + 1)$ possible positions for the dot in the antecedent A-items. Note that, once the A-production is fixed, the position of the dot determines the left-hand side symbol of the second production. Let $m_{rhs} = max_{A \in N}|\{A \to \alpha \in P\}|$. Then we have $\leq l_{rhs} \cdot |P| \cdot m_{rhs}(n+1)^3$ possible different applications of **complete**. Consequently, as in the CYK case, the time complexity of the fixed recognition problem is $\mathcal{O}(n^3)$.

Problems of Chapter 4

4.1

1. TAG for L_3:

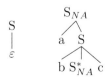

2. Assume that a TAG G for L_3 without adjunction constraints exists. Assume without loss of generality that G contains no substitution nodes. G has at least one auxiliary tree β with leaves labeled with terminals. β must contain equal numbers of as, bs and cs. (Otherwise one could derive a word with different numbers of as, bs and cs.) One can adjoin β at its root, which leads to a derived auxiliary β'. If the yield of β is $a^i b^i c^i$ ($i \geq 1$), there are the following possibilities for the foot node:
   a) The foot node is left of all as or right of all cs $\Rightarrow$ using β' a word with substring $a^i b^i c^i a^i b^i c^i$ can be derived. Contradiction.
   b) The foot node is right of the kth a for some k, $1 \leq k \leq i$ $\Rightarrow$ using β' a word with substring $a^{i-k} b^i c^i a^{i-k} b^i c^i$ can be derived. Contradiction.
   c) The foot node is right of the kth b for some k, $1 \leq k \leq i$ $\Rightarrow$ using β' a word with substrings $a^i b^k a^i b^k$ and $b^{i-k} c^i b^{i-k} c^i$ can be derived. Contradiction.
   d) The foot node is left of the kth c for some k, $1 \leq k \leq i$ $\Rightarrow$ using β' a word with substring $a^i b^i c^{k-1} a^i b^i c^{k-1}$ can be derived. Contradiction.

   Consequently, there is no TAG without adjunction constraints for L_3. □

4.2 L_3 is a TAL $\Rightarrow$ with closure under concatenation $\{w_1 w_2 \mid w_1, w_2 \in L_3\} = \{a^n b^n c^n a^m b^m c^m \mid n, m \geq 0\}$ is a TAL. □

4.3 The copy language is a TAL and $a^* b^* a^* b^*$ is a regular language $\Rightarrow$ with closure under intersection with regular languages, $\{ww \mid w \in \{a, b\}^*\} \cap a^* b^* a^* b^* = \{a^i b^j a^i b^j \mid i, j \geq 0\}$ is a TAL. □

4.4 Assume that L is a TAL. Then the weak pumping lemma holds for some constant c. $\Rightarrow$ For each word $w \in L$ with $|w| \geq c$ there is a $w' \in L$ with $|w'| \leq |w| + c$. This is a contradiction since for all $w \in L$ with $|w| > c$ this is not the case (for each $w \in L$ the $w' \in L$ following it wrt word length has twice its length). □

4.5

1. TAG for L_4:

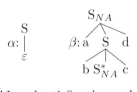

2. Assume that L_5 is a TAL and satisfies the weak pumping lemma with some constant c. Take $w = a^{c+1} b^{c+1} c^{c+1} d^{c+1} e^{c+1}$. According to the pumping lemma one can find $w_1, \ldots w_4$, at least one of them not empty, such that they can be inserted repeatedly at four positions into w yielding a new word in L_5. At least one of the $w_1, \ldots w_4$ must contain two different terminal symbols since they altogether must contain equal numbers of as, bs, cs, ds and es. Then, when doing a second insertion of the $w_1, \ldots w_4$,

the as, bs, cs, ds and es get mixed and the resulting word is not in L_5. Contradiction. □

4.6

(30) John saw a man with a telescope

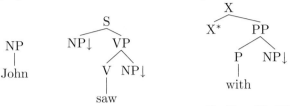

X=N or X=VP

Concerning the determiners, there are three possibilities:

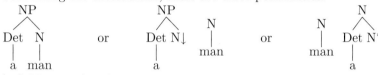

(31) Mary took a decision

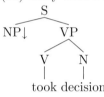

4.7

Since extraction out of sentential subjects is not allowed, it makes sense to add them by substitution. Otherwise one could adjoin them to a sentence with wh-extracted elements. (Of course such an adjunction could also be prevented with appropriate adjunction constraints.)

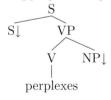

4.8

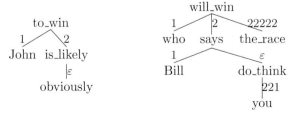

4.9
$S_0 \to S[\#]$
$S[..] \to aS_x[..]d$ $\quad S_x[..] \to S[x..]$
$S \to T$ $\quad T[x..] \to bT[..]c$
$T[\#] \to \varepsilon$

Problems of Chapter 5

5.1 Replace the deduction rules **move-unary** and **move-binary** with a single new rule **move-up**:

$$\frac{[\gamma, (p \cdot 1)_\top, i_0, f_{11}, f_{12}, i_1], \ldots, [\gamma, (p \cdot m)_\top, i_{m-1}, f_{m1}, f_{m2}, i_m]}{[\gamma, p_\bot, i_0, f_{11} \oplus \cdots \oplus f_{m1}, f_{12} \oplus \cdots \oplus f_{m2}, i_m]}$$

As a side condition, we require that the node address $p \cdot (m+1)$ does not exist in γ.

5.2

We keep the items $[\gamma, p_t, i, f_1, f_2, j]$ we had before (passive items) and add new active items $[\gamma, p, k, i, f_1, f_2, j]$ with

- γ an elementary tree, p a node position in γ, k the number of daughters of the node at p in γ that we have already seen;
- i, f_1, f_2, j as before.

The rules **move-unary** and **move-binary** are replaced with the following new rules:

1. A rule **left-corner predict** that, once we have seen the first daughter of a node, predicts the appropriate active item for its mother with $k = 1$.

   Left-corner predict: $\dfrac{[\gamma, (p \cdot 1)_\top, i, f_1, f_2, j]}{[\gamma, p, 1, i, f_1, f_2, j]}$

2. A rule **complete** that, from an item telling us that we have seen the first k daughters of a node and another item telling us that we have the passive item of the $(k+1)$th daughter, deduces the active item telling us that we have seen the $k+1$ daughters of the mother.

   Complete: $\dfrac{[\gamma, p, k, i_1, f_1, f_2, i_2][\gamma, (p \cdot (k+1))_\top, i_2, f_3, f_4, i_3]}{[\gamma, p, k+1, i_1, f_1 \oplus f_3, f_2 \oplus f_4, i_3]}$

3. A rule **convert** that converts an active item where we have seen all the daughters into a passive item.

   Convert: $\dfrac{[\gamma, p, k, i, f_1, f_2, j]}{[\gamma, p_\bot, i, f_1, f_2, j]}$ $\quad$ address $p \cdot (k+1)$ not defined in γ

Anything else remains as before.

5.3

In our items we have only three indices, i, j, k, where i and k delimit the total span of the relevant part of the tree (these were i and l in the original algorithm). j gives the start position of the part below the foot node for left auxiliary trees.

The *Scan* and *Predict* rules remain more or less the same except for the reduced number of indices:

$ScanTerm \quad \dfrac{[\alpha, p, la, i, j, k, 0]}{[\alpha, p, ra, i, j, k+1, 0]} \quad \alpha(p) = w_{k+1}$

$Scan\text{-}\varepsilon \quad \dfrac{[\alpha, p, la, i, j, k, 0]}{[\alpha, p, ra, i, j, k, 0]} \quad \alpha(p) = \varepsilon$

$PredictAdjoinable \quad \dfrac{[\alpha, p, la, i, j, k, 0]}{[\beta, 0, la, k, -, k, 0]} \quad \beta \in f_{SA}(\alpha, p)$

$PredictNoAdj \quad \dfrac{[\alpha, p, la, i, j, k, 0]}{[\alpha, p, lb, k, -, k, 0]} \quad f_{OA}(\alpha, p) = 0$

$PredictAdjoined \quad \dfrac{[\beta, p, lb, k, -, k, 0]}{[\delta, p', lb, k, -, k, 0]} \quad p = foot(\beta), \beta \in f_{SA}(\delta, p')$

For the *Complete* rule, we obtain the following:

Complete

$\dfrac{[\alpha, p, rb, i, j, k, 1][\beta, p', lb, i, -, i, 0]}{[\beta, p', rb, i, i, k, 0]} \quad p' = foot(\beta), \beta \in f_{SA}(\alpha, p)$

Complete2 (remains the same)

$\dfrac{[\beta, p, rb, i, j, k, sat?][\beta, p, la, h, -, i, 0]}{[\beta, p, ra, h, j, k, 0]} \quad \beta(p) \in N$

For the *Adjoin* rule, we obtain the following:

Adjoin

$\dfrac{[\beta, 0, ra, i, j, k, 0][\alpha, p, rb, j, l, k, 0]}{[\alpha, p, rb, i, l, k, 1]} \quad \beta \in f_{SA}(\alpha, p)$

The *Move* rules and also the *Initialize* rule and the goal item remain the same, except for the reduced number of indices.

5.4

PredictSubstituted:

$\dfrac{[\gamma, p, la, \sim, \sim, \sim, \sim, i, 0]}{[\alpha, \varepsilon, la, i, i, -, -, i, 0]} \quad \alpha \in I, \gamma(p) \text{ substitution node}, \ l(\gamma, p) = l(\alpha, \varepsilon)$

Substitute:

$\dfrac{[\gamma, p, la, \sim, \sim, \sim, \sim, i, 0], [\alpha, \varepsilon, ra, i, i, -, -, j, 0]}{[\gamma, p, rb, \sim, i, -, -, j, 0]} \quad \alpha \in I, \gamma(p) \text{ substitution node}, \ l(\gamma, p) = l(\alpha, \varepsilon)$

Note that adjunction is not allowed at substitution nodes; therefore the adjunction flag 0 in the consequent item does not cause any problems.

5.5

Multiple adjunctions are avoided since *reduce_subtree* is applied only if $X_1 \ldots X_m \in CS^+(N)$, i.e., if the stack contains a cross-section of the node N that is not N itself. After having traversed the tree adjoined at N and having returned to the node N by applying *reduce_aux_tree*, it is the node N itself that is on the stack.

5.6

1.

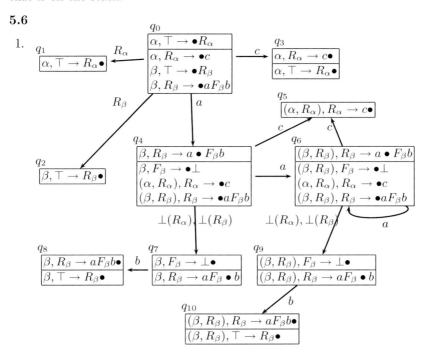

2.

Stack	remaining input	operation
q_0	$aacbb$	shift
$q_0 a q_4$	$acbb$	shift
$q_0 a q_4 a q_6$	cbb	shift
$q_0 a q_4 a q_6 c q_5$	bb	reduce_subtree
$q_0 a q_4 a q_6 (\bot [R_\alpha]) q_9$	bb	shift
$q_0 a q_4 a q_6 (\bot [R_\alpha]) q_9 b q_{10}$	b	reduce_subtree
$q_0 a q_4 (\bot, [R_\beta, R_\alpha]) q_7$	b	shift
$q_0 a q_4 (\bot, [R_\beta, R_\alpha]) q_7 b q_8$	ε	reduce_aux_tree
$q_0 (R_\beta, [R_\alpha]) q_2$	ε	reduce_aux_tree
$q_0 R_\alpha q_1$	ε	accept

Problems of Chapter 6

6.1 There are of course different possibilities, for instance the following two MCFGs:

1. Rewriting rules: $S \to f_1[A] \quad A \to f_2[A] \quad A \to f_3[\,]$
   Operations:
   $f_1[\langle X,Y,Z,U\rangle] = \langle XYZU\rangle$
   $f_2[\langle X,Y,Z,U\rangle] = \langle aX, bY, cZ, dU\rangle$
   $f_3[\,] = \langle a,b,c,d\rangle$
2. Rewriting rules: $S \to f_1[A] \quad A \to f_2[A] \quad A \to f_3[\,]$
   Operations:
   $f_1[\langle X,Y\rangle] = \langle XY\rangle$
   $f_2[\langle X,Y\rangle] = \langle aXb, cYd\rangle$
   $f_3[\,] = \langle ab, cd\rangle$

6.2

Clauses:
$S(XYZ) \to A(Y)B(X,Z)$
$A(aX) \to A(X) \qquad A(a) \to \varepsilon$
$B(bX, bYb) \to B(X,Y) \quad B(\varepsilon,\varepsilon) \to \varepsilon$

1. $yield(A) = \{\langle a^n\rangle \mid n \geq 1\}$
   $yield(B) = \{\langle b^n, (bb)^n\rangle \mid n \geq 0\}$.
2. $\{b^m a^n (bb)^m \mid n \geq 1, m \geq 0\}$.
3. For $w = abbb$,
   $r\text{-}yield(B) = \{(\langle i,i\rangle, \langle j,j\rangle) \mid 0 \leq i,j \leq 4\} \cup \{(\langle 1,2\rangle, \langle 2,4\rangle), (\langle 3,4\rangle, \langle 1,3\rangle)\}$.

6.3

1. $\{a^n b^n c^m d^m a^n b^n c^m d^m \mid n,m \geq 0\}$
2. $\{w_1 w_2 \mid w_1 \in \{a,b\}^*, w_2$ is the image of w_1 under the homomorphism f with $f(a) = b, f(b) = a\}$

6.4

1. Instantiations of $A(aX, bY) \to A(X,Y)$:
   $A(\langle 0,1\rangle, \langle 1,2\rangle) \to A(\langle 1,1\rangle, \langle 2,2\rangle)$
   $A(\langle 0,1\rangle, \langle 2,3\rangle) \to A(\langle 1,1\rangle, \langle 3,3\rangle)$
   $A(\langle 0,2\rangle, \langle 2,4\rangle) \to A(\langle 1,2\rangle, \langle 3,4\rangle)$
   $A(\langle 3,4\rangle, \langle 1,2\rangle) \to A(\langle 4,4\rangle, \langle 2,2\rangle)$
   $A(\langle 3,4\rangle, \langle 2,3\rangle) \to A(\langle 4,4\rangle, \langle 3,3\rangle)$
2. Derivation of $abba$:
   $S(\langle 0,4\rangle) \Rightarrow A(\langle 0,2\rangle, \langle 2,4\rangle)$
   $\Rightarrow A(\langle 1,2\rangle, \langle 3,4\rangle)$
   $\Rightarrow A(\langle 3,4\rangle, \langle 1,2\rangle)$
   $\Rightarrow A(\langle 4,4\rangle, \langle 2,2\rangle)$
   $\Rightarrow \varepsilon$

6.5 Let $k > 0$ be fixed.

We assume that the language $L = \{w^{2k+1} \mid w \in \{a,b\}^*\}$ is a k-MCFL.

Then its intersection with the regular language $(a^+ b^+)^{2k+1}$ must be a k-MCFL as well. This intersection yields $L' = \{(a^n b^m)^{2k+1} \mid n,m > 0\}$.

If L' is a k-MCFL, then it satisfies the pumping lemma for k-MCFLs. I.e., there must be a word $(a^n b^m)^{2k+1}$ for some $m, n > 0$ such that $2k$ substrings of this word can be iterated. At least one of these strings is not empty and none of them can contain different terminals, otherwise pumping would immediately lead to strings not in L'. However, if at most $2k$ strings are pumped, each of them containing only as or only bs, we necessarily obtain strings that are not in the language L'. This contradicts the assumption that L' satisfies the pumping lemma for k-MCFLs.

Consequently, neither L' nor L are k-MCFLs. □

6.6 The string language is the regular language

$$\textit{whom Peter painted ((a copy of)} + \textit{(a picture of)})^*$$

For the string *whom Peter painted a copy of a picture of* (of length 9), we obtain the following derivation tree:

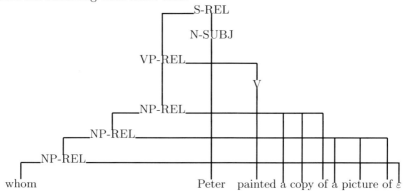

Problems of Chapter 7

7.1 The only unconstrained prediction concerns S predicates starting at position 0:

Initialize: $\dfrac{}{[S \to f[\mathbf{B}]; (R_1 = \langle 0, 0 \rangle \bullet x); \Gamma_\mathbf{B}]} \quad S \to f[\mathbf{B}] := (x)$

Predictions are now triggered by the dot preceding a component variable $B_k^{(i)}$:

Predict: $\dfrac{[A \to g[\mathbf{B}]; (\Phi_1, R_l = \alpha \bullet B_k^{(i)} x, \Phi_2); \Gamma]}{[B_k \to f[\mathbf{C}]; (R_i = \langle j, j \rangle \bullet y, \Psi_1, \Psi_2); \Gamma_\mathbf{C}]} \quad \begin{array}{l} B_k \to f[\mathbf{C}] := \\ (\Psi_1, y, \Psi_2) \\ \text{with } y \text{ the } i\text{th element,} \\ j \text{ greatest range} \\ \text{boundary in } \alpha \end{array}$

The same holds for **complete**:

Solutions   229

Complete:
$$\frac{[A \to g[\mathbf{B}]; (\Phi_1, R_j = \alpha \bullet B_k^{(i)}x, \Phi_2); \mathbf{\Gamma}],}{[B_k \to f[\mathbf{C}]; (\Psi, R_l = \langle l_l, r_l \rangle \bullet, \Psi_1, y, \Psi_2); \mathbf{\Gamma}']}$$
$$[B_k \to f[\mathbf{C}]; (\Psi, R_l = \langle l_l, r_l \rangle, R_i = \langle m, m \rangle \bullet y, \Psi_1, \Psi_2); \mathbf{\Gamma}']$$

y is the ith element in the range constraint vector of $B_k \to f[\mathbf{C}]$, m is the greatest range boundary in α

The other operations and the goal item are the same as in the incremental algorithm with unconstrained prediction.

7.2

$S(XYZU) \to A(X,Z)B(U,Y)$ $S(XYZ) \to A(X,Z)C(Y)$
$A(aX, aZ) \to A(X,Z)$ $A(\varepsilon, c) \to \varepsilon$
$B(Xb, Yb) \to B(X,Y)$ $B(\varepsilon, c) \to \varepsilon$
$C(aXY) \to D(X)C(Y)$ $D(d) \to \varepsilon$

1. Simplifying the grammar:
   a) Transform the grammar into an ordered simple RCG. (If the superscript is the identity, we omit it.)
      The only problematic rule is $S(XYZU) \to A(X,Z)B(U,Y)$. It transforms into $S(XYZU) \to A(X,Z)B^{\langle 2,1 \rangle}(Y,U)$.
      Add $B^{\langle 2,1 \rangle}(Yb, Xb) \to B(X,Y)$ and $B^{\langle 2,1 \rangle}(c, \varepsilon) \to \varepsilon$.
      Then, $B^{\langle 2,1 \rangle}(Yb, Xb) \to B(X,Y)$ transforms into $B^{\langle 2,1 \rangle}(Yb, Xb) \to B^{\langle 2,1 \rangle}(Y,X)$.
      In the following, for reasons of readability, we replace $B^{\langle 2,1 \rangle}$ with a new symbol E.
      Result:
      $S(XYZU) \to A(X,Z)E(Y,U)$ $S(XYZ) \to A(X,Z)C(Y)$
      $A(aX, aZ) \to A(X,Z)$ $A(\varepsilon, c) \to \varepsilon$
      $B(Xb, Yb) \to B(X,Y)$ $B(\varepsilon, c) \to \varepsilon$
      $E(Yb, Xb) \to E(Y,X)$ $E(c, \varepsilon) \to \varepsilon$
      $C(aXY) \to D(X)C(Y)$ $D(d) \to \varepsilon$
   b) Remove useless rules.
      - $N_T = \{A, B, E, D, S\}$.
        Consequently, remove $S(XYZ) \to A(X,Z)C(Y)$ and $C(aXY) \to D(X)C(Y)$.
      - In the result, $N_S = \{S, A, E\}$.
        Consequently, remove also $D(d) \to \varepsilon$, $B(Xb, Yb) \to B(X,Y)$ and $B(\varepsilon, c) \to \varepsilon$.
      Result:
      $S(XYZU) \to A(X,Z)E(Y,U)$
      $A(aX, aZ) \to A(X,Z)$ $A(\varepsilon, c) \to \varepsilon$
      $E(Yb, Xb) \to E(Y,X)$ $E(c, \varepsilon) \to \varepsilon$
   c) Remove ε-rules.
      $N_\varepsilon = \{A^{01}, A^{11}, E^{10}, E^{11}, S^1\}$.
      Resulting productions:

$$S^1(XYZU) \to A^{11}(X,Z)E^{11}(Y,U) \quad S^1(YZU) \to A^{01}(Z)E^{11}(Y,U)$$
$$S^1(XYZ) \to A^{11}(X,Z)E^{10}(Y) \quad S^1(YZ) \to A^{01}(Z)E^{10}(Y)$$
$$A^{11}(aX,aZ) \to A^{11}(X,Z) \quad A^{11}(a,aZ) \to A^{01}(Z)$$
$$A^{01}(c) \to \varepsilon$$
$$E^{11}(Yb,Xb) \to E^{11}(Y,X) \quad E^{11}(Yb,b) \to E^{10}(Y)$$
$$E^{10}(c) \to \varepsilon$$

2. The string language generated by this grammar is

$$\{a^n cb^m a^n cb^m \mid n, m \geq 0\}.$$

7.3

We have to consider the maximal number of possible applications of the complete rule.

Complete: $\dfrac{[B, \rho_B], [C, \rho_C]}{[A, \rho_A]}$ $A(\rho_A) \to B(\rho_B)C(\rho_C)$ is an instantiation of a $c \in P$ wrt. w

Since the maximal arity is k, we have maximal $2k$ range boundaries in each of the antecedent items of this rule. For variables X_1, X_2 being in the same left-hand side argument of the clause c, X_1 left of X_2 and no other variables in between, the right boundary of X_1 gives us immediately the left boundary of X_2. In the worst case, A, B, C all have arity k and each left-hand side argument contains only two variables. This leads to $3k$ independent range boundaries and consequently a time complexity of $\mathcal{O}(n^{3k})$ for the entire algorithm.

7.4

The antecedent of the **Suspend** operation

$$\dfrac{[B(\boldsymbol{\psi}) \to \boldsymbol{\Psi}, pos', \langle i,j \rangle, \rho_B], [A(\boldsymbol{\phi}) \to \ldots B(\boldsymbol{\xi}) \ldots, pos, \langle k,l \rangle, \rho_A]}{[A(\boldsymbol{\phi}) \to \ldots B(\boldsymbol{\xi}) \ldots, pos', \langle k, l+1 \rangle, \rho]}$$

contains two active items, the A-item and B-item.

Since our grammar is ε-free, all daughters (here the B-item) have yields with non-empty components. Therefore the position of the B-item is greater than the one of the A-item, $pos' > pos$, in a **suspend** operation. Consequently, the A-item is always added first to the chart and it is therefore sufficient to trigger **suspend** operations by the B-items.

Problems of Chapter 8

8.1 Clauses:
$$S(XY) \to A(X,Y)B(X,Y)$$
$$A(aX,aY) \to A(X,Y) \qquad B(bX,bY) \to B(X,Y)$$
$$A(bX,Y) \to A(X,Y) \qquad B(aX,Y) \to B(X,Y)$$
$$A(X,bY) \to A(X,Y) \qquad B(X,aY) \to B(X,Y)$$
$$A(\varepsilon,\varepsilon) \to \varepsilon \qquad B(\varepsilon,\varepsilon) \to \varepsilon$$

Input: $w = abba$

Instantiated clauses used:

instantiation	clause
1. $S(\langle 0,4\rangle) \to A(\langle 0,2\rangle,\langle 2,4\rangle)B(\langle 0,2\rangle,\langle 2,4\rangle)$	$S(XY) \to A(X,Y)B(X,Y)$
2. $A(\langle 0,2\rangle,\langle 2,4\rangle) \to A(\langle 0,2\rangle,\langle 3,4\rangle)$	$A(X,bY) \to A(X,Y)$
3. $A(\langle 0,2\rangle,\langle 3,4\rangle) \to A(\langle 1,2\rangle,\langle 4,4\rangle)$	$A(aX,aY) \to A(X,Y)$
4. $A(\langle 1,2\rangle,\langle 4,4\rangle) \to A(\langle 2,2\rangle,\langle 4,4\rangle)$	$A(bX,Y) \to A(X,Y)$
5. $A(\langle 2,2\rangle,\langle 4,4\rangle) \to \varepsilon$	$A(\varepsilon,\varepsilon) \to \varepsilon$
6. $B(\langle 0,2\rangle,\langle 2,4\rangle) \to B(\langle 1,2\rangle,\langle 2,4\rangle)$	$B(aX,Y) \to B(X,Y)$
7. $B(\langle 1,2\rangle,\langle 2,4\rangle) \to B(\langle 2,2\rangle,\langle 3,4\rangle)$	$B(bX,bY) \to B(X,Y)$
8. $B(\langle 2,2\rangle,\langle 3,4\rangle) \to B(\langle 2,2\rangle,\langle 4,4\rangle)$	$B(X,aY) \to B(X,Y)$
9. $B(\langle 2,2\rangle,\langle 4,4\rangle) \to \varepsilon$	$B(\varepsilon,\varepsilon) \to \varepsilon$

Derivation:
$$\begin{aligned}
S(\langle 0,6\rangle) &\Rightarrow A(\langle 0,2\rangle,\langle 2,4\rangle)B(\langle 0,2\rangle,\langle 2,4\rangle) &&\text{(with 1.)}\\
&\Rightarrow A(\langle 0,2\rangle,\langle 3,4\rangle)B(\langle 0,2\rangle,\langle 2,4\rangle) &&\text{(with 2.)}\\
&\Rightarrow A(\langle 1,2\rangle,\langle 4,4\rangle)B(\langle 0,2\rangle,\langle 2,4\rangle) &&\text{(with 3.)}\\
&\Rightarrow A(\langle 2,2\rangle,\langle 4,4\rangle)B(\langle 0,2\rangle,\langle 2,4\rangle) &&\text{(with 4.)}\\
&\Rightarrow B(\langle 0,2\rangle,\langle 2,4\rangle) &&\text{(with 5.)}\\
&\Rightarrow B(\langle 1,2\rangle,\langle 2,4\rangle) &&\text{(with 6.)}\\
&\Rightarrow B(\langle 2,2\rangle,\langle 3,4\rangle) &&\text{(with 7.)}\\
&\Rightarrow B(\langle 2,2\rangle,\langle 4,4\rangle) &&\text{(with 8.)}\\
&\Rightarrow \varepsilon &&\text{(with 9.)}
\end{aligned}$$

8.2

- G_1 is simple since in all clauses, RHS arguments are single variables and each variable occurring in the clause occurs exactly once in its LHS and exactly once in its RHS.
  $L(G_1) = \{ca^{2n}b^k ca^{2n}b^k ca^{2n} \mid n > 0, k \geq 0\}$.
- G_2 is a non-simple RCG, since the variable X is used twice in the RHS of $S(X) \to S_1(X)S_2(X)$ and therefore the grammar is not linear.
  $L(G_2) = \{a^n b^n c^k \mid n \geq 0, k \geq 1\} \cap \{a^k b^n c^n \mid k \geq 1, n \geq 0\} = \{a^n b^n c^n \mid n \geq 1\}$

8.3

1. L_1 can be generated by a simple RCG G_1:
   $G_1 = \langle \{S,A\}, \{c,d\}, \{X,Y,U,V\}, S, P\rangle$ with P the following set of clauses:
   $$S(XYUV) \to A(X,Y,U,V)$$
   $$A(cX,cY,cU,cV) \to A(X,Y,U,V)$$
   $$A(dX,dY,dU,dV) \to A(X,Y,U,V)$$
   $$A(\varepsilon,\varepsilon,\varepsilon,\varepsilon) \to \varepsilon$$

2. L_2 can only be generated by a non-simple RCG G_2.
   $G_2 = \langle \{S, eq\}, \{a\}, \{X,Y,Z\}, S, P\rangle$ with P the following set of clauses:
   $$S(XYZ) \to S(X)eq(X,Y,Z)$$
   $$S(a) \to \varepsilon$$
   $$eq(aX,aY,aZ) \to A(X,Y,Z)$$
   $$eq(a,a,a) \to \varepsilon$$

8.4

1. L_1 can be generated by a linear non-erasing simple LMG G_3 containing the same clauses as the simple RCG for the same language.
2. L_2 can be generated by the following simple LMG G_4.
   $G_4 = \langle \{S\}, \{a\}, \{X\}, S, P \rangle$ with P the following set of clauses:
   $S(XXX) \to S(X)$
   $S(a) \to \varepsilon$

8.5

Equivalent simple 2-RCG:
$S(X) \to \langle\alpha\rangle(X)$
$\langle\alpha\rangle(LR) \to \langle adj, \alpha, \varepsilon\rangle(L, R)$
$\langle\beta\rangle(aLb, cRd) \to \langle adj, \beta, 2\rangle(L, R)$
$\langle adj, \alpha, \varepsilon\rangle(L, R) \to \langle\beta\rangle(L, R)$
$\langle adj, \beta, 2\rangle(L, R) \to \langle\beta\rangle(L, R)$
$\langle adj, \alpha, \varepsilon\rangle(\varepsilon, \varepsilon) \to \varepsilon$
$\langle adj, \beta, 2\rangle(\varepsilon, \varepsilon) \to \varepsilon$

Problems of Chapter 9

9.1

Assume that we have a k-RCG.

For binarized RCGs, the **complete** rule amounts to the following:

Complete: $\dfrac{[A_1, \boldsymbol{\rho}_1], [A_2, \boldsymbol{\rho}_2]}{[A_0, \boldsymbol{\rho}]}$ $A_0(\boldsymbol{\rho}_0) \to A_1(\boldsymbol{\rho}_1) A_k(\boldsymbol{\rho}_2)$ an instantiated clause

In contrast to simple RCG, we cannot assume that the variables in the left-hand side occur also in the right-hand side. Therefore, in the worst case, there is no relation at all between these variables. We then obtain for the left-hand side that we have ≤ 3 range boundaries per argument and $\leq 3k$ range boundaries per clause. For the right-hand side, we get ≤ 2 range boundaries per argument and therefore $\leq 2 \cdot 2k$ range boundaries per clause. Consequently, we have a total of $\leq 3k + 4k = 7k$ range boundaries per clause that can have values between 0 and n.

Therefore, parsing with this algorithm for the restricted type of RCG considered here is $\mathcal{O}(n^{7k})$.

9.2

Clause $A(aX, Ya, \varepsilon) \to C(XY)$.
Range constraint vector $\langle \mathbf{r}, C \rangle$ with

- $\mathbf{r} = (\langle r_1, r_2\rangle, \langle r_3, r_4\rangle, \langle r_5, r_6\rangle, \langle r_7, r_8\rangle, \langle r_9, r_{10}\rangle)$,

- $C = \{r_1 \leq r_2, \ldots, r_9 \leq r_{10},$
  $r_1 + 1 = r_2, r_7 + 1 = r_8,$
  $r_2 = r_3, r_4 = r_5, r_6 = r_7,$
  $r_9 = r_{10}\}$

9.3

Clauses of the RCG G:
$S(XY) \to A(X,X)B(Y,Y)$
$A(aX, bY) \to A(X, Y)$ $B(cX, dY) \to B(X, Y)$
$A(bX, Y) \to A(X, Y)$ $B(dX, Y) \to B(X, Y)$
$A(X, aY) \to A(X, Y)$ $B(X, cY) \to B(X, Y)$
$A(\varepsilon, \varepsilon) \to \varepsilon$ $B(\varepsilon, \varepsilon) \to \varepsilon$

1. $L(G) = \{w_1 w_2 \mid w_1 \in \{a,b\}^*$ with $|w_1|_a = |w_1|_b$ and $w_2 \in \{c,d\}^*$ with $|w_2|_c = |w_2|_d\}$.
2. $First(A, 1) = First(A, 2) = \{a, b, \varepsilon\}$,
   $First(B, 1) = First(B, 2) = \{c, d, \varepsilon\}$.
3. Possible filters:
   - The components of A belong to $\{a,b\}^*$ while the components of B belong to $\{c,d\}^*$.
   - For every range vector $(\langle l_1, r_1 \rangle, \langle l_2, r_2 \rangle)$ in the yield of A or B, it holds that $r_1 = r_2$.

Problems of Chapter 10

10.1

Let $M = \langle Q, \Sigma, \Gamma, \delta, q_0, Q_F, Z_0 \rangle$ be the original EPDA.
$M' = \langle Q \cup \{q_0', q_f\}, \Sigma, \Gamma \cup \{Z_0'\}, \delta', q_0', \{q_f\}, Z_0' \rangle$ with

- $q_0' \neq q_f, q_0', q_f \notin Q, Z_0' \notin \Gamma$;
- δ' extends δ as follows:
  $\delta'(q_0', \varepsilon, Z_0') = \{(q_0, \varepsilon, Z_0', \ddagger\#)\}$
  $\delta'(q_3, \varepsilon, Z_0') = \{(q_f, \varepsilon, Z_0', \varepsilon)\}$
  In all other cases, δ' is defined as the original δ.

10.2

$M = \langle \{q_0, q_1, q_2, q_3\}, \{a, b\}, \{\#, A, B\}, \delta, q_0, \{q_3\}, \# \rangle$ with
$\delta(q_0, \varepsilon, \#) = \{(q_3, \varepsilon, \varepsilon, \varepsilon), (q_1, \varepsilon, \#, \varepsilon)\}$
$\delta(q_1, a, X) = \{(q_1, \varepsilon, XA, \varepsilon)\}$
$\delta(q_1, b, X) = \{(q_1, \varepsilon, XB, \varepsilon)\}$
$\delta(q_1, \varepsilon, X) = \{(q_2, \varepsilon, X, \varepsilon)\}$
$\delta(q_2, \varepsilon, A) = \{(q_2, \ddagger A, \varepsilon, \varepsilon)\}$
$\delta(q_2, \varepsilon, B) = \{(q_2, \ddagger B, \varepsilon, \varepsilon)\}$
$\delta(q_2, \varepsilon, \#) = \{(q_3, \varepsilon, \varepsilon, \varepsilon)\}$
$\delta(q_3, a, A) = \{(q_3, \varepsilon, \varepsilon, \varepsilon)\}$
$\delta(q_3, b, B) = \{(q_3, \varepsilon, \varepsilon, \varepsilon)\}$

where $X \in \Gamma$

10.3

1. The language is $\{ww^R \mid w \in \{a,b\}^+\}$.
2. Successful configurations for $w = abba$:

thread set	remaining input	operation
$\varepsilon : S$	abba	
$\varepsilon : S, \mathbf{1 : S'}$	abba	$S \longrightarrow [S]S'$
$\varepsilon : S, \mathbf{1 : S_A}$	bba	$S \xrightarrow{a} S_A$
$\varepsilon : S, 1 : S_A, \mathbf{11 : S'}$	bba	$S_A \longrightarrow [S_A]S'$
$\varepsilon : S, 1 : S_A, \mathbf{11 : B_2}$	ba	$S' \xrightarrow{b} B_2$
$\varepsilon : S, 1 : S_A, \mathbf{11 : ret}$	a	$B_2 \xrightarrow{b} ret$
$\varepsilon : S, \mathbf{1 : A_2}$	a	$[S_A]ret \longrightarrow A_2$
$\varepsilon : S, \mathbf{1 : ret}$	ε	$A_2 \xrightarrow{a} ret$

References

Abeillé, Anne. 1988. Parsing French with Tree Adjoining Grammar: some linguistic accounts. In *Proceedings of COLING*, pages 7–12, Budapest.

Abeillé, Anne. 2002. *Une Grammaire Électronique du Français*. CNRS Editions, Paris.

Aho, A. V. 1968. Indexed grammars – an extension of context-free grammars. *Journal of the ACM*, 15(4):647–671.

Alonso Pardo, M. A., M.-J. Nederhof, and E. Villemonte de la Clergerie. 2000. Tabulation of automata for Tree-Adjoining Languages. *Grammars*, 3:89–110.

Barthélemy, François, Pierre Boullier, Philippe Deschamp, and Éric de la Clergerie. 2001. Guided parsing of Range Concatenation Languages. In *Proceedings of the 39th Annual Meeting on Association for Computational Linguistics*, pages 42–49.

Barton, G. Edward, Jr. 1985. The computational difficulty of ID/LP parsing. In *Proceedings of the 23rd Annual Meeting of the Association for Computational Linguistics*, pages 76–81, Chicago.

Becker, Tilman. 1994. A new automaton model for TAGs: 2-SA. *Computational Intelligence*, 10(4):422–430.

Becker, Tilman, Aravind K. Joshi, and Owen Rambow. 1991. Long-distance scrambling and Tree Adjoining Grammars. In *Proceedings of ACL-Europe*.

Becker, Tilman, Owen Rambow, and Michael Niv. 1992. The Derivational Generative Power of Formal Systems or Scrambling is Beyond LCFRS. Technical Report IRCS-92-38, Institute for Research in Cognitive Science, University of Pennsylvania.

Bellman, Richard 1957. *Dynamic Programming*. Princeton University Press.

Bertsch, Eberhard and Mark-Jan Nederhof. 2001. On the complexity of some extensions of RCG parsing. In *Proceedings of the Seventh International Workshop on Parsing Technologies*, pages 66–77, Beijing, China, October.

Boullier, Pierre. 1996. Another facet of LIG parsing. In *Proceedings of ACL 1996*.

Boullier, Pierre. 1998a. A generalization of mildly context-sensitive formalisms. In *Proceedings of the Fourth International Workshop on Tree Adjoining Grammars and Related Formalisms (TAG+4)*, pages 17–20, University of Pennsylvania, Philadelphia.

Boullier, Pierre. 1998b. A Proposal for a Natural Language Processing Syntactic Backbone. Technical Report 3342, INRIA.

Boullier, Pierre. 1999a. Chinese numbers, mix, scrambling, and range concatenation grammars. In *Proceedings of the 9th Conference of the European Chapter of the Association for Computational Linguistics (EACL'99)*, pages 53–60, Bergen, Norway, June.

Boullier, Pierre. 1999b. On TAG Parsing. In *TALN 99, 6ᵉ conférence annuelle sur le Traitement Automatique des Langues Naturelles*, pages 75–84, Cargèse, Corse, July.

Boullier, Pierre. 2000a. A cubic time extension of context-free grammars. *Grammars*, 3(2/3):111–131.

Boullier, Pierre. 2000b. Range Concatenation Grammars. In *Proceedings of the Sixth International Workshop on Parsing Technologies (IWPT2000)*, pages 53–64, Trento, Italy, February.

Boullier, Pierre and Benoît Sagot. 2009. Multi-Component Tree Insertion Grammars. In *Proceedings of Formal Grammar 2009*, Bordeaux, France, July. To appear in Lecture Notes in Computer Science, Springer.

Bresnan, Joan. 2001. *Lexical-Functional Syntax*, volume 16 of *Blackwell Textbooks in Linguistics*. Blackwell.

Bresnan, Joean, Ronald M. Kaplan, Stanley Peters, and Annie Zaenen. 1982. Cross-serial dependencies in Dutch. *Linguistic Inquiry*, 13(4):613–635. Reprinted in (Savitch et al., 1987).

Burden, Håkan and Peter Ljunglöf. 2005. Parsing linear context-free rewriting systems. In *IWPT'05, 9th International Workshop on Parsing Technologies*, Vancouver, Canada, October.

Candito, Marie-Hélène and Sylvain Kahane. 1998. Can the TAG derivation tree represent a semantic graph? An answer in the light of Meaning-Text Theory. In *Fourth International Workshop on Tree Adjoining Grammars and Related Frameworks, IRCS Report 98-12*, pages 25–28, University of Pennsylvania, Philadelphia.

Chiang, David and Tatjana Scheffler. 2008. Flexible composition and delayed tree-locality. In *TAG+9 Proceedings of the Ninth International Workshop on Tree-Adjoining Grammar and Related Formalisms (TAG+9)*, pages 17–24, Tübingen, June.

Chomsky, Noam. 1956. Three models for the description of language. *IRE Transactions on Information Theory*, 2:113–124.

Chomsky, Noam. 1995. *The Minimalist Program*. MIT Press.

Crabbé, Benoit. 2005. *Représentation informatique de grammaires d'arbres fortement lexicalisées : le cas de la grammaire d'arbres adjoints*. Ph.D. thesis, Université Nancy 2.

Cremers, Armin B. and Otto Mayer. 1973. On matrix languages. *Information and Control*, 23:86–96.

Dassow, Jürgen and Gheorghe Păun. 1989. *Regulated Rewriting in Formal Languages Theory*, volume 18 of *EATCS Monographs on Theoretical Computer Science*. Springer.

de Groote, Philippe. 2001. Towards abstract categorial grammars. In *Association for Computational Linguistics, 39th Annual Meeting and 10th*

Conference of the European Chapter, Proceedings of the Conference, pages 148–155.

Dras, Mark, David Chiang, and William Schuler. 2004. On relations of constituency and dependency grammars. *Journal of Language and Computation*, 2(2):281–305.

Frank, Anette and Josef van Genabith. 2001. GlueTag. Linear logic based semantics for LTAG – and what it teaches us about LFG and LTAG. In Miriam Butt and Tracy Holloway King, editors, *Proceedings of the LFG01 Conference*, Hong Kong.

Frank, Robert. 1992. *Syntactic Locality and Tree Adjoining Grammar: Grammatical, Acquisition and Processing Perspectives*. Ph.D. thesis, University of Pennsylvania.

Frank, Robert. 2002. *Phrase Structure Composition and Syntactic Dependencies*. MIT Press, Cambridge, Mass.

Gallo, G., G. Longo, S. Nguyen, and S. Pallottino. 1993. Directed Hypergraphs and Applications. *Discrete Applied Mathematics*, 42:177–201.

Gazdar, Gerald. 1988. Applicability of indexed grammars to natural languages. In Uwe Reyle and Christian Rohrer, editors, *Natural Language Parsing and Linguistic Theories*. D. Reidel, pages 69–94.

Gazdar, Gerald, Ewan Klein, Geoffrey Pullman, and Ivan Sag. 1985. *Generalized Phrase Structure Grammar*. Harvard University Press, Cambridge, Massachusetts.

Ginsburg, Seymour 1966. *The Mathematical Theory of Context Free Languages*. McGraw Hill, New York.

Gómez-Rodríguez, Carlos, Marco Kuhlmann, Giorgio Satta, and David Weir. 2009. Optimal reduction of rule length in linear context-free rewriting systems. In *Proceedings of the North American Chapter of the Association for Computational Linguistics – Human Language Technologies Conference (NAACL'09:HLT)*, pages 539–547, Boulder, Colorado.

Groenink, Annius Victor. 1995. Literal movement grammars. In *Proceedings of the 7th EACL Conference*.

Groenink, Annius Victor. 1996. Mild context-sensitivity and tuple-based generalizations of context-free grammar. Report CS-R9634, Centrum voor Wiskunde en Informatica, Amsterdam.

Groenink, Annius Victor. 1997. *Surface Without Structure. Word Order and Tractability in Natural Language Analysis*. Ph.D. thesis, Utrecht University.

Grune, Dick and Ceriel Jacobs. 2008. *Parsing Techniques. A Practical Guide*. Monographs in Computer Science. Springer. Second Edition.

Han, Chung-Hye. 2002. Compositional semantics for relative clauses in lexicalized Tree Adjoining Grammars. In *Proceedings of the Sixth Interna-*

tional Workshop on Tree Adjoining Grammars and Related Frameworks (TAG+6), pages 1–10, Venice, May.

Hopcroft, John E. and Jeffrey D. Ullman. 1979. *Introduction to Automata Theory, Languages and Computation*. Addison-Wesley.

Huang, Liang and David Chiang. 2005. Better k-best parsing. In *Proceedings of IWPT 2005*, Vancouver, Canada.

Jäger, Gerhard and Jens Michaelis. 2004. An introduction to mildly context-sensitive grammar formalisms. Course Material at ESSLLI 2004, Nancy, France.

Joshi, Aravind K. 1985. Tree adjoining grammars: How much context-sensitivity is required to provide reasonable structural descriptions? In D. Dowty, L. Karttunen, and A. Zwicky, editors, *Natural Language Parsing*. Cambridge University Press, pages 206–250.

Joshi, Aravind K., Laura Kallmeyer, and Maribel Romero. 2003. Flexible composition in LTAG: Quantifier scope and inverse linking. In Harry Bunt, Ielka van der Sluis, and Roser Morante, editors, *Proceedings of the Fifth International Workshop on Computational Semantics IWCS-5*, pages 179–194, Tilburg.

Joshi, Aravind K., Leon S. Levy, and Masako Takahashi. 1975. Tree Adjunct Grammars. *Journal of Computer and System Science*, 10:136–163.

Joshi, Aravind K. and Yves Schabes. 1997. Tree-Adjoining Grammars. In G. Rozenberg and A. Salomaa, editors, *Handbook of Formal Languages*. Springer, Berlin, pages 69–123.

Joshi, Aravind K. and K. Vijay-Shanker. 1999. Compositional semantics with lexicalized Tree-Adjoining Grammar (LTAG): How much underspecification is necessary? In H. C. Blunt and E. G. C. Thijsse, editors, *Proceedings of the Third International Workshop on Computational Semantics (IWCS-3)*, pages 131–145, Tilburg.

Kahane, Sylvain, Marie-Hélène Candito, and Yannick de Kercadio. 2000. An alternative description of extraction in TAG. In *Proceedings of TAG+5*, pages 115–122, Paris.

Kallmeyer, Laura. 2005. Tree-local multicomponent tree adjoining grammars with shared nodes. *Computational Linguistics*, 31(2):187–225.

Kallmeyer, Laura. 2009. A Declarative Characterization of Different Types of Multicomponent Tree Adjoining Grammars. *Research on Language and Computation*, 7(1):55–99.

Kallmeyer, Laura and Aravind K. Joshi. 2003. Factoring Predicate Argument and Scope Semantics: Underspecified Semantics with LTAG. *Research on Language and Computation*, 1(1–2):3–58.

Kallmeyer, Laura and Wolfgang Maier. 2009. An incremental Earley parser for simple Range Concatenation Grammar. In *Proceedings of IWPT 2009*.

Kallmeyer, Laura and Wolfgang Maier. 2010. Data-driven parsing with probabilistic Linear Context-Free Rewriting Systems. In *Proceedings of the 23rd International Conference on Computational Linguistics (COLING 2010)*, Beijing, China.

Kallmeyer, Laura, Wolfgang Maier, and Yannick Parmentier. 2009a. An Earley Parsing Algorithm for Range Concatenation Grammars. In *Proceedings of ACL 2009*, Singapore.

Kallmeyer, Laura, Wolfgang Maier, and Yannick Parmentier. 2009b. Un algorithme d'analyse de type Earley pour grammaires à concaténation d'intervalles. In *Actes de la 16ème conférence sur le Traitement Automatique des Langues Naturelles (TALN 2009)*, Senlis, France.

Kallmeyer, Laura and Yannick Parmentier. 2008. On the relation between Multicomponent Tree Adjoining Grammars with Tree Tuples (TT-MCTAG) and Range Concatenation Grammars (RCG). In Carlos Martín-Vide, Friedrich Otto, and Henning Fernaus, editors, *Language and Automata Theory and Applications. Second International Conference, LATA 2008*, number 5196 in Lecture Notes in Computer Science. Springer, Heidelberg Berlin, pages 263–274.

Kallmeyer, Laura and Maribel Romero. 2008. Scope and situation binding in LTAG using semantic unification. *Research on Language and Computation*, 6(1):3–52.

Kallmeyer, Laura and Giorgio Satta. 2009. A polynomial-time parsing algorithm for TT-MCTAG. In *Proceedings of ACL*, Singapore.

Kanazawa, Makoto. 2008. A Prefix-Correct Earley Recognizer for Multiple Context-Free Grammars. In *Proceedings of the Ninth International Workshop on Tree Adjoining Grammars and Related Formalisms (TAG+9)*, pages 49–56, Tübingen, June.

Kanazawa, Makoto. 2009. The pumping lemma for well-nested Multiple Context-Free Languages. In V. Diekert and D. Nowotka, editors, *DLT 2009*, volume 5583 of *LNCS*, pages 312–325, Berlin Heidelberg. Springer.

Kaplan, Ronald M. and Joan Bresnan. 1982. Lexical-Functional Grammar: A Formal System for Grammatical Representations. In *The Mental Representation of Grammatical Relations*. MIT Press, pages 173–281.

Kato, Yuki, Hiroyuki Seki, and Tadao Kasami. 2006. Stochastic multiple context-free grammar for RNA pseudoknot modeling. In *Proceedings of The Eighth International Workshop on Tree Adjoining Grammar and Related Formalisms (TAG+8)*, pages 57–64, Sydney, Australia, July.

Kay, Martin. 1986. Algorithm schemata and data structures in syntactic processing. In Barbara J. Grosz, Karen Sparck-Jones, and Bonnie Lynn Webber, editors, *Readings in Natural Language Processing*. Morgan Kaufmann, Los Altos, pages 35–70.

Klein, Dan and Christopher D. Manning. 2003. A* Parsing: Fast exact Viterbi parse selection. In *HLT-NAACL*.

Klein, Dan and Christopher D. Manning. 2004. Parsing and hypergraphs. In *New Developments in Parsing Technology*. Kluwer Academic Publishers, Norwell, MA, USA, pages 351–372.

Kracht, Marcus. 2003. *The Mathematics of Language*. Number 63 in Studies in Generative Grammar. Mouton de Gruyter, Berlin.

Kroch, Anthony. 1989. Asymmetries in long-distance extraction in a Tree Adjoining Grammar. In Baltin and Kroch, editors, *Alternative Conceptions of Phrase Structure*. University of Chicago.

Kroch, Anthony and Beatrice Santorini. 1991. The derived constituent structure of the West Germanic verb raising construction. In R. Freidin, editor, *Principles and Parameters in Comparative Grammar*. MIT Press, Cambridge, Mass., pages 268–338.

Kroch, Anthony S. 1987. Unbounded dependencies and subjacency in a Tree Adjoining Grammar. In A. Manaster-Ramer, editor, *Mathematics of Language*. John Benjamins, Amsterdam, pages 143–172.

Kroch, Anthony S. and Aravind K. Joshi. 1987. Analyzing extraposition in a tree adjoining grammar. In Geoffrey J. Huck and Almerido E. Ojeda, editors, *Syntax and Semantics: Discontinuous Constituency*. Academic Press, Inc., pages 107–149.

Kuhlmann, Marco. 2007. *Dependency Structures and Lexicalized Grammars*. Ph.D. thesis, Saarland University.

Kuhlmann, Marco and Giorgio Satta. 2009. Treebank grammar techniques for non-projective dependency parsing. In *Proceedings of EACL*.

Kuno, Susumu 1965. The predictive analyzer and a path elimination technique. *Communications of the ACM*, 8(7):453–462, July.

Langer, Hagen. 1998. Experimente mit verallgemeinerten Lookahead-Algorithmen. In Bernhard Schröder, Winfried Lenders, Wolfgang Hess, and Thomas Portele, editors, *Computers, linguistics and phonetics between language and speech / KONVENS 98*, pages 69–82, Bonn.

Levy, Roger. 1999. *Probabilistic Models of Word Order and Syntactic Discontinuity*. Ph.D. thesis, Stanford University.

Lichte, Timm. 2007. An MCTAG with Tuples for Coherent Constructions in German. In *Proceedings of the 12th Conference on Formal Grammar 2007*, Dublin, Ireland.

Ljunglöf, Peter. 2004. *Expressivity and Complexity of the Grammatical Framework*. Ph.D. thesis, Department of Computer Science, Gothenburg University and Chalmers University of Technology, November.

Ljunglöf, Peter. 2005. A polynomial time extension of parallel Multiple Context-Free Grammar. In *Logical Aspects of Computational Linguistics*, volume 3492 of *Lecture Notes in Computer Science*. Springer, Berlin/Heidelberg, pages 177–188.

Maier, Wolfgang. 2010. Direct parsing of discontinuous constituents in German. In *Proceedings of the NAACL HLT 2010 First Workshop on Statistical Parsing of Morphologically-Rich Languages*, pages 58–66, Los Angeles, CA, USA, June. Association for Computational Linguistics.

Maier, Wolfgang and Laura Kallmeyer. 2010. Discontinuity and non-projectivity: Using mildly context-sensitive formalisms for data-driven parsing. In *Proceedings of the Tenth International Workshop on Tree Adjoining Grammars and Related Formalisms (TAG+10)*, New Haven.

Maier, Wolfgang and Timm Lichte. 2009. Characterizing discontinuity in constituent treebanks. In *Proceedings of Formal Grammar 2009*, Bordeaux, France, July. To appear in Lecture Notes in Computer Science, Springer.

Maier, Wolfgang and Anders Søgaard. 2008. Treebanks and mild context-sensitivity. In *Proceedings of the 13th Conference on Formal Grammar 2008*, Hamburg, Germany.

McAllester, David 2002. On the complexity analysis of static analyses. *Journal of the ACM*, 49(4):512–537.

Merlo, Paola, Harry Bunt, and Joakim Nivre. 2010. *Current Trends in Parsing Technology*. Springer.

Michaelis, Jens. 1998. Derivational minimalism is mildly context-sensitive. In *Proceedings. Logical Aspects of Computational Linguistics*, Grenoble.

Michaelis, Jens. 2001a. Derivational minimalism is mildly context-sensitive. In Michael Moortgat, editor, *Logical Aspects of Computational Linguistics*, volume 2014 of *LNCS/LNAI*, pages 179–198, Berlin, Heidelberg. Springer.

Michaelis, Jens. 2001b. Transforming linear context-free rewriting systems into minimalist grammars. In Philippe de Groote, Glyn Morrill, and Christian Retoré, editors, *Logical Aspects of Computational Linguistics*, volume 2099 of *LNCS/LNAI*, pages 228–244, Berlin, Heidelberg. Springer.

Michaelis, Jens and Marcus Kracht. 1997. Semilinearity as a syntactic invariant. In Christian Retoré, editor, *Logical Aspects of Computational Linguistics. First International Conference, LACL '96, Nancy, France, September 23-25, 1996. Selected Papers*, volume 1328 of *LNCS/LNAI*, Berlin, Heidelberg. Springer.

Nederhof, Mark-Jan. 1997. Solving the correct-prefix property for TAGs. In T. Becker and H.-U. Krieger, editors, *Proceedings of the Fifth Meeting on Mathematics of Language*, pages 124–130, Schloss Dagstuhl, Saarbrücken, August.

Nederhof, Mark-Jan. 1998. An alternative LR algorithm for TAGs. In *Proceedings of ACL*, Montreal, Canada.

Nederhof, Mark-Jan. 1999. The computational complexity of the correct-prefix property for TAGs. *Computational Linguistics*, 25(3):345–360.

Nesson, Rebecca, Giorgio Satta, and Stuart Shieber. 2008. Complexity, parsing, and factorization of tree-local multi-component tree-adjoining grammar. Technical Report TR-05-08, School of Engineering and Applied Sciences, Harvard University, Cambridge, MA.

Nesson, Rebecca and Stuart M. Shieber. 2006. Simpler TAG semantics through synchronization. In *Proceedings of the 11th Conference on Formal Grammar*, Malaga, Spain, 29–30 July.

Parikh, Rohit 1966. On context-free languages. *Jounal of the ACM*, 13:570–581.

Parmentier, Yannick and Wolfgang Maier. 2008. Using constraints over finite sets of integers for range concatenation grammar parsing. In Bengt Nordström and Aarne Ranta, editors, *Advances in Natural Language Processing*, volume 5221 of *LNCS/LNAI*, Gothenburg, Sweden, August. Springer.

Pereira, Fernando C. N. and David Warren. 1983. Parsing as deduction. In *21st Annual Meeting of the Association for Computational Linguistics*, pages 137–144, MIT, Cambridge, Massachusetts.

Pollard, Carl and Ivan A. Sag. 1994. *Head-Driven Phrase Structure Grammar*. Studies in Contemporary Linguistics. The University of Chicago Press, Chicago, London.

Prolo, Carlos. 2000. An efficient LR parser generator for Tree Adjoining Grammars. In *Proceedings of the 6th International Workshop on Parsing Technologies (IWPT-2000)*, pages 207–218, Trento, Italy.

Prolo, Carlos. 2003. *LR Parsing for Tree Adjoining Grammars and Its Application to Corpus-Based Natural Language Parsing*. Ph.D. thesis, University of Pennsylvania.

Radzinski, Daniel. 1991. Chinese number-names, tree adjoining languages, and mild context-sensitivity. *Computational Linguistics*, 17:277–299.

Rambow, Owen. 1994. *Formal and Computational Aspects of Natural Language Syntax*. Ph.D. thesis, University of Pennsylvania.

Rambow, Owen, K. Vijay-Shanker, and David Weir. 1995. D-Tree Grammars. In *Proceedings of ACL*.

Rambow, Owen, K. Vijay-Shanker, and David Weir. 2001. D-Tree Substitution Grammars. *Computational Linguistics*.

Sagot, Benoît. 2005. Linguistic facts as predicates over ranges of the sentence. In *Proceedings of LACL 05*, number 3492 in Lecture Notes in Computer Science, pages 271–286, Bordeaux, France. Springer.

Savitch, Walter J., Emmon Bach, William Marxh, and Gila Safran-Naveh, editors. 1987. *The Formal Complexity of Natural Language*. Studies in Linguistics and Philosophy. Reidel, Dordrecht, Holland.

Schabes, Yves. 1990. *Mathematical and Computational Aspects of Lexicalized Grammars*. Ph.D. thesis, University of Pennsylvania.

Schabes, Yves and Aravind K. Joshi. 1988. An Earley-type parsing algorithm for Tree Adjoining Grammars. In *Proceedings of the 26th Annual Meeting of the Association for Computational Linguistics*, pages 258–269.

Schabes, Yves and K. Vijay-Shanker. 1990. Deterministic left to right parsing of tree adjoining languages. In *Proceedings of ACL*, Pittsburgh.

Seki, Hiroyuki and Yuki Kato. 2008. On the generative power of multiple context-free grammars and macro grammars. *IEICE Transactions on Information and Systems*, E91-D(2):209–221, February.

Seki, Hiroyuki, Takahashi Matsumura, Mamoru Fujii, and Tadao Kasami. 1991. On multiple context-free grammars. *Theoretical Computer Science*, 88(2):191–229.

Seki, Hiroyuki, Ryuichi Nakanishi, Yuichi Kaji, Sachiko Ando, and Tadao Kasami. 1993. Parallel multiple context-free grammars, finite-state translation systems, and polynomial-time recognizable subclasses of lexical-functional grammars. In *31st Meeting of the Association for Computational Linguistics (ACL'93)*, pages 121–129.

Shieber, Stuart M. 1984. Direct parsing of ID/LP grammars. *Linguistics and Philosophy*, 7(2):135–154.

Shieber, Stuart M. 1985. Evidence against the context-freeness of natural language. *Linguistics and Philosophy*, 8:333–343. Reprinted in (Savitch et al., 1987).

Shieber, Stuart M. 1994. Restricting the weak-generative capacity of synchronous Tree-Adjoining Grammars. *Computational Intelligence*, 10(4):271–385.

Shieber, Stuart M., Yves Schabes, and Fernando C. N. Pereira. 1995. Principles and implementation of deductive parsing. *Journal of Logic Programming*, 24(1 and 2):3–36.

Sikkel, Klaas. 1997. *Parsing Schemata*. Texts in Theoretical Computer Science. Springer, Berlin, Heidelberg, New York.

Sippu, Seppo and Eljas Soisalon-Soininen. 1990. *Parsing Theory*, volume 20 of *EATCS Monographs on Theoretical Computer Science*. Springer-Verlag, Berlin, Heidelberg.

Søgaard, Anders. 2007. *Complexity, expressivity and logic of linguistic theories*. Ph.D. thesis, University of Copenhagen, Copenhagen, Denmark.

Søgaard, Anders. 2008. Range concatenation grammars for translation. In *Proceedings of the 22nd International Conference on Computational Linguistics*, Manchester, England.

Søgaard, Anders, Timm Lichte, and Wolfgang Maier. 2007. The complexity of linguistically motivated extensions of tree-adjoining grammar. In *Recent Advances in Natural Language Processing 2007*, Borovets, Bulgaria.

Stabler, Edward P. 1997. Derivational Minimalism. In Christian Retoré, editor, *Logical Aspects of Computational Linguistics. First International Conference, LACL '96, Nancy, France, September 23-25, 1996. Selected Papers*, volume 1328 of *LNCS/LNAI*, pages 68–95, Berlin, Heidelberg. Springer.

Steedman, Mark. 2000. *The Syntactic Process*. MIT Press.

Vijay-Shanker, K. 1987. *A Study of Tree Adjoining Grammars*. Ph.D. thesis, University of Pennsylvania.

Vijay-Shanker, K. and Aravind K. Joshi. 1985. Some computational properties of Tree Adjoining Grammars. In *Proceedings of the 23rd Annual Meeting of the Association for Computational Linguistics*, pages 82–93.

Vijay-Shanker, K. and David J. Weir. 1993. Parsing some constrained grammar formalisms. *Computational Linguistics*, 19(4):591–636.

Vijay-Shanker, K. and David J. Weir. 1994. The equivalence of four extensions of context-free grammars. *Mathematical Systems Theory*, 27(6):511–546.

Vijay-Shanker, K., David J. Weir, and Aravind K. Joshi. 1987. Characterizing structural descriptions produced by various grammatical formalisms. In *Proceedings of ACL*, Stanford.

Villemonte de la Clergerie, Éric. 2002. Parsing mildly context-sensitive languages with thread automata. In *Proceedings of COLING'02*, August.

Villemonte de la Clergerie, Eric. 2006. Designing tabular parsers for various syntactic formalisms. ESSLLI Lecture Notes.

Villemonte de la Clergerie, Éric and Alonso M.A. Pardo. 1998. A tabular interpretation of a class of 2-stack automata. In *Proceedings of COLING-ACL*, pages 1333–1339.

Weir, David J. 1988. *Characterizing Mildly Context-Sensitive Grammar Formalisms*. Ph.D. thesis, University of Pennsylvania.

Weir, David J. 1992. A geometric hierarchy beyond context-free languages. *Theoretical Computer Science*, 104:235–261.

XTAG Research Group. 2001. A Lexicalized Tree Adjoining Grammar for English. Technical report, Institute for Research in Cognitive Science, Philadelphia.

Index

Abstract Categorial Grammar, 7

chart parsing, 46, 47
Combinatory Categorial Grammar, 7, 73
  backward application, 73
  backward composition, 73
  forward application, 73
  forward composition, 73
computation sharing, 46
constant growth property, 23
Context-Free Grammar, 11
  Chomsky Normal Form, 12, 41
  closure properties, 12
  CYK parsing, 41, 42
  derivation tree, 15
  Earley parsing, 43
  Greibach Normal Form, 12, 21
  LR parsing, 98
  parse tree, 15
  pumping lemma, 12
  string language, 11
  tree language, 15
  useful symbol, 11
cross-serial dependencies, 17
  – in Dutch, 17
  – in Swiss-German, 18
  – with TAG, 28
CYK parsing
  – for CFG, 42
  – for MCFG, 131
  – for RCG, 178
  – for TAG, 77

dependency parsing, 8
dynamic programming, 44

Earley parsing
  – for CFG, 43
  – for MCFG, 141
  – for RCG, 188
  – for TAG, 82
Embedded Push-Down Automaton, 193, 195
  k-order –, 199
  bottom-up –, 197
  language, 195
  transition, 195
equivalence
  strong –, 15
  weak –, 15

Finite State Automaton, 13
finitely ambiguous, 21
fixed recognition problem, 49

graph
  directed –, 14
  in-degree, 14
  out-degree, 14

Head-Driven Phrase Structure Grammar (HPSG), 7

Indexed grammar, 31, 72
  Linear –, 31, 72

language, 10

alphabet, 10
empty word, 10
homomorphism, 11
length of a word, 11
letter equivalent, 24
Parikh mapping, 24
semilinear, 25
word, 10
Lexical Functional Grammar, 126
  c-structure, 126
  f-structure, 127
  finite-copying –, 127
Lexical Functional Grammar (LFG), 7
lexicalization, 21
  strong lexicalization, 21
  weak lexicalization, 21
lexicalized grammar, 20
  anchor, 20
  multicomponent anchor, 21
Linear Context-Free Rewriting System, 24, 33, 111
  fan-out, 117
  CYK parsing, 131
  monotone –, 145
  rank, 147
  well-nested –, 122
Literal Movement Grammar, 167
  clause instantiation, 168
  linear –, 169
  non-combinatorial –, 169
  non-erasing –, 169
  simple –, 169
  string language, 168
LR parsing
  – for CFG, 98
  – for TAG, 96

Matrix Grammars, 7
mildly context-sensitive, 23
Minimalist Grammar, 126
Multicomponent TAG, 33, 70
  k-TT-MCTAG, 71
  k-delayed tree-local –, 71
  non-local –, 35
  set-local –, 24, 35, 125
  tree-local –, 35, 71
  tree-local – with flexible composition, 71

Multiple Context-Free Grammar, 24, 36, 110
  r-*yield*, 114
  k-MCFG, 110
  closure properties, 119
  CYK parsing, 131
  incremental CYK parsing, 139
  incremental Earley parsing, 141
  left-corner parsing, 142
  mcf-function, 111
  parallel –, 169
  pumping lemma, 118
  range, 113
  string language, 111, 114

NP-complete, 50

Parikh Theorem, 25
parsing
  $LL(k)$, 44
  – and hypergraphs, 48
  – as deduction, 6, 41
  active item, 44
  chart –, 6
  completeness, 48
  complexity, 49
  deduction rules, 44
  dependency –, 8
  dotted production, 43
  item, 42
  passive item, 44
  soundness, 48
pseudo-code, 41
PTIME, 37, 50
pumping lemma
  – for CFG, 12
  – for MCFG, 118
  – for TAG, 61
Push-Down Automaton, 13

Range Concatenation Grammar, 36, 157
  $(2,2)$-BRCG, 166
  arity, 117
  clause, 117
  bottom-up linear –, 162
  bottom-up non-erasing –, 162
  clause instantiation, 160
  combinatorial clause, 159

CYK parsing, 178
derivation, 161
Earley parsing, 188
erasing clause, 157
filters for parsing, 183
linear –, 162
negative –, 159
non-combinatorial –, 162
non-erasing –, 163
non-linear clause, 158
positive –, 159
range, 113
range constraint vector, 185
range language, 161
simple –, 24, 37, 163
string language, 161
top-down linear –, 162
top-down non-erasing –, 163
top-down parsing, 179

Simple Range Concatenation Grammar, 111, 112
ε-free –, 143
ε-clause, 143
arity, 117
derivation tree, 115, 116
eliminating ε-rules, 143
gap degree, 121
ordered –, 145
tree language, 117
well-nested, 122
binarization, 147
clause instantiation, 115
eliminating useless rules, 142
filters for parsing, 154
simple k-RCG, 112
transformation into an ordered –, 146
substitution, 22
substitution node, 22

tabulation, 46
Thread Automaton, 204, 206
– for LCFRL, 209
– for TAL, 208
configuration, 206
language, 208

thread, 206
transitions, 207
tree, 14
completed –, 22
labeling, 15
ordered tree, 14
syntactic tree, 15
Tree Adjoining Grammar, 26, 55
adjunction, 55
adjunction constraints, 55
auxiliary tree, 54
closure properties, 58
Condition on Elementary Tree Minimality, 64
cross-serial dependencies, 28
CYK parsing, 77
derivation tree, 56, 68
derived tree, 56, 68
Earley Parsing, 82
elementary tree, 55
extended domain of locality, 30, 65
factoring of recursion, 65
initial tree, 54
LR parsing, 96
Predicate Argument Co-occurrence Principle, 63
prefix valid Earley parsing, 93
pumping lemma, 61
string language, 58
tree language, 58
Tree Substitution Grammar, 22
elementary tree, 22
tree language, 22
Two-Stack Automaton, 200
strongly-driven –, 203
two-stack automaton, 200

universal recognition problem, 50
unordered Vector Grammars, 7

valid prefix property, 51
Earley parser for TAG, 92
LR parser for TAG, 107
Vector-TAG with dominance links, 7

Weir Hierarchy, 199